LET A THOUSAND FLOWERS BLOOM

© 2008 IOS Press and the Authors. All rights reserved.

Legal notice
The publisher is not responsible for the use which might be made of the following information.

Design
Renssen [typo]grafische ontwerpen, Rijswijk

Publisher
IOS Press BV
Nieuwe Hemweg 6b   1013 BG Amsterdam   The Netherlands
tel: +31-20-688 3355   fax: +31-20-687 0019   email: info@iospress.nl
www.iospress.nl   www.dupress.nl

ISBN 978-1-58603-879-3
Published by IOS Press under the imprint Delft University Press

Printed in the Netherlands

LET A THOUSAND FLOWERS BLOOM
Essays in commemoration of prof. dr. René Wagenaar

EDITED BY
Harry Bouwman
Roger Bons
Martijn Hoogeweegen
Marijn Janssen
Hans Pronk

Je prachtige kostuums, die we samen uitzochten; je toga met de baret en de sjerp, altijd zorgvuldig opgehangen; je zachte zomerbroeken, die zo lekker zaten; rijen fel gekleurde stropdassen, om toch te kunnen opvallen ondanks de grijze pakken – stapels en stapels kleren, niemand wil ze, maar weg doen is te moeilijk, je hield zo van je kleren. Ik kijk of er geen dingen meer in je zakken zitten. Soms vind ik daar nog geeltjes, jouw manier om de chaos in je hoofd te structureren. Voortdurend zag je om je heen allerlei kansen en mogelijkheden. Altijd had je originele gedachtesprongen en een constante ideeënstroom. Op de onmogelijkste momenten kreeg je creatieve ingevingen en die werden dan snel op een geeltje gekalkt.

In je werkkamer op de TU heb ik je logboeken gevonden – schriften waarin je van alles in opschreef. Aantekeningen over gemaakte afspraken tijdens overlegsessies. Je deed dat niet netjes en puntsgewijs, maar spontaan en rommelig. Soms in het Engels, dan weer in het Nederlands. Elk overleg resulteerde in een geweldige hoeveelheid krabbels en opmerkingen. Overal heb je kreten omcirkeld, onderstreept of juist weer doorgestreept. Je schriften borrelen van de plannetjes van wat je nog allemaal kon opstarten. Ze zitten vol met onmogelijke schetsjes en schemaatjes. Ze zitten vol met toekomst en levenslust.

Je wilde nog zoveel ...

WIE ZIJN TIJD ALLEEN MAAR VOORUIT IS
WORDT EENS DOOR HAAR INGEHAALD

From *Virtual Merchant*

Arne Zimmermand → u
XSYAU
Brietje von Claudia → Recto
 T Crisismgmt - Travestrines
 (mons)

Contents

Wim Dik
Preface – 13
Jeroen van den Hoven
René Wagenaar and The Quest for Value Sensitivity – 15

Harry Bouwman, Roger Bons, Martijn Hoogeweegen, Marijn Janssen, Hans Pronk
Introduction – 13

1 – THE VIRTUAL MERCHANT
Peter Vervest
Trust in the network – 45
Martijn Hoogeweegen, Peter Vervest
Modularity in Business Networks – 55
Wout Hofman
Forget about chains, business webs are the future! – 65
Lorike Hagdorn – van der Meijden
Strength and weakness in networks – 83
Wil Janssen, Erwin Fielt, Marc Lankhorst
Transparancy in Services Networks, Combining Choice and Obligation – 97
Eric van Heck
The Virtual Merchant Is Searching for Profit – 115

2 – THE VIRTUAL CIVIL SERVANT
Roland Traunmüller, Maria Wimmer, Gerti Orthofer
Managing Change in e-Government: Policies and Strategies – 125
Arjan van Venrooij
ICT and new forms of inter-organizational public service provisioning – 143
René Matthijsse
In search of network government: discussion and future outlook – 159
Norien Kuiper
New Government needs new Architectural Models – 173
Ronald Lee, Roger Bons, Elizabeth Dominguez, Kenneth Henry, Vu Nguyen
Navigating the bureaucratic maze: a messenger model for e-Government – 187

Andreas Mitrakas
Heidi: an electronic identity intermediary model in e-Government – 203
Yao-Hua Tan, Helle Zinner Henriksen
Let a Thousand Flowers Bloom for e-Government – 223
Nitesh Bharosa, Ralph Feenstra, Jeffrey Gortmaker, Bram Klievink, Marijn Janssen
Rethinking Service-Oriented Government: is it really about services? – 237

3 – SOCIO-TECHNICAL DESIGN
Patrick Dewilde
Are Technology and Service Management compatible? – 259
John Groenewegen, Rolf Künneke
Exploring the public value of broadband – 267
Zofia Lukszo, Koen van Dam, Margot Weijnen, Gerard Dijkema
Agent-based models for crisis management – 281
Paulien Herder, Uldrik Speerstra
Design and Evaluation of the Information Architecture Program – 301
Eric Bun, Tim de Koning, Ton Monasso, Pim Veldhoven, Alex Verheij
Infectious diseases and ICT – 319

4 – LET A THOUSAND FLOWERS BLOOM
Harry Bouwman, Mark de Reuver, Guadalupe Flores Hernández
Strategy and business models: mobile telecommunication – 341
Christer Carlsson, Pirkko Walden
Smart Adaptive Mobile Life Enhancements – 357
Els van de Kar, Bart Nieuwenhuis
Does Service Innovation require more than ICT? – 373
Jolien Ubacht
Next generation ICT users: inspiration and challenges for policy makers – 391
Hans Pronk
Thoughts about Identity, privacy and virtualisation – 407
Kees van de Meer
'If only we knew what we knew...' – 419

Biographies – 428
List of Publications René Wagenaar – 434

Preface

When interesting people retire or celebrate an important milestone, it is a good habit to construct a 'liber amicorum' in which colleagues, business relations, science-relations and plain friends picture the person in question with his or her positive and negative sides.
Our friend René Wagenaar did not get the chance to reach a jubilee or his super-annuation; an awful disease pulled him away. So now his friends and relations build a modest monument for him. The man René as he was in other people's eyes: a contradiction in itself.
From a distance modest, almost shy, always seemingly lightly confused, slightly disorganised, not a good timekeeper. Certainly not pushing himself to the foreground, keeping his knowledge to himself even when he knew better than what was laid out. As a colleague at KPN Research he was one of the least outspoken professors there, but always participating, always contributing and listening very well.
But when you came closer to him, got to know him better, he was lively; he could be harsh and direct in his approach, someone who lived life intensely, a strong family man who, besides that, took a great interest in other people. And more important for our TU Delft: a man with the basic curiosity to drive research forward, to motivate colleagues and students and make the space available in which they could excel, like a father.
I hope and trust that this book will show its readers that the progress of science – albeit that we remember the icons better – has much more to thank to relatively ordinary people like René, provided they have the motivation and drive he had.

Wim Dik

René Wagenaar and The Quest for Value Sensitivity

Jeroen van den Hoven
Acting Dean, Faculty of Technology Policy and Management,
Delft University of Technology

My recollections of debates with René about the topics of our shared interest are both vivid and dear to me. René had a strong presence and style in academic discussions, which was gentle, generous and not dominating. This I only fully realized when I knew there would be no more of such conversations between us. He combined an analytical intellect with a reflective cast of mind and knew how to reconcile attention for what in philosophy is called the pars destruens and the pars construens in the analysis of arguments or a debate: the criticism of the old and the construction of something new.

When we met after many years we immediately started to think about a common passion: Philosophy and IT. We knew each other from the years in the nineties in which we were both affiliated with Erasmus University where Ron Lee had established the EURIDIS institute. After a couple of sustained discussions René convinced me that it was a good idea to come to Delft University of Technology and join the Faculty of Technology, Policy and Management. His persuasive enthusiasm, warm collegiality and the prospect of working together were important for me to make the step from Rotterdam to Delft.

I had started to think about new lines of research at the intersection of the ethics of ICT and Software Engineering and René was an ideal intellectual sparring partner. We started to discuss the importance of systems design and information architectures in conformity with public moral values and we soon agreed upon a research program 'Value Sensitive Design', which would study moral ideals and their realization and implementation in software. After a phase where we critically examined the research topics and actively pursued new areas, we started to think about joint research efforts into the privacy and security, trust, identity, accountability, usability, autonomy and their role in the shaping architectures and systems. We both realized that something more was needed to make complex information systems work – especially in the public sector – than was found in available approaches in systems design.

When the computer was introduced around the middle of the twentieth century, scholarly attention was focused on the technology simpliciter. The computer was developed without too much thought about (1) the use and application in real life and (2) the social, organisational and political changes it would require or that it would bring about. In the early days computers were a new and fascinating technology: solutions looking for problems. Later, in the seventies and eighties attention was increasingly given to the context of the technology, to the real organizations, the real human user needs and work conditions, usability, etc. The social and behavioural sciences became involved with Information Technology in the form of Human-Computer Interaction and Participatory Design and Social Informatics. However, the focus of these efforts and commitments was mainly on functional and instrumental values, such as user-friendliness and worker-safety. Social and organizational context was often taken into account merely as a way to identify potential barriers to the successful implementation of systems and to prevent costly failures. Attention for human and social context of computing was thus largely determined by fear of failures in implementation.

In the last decade of the 20th century the successful application of information technology was increasingly seen as dependent on its capacity to accommodate human values. Human beings, whether in their role as employers, consumers, citizens, or patients, have moral values, moral preferences and ideals. There are moral and public debates in society about liability, equality, property, privacy, autonomy and accountability. Successful implementation should therefore be construed in terms of how and to what extent values are taken into account in the design and architecture of systems. Values may even become driving factors in the development of IT instead of impediments in the design and developments of information technology. We seem to be entering a third phase in the development of IT systems, that might be referred to as 'The Value Turn in IT', where the needs and values of human users, as citizens, patients, are considered in their own right.

We are continuing the work in Delft on Value Sensitive Design (VSD) that René and I had identified as worthwhile pursuing, with the help of PhD's who have been supervised by René, such as Noemi Manders, Vincent Wiegel and Luuk Simons.

VSD is an approach to systems development and software engineering which was developed in the last decade of the 20th century. In VSD the focus is on incorporating human and moral values into design of (information) technology, by looking at the endeavours of the design from an ethical perspective concerned with the way moral values such as freedom from bias, trust, autonomy, privacy, and justice, are facilitated or constrained. Where other research and technical communities have also been working on the value implications of computer technology, such as computer ethics, computer-supported cooperative work (CSCW) and participatory design (PD), VSD focuses primarily and specifically on addressing values of moral import. Other (mainly older) frameworks tend to focus more on functional and instrumental values, such as user-friendliness and worker-safety. Although building a user-friendly technology might have the side-effect of increasing a user's trust or sense of autonomy, in VSD incorporating moral values into the design is the primary goal instead of a by-product.

According to Friedman, "Value-Sensitive Design is primarily concerned with values that center on human well being, human dignity, justice, welfare, and human rights. Value-Sensitive Design connects the people who design systems and interfaces with the people who think about and understand the values of the stakeholders who are affected by the systems. Ultimately, Value-Sensitive Design requires that we broaden the goals and criteria for judging the quality of technological systems to include those that advance human values." (Friedman 1997).

I had high hopes to make progress with René as an intellectual companion and trusted fellow traveller in exploring this new and morally significant terrain in IS. We will continue the quest for value sensitivity in Delft and will always remember René, grateful for what he contributed to our work and who has been to us.

REFERENCES

Flanagan, Mary, Howe, Daniel, and Nissenbaum, Helen. Values in Design: Theory and Practice. In *Information Technology and Moral Philosophy*. Jeroen van den Hoven and John Weckert (Eds.), Cambridge University Press, 2008.

Friedman, Batya. *Human values and the design of computer technology* New York: Cambridge University Press, 1997.

Friedman, Batya, Kahn, Peter and Borning, Alan. Value Sensitive Design and Information Systems. In *Human-Computer Interaction in Management Information Systems: Foundations*, P. Zhang & D. Galletta (eds.). M.E. Sharpe, Inc. 2005.

Friedman, Batya, Kahn, Peter. Human Values, Ethics, and Design. In *The Human-Computer Interaction Handbook* Jacko, J.A. and Sears A. (eds.), Lawrence Erlbaum Associates, 2003, 1177-1201.

Nissenbaum, Helen. How computer systems embody values. *IEEE Computer* 2001, 34, 3, 118-120.

Van den Hoven, Jeroen. Moral Methodology and Information Technology. In *Handbook of Computer Ethics*. Herman Tavani and Ken Himma (eds.) Hoboken, NJ: Wiley, 2008.

You know of all our friends who left
Leaving their thoughts in your mind
remembering who wrote the scenes
They always left behind.

Walk to the table and ask, my friend,
Why we why we never talked again;
Why we echo yesterday
And only we remain.

Walk to the table again, my friend,
Walk over and take the glass,
The lip is chipped with memories,
The wine is from the past.

Walk to the table again, my friend
Walk over and take my hand,
We are so deep in memories,
We cannot understand.

Al Dunn

Introduction

Harry Bouwman, Roger Bons, Martijn Hoogeweegen,
Marijn Janssen, Hans Pronk

With this book, we want to commemorate Prof. Dr. René Wagenaar. After his university study and promotional research in experimental physics, René began his career in ICT as a computer network architect at Philips Data and Telecommunications Systems in the Netherlands and Sunnyvale, USA. After a brief period as a university lecturer with the ICT group of the Economics Faculty at Erasmus University in Rotterdam, he moved on to the Management Faculty in 1989, where he started working as an associate professor in Business Telecommunications. Under his leadership, new research was set up into the impact of electronic communication and EDI within trade and transport chains, which resulted in a large number of publications. René was one of the key inspirators and contributors to the Erasmus University Research Institute for Decision and Information Systems, an interfaculty institute lead by Ronald Lee. In addition, René developed the concept for the management simulation game called 'Port of Rotterdam', which became very popular in the business community. In 1996, René moved to KPN, and at the same time he was appointed to a special chair 'Tele-services, in particular their economic aspects' at the Free University of Amsterdam. Within KPN, he filled the staff position of corporate R&D strategy, where he was especially involved in the development of new e-business concepts and services.

Since his appointment at the TPM Faculty, in October 2001, René worked with great enthusiasm on building a dynamic ICT section and high quality education and research programs at the crossroads of ICT, policy and management. Together with the EWI Faculty, he created the interfaculty study program Information Architecture. Under his leadership, the research within the section was aimed at the core clusters of ICT Infrastructure Development, ICT Service Architectures and ICT Service

Management. René thus also made constituent contributions to the DRC Service Architectures and the DRC Next Generation Infrastructures. His personal areas of interest included technological innovation, organisational redesign and management regarding electronic service provision. Recently, he was involved, among other things, in developing research projects surrounding innovative concepts for Digital Government and Crisis Management. Together with KPN, TNO ICT, the EWI Faculty and the Philosophy section of the TPM Faculty, he helped create the knowledge center for trans-sector innovation through ICT.

René was also very active internationally, among other things in setting up the European E-Government Society and in the European road-mapping project called E-Government 2002. Within these communities, he was an important motivator and sounding board. In addition, René was much in demand as a speaker at international conferences, and he was involved with various journals. In short, René was a researcher of international standing.

This bundle of essays illustrates the impact René had on research and discussions on research topics. They are divided into four parts, each part relating to a specific area of René career, and also more or less reflecting the work he did at the three universities that played a role in his career, i.e. Erasmus University of Rotterdam, the Free University of Amsterdam, and Delft University of Technology. He held a chair at all three universities for a shorter or longer period. At Erasmus University, René started working on EDI and inter-organizational systems (IOS) (see Part I). At the Free University, his research coincided with the Internet growth and hype, and he became focused on eCommerce and the role of Virtual Merchant, as discussed in part II. In 2001, he assumed his position at Delft, and refocused his research on e-Government, and on infrastructure and service-related projects. At Delft, socio-technological designs have a prominent position in both education and research. René's involvement in and impact on research and education starting from a socio-technical approach are discussed in contributions in Part III. In Part IV, some contributions are bundled that address a number of issues in which René was interested and left his marks on, like mobile technologies, business models, privacy issues and standardization.

PART I: THE VIRTUAL MERCHANT
In part I, we have grouped all the essays that are related to EDI, e-Commerce and e-Business. The concept of the Virtual Merchant, as introduced in 1997 by René, still proves to be relevant 10 years later.

In his contribution, Peter Vervest makes an assessment of René's Inaugural Address, 'Virtual Merchant, fiction or reality' in which the concept of the Virtual Merchant was introduced. In his assessment, Vervest places the concept of trust in a central position. He demonstrates the vulnerability of linear value chain based electronic trading systems, even though René expected Trusted Third Parties to play a key role. These would govern the electronic trade and set the rules. However, this did not become a reality. As an alternative, Vervest starts to discuss trust in a networked environment, a topic that definitely merits further research. In a similar grain, Wil Janssen, Erwin Fielt and Marc Lankhorst plead for transparency in a networked environment. Their contribution can be found in the second part.

One of the earliest research programs that René was involved in was inspired by the concept of building blocks, and their possible re-use. The building block concept was important in René's vision on IT-system development. In their contribution, Martijn Hoogeweegen and Peter Vervest discuss the relevance of the business modularity concept, looking for modularity in services and processes that are offered in a network environment. Of course, a concept like coordinator, or in more recent René speech, orchestrators, can already be found in this early research project. The ideas proposed by Hoogeweegen and Vervest about network organizations that produce and deliver services to customers are still relevant, as is the debate about the level of granularity, governance of networks and the orchestration of service elements.

Also, Wouter Hofman, in his contribution, discusses the network aspects of modern business, starting from an operational level, where as Hagdorn in the next contribution takes a more strategic view. The introduction and implementation of EDI was in the view of Hofman a starting point of developments that have resulted in the networked society. The main difference is that, whereas EDI was hierarchical in nature, the new standards enable more flexible networks. Standards related to the Service Oriented Architecture and the Semantic web make new standards like ebXML possible, enabling a more flexible use of EDI. Basically, EDI is broken down into a number of components that can be composed and used more flexible, leading to reduced development time and re-use. On the other hand, Hofman discusses developments in the Web 2.0 domain, and the role end-users play in developing their own content, applications and services. Again, components and combination of components (or services) make this trend possible. The challenges defined are related to service composition semantics, which means that software applications are more in-sync, and the business process alignment in a networked environment.

In her contribution, Lorike Hagdorn specifically focuses on networks. She discusses primary or production networks, secondary or support networks, and tertiary or stakeholder networks, and analysis on a generic level the nature and role of power within networks. Based on empirical research, she concludes that organizations in networks only have insight into operational issues, and not the strategies of their network partners. Hagdorn discusses how individual organizations can pursue certain strategic options within a network, and what strategic roles can be fulfilled. She specifically looks at the role of organizations that can play a bridging role, and that can fill 'structural holes'. Finally, she discusses some ways to obtain such a strategic position.

Whereas, Hofman discusses semantics, Wil Jansen, Erwin Fielt and Marc Lankhorst focus on transparency of information. They assume that semantic clarity has already been achieved. They focus on what information is made available in a network and in which form, the routes information takes, as well the ways in which information is processed, and the rules that are applied. As mentioned before, there is a clear relationship between transparency and trust. In their essay, Janssen et al. look at transparency in business and in government processes. These processes are intermingling more and more. However, the rules and conditions under which information is used varies between processes in which business and customers are involved, from those in which government and citizens play a role. The use of information as required by the government opens the way to invasion of privacy.

Extensive use of information acquired from customers is the key element of Google's business model. Eric Van Heck illustrates the shift in thinking from EDI toward the Virtual Merchant, by addressing Google's business model and the database technology that makes this possible. The fact that the availability of technology, either network technology, or smart algorithms and agents that enable the construction and use of distribute databases for search purposes does not mean that a service will attract a stable user community and enable a robust and sustainable business mode, becomes clear from Van Heck's analysis. Finding the right revenue model, in this case based on auction concepts, is as relevant as the technology itself, providing customer and network value, the value provided to Google and their partners.

Part II: The Virtual Civil Servant
In their contribution, Roland Traunmüller, Maria A. Wimmer and Gerti Orthofer set the European stage for e-Government policies and strategies. In their contribution they described the role of the Lisbon agenda for e-Government, focusing on e-Participation, intelligent, inclusive and personalized service provisioning, adaptive and proactive support systems as well as pan-European architectures and applications. They discuss developments in Austria in the e-Government domain. Issues at stake are amongst others interoperability, collaboration between several government institutions and layers, data models and file exchange formats. Next, they discuss European initiatives that are expected to have a considerable impact, like ministerial conferences, knowledge transfer by means of a European awards competition, work on interoperability, and the development of visions and roadmaps for e-Government research. René was an important collaborator and motivator for this project.

The next contribution is directed at electronic service delivery by the government in the Netherlands. Autonomy of governmental organizations is one of the four alternatives Arjan van Venrooij deals with in his paper to understand models for inter-organizational public service provisioning and delivery. He also discusses the concentration, franchise and exchange model. The four models are based on two dimensions dealing with the organization of service provisioning. One dimension deals with centralization versus decentralization, the other with standardization versus diversification. Van Venrooij's approach is more organizational in nature, and contributions of ICT are discussed on the basis of these organizational models. In discussions with René, the focus was more on the role of governments in the hollow state, a metaphor for the increased use of their parties by government.

René Matthijsse takes the discussion that was started by Van Venrooij one step further. In his paper, he not only discusses cooperation between organizational networks, but also focuses on information management and governance mechanisms. Matthijssse focuses preliminarily on the implementation of policy and the lack of flexibility. Flexibility can be achieved by new forms of formal and informal cooperation. Matthijsse tries to answer the question which core activities are involved and who should carry out these activities to achieve the required flexibility? New forms of cooperation, standardization of work processes, and information management are core issues he discusses. Matthijsse uses the concept of information director, and addresses the relevance of ICT governance and assurance to be part of the policy agenda. Referring to the PhD thesis by Van Venrooij and Matthijsse, management related aspects related to organizing and implementing arrangement for policy implementation are discussed in relation to accountability.

In her contribution, Norien Kuiper is enacting a debate between defenders and opponents of architectural models in the e-Government domain. The proposition to be debated is framed as 'New government needs new architectural models. The current single actor architectural model results in no cooperation at worst, or in low levels of cooperation at best'. Although the debate is imaginary, it is clear that e-Government needs architectural thinking. The next four contributions adopt an architectural approach.

Whereas, in his research on e-Government, René had an interest in services-oriented architectures in relation to orchestration approaches in order to deal with rules and procedures of multiple government agencies with whom many citizens as well as businesses are confronted on a regular and sometimes recurrent basis. Ronald Lee, Roger Bons, Elizabeth Dominguez, Kenneth Henry, and Vu Nguyen focus on how artificial intelligence technology can help to deal with exceptional cases. The core element in their approach is the concept of a messenger (in web 2.0 applications this would be the virtual alter ego of the citizen) acting on behalf of citizens. Based on a scenario, they illustrate the opportunities as well as the problems of a web services based approach and a regime approach. A regime is the collected procedural requirements of an individual agency. The complementary approach proposed in this paper offers a customized, integrated view of the procedure to the citizen, even though this may actually involve numerous back office activities of a variety of agencies.

The contribution by Andreas Mitrakas deals with the reality of multiple identities, physical and electronic, and the need to manage these identities. Mitrakas discusses an architecture that enables the exchange of identity information with the aim of establishing trust. The Hub eID Intermediary is developed to overcome existing shortcomings in communication applications by using certificate management for establishing identities. A lack of interoperability with regard to authentication and non-repudiation are among the core problems that can slow down the further development of the shared services approach

In the contribution by Yao-Hua Tan, and Helle Zinner Henriksen, other less specific hurdles with regard to integrated service delivery, as proposed by René, are discussed, including interoperability, a lack of orchestration and autonomy of public agencies. Based on the Information Technology for Adoption and Intelligent Design for e-Government (ITAIDE), a project focused on e-Customs, these hurdles are discussed in different Living Labs settings, with a main focus is on the Dutch Beer Living Lab. The case description illustrates how the first two of the three hurdles may be overcome by orchestrating web services. Autonomy of public agencies may lead to businesses opening their ERP systems to Customs and Excise, rather than the other way around. Furthermore, Tan and Henriksen illustrate some additional advantages of the Living Labs concept, for instance co-creation, which are typical of open innovation approaches, overcoming information asymmetry and dealing with sticky information.

In the final contribution on e-Government, Nitesh Bharosa, Ralph Feenstra, Jeffrey Gortmaker, Bram Klievink, and Marijn Janssen articulate the ideas René had on a flexible, transparent and responsive e-Government.

An architecture based on generic, standardized components would contribute to such a government. The research defined by René in close collaboration with Marijn Janssen provides insight into the issues that concerned René. In the final contribution, the initial scope of the research on e-Government is discussed in terms of public services delivered by public service networks, as are the role service-oriented government and the relevance of architectures. Conceptually, the research is closely related to Malone and Crowston's coordination theory. Starting from this approach, web service orchestration 'can be viewed as the coordination of a sequence of web service invocations, i.e. managing the dependencies between the web services'. Several coordination mechanisms can be used to manage dependencies between services, and alternative service compositions can be attributed to different coordination mechanisms. These different compositions of web services may lead to different outcomes. Building a portfolio of service can help develop roadmaps to the e-Government 'to be', and it can be re-used in the design of new business processes, in combination with the applications to be provided. The authors illustrate how the different PhD projects contribute to the vision, taking in account the specificities of government, e-Government technological capabilities and the societal needs and impacts. Combining technology with more social approaches was a key element in René's work.

PART III: SOCIO-TECHNOLOGICAL DESIGN
In Part III we bundled a number of essays that address a range of topics that may at face value seem quite different, have that have a lot in common. Recurring themes are related to infrastructure issues, services in the mobile, software or crisis management domain, to building blocks, ontologies, business models and business cases, modelling and architectural issues. However, in all these areas, the socio-technological design approach plays a key role.

In his contribution, Patrick de Wilde engages in an imaginary dialogue with René, discussing the relationship between technology, more specifically Information and Communication Technology, and management-related and organizational issues. Technological developments in network technology, middleware, architectural thinking and service approach, like WiFi, 3G+, service-oriented architectures, software as services, etc., offer opportunities for business and governments, as well as raising questions as to how these technologies have to be absorbed and managed, while having an impact on service innovation, business processes and business models. Patrick de Wilde specifically addresses the work René started in the area of Crisis Management and Information and Communication Technology, and his support for the line of research in the mobile domain that already had the attention of the Information and Communication Technology section before René came to Delft. Managing collaboration between researchers with different backgrounds, ranging from Physics to Social Science, is necessary to achieve scientific breakthroughs. It is only when we succeed in bringing researchers with different backgrounds together that we will be able to solve scientific as well as societal problems in the field of mobile technology, crisis management and the intelligent enabling technologies that are necessary to support sustainability projects, energy, water, transport, logistics or even ICT infrastructures themselves, in the private as well as the public domains.

An example of such an approach is described in the contribution by John Groenewegen and Rolf Künneke. They describe how the public value of broadband can be analyzed from a New and Original Institutional Economics perspective. In their approach, they try to assess the social benefits of broadband roll-outs. The two options with regard to broadband roll-out, a disruptive and an evolutionary approach, raise a number of questions with regard to the risks and uncertainties involved in these investment, while the social benefits can only be assessed in the long run. Their approach is an interesting alternative to the work provided by the Central Planning Bureau (CPB), which appears to be rooted in neo-classical economics. The CPB approach clearly misses the essence of the opportunities provided by broadband roll-out. It is clear that there has to be agreement on the economic and social value of broadband. The two paths Groenewegen and Künneke describe for institutional change are quite interesting, all the more so because one of the PhD projects in which René was involved specifically addressed one of these paths, i.e. the path in which uncertainty and risk perceptions with respect of future investments in broadband could be determined. The second path appears to involve a more long-term approach. Nevertheless, René's involvement in the public value of broadband projects is an illustration of the kind of broad open multi-disciplinary approach that is needed to deal with enabling infrastructures.

The next paper illustrates René's interest in ontologies and architectural approaches, and system design and crisis management. Zofia Lukszo, Koen Van Dam, Margot Weijnen and Gerard Dijkema describe an agent modelling approach for dealing with efficient and reliable operations of critical infrastructures. This approach is an example of what a socio-technical system can achieve. Starting from an ontology, a generic framework is developed. This generic framework enables the re-use of generic building blocks. The framework is used to present two example cases. The first case deals with inter-modal freight transport, the second with supply chain analyses for an oil refinery. Based on these cases, lessons are drawn that can help develop agent behavior models in crisis management. These models can in turn be used in training and decision-making processes.

Socio-technological design is also a core topic in the Systems Engineering, Policy Analysis and Management education program, as well as in the Information Architecture Master's program that was set up by and co-directed by René and Jan Dietz. This collaboration between the ICT group of the TBM faculty and the Computer Science department is discussed in the contribution by Paulien Herder and Uldrik Speerstra, who discuses the multi-disciplinary background of the education programs, and take a close look at the role of the capstone project, and the principals behind this project. Both the design process and the socio-technological systems perspective are discussed. It is impossible to combine the technological, institutional and process-related perspectives on existing approaches and methods. In a sense, this would be like inventing the wheel while cycling.

An example of how a socio-technological design is dealt with within the Information Architecture program is provided by Eric Bun, Tim de Koning, Ton Monasso, Pim Veldhoven & Alex Verheij. In their essay, they present the results from a project they were involved in with René. The authors pay attention to the concerted designs of the institutional and the technological systems that have to be in place to combat the outbreak of an infectious disease. The essay is an illustration of the points made earlier by Patrick de Wilde, and shows how technological expertise should be combined with management and organizational science. The authors come up with two systems, a more process-oriented one and a more technical one, to solve problems with regard to the containment of infectious diseases. The essay is an example of the design work carried out at the Technology Policy and Management Faculty, and of the approach René was defining.

PART IV: LET THOUSAND FLOWERS BLOOM

A topic that was close to René's heart, and that is still a core subject for the Information and Communication technology group, is that of mobile telecommunication, and (mobile) services innovation and design. User behavior is an important issue in this regard, as is standardization. In the last part of this book we discuss some of the marks that René left in these three domains: mobile (service) innovation, user involvement and standardization.

In the area of mobile telecommunication Harry Bouwman, Mark De Reuver and Guadalupe Flores Hernández discuss the troublesome relationship between business models and strategy. They suggest that mobile web services, being one of the exponents of component thinking, will have a huge impact on business models in the mobile telecommunication domain. Mobile web services will lead to the decomposition of services in the mobile domain. Services that have traditionally been offered by telecommunication providers can (in a modular network) be offered by other parties as well. As a result, a number of strategic questions have to be answered, again illustrating the interrelatedness between technological and business-related choices.

Christer Carlsson and Pirkko Walden also discuss the added value of mobile services in relation to enabling technologies, for instance SmartAMLETS, which refer to smart and adaptive mobile technologies that will help users make better decisions. Carlsson and Walden are highly interested in questions regarding the value of mobile services, which they explain by referring to Fernand Braudel, the French historian from L' Ecole des Annales. This rule implies that only when new technologies enable the behavior of users to expand ordinary routines and behavior in another direction, this technology is of value to the user. The multi agent SmartAMLETS are software modules that are assumed to expand the opportunities of businesses as well as the end-users of mobile services. The authors show how SmartAMLETS could change everyday life. Although the SmartAMLETS did not make it as a EU-project, a proposal in which René was involved, many of the attributes and functionalities are built into the mobile services that are brought to the Finnish mobile market.

In the contribution by Els van de Kar and Bart Nieuwenhuis, the scope is broadened to include the concept of service innovation, i.e. moving away from the mobile infrastructure to the broadband infrastructure, and focusing more on service innovation, rather than service design. Van de Kan and Nieuwenhuis look at the economic relevance of the service industry and, based on a service innovation framework, they analyze the obstacles to innovation in service companies. Based on data from twenty-six companies, they discuss service innovation strategies and management, as well as the innovations that are enabled by the service systems. Their results confirm earlier studies, as well as offering new observations. The results of the study will contribute to the development of a service innovation center, an initiative that René would have enjoyed and supported.

Closely related to service innovation is the concept of user-generated content, which is associated with Web 2.0 applications, in which users are actively involved, as content generators as well as potential providers of parts of the infrastructure. Jolien Ubacht, in her contribution, deals with the blurring roles between public and private spaces, physical and virtual worlds, consumer and producer roles, social and economic interactions, and in the motile roles people can play in Web 2.0 reality. In her paper, Ubacht raises the kinds of questions René would have asked: what is the relevance of your typology?; So what?; What is the next (research) step? In short, the blurring of borders between traditional domains raises a number of relevant (negative and positive) issues for policy-makers and regulators. In her paper, Ubacht focuses on the positive trends, arguing that end-user initiatives should be supported and explored to open new open avenues for innovation. These new avenues will have consequences for a number of economic sectors as well for trans-sectoral innovations, for education, but also for the governance of, for instance, infrastructures, as well as for new modes of government regulation.

Whereas Ubacht focuses on the role of end-users, Hans Pronk discusses some interesting new technologies, in an attempt to assess the impact of new technology concepts like cloud-computing, a subset of utility-oriented grid-computing. Sharing computing resources in a grid environment is a trend that may reinforce the dominant position of a very limited number of dominant players in the computing and platform domains. Amazon Elastic Compute Cloud creates, launches and terminate sserver instances on demand, raising questions with regard to where information is stored and where processing takes place, as well as raising regulatory issues. In the second part of his paper, Pronk raises some interesting points with regard to the virtual identity, virtual world and virtual economies. In the third part of his paper, he discusses the role of ICT in the physical domain and how this can threaten privacy, for instance through large-scale video surveillance, in combination with facial recognition. All three topics addressed by Pronk are issues that René would have liked to explore in greater detail, trying to understand dilemma's privacy versus the necessary protection against terrorism.

Kees van de Meer starts by bringing the horrifying events of 9/11 back to memory, not to address crisis management issues, but to discuss issues that are relevant in the aftermath of a crisis, i.e. the recovery phase. He specifically addresses issues of regarding the recovery of information that is available in physical and electronic systems. He proposes the concept of building blocks for records management, and discusses how standards can play a role in defining the technological building blocks. Although the relevance of building blocks with regard to records management and the underlying business case are clear, there are still a large number of research questions that need to be answered before the concept can be put in practice.

This book offers a broad range of topics in which René Wagenaar was interested. Topics he liked to debate and explore, both with an eye for the practical and the scientific relevance. Many people will miss René and his eagerness to debate and discuss the topics that had his interest.

Delft, February 27, 2008

Professor René W. Wagenaar ePrototype Bazaar:
The Undergraduate and Graduate Students Prototype Presentation

The Bled eConference Committee has learned about how the graduate students could be involved in the conference by an example which Professor René W. Wagenaar has provided in 1992.

Professor René W. Wagenaar first came to Bled in 1992, when he attended the second symposium on Research and Teaching Electronic Data Interchange–EDI, organized a day before the Fifth international conference 'EDI and Interorganizational Systems in the Global Environment'. Coauthoring with two of his PhD students at that time, Haydee Sheombar and Hans van der Heijden, he has participated with a paper titled Research on EDI at the Faculty of Business Administration, Erasmus University of Rotterdam.

After the conference, he has offered an opportunity to one of the University of Maribor students, Tomaž Borštner, to visit the Erasmus University in Rotterdam (René's university at that time) for two weeks. A day after the Bled conference, Tomaž Borštner was in a car with the René's group on their way to Rotterdam; currently he is Director of IT, Bankart Ljubljana.

That experience has meant a major change in a way we were involving students into the Bled eConference program since than. One of the results of working with René was a formalization of the prototypes presentations, named 'Students Bazaar' in recent years.

Among the chairs of the Students Bazaar there were:
Matt Glowatz, University College Dublin
Eric van Heck, Erasmus University Rotterdam
Jukka Heikkilä, University of Jyväskylä
Niels Christian Juul, Copenhagen Business School & Roskilde University
Gregor Lenart, University of Maribor
Robert Leskovar, University of Maribor
Andreja Pucihar, University of Maribor
Paula Swatman, Stuttgart Institute of Management and Technology & Deakin University

From 2007 on, the ePrototype Bazaar of the annual Bled eConference is named in the René's honor "Professor René W. Wagenaar ePrototype Bazaar: The Undergraduate and Graduate Students Prototype Presentation" (http://BledConference.org/2007/StudentsBazaar).

Professor René Wagenaar had a sense for the upcoming innovative ways of interorganizational collaboration provided by the eTechnologies. He was anxious about developing the appropriate methods of conveying knowledge and experience to the students. In order to document his early insights into what is very obvious today, his text, published in the proceedings of the second symposium on Research and Teaching EDI in 1992, is reprinted in this publication in 2008.

On behalf of the Bled eConference Committee we are expressing the appreciation of the René's contributions to the conference.

Andreja Pucihar, Gregor Lenart, Jože Gričar
eCenter, Faculty of Organizational Sciences, University of Maribor, Slovenia

Enclosure
Reprint of 1992

Researching and Teaching EDI

Second Symposium

**The Fifth International EDI –
Electronic Data Interchange Conference**

**INTERORGANIZATIONAL SYSTEMS
IN THE GLOBAL ENVIRONMENT**

Bled, Slovenia, September 5, 1992

Hotel Toplice

RESEARCH ON EDI AT THE FACULTY OF BUSINESS ADMINISTRATION, ERASMUS UNIVERSITY OF ROTTERDAM

R.W. Wagenaar
Faculty of Business Administration, Erasmus University, The Netherlands

I. INTRODUCTION

Telematics, in particular EDI and more generally Value Added Services, is rapidly altering business environments. The issue is not only to have better communications between human beings: equally important is the interconnection of different organizational processes both within and between organizations. Just-In-Time management of logistics processes, electronic interchange of data between trading partners, electronic funds transfer and the integral control of goods flows are exemplary of the trend towards strategically interlinking business processes.

To establish such strategic electronic links between organizations, so-called Inter Organizational Information Systems (IOS) have to be implemented. Viewed another way, IOS can be considered as a strategic tool, by which organizations can reinforce their competitive posture. Making such systems effective however, requires a thorough evaluation of both the existing relations between the functional areas within a company, as well as the companies' relations with its environment. The outcome of such an internal as well as external analysis often points at considerable changes to be made in the companies' existing operations. Companies' top management should be aware of the opportunities IOS's might offer to the business in terms of creating an improved service level or even new services to their customers.

Although more and more account is made in the literature of successful implementations of IOS's, many organizations still lack the skills to perform an in-depth strategic planning study regarding the impact of information technology, and telematics in particular, on their business performance, and to subsequently incorporate this into information systems plans.

In-depth research on, as well as education and training of (future) managerial staff in these strategic issues is therefore urgently required. Those tasks are undertaken since 1988 by the Faculty of Business Administration at the Erasmus University in Rotterdam.

II. RESEARCH FRAMEWORK

Currently, our research and educational activities are focusing on the following three 'scope of analysis' levels:

1. The single company level:
how to re-engineer the intracompany processes, give the capabilities of EDI and other Value Added Services.

2. The dyadic company level
how may the intercompany processes be coordinated by EDI in case two companies decide to redesign their operations in partnership.

3. The business network level:
which transformations among existing roles within a business network may be driven by EDI and which new roles may emerge?

Below a description is give of three research projects, which are currently in progress.

A. EDI and logistics design; A Theory of Logistical Coordination and Design Aids in Dyadical Partnerships

RESEARCH ASSISTANT: HAYDEE SHEOMBAR, M.SC.

Electronic Data Interchange (EDI) enables organizations to redesign their current ways of working, especially the way they interface to other organizations. EDI, together with the trend of organizations going back to their core business, makes the design of inter organizational relationships and the inherent communication using the capabilities of EDI a key factor for a firm's success. For the business redesigner a thorough understanding of the principles underlying boundary crossing communication is a necessity. This research aims at providing this understanding in the form of a theory of coordination at an operational level between organizational units.

In order to keep the research tractable the application domain of the theory has been limited. As an outset for the theory development two logistical organizations which cooperate closely together to jointly manage their boundary crossing goods flows, a dyadical Value Adding Partnership (VAP), is taken. Such a VAP is governed by a long term contract of which the operational aspects are the subject of this research.

The theory describes the coordination problem that two interacting logistical systems have to deal with, and derives from (internal) organization theory three basic coordination mechanisms for accomplishing this coordination. The factors determining the choice of a coordination mechanism are identified, along with a set of evaluation variables for selecting the best mechanism under certain circumstances. Simulation will be used as a means to test certain hypotheses derive from the theory. To this end a simulation tool based on a modeling approach for logistical processes has been developed. This approach allows for an integrated specification of information and physical tasks, and is able to include among others the coordination schemes encountered in business practice. The simulation tool could also be used as a redesign support tool.

This logistical coordination theory should provide the business redesigner with the insight necessary to, given the improved internal operations of both parties in the VAP and the logistical performance requirements, design the business communication protocol (messages and scenarios for their exchange) between both organizational units. To mange the design process for more intense inter organizational relationships, a method for redesign which builds on the coordination theory is proposed. Key components of this method are a design aid and accompanying guidelines for the specification of the business communication protocol, and a set of guidelines pertaining to the handling of exceptions and the resulting informal communications.

B. Participation in Electronic Markets
RESEARCH ASSISTANT: HANS VAN DER HEIJDEN M.Sc.

Electronic markets, broadly defined as inter-organizational information systems that support participating buyers and sellers in their trading processes, can be scientifically analyzed along various approaches.
Strategic and economic approaches dominate the emerging body of knowledge, but legal and modeling issues are also starting to be covered.

The PhD-research project 'Electronics market participation' deals with the economics issues of joining an electronics market. A conceptual framework has been constructed that explains both buyer and seller behaviour in this context. The framework springs from transaction cost economics, network externalities and previous research at the department.

Using transaction cost economy, it is argued that the degree of buyer participation depends on the savings that electronic markets provide on market transaction costs. The same argument holds for sellers, since sellers incur market transaction costs as well. For buyers, savings in market transaction costs increase as more sellers join the system. For sellers, the savings in market transaction costs increase as more buyers join the system. This makes an electronic market subject to positive consumption externalities, or network externalities as it is frequently called: the degree of participation depends on the degree of participation of the organization's trading partners. Furthermore, savings in the market transaction costs are reduced by the investments that an electronic market system demands, including hardware, software, organizational learning and organizational change.

So far, the participation problem has been expressed using transaction cost economy. Previous research at the department, however, enables us to assert that additional inhibiting determinants affect the degree of participation of both buyers and sellers. We assert that the degree of buyer participation is negatively influence by seller's market transaction savings and that the degree of seller participation is negatively influenced by buyer's market transaction savings. The main rationale behind these affections is that organizations fear to be evaluated more easily.

Empirical evidence is sought for the above statements by doing explanatory, multiple case study research on a number of electronic markets in The Netherlands. Design and implementation are currently under way.

C. The Port of Rotterdam management simulation game
PRIME RESEARCHER: DR. RENÉ W. WAGENAAR

With financial aid from the Dutch Ministry of Economic Affairs and the Directorate General XIII of the Commission of the European Communities, a management simulation game has been developed in partnership with Bakkenist Management Consultants, a leading management consultancy firm in The Netherlands and involved in many EDI-project. The game addresses the strategic issues involved in by introducing Electronic Data Interchange (EDI) for the control of multimodal, global transport. Its objectives are to create widespread awareness of the catalyst role EDI may play in restructuring business operations. It is based on studies of the information flows controlling the flow of goods through the Port of Rotterdam. The game leads participants through a learning process starting from a traditional paper document processing environment into a fully integrated EDI work environment.

So far, experiences from playing the game at seminars, international courses as well as within the regular programmes of the Faculty, are very encouraging and clearly demonstrate managers' needs for such training tools. Further research will focus on extending the current business protocol in the game with the contracting phase and payment phase. Next or in parallel, a 'meta-modelling' technique will be developed, which enables fast prototyping of business networks and their protocols.

PART 1

THE VIRTUAL MERCHANT

THE NEED TO PAY MORE ATTENTION TO GENERATING THE 'TRUST' THAT IS INDISPENSABLE IN TRADE IN THE CURRENT CONSTRUCTION PHASE OF THE ELECTRONIC HIGHWAY.

From Virtual Merchant

Trust in the network

Peter H.M. Vervest

Introduction

On 14 March 1997 René Wagenaar accepted his position as professor of 'tele-informatics' at the Free University of Amsterdam. With pride and regret we saw him depart from our faculty of Information and Decision Sciences, RSM Erasmus University: A good colleague and friend left but promoted to an important position. René's inaugural speech 'The Virtual Merchant, fiction or reality' (1997) inspired us all. The speech remains memorable today: Both its content as well as the immaculate and inspiring graphical design by Brenda, René's lifelong wife and companion. René's key theme: "*New communication services such as the Internet challenge the traditional principles that have shaped our production and customer processes since Alfred Sloan and Henry Ford. Communication will be an integral part of future primary production processes ... and trust is an un-dervalued component of that future*".

In memory of René I will review a number of his positions in this memorable speech against the reality of today, more than ten years hence. Internet trade is now a fact, larger and bigger than many of us foresaw in 1997. Mobile and wireless communications – then not yet a factor in e-commerce – have grown at incredible speed. We see – and experience – the vulnerability of the global interdependence that the electronic highways have created, every day, from personal hazards as spam or global catastrophes as today's crises in our financial systems. None would have happened if today's communication means would not have provided such unprecedented speed to spread commerce around the globe. The electronic silk routes, the cyber routes in the words of René, have changed our world. René was convinced that it would only prosper in a world of trust: How do you get to a world of trust, and what happens if that 'trust' is not given?

I will first review René's speech and then assess trust as an essential condition for major growth of electronic trade. I will argue that our management and control systems are not geared to handle massive electronic trade. We need to understand – and to manage – the complexity of global business networks – or we will risk to fail without knowing where – or what – broke the chain.

Is the 'virtual merchant' real?

A market is a place where buyers and sellers meet; and the ownership, or risk, of products is being exchanged. That is the simple definition. Markets developed when cities formed, and farmers came to trade their merchandise on the local market. The city authorities facilitated the market: By allowing the physical space for the market itself, by providing and controlling access, by regulating the trade process. The authorities were paid by way of levies and duties on the transactions, or by charging persons for access to the market. The merchant is the person who populates the market to buy or sell goods not originally produced by himself. Merchants are intermediaries between the producer and the consumer, they take risk in matching supply and demand, they bridge positions between different trade parties in different locations and different time zones.

According to René it is a ground rule for any trade that price increases as the goods move from location (Wagenaar, 1997, p. 8). Simply to compensate for the move of the goods...! The merchant was required to assess exante if there was profit in moving the goods. Trade meant that goods would change 'hands' (or ownership) many times on their destiny to the 'end', or final, consumer. The 'end' of the value chain. Every change of hands is seen as a transaction cost. The ultimate price for the consumer usually was many times the initial price – and the sum of transaction costs was huge.

The 'silk route' is a phrase coined by Ferdinand von Richthofen (Wagenaar, 1997, p.9): It is a network of trade routes – in this case: transport routes – to connect the origin of the silk, China, to the ultimate consumer, Europe. The Parthans dominated the routes in the Roman days and efforts to circumvent this powerful nation, via sea, or otherwise, failed many times. In 762 AD the Arabs founded what we now know as Baghdad – and they succeeded in creating alternative routes via sea. Their dominance resulted in equally high costs and it was not until the mongol ruler Koebilai Chan around 1250 created a world empire from Central Asia to Hungary that a new corridor developed. This was what Marco Polo discovered. And a lot more: Close to

the new emperor he understood their ways of regulation and trade.
As trade developed on a global scale, due to the discovery of the Americas at the end of the 15th century and the development of sea going vessels, the trade routes required a new organization. They required capital in the transport system (expensive ships) and an organization to 'securitize' the risks associated with wide sea-going transport in those days. Amsterdam realized in 1611 the first-ever 'bourse', an exchange to trade goods-on-the-move. The bill-of-lading, the 'cognossement', it came from that time. It generated 'trust', a more or less justifiable expectation that trade would be as had been agreed: That risk would be allocated according to agreed and set rules. The 'company' was invented to group individual persons together and to rule the risks that they jointly – as a company – and individually had taken. No longer the (wealthy) individual was the point of gravity in economic life: Companies would become equally, and over time even more, important...

René believed profoundly that the modern cyberroutes will change all this. In ancient trade – as well as during the industrial era – traders aimed to control the trade routes. Control of transport meant control of transaction costs. Information on the transport routes meant one could dominate access to resources as well as the prices for exchange of those resources. According to René instant communication and accurate information on a global scale would change the essence of trade. First, as a result of electronic data interchange (EDI) the chain of events between trade partners, the value chain, can be highly rationalized, reducing slack, throughput times and inventories while maintaining customer-order identities high-up in the chain (Wagenaar, 1997, p. 21). Second, increased information-richness, e.g. via multimedia representation of goods and services, facilitates direct interaction between producers and consumers: "... *The fact that you as ultimate consumer direct the production, as a 'virtual visitor' of the producer or his agent, is an entirely new phenomenon, unprecedented in history ...*" (Wagenaar, 1997, p. 28). In early times 'made-to-order' was generally done, but it required local presence, the customer to visit the nearby production shop: The cyberworld removed distance as a key factor of organizing production and customer processes. The merchant became 'virtual', no longer a real entity, but a function embedded in the cyberroutes: Consumers interacting directly with producers and between themselves, a market economy (re-)turning into a transaction economy, ultimate personalization of everything that would be 'produced' ...! A new intermediary would emerge, the 'cybermediary' such as Amazon (Wagenaar, 1997, p. 33).

Internet trade has grown far beyond the expectations of those days, 1997. It succeeded despite the pitfalls and issues so well enumerated (Wagenaar, 1997, p. 39 – 47), such as failing security, non-warranted authorization, lack of privacy, non-reliability, low system-response times. Internet trade has become an accepted way of buying and selling goods. But one issue from the list still stands out: Trust. Or put differently, the vulnerability of today's electronic trade systems. How much do we really know of fraudulent transactions, identity theft, breaches of privacy, or electronic burglary? It may not be in the interest of the virtual merchants to have us fully informed on the vulnerabilities of the very systems that make them exist. Where are the 'trusted third parties' (Wagenaar, 1997, p. 52) and why is the cyberworld of trade so seemingly unregulated?

Trust as essential condition of massive electronic trade

What is 'trust'? One of René's PhD students, Roger Bons (1997), defines trust as *"a particular level of subjective probability with which an agent assesses that another agent or group of agents will perform a particular action ..."*. Trust in other words is the likelihood that the counterparty in a transaction will not display 'opportunistic' behavior, i.e. do not what has been agreed because it is more beneficial for him to dishonor the commitment. Electronic trade is trustworthy if transactions have a high probability to deliver what has been agreed between actors.

Let us imagine a world where all trade transactions are fully 'virtual', i.e. even if you buy a physical good, all that goes to trade that good, from search to the actual purchasing decision, all logistical processes involved in physical delivery, every part of the financial transactions, all administrative handling, return shipments, all is done fully electronic, or rather: 'virtual'. You cannot see any part of the transaction, have no record other than what is somewhere contained in the network. You do not physically 'know' the person that sells, or buys, or any of the intermediaries. You do not know the parties who produce or deliver the goods. It is an unknown world of production processes linked to yours as a customer. The only remarkable thing is 'it happens', you get your delivery, on time, against the set price and conditions. Over time you develop 'trust'. If it works again and again. Until it does not work. What then?

This in a nutshell is the enormous vulnerability that we face. One, if something goes wrong, where do you start? Thousands and thousands of computer systems have been interlinked to guide all the processes that collectively should ensure that the transaction works for you, individually. But you are not able – if you were at all capable – to inspect these systems and investigate where it went wrong. You are lost on the cyberroutes. And nobody tells you. You require end-to-end process control – the first condition for massive electronic trade.

Second, once you found out it is wrong and what is wrong, how do you remedy the situation? What alternatives do you have? How do you choose? And when are you relieved from the agreement with the other party whose identity you may not know? This is condition two for massive electronic trade: Contingency management.

Third, now that you have opted for an alternative, how can you actually enforce that this will work? That parties that you may not know, do as is actually agreed? From a distance, with no direct interface, in a different place, with different governance? How much redundancy is required in order to be able to generate satisfactory outcomes of interconnected organizational systems with a satisfying probability that it will happen: Condition three for massive electronic trade, managerial command in the hands of the customer.

These three conditions for massive electronic trade: End-to-end process control, contingency management; and customer managerial command, seem self-explanatory in an e-commerce system under central control, or in single ownership. But that is not the reality of our global trade systems. Many organizations are involved, each their own boss, each having a role to play, holding a part of the puzzle, each needing to link, and to synchronize, their section of the process chain. It will not help to call the call centre – they have the same problem.

The risk of broken chains is not only apparent in trade of physical goods. It is more so if services, or digital products, are being transacted, watermarked or copy-protected, or not. Digital products seem easier to handle on the cyberroutes, simply because no physical delivery is involved. But how long will customers accept that they do no longer 'own' the digital products that they buy, but only get temporary access. If you loose your iPod with a fortune of iTunes on it, can I get a copy and not pay the full price, can I sell it to someone else? Is the digital world purely a temporary subscription to something that I cannot use to add value? Am I allowed to use the electronic design of my kitchen from one kitchen manufacturer to ask for competitive bids from another one? Or to use this design in an Internet auction to get the best bids for the services and goods that I need? And what if that design or the tool is faulty?

It is interesting to note that René did not address the need for command and control systems in electronic trade. In years thereafter this became much debated as electronic commerce generated many issues around fulfillment management (Vervest and Dunn, 2001). Trust will not develop as long as managerial command – at the customer level – across different e-trade systems, is not provided. End-to-end process control, straight-through from customer interaction to production process, and contingency management need much improvement to avoid that massive use of electronic trade systems result in massive vulnerabilities to all concerned. This is one of the reasons why real time Business Process Management is so important (Fisher, 2005) and operating environments are required that enable to swap process elements in real time (Vervest, 2005). We are not yet there.

Trust as a network issue

When René wrote his inaugural speech the general view was that 'trust' could be provided by establishing 'trusted third parties', entities that would govern electronic trade by establishing the rules. These 'TTP's' would act as the old city authorities that governed the physical markets: The TTP would define where the market takes place, who can participate, they would regulate the trade processes, including acting as the ultimate authority to settle disputes. It is remarkable how few TTP's actually developed. It is difficult to provide a good example. The reality seems to be that trust in today's electronic trade systems is generally established by the platform providers themselves, in particular the large ones such as Amazon, eBay, Expedia, etc. They use a variety of methods such as reputation cards, arbitrage, payment settlement, identity management. However, the dependence on these platforms is becoming huge while these companies are largely self-regulated. Mostly these platforms do not provide management functionality beyond their own platform. So what can be done to establish trust across different platforms?

In a way René has pointed to an innovative way for establishing trust by investigating the silk routes and Marco Polo's impact on it. Marco Polo did not only provide knowledge on the 'full' route (meaning, he went from Venice in Italy to today's Beijing in China, and returned), he also understood the different relays that had been taken, and developed, however primitive, a 'map' of the various routes, or paths, that can be taken. He may have understood that trade routes form part of a 'network' of interconnected nodes (the cities, or relays), each linked via pathways, with different properties like the mode of transport, the difficulty in different seasons, local circumstances such as safety, retributions to be paid, etc. The network can be more or less 'robust', i.e. able to provide an end-to-end path under many different circumstances (Bar-Yam, 1997).

The notion of network is important: Trust can develop if different routes are generally available in a system in such a way that the desired result can be achieved under a variety of unforeseen circumstances, so that the chain need not be broken. Over the last years significant research has been – and is being – carried out to understand how organizations and people perform as 'networks' rather than as individual actors (Vervest et al., 2005). The intriguing theme of this 'business network' research is that the individual firm can exhibit properties that cannot be discovered or understood by studying them in isolation. If two cars are distanced, the speed of one car has no or little influence on the other. But if they are close, the driver must interact with the other, braking when the car before does, or accelerating to keep up. Seen from a distance, a group of cars forms a wave – with properties that cannot be studied by analyzing the individual cars. The same applies to the 'business network' (Van Heck and Vervest, 2007). The network, not the individual company, becomes the point of gravity.

It could be postulated that trust in a business network is related to the structure of that network (defined loosely as who links to whom): As an example, it can be argued that some network structures are better suited to ensure that the contracted result between actors is delivered than other structures. Trust, defined as the likelihood that 'you get what you expect', can be seen as the result of the links – or paths – in a network. The person who holds the best map of those links in the network, would be able to get the best position (Van Liere, 2007).

Braha (2005) provided an interesting assessment of how structural properties of networks can be analyzed: Studying the topology of product development networks he finds that the distribution of incoming communication links always has a cutoff point while the distribution of outgoing communication links is scale-free with or without a cutoff point. In other words, actors are limited in their ability to process information, but unrestricted in their ability to communicate information. Braha compares this to Simon's bounded rationality argument, i.e. actors are limited in their ability to process incoming information. If we put this to trade networks, it would therefore be important to see the distribution of incoming and outgoing trade links – and see if similar unbalances are present. Van Liere (2007) argues that network actors each have different 'network horizons': The number of actors (also called alters – referring to the direct neighboring alter and to the alter's alter, and so on) that can be seen in the network. Like Braha he finds in his study of the insurance world a trade-off point: There is an optimum of how much an actor should invest in his network horizon, more is not always better.

We still do not adequately understand the relationship between network topologies (and the availability of maps) and the development of trust in electronic trade systems. It will be an important challenge to find out.

Concluding Remarks

The 'virtual' merchant has become real. Electronic trade is a multi-trillion Euro business. Remarkably few disasters have hit us. But multi-party electronic trade systems still do not provide essential cross-platform management facilities such as customer command, end-to-end control, contingency management. Trust comes by foot and leaves by horse: As trust is so under-engineered in our systems, we risk that once big failures happen, complete economic systems will be affected, perhaps wiped out. Like many trade routes were foreclosed by governments or the trade parties themselves, this could also happen to global electronic trade. René's inaugural speech still is valid over ten years since it was delivered in Amsterdam. Analogous to the silk routes of Marco Polo, let us try to understand the impact of today's network structures on the development of trust in global cooperation.

References

Bar-Yam, Y. (1997). *Dynamics of Complex Systems*, Westview Press, Boulder, USA.

Bons, R., (1997). *Designing Trustworthy Trade Procedures for Open Electronic Commerce*, PhD-Series in General Management 27, Rotterdam School of Management, TRAIL Research School, EURIDIS, Rotterdam.

Braha, D., Bar-Yam, Y. Information Flow Structure in Large-Scale Product Development Organizational Networks, pp. 106 - 126, in: Vervest, P.H.M., Van Heck, E., Preiss, K., Pau, L-F., eds., (2005). *Smart Business Networks*, Heidelberg: Springer Verlag.

Fisher, L., ed., (2005). *Workflow Handbook*, Future Strategies, USA, wfmc@wfmc.org.

Van Heck, E., Vervest, P. H. M., (2007). How the Network Wins, *Communications of the ACM*, 50(6), 29 - 37.

Van Liere, D. W., (2007). *Network Horizon and the Dynamics of Network Positions*, Doctoral Dissertation, Erasmus Research Institute of Management ERIM, Rotterdam (NL)

Vervest, P. H. M., Dunn A. F., (2000). *How to win customers in the digital world: total action or fatal inaction?*, Springer Verlag, Heidelberg.

Vervest, P. H. M., Van Heck, E., Preiss, K., Pau, L-F., eds., (2005). *Smart Business Networks*, Springer Verlag, Heidelberg.

Wagenaar, R. W., (1997). *De Virtuele Koopman, Fictie of Werkelijkheid – Ontwikkelingen in het elektronisch handelsverkeer vanuit economisch en strategisch perspectief*, Inaugural Speech.

SOLUTIONS TO THIS ... DILEMMA ARE SOUGHT IN FLEXIBLE PRODUCTION TECHNOLOGIES THAT MAKE IT POSSIBLE TO ASSEMBLE STANDARD ELEMENTS IN VARIOUS COMBINATIONS. IN ADDITION, ATTEMPTS ARE MADE TO WORK TOGETHER WITH PARTNERS IN NETWORKS TO REDUCE TRANSACTION COSTS AND TO SHARE PART OF THE PRODUCTION PROCESS OR THE INFRASTRUCTURE THAT IS REQUIRED WITH COMPETITORS.

From *Virtual Merchant*

Modularity in Business Networks

Martijn R. Hoogeweegen & Peter H.M. Vervest

ABSTRACT

In the last 15 years we have had the opportunity the work a lot with René. We started with an EDI cost/benefit analysis project (resulting in the Edialysis decision support tool), followed by Martijn's PhD project, and then the Business Networking Game. René was always looking for the perfect contribution: it should be innovative, it should be scientifically rigorous and last but not least it should be relevant to practice. In this paper we would like to discuss whether, with hindsight, we actually met these requirements for the main ideas of Martijn's PhD project, centered around the concept of business modularity. And more importantly, looking to the future, which topics regarding business modularity are of interest to further research.

INTRODUCTION

In the last 15 years we have had the opportunity the work a lot with René. We started with an EDI cost/benefit analysis project (resulting in the Edialysis decision support tool), followed by Martijn's PhD project, and then the Business Networking Game.

René was always looking for the perfect contribution: it should be innovative, it should be scientifically rigorous and last but not least it should be relevant to practice. He was convinced that only by meeting at least these three criteria success was 'guaranteed' (in terms of journal publications and presentations at international conferences).

In this paper we would like to discuss whether, with hindsight, we actually met these three criteria for the main 'product' of Martijn's PhD project, the Modular Network Design (MND) approach. Based on these insights we would like to discuss how we could or should continue our MND research in pursuing for the perfect contribution.

Modular Network Design

Martijn's PhD research was focused on how a network of organizations could organize for fulfilling customized demand in an efficient and effective way. The idea we proposed and tested was to define the offerings of a network in modular services as well as the fulfilment processes in modular process steps. This would allow the client to select, mix and match those elements of the product offering he/she really wants, and the network / organizations to select and execute exactly those modular fulfilment processes that together would produce the requested product elements. The idea was worked out in an approach we called 'Modular Network Design' (see figure 1).

The idea is as follows. A customer places an order with one of the organizations of the network. This organization will act as the coordinator for the fulfilment of this particular order. The order is a selection of service elements offered by this organization and will be translated by the coordinator into production elements. The coordinator then will outsource the

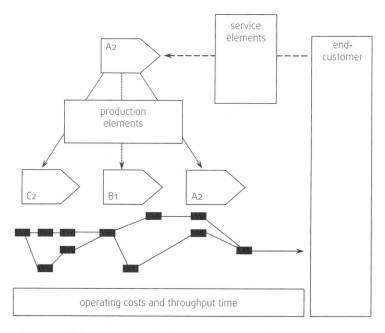

Figure 1. Modular Network Design (see Hoogeweegen et al. 1999)

actual fulfilment of these production elements to specific partners in the coordinator's network. In turn, these partners will translate the requested production elements into process elements and will, by executing these process elements, collectively produce and deliver the requested service elements by the customer.

Any specific set of service elements could be requested by a customer at any coordinator, who will translate the service elements into a specific set of production elements and will approach specific fulfilling partners. The fulfilling network of organizations will be tailored to the exact requested set of service elements.

In essence, the MND approach illustrates how business modularity enables a network to become more flexible in offering customized products and services, while keeping costs low by only fulfilling those processes that exactly will fulfil the requested service elements (nothing more, nothing less).

Evaluation
In this section we would like to discuss to what extent we have met the criteria for a 'perfect' contribution regarding our MND approach. First we discuss the degree of innovativeness, than the level of scientific rigidness, and then to what degree the developed approach is relevant to practice and also relatively easy to apply by practice.

MND: *innovative?*
The original question we were addressing when developing MND was why a network or value chain of organizations should consider adopting ICT applications like EDI. Using ICT would decrease costs along the value chain and also decrease throughput times towards the end-customer. We wanted to develop a method to be able to assess the impact of ICT in a value chain of organizations prior to actual implementation, and to assess how costs and benefits would be divided among these organizations. The hypothesis was that if we can upfront show that costs and benefits are more or less equally spread (or we can define implementation scenarios to achieve such an equal spread) that organizations would become more inclined to start implementing ICT solutions. However, we realized that

before developing such a method we should first understand the primary goal of a value chain, otherwise you do not know how to optimize (in terms of efficiency and effectiveness) a value chain with ICT. We defined the primary goal of a value chain to meet end-customer requirements, preferably in a cost efficient way. Meeting the exact requirements of customers increasingly is a challenge because customers more and more ask for personalised goods and services. More flexibility is required in fulfilment, while costs should not increase disproportionately.

Therefore, the concept of business modularity was adopted. At that time not a well spread or commonly known concept (1993). The idea of modularity is to standardize the components of a system (a product or process) in such a way that they can be separated and recombined fairly easily. This makes modularity a powerful approach to organize complex products and processes efficiently (see Venkatraman & Henderson 1998). The main benefits of applying modularity are increasing customer satisfaction, decreasing coordination costs and decreasing production costs. Garud and Kumaraswamy (1993) referred in this respect to the economies of substitution: in a modular process design only parts of a process have to be substituted by other processes to produce a different product. Modularity allows the mixing and matching of service elements to the customer's requirements and establish with a 1:1 relationship to the associated capabilities.

Although the idea of modularity was not totally new, see for instance the developments in the computer sector, with the mainframes of IBM for instance, the idea of applying modularity to business was quite new. At that time, around the mid 90s, business modularity became a popular topic, with all kinds of first movers in publishing books, proposing theories, etc. (see for instance O' Grady 1999 and Schilling 2000). Nowadays, more and more companies are adopting modular product and service designs to offer their customers the possibility to tailor products and services to their own requirements. Especially on the web, the examples of online 'product configurators' are countless. Take Dell, Nike, Sony or any car manufacturer, they all offer us to tailor our own products (see f.i. Morcott 2000). Services like insurance or logistics show a similar picture. The strength of a modular product and service design is to let customers optimally choose of a large variety of standardized options and features (see for instance Baldwin & Clark 1997). Analogously, the concept of modularity is also advocated for the design of fulfillment processes (see Venkatraman & Henderson 1998). A modular process that is triggered through a modular service portfolio, via a one-on-one relationship between process steps and service options delivers both flexibility as well as efficiency.

MND: *scientific rigor?*
For the development of the MND approach we used different sources in literature. We looked at contributions that introduced the concept of modularity (see previous sections), that analysed the impact of ICT on business networks, that developed theories of network formation and coordination and that elaborated on the concept of strategic flexibility.

Malone et al. (1987) and Clemons et al. (1993) were the key contributions regarding ICT impact on business networks. Malone argues that ICT decreases coordination costs and therefore markets become relatively more efficient than hierarchies. Following the Transaction Cost Economics approach of Williamson, Clemons et al (1993) argue that ICT impacts the trade-off between the advantage of low transaction costs in case of internal production and the low production costs of outside procurement, by lowering the transaction costs. We applied these contributions by arguing that small, modular, organizations emerge in a network that all are specialized in (one or more) capabilities (or production elements) which they quickly can be connected to other capabilities / modular organizations in the same network.

Some key contributions on network formation and coordination helped us developing the main idea of MND: to first let end-customers specify their order before actual production (see concept of 'thinking in reverse' of Jarvenpaa & Ives 1994), and then to form a 'temporary alignment' of network partners for the production of the order (see Miles & Snow 1992). After fulfilment the 'temporary alignment' dissolves again and is ready to form / participate in new alignments. Further, we adopted the concept of 'network horizon' (see Anderson et al. 1994) to describe which other network participants are known to a particular network organization. Quite relevant when looking at who to consider in a network for participation in the fulfilment of a particular customer order.

The concept of strategic flexibility as defined by Evans (1991) supported us to further specify the aim for flexibility in fulfilment to meet customized demand. With the MND approach we tried to specify the concepts of 'agility' (referring to the ability to act quickly to new opportunities) and 'versatility' (referring to the ability to do apply different capabilities depending on the needs of a particular situation – see also Bahrami 1992).

Relevant to practice?
The concept of business modularity seems highly relevant to business. As indicated in an earlier section, more and more companies are adopting modular product and service designs. Also the case studies in the logistics sector, with KLM Cargo being one of the organizations we have analysed, show how modular services are successfully applied in practise (see for instance the modular service portfolio current being offered via the internet by KLM Cargo). However, we experienced in these case studies and also later in other cases that the concept of business modularity and the way we used it in MND is quite difficult to comprehend. The application of modularity in a business context seems quite complex, although the idea of modularity seems very powerful. Questions arise like how to define service elements, and how 'granular' should they be? How to manage the interoperability of modules? How to realize a 'quick connect' with other (modular) organizations in a network? These type of questions let us realize that indeed the idea of MND is powerful, however we need more elaboration to let (potential) users fully understand why it is important and how to apply the approach in their business context.

In summary we judge MND to be an innovative idea (especially at the time we introduced the approach), to be scientific rigor in a sense that we accurately embedded the approach in literature and that the approach indeed is relevant to practice, provided that business modularity seems to be a difficult concept to comprehend.

Next steps

Based on the evaluation of the MND concept we think there are three main areas for follow up, and trust that René would have agreed... The first one is to develop new tools to further foster the understanding of why and how MND will support (organizations of) networks to become more flexible towards customized demand, while keeping current costs and throughput times low. Therefore we developed the Business Networking Game (see Hoogeweegen et al. 2006) and René was one of the main experts we consulted in the definition phase. This game simulates the changing dynamics of business networks and stimulates the players thinking whether and how to develop a strategy to cope with the mass customization trend within their own businesses. They can acquire and dismantle capabilities (modularly designed in production elements) and they can consider forming new alignments with other business in the network (by mixing and matching their production elements with other players). The game illustrates that changing customer demand both delivers opportunities and threats. It is the total set of decisions taken by the individual organizations in a particular network that will make a specific strategic choice a winning one or not. By playing this game the players experience the power of modularity and start thinking about how modularity could change their network and how they interact with others in their network.

The second one is to further research how a modular service portfolio should be defined as well as how to define modular process modules. What is an accurate level of granularity? Too little modularization restricts the possibility to mix and match with other organizations in temporary alignments. Too much modularity on the other hand fosters the transparency of your product and service offerings. Transparency will lead to increasing competition resulting in lower margins and the danger of imitation by others (see also Hoogeweegen & Vervest 2004).

The third one is to further research how indeed networks will change enabled by ICT to respond to customized demand. One of the theories is that organizations will focus on their core capabilities and outsource less relevant activities. Supported by ICT, transaction costs will decrease and thus the search costs to find relevant business partners decrease. Hierarchies will move towards markets, and networks will emerge with an increasing number of participating organizations (more organizations, with on average less capabilities than before). Baldwin et al. (2003) have also looked at this topic and came with some interesting insights. They speak of 'modular clusters' (we called them modular organizations) and they tried to answer the question of what an optimal configuration should be for a given supply market given its current level of modularity. A supply market can be defined in terms of number of steps in a value chain from raw materials to end-customer and in terms of the number of suppliers per step in the value chain (see figure 2). The higher the number of steps the more granular and the lower the number of capabilities present within each step of the value chain. The higher the number of steps, the more modular clusters are specialized, the higher the expected price per capability. The higher the number of suppliers per step the higher the intensity of the competition, the lower the expected price. Baldwin et al. (2003) agrue that for each supply market a different modular configuration could be responsible for realizing the optimal price, and therefore profitability.

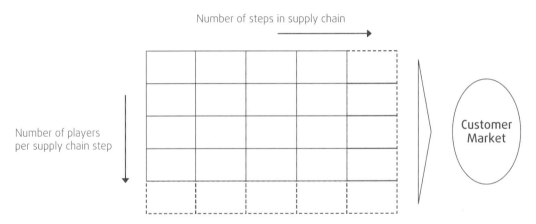

Figure 2. Modular granularity in a supply network (after Baldwin et al. 2003)

All three directions for further research we think still are very relevant and worth while further researching. In the end, if applied well, MND could really support networks of organizations to be agile and versatile towards customized demand at the same time, while keeping costs and throughput times low: adding the maximum possible value (that is personalized) and achieving high levels of profitability at the same time.

REFERENCES

Anderson, J.C., H. Håkansson, J. Johanson (1994). Dyadic Business Relationships Within a Business Network Context, *Journal of Marketing*, 58, October 1994, pp. 1-15

Bahrami, H. (1992), The Emerging Flexible Organization: Perspectives from Silicon Valley, *California Management Review*, Summer 1992, pp. 33-52

Baldwin, C. Y., Clark, K. B. (1997). Managing in an age of modularity. *Harvard Business Review*, September-October 84-93

Baldwin, C.Y., K.B. Clark, C.J. Woodard (2003). The Pricing and Profitability of Modular Clusters, HBS internal report, August 2003

Clemons, E.K., S.P. Reddi, M.C. Row (1993). The Impact of Information Technology on the Organization of Economic Activity: the 'Move to the Middle' Hypothesis, *Journal of Management Information Systems*, 10, 2, pp. 9-35

Evans, J.S. (1991). Strategic Flexibility for High Technology Manoeuvres: A Conceptual Framework, *Journal of Management Studies*, 28, 1, pp. 69-89

Garud, R., A. Kumaraswamy (1993). Changing Competitive Dynamics in Network Industries: an Exploration of Sun Mircosystems' Open Systems Strategy, *Strategic Management Journal*, 14, pp. 351-369

Hoogeweegen, M.R., W.J.M. Teunissen, P.H.M. Vervest, R.W. Wagenaar (1999). Modular Network Design: Using Information and Communication Technology to Allocate Production Tasks in a Virtual Organization, *Decision Sciences*, 30, 4, pp. 1073-1103

Hoogeweegen, M.R., P.H.M. Vervest (2004). *How Much Modularity?*, in: Smart Business Networks, editors: P.H.M. Vervest, E. van Heck, K. Preiss, and L.F. Pau, Springer, pp. 339-348

Hoogeweegen, M.R., Liere, D. van, L. Hagdorn, P.H.M. Vervest (2006). Strategizing for Mass Customisation by Playing the Business Networking Game, *Decision Support Systems*, 42, 3, pp. 1402-1412

Jarvenpaa, S.L., B. Ives (1994). The Global Network Organization of the Future: Information Management Opportunities and Challenges, *Journal of Management Information Systems*, 10, 4, pp. 25-57

Malone, T.W., J. Yates, R.I. Benjamin (1987). Electronic Markets and Electronic Hierarchies, *Communications of the ACM*, 30, June, pp. 484-497, 1987

Miles, R.E., C.C. Snow (1992). Causes of Failure in Network Organizations, *California Management Review*, Summer 1992, pp. 53-72

Morcott, S.J. (2000). Today's Automotive Supply Industry, *Vital Speeches of the Day*, 14, 4, pp. 431-434

Schilling, M.A. (2000). Towards a general modular systems theory and its application to inter-firm product modularity. *Academy of Management Review*, Vol 25:312-334.

O'Grady, P. (1999), The Age of Modularity, Adam and Steele Publishers, 1999

Venkatraman, N., Henderson. J. C. (1998), Real strategies for virtual organizing. *Sloan Management Review*, Fall 33-48

THE INTERNET HAS ERASED THE TEMPORAL AND GEOGRAPHICAL BOUNDARIES AND IS NOW THE ENGINE THAT MAKES THE VALUE CHAIN MORE DYNAMIC.

From Virtual Merchant

Forget about chains, business webs are the future!

Wout Hofman

Abstract

René has always been interested in the creation of organizational networks of business, government, and citizens. These organizational networks are the future. René's first interests in this particular area were with the Port of Rotterdam game, on which I have worked with him. With respect to this subject he wrote in his foreword of Hofman (2003) that a good combination of business issues and technical knowledge is required. Formerly, EDI messaging has been the paradigm to support business between different organizations, but currently other technical standards apply. Implementation of EDI meant large investments and thus gave high switching costs. The web has enabled consumers with the ability of switching quickly between different suppliers utilizing browser software. A shift in business chains was always the promise (Wagenaar, 1997). Business to business relations still needs high investments, but standards are improving. Service Oriented Architecture promises the creation of a business web. Challenges are service description and discovery, interoperability, which include semantics, mappings, and choreography, run time process design and operation, verification of run-time processes against the expected choreography. First of all, integration aspects of in a networked economy with available standards during the inauguration of René will be discussed (Wagenaar, 1997). Secondly, this contribution will address changes in standards and how these changes will affect business to business integration (section 2). Changes in the usage of the World Wide Web based on these new standards are discussed in section 3. It will also address issues for future research that reflect discussions I had with René on the subject of business process modeling (section 4).

Networked economy

Business approaches to integration

In the 80-s and 90-s of the previous century, a lot of effort in terms of time and money was spent on development and implementation of EDI (Electronic Data Interchange. In 1986, the exchange syntax EDIfact (EDI for administration, commerce, and transport, ISO 9735,1987) became an ISO standard. Hereafter, quite a number of successful implementations have been made and a lot are still operational. The EU Transit system for transit of goods between EU countries is a very good example (EC – DG Taxud). Other examples are in shipping, e.g. PortInfoLink. However, also a lot of effort and money has been wasted. Intis, International Transport Information System, established in 1985 is one of those examples. It lasted till mid 90-s and came up with a limited number of successful links, e.g. for the Rotterdam Customs System Rodos (PortInfoLink). Rodos has been taken over by a new system, Sagitta Binnenbrengen (Belastingdienst), which interfaces to traders, liners, etc. and is supported by PortInfoLink. EDI has been very promising. The promises that are currently stated for eBusiness also applied to EDI. Shorter time-to-market for new business services, efficiency improvement by business process redesign, and effectiveness improvement by performing the right processes are some of the promises. These promises were to be implemented by for instance reducing errors and focusing efforts of persons on exceptions instead of handle standard cases, which could be handled (semi-)automatically.

Reality was different. EDI implementation was in many cases considered a technical issue, and consequently left to the technicians, without realizing that the real challenge lay business process alignment. One should have specific knowledge of the standards, apply specific software, and more often the business case was not clear. On a business level, organizations had to discuss semantics and processes: what is a delivery date, how do we deliver, etc. These semantic discussions were intermingled by technical discussion; some persons were talking in codes, e.g. 1136 and 3161 identifying a code set to be used and the maintenance organization for that code set. From a business perspective, the main advantages seemed to be with the sender of a message, because of reduction of handling costs (mail, fax, etc.). The following approaches are considered (see figure 1, van der Vlist, 1987):

— Most successful implementations were driven by a strong partner that enforced the implementation, e.g. customs, a large retailer, and the strongest stevedore with its large customers in a port.

— Other implementations were based on combinations of different approaches, namely consensus ('subsidiarity') with a strong business case enforced by EU parliament and EU ministers, e.g. EU Transit promised fraud prevention with high raise of VAT income for customs authorities.

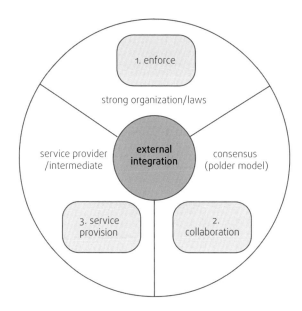

Figure 1. EDI implementations

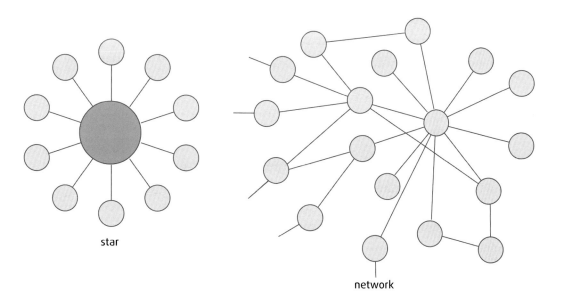

Figure 2. From star tot business web

— The last approach was based on a service provision model. A central organization developed open standards and provided them to the market on behalf of its stakeholders. These stakeholders most often participate in a service provider. Such a service provider not only offers standards, but also tools for integration (EDI adapters) and communication. The network for insurance agents (ADN: Assurantie Data Netwerk) was an example of such an approach driven by all major insurance companies. It resulted in a technology provider, ABZ. The establishment of such a service provider most often was the result of a failing EDI implementation by a strong organization with its suppliers. Such an organization realized it operates in a network with competitors and suppliers.

Because of its technical nature and implementation of business process aspects in technical data semantics, all EDI implementations were and are still bilateral or star-based implementations (figure 2). Bilateral implementations are for instance in a business relation between two companies. Extending bilateral implementations to a star-based approach was time consuming. One of the companies driving the implementation needs to extend its implementation to other business partners. Star-based implementations are with the strong partner in the centre. Extending a star-based approach to a network is feasible, but depends on the buying power and competition between two or more potential hubs in the network.

It has been feasible for a limited number of container stevedores in the Rotterdam port, enforced by customers of the port. The Transit system is an example of such a business network, although customs authorities play the role of 'hub' in the network.

Requirements: forming a business web

We have already discussed that EDI implementation was expensive and therefore had high switching costs. It can only be applied in situations with for instance contractual agreements between business partners. On the other hand, in a market where supply is greater than demand and quality of all suppliers is almost equal, buyers tend to do business on a transaction basis. In such a situation, business support by electronic messaging has to be available. Organizational networks have to be supported by electronic business transactions with zero implementation effort per transaction. Open standards are a solution, but the main issue is semantics of these standards.

Looking closely at EDI projects, they have to support such organizational networks, also called business web. Take for instance shipping and ports. This particular application area consists of many actors with different roles. A role of a particular actor will also differ per consignment, e.g. for one consignment an actor is 'forwarder' and for another 'liner-agent'. The potential number of actors serving a port is also large (over 200), so a business network needs to be established (Hofman, 1994).

A government is a similar case of a network that have to support business transactions. Currently, many departments of the Dutch Government have initiated the establishment of chains. These chains are enforced by law, both EU and/or national directives and laws. Examples are the EU Service Directive (EU, 2006) and the environmental permit (Wabo, 2006). Basically, they try to support these laws by service provision. Intermediates are raised that offer mandatory services. These intermediates serve as front end and/or central hub for (part of the) Dutch government organizations. Technically, one could say that it is chain integration. Business wise, it is support of a government network by technology, also called federation. Each chain represents a set of business transactions with identical features. The number of chains is large in case many organizations are involved and the number of features per business transaction is high. Dutch government is relatively small with some 1200 organizations, but the number of chains will be high. With the individualization trend, the number of chains will only grow.

Evolving standards

Technically, a number of changes has taken place since the 80-s of the past century. The most important is of course the introduction of the World Wide Web that not only supports sharing of information, but also allows shopping. The latter is called ecommerce. XML, eXtensible Markup Language (Bray, T., & Paoli, J. & Sperberg-McQueen, C.M. & Maler, E., NY), was the new syntax for data exchange between applications. Besides these changes of standards, technology is changing fast and services are already provided on the Internet. These changes also forced the UN/Cefact community to transform its standards. We will briefly discuss these changes in the next pages. It is not feasible to discuss all developments in the context of this article. We will only touch upon those that we think are relevant to external integration. For those that are interested, the Object Management

Group (OMG) is developing various technical standards that have a relation with the ones mentioned here.

W3C standards

In the World Wide Web community, one can basically consider two classes of standards. The first class enables the Service Oriented Architecture (SOA, Erl, 2005), whereas the second class supports semantics. Both will be discussed in this section.

The SOA stack consists of the following standards (see figure 3):

— Standards for the exchange and integration of data between different applications. XML, the eXtensible Markup Language, is the standard for structuring data. SOAP adds control information for the actual data exchange. The control information is used by receiving applications to take the appropriate action. A WSDL document specifies messages as operations supported by SOAP and the actual data exchange protocols. Finally, a BPEL document defines the sequence in which WSDL messages will be processed by an application and/or humans, and actions to be performed.

— Standards for description and discovery of services. UDDI was the first standard, which seemed promising. It specified the interface to a repository for services. Services are specified by their WSDL documents. However, due to its lack of semantics, it is not used in an open (Internet) environment and is succeeded by WSMO. The actual interpretation of this

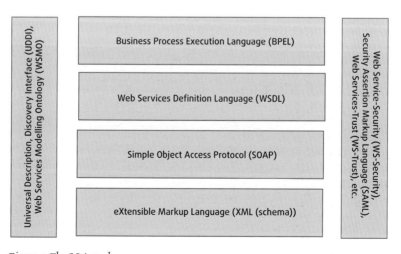

Figure 3. The SOA stack

standard is not yet clear; it can be used in several ways (see for instance Hofman, 2007 and Krämer, 2007).

— Security standards. There is a set of security standards developed, which is supported by the latest version of SOAP (SOAP 2.0). Furthermore, a federated approach is taken to identification and authentication as specified by SAML.

These are basically technical standards for integration. They have to be applied in the context of an architectural framework, like for instance Archimate (Lankhorst (2005). Such a framework also considers the application of for instance Business Process Modelling notation (BPMn, 2006) for conceptual modelling of business processes. Business process models can be transformed to BPEL documents.

The second class of standards is the Semantic Web stack (figure 4), originally conceived by Berners-Lee (2001), the founder of the World Wide Web. It is the objective that the Semantic Web supports computer applications

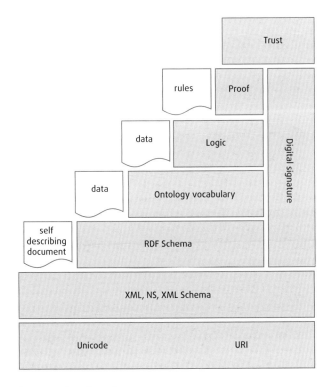

Figure 4. The Semantic Web stack

to understand each others semantics and by means of logic make decisions. A simple example as imagined by Berners-Lee describes the making an appointment for a general practitioners' consult. The stack consists of a number of standards specifying data and documents, relations to other sources (RDF Schema, Resource Description Framework), and semantics of the data. The semantics is specified by ontology. Reasoning about the semantics is in logic and a set of rules. In the end, trust needs to be established. There is already a number of applications that work with ontology's, e.g. a Product Modelling Ontology for building design (Katranuschkov et. al., 2003). Whereas the SOA stack basically specifies process aspects of integration, the Semantic Web stack has its focus on data. Data is specified by XML messages in the SOA stack, whereas the Semantic Web stack can be used

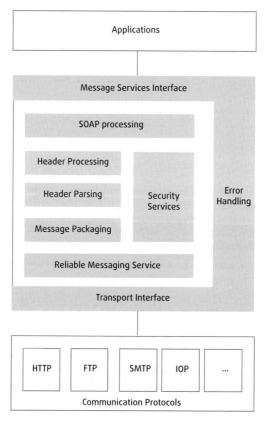

Figure 5. ebXML messaging stack

to generate XML structures. Both stacks have identity, authentication, and also authorisation in common. Processes, data with their semantics, and security issues need to be solved in a business web. Thus, we require both the SOA and the Semantic Web stack.

UN/Cefact community
From its very nature, the main focus of UN/Cefact has been on cross border information exchange for international trade. As such, they have the intention to facilitate international trade with open standards. They have always been aware that semantics and business processes are the main issues in cross border integration. To cope with the introduction of XML and focus on data semantics for integrating business processes, UN/Cefact has, in cooperation with OASIS, developed ebXML (electronic business XML, OASIS, 2006). To decrease message development time and re-use already defined semantics, they developed standard artifacts called 'Core Components' as part of ebXML. Additionally, they developed a method to specify data exchange semantics and transform these semantics into syntax. The method is called UMM (UN EDIfact Modelling Method). We will briefly discuss ebXML with Core Components and UMM.

ebXML consists of the following relevant parts: a modelling method, a message transfer service, and Core Components. The first part specifies a modelling method. It has a focus on process modelling for business chains. This part seems to be preceded by other methods like BPMn. The UN/Cefact community had several initiatives for the application of the ebXML process modelling method, for instance by drafting a supply chain reference model. The status of these reference models is unknown. These models also support only particular chains describing a particular set of business transactions (see before). Other initiatives have been in the so-called open-EDI modelling. Reference models consisting of business processes and data should be the basis for negotiating semantics and establishing a trading partner relation. The result of open-EDI is also still unknown. The second part of ebMXL specifies a reliable and secure transfer service, the Messaging Service. It has several extensions to SOAP for reliability and security. A number of governmental organizations is implementing this standard because of its reliability and security. ebXML/MS and the SOA stack are currently evolving towards each other and will in the near future become compatible.

The last relevant part of ebXML is 'Core Components'. These are artifacts specifying certain syntax independent data structures. A well known example is a Core Component specifying names and addresses of organizations, independent of roles. Another example is the specification catalogue articles. A simple Core Component is specifying date and time with its time zone identifier, which is most often a data type. A number of EDIfact segments and segment groups are transformed to Core Components. The intention is to construct message structures and/or XSDs based on these Core Components. Thus, one needs only to specify the possible roles of organizations in data exchange and their name and address structure is available. In terms of XML Schema: one could work with import constructions for Core Components. Core Components could not only be used in constructing XSDs, but could also serve as portlets in a portal environment. In case these portlets are remote, one should be able to access them by open standards, e.g. Web Services for Remote Portlets. It would greatly simplify the construction of a portal based on existing artifacts. Both for message development and portal construction, one needs a repository of Core Components with metadata specifying each Core Component. This metadata should encompass the semantics expressed by the Core Component. UMM, the UN EDIfact Modelling Method, specifies a UML profile (UML: Unified Modelling Language) for development of a UML class diagram as the basis for deriving XML messages. Basically, a class diagram needs to be developed per XSD (XSD: XML Schema Definition), whereas such an XSD specifies one message of a WSDL. This approach is successfully supported by many UML tools, e.g. MagicDraw and Enterprise Architect. It is also successfully applied in many areas like Telecommunications (eTOM (2007) and Traffic Information (Datex, 2006). These approaches are also supported by integration software, where they are called Common Data Model (Hohpe et.al., 2004). However, semantics is of course shared between several messages and XSDs. Thus, a data model for a particular application area needs to be constructed as the basis for a set of XSDs/messages. We dare to state that tool support for creating various hierarchical structures on a data structure is not yet available.

Services on the Web
Wagenaar (1997) stated that Internet would rapidly decrease transaction costs and change current business structures. These statements were

based on assumptions that the networked economy could be established. Wagenaar could not predict that 10 years later, standards were still under development, but the World Wide Web would emerge into a community of prosumers (Tapscott and Williams, 2006). The current technology integrates applications hiding implementation specifics of those applications and specifies integration semantics. It seems that the W3C and the UN/Cefact technology will converge, although it is not yet clear how. The W3C technology is already used on the World Wide Web, which is, besides information and ecommerce applications, rapidly evolving into stand alone social communities (web sites). Social communities are a relative new arena based on the open standards discussed before (Tapscott and Williams, 2006). Examples of social communities are Hyvess, Plaxo, Facebook, and LinkedIn. They are used for personal networking, but others are already evolving to virtual networks of professionals. These communities can already interface with each other utilising a set of Application Programming Interfaces provided by Google.

The communities are already open to other environments like YouTube, Hearmymusic.nl, and Wikipedia. These environments offer all kinds of people to post whatever information they want, which in its turns leads to unreliable information in encyclopaedias' like Wikipedia. Some sites support new artists by publishing their work, e.g. music. Blogging, office automation, data storage, etc. are already offered as services. Access to that data is by means of different devices, as long as they have Internet connection.

These social communities all support users, the so-called prosumers (Tapscott and Williams, 2006). These communities do not yet fully integrate services of other providers in their service offering. In many cases, content integration of different providers is still by links edited by users. We have already explained that Google is providing APIs for integrating different sites. Other providers offer functionality for reliable data transfer, e.g. Amazon, integration of several services by simple processes, Yahoo pipes, and integration of services into end-user software products. The latter is called 'mash-up' and the resulting software is known as 'gadget'. It is the purpose of these environments to offer end-users a simple way of writing their particular software based on services available on the Web. These services are specified by the SOA stack. Finding the proper reliable services, in terms that they will be provided for a given period of time, is still a challenge. The WSMO, service quality, and service level agreements have to cater for those problems.

A future outlook can be drafted for many application areas. However we will limit us to government, since this area had the special attention of René. One would preferably like to combine social networks with service provision of different governmental organizations. On the one hand, citizens should be able to tag and add relevant information and their favourite services on their personal website, e.g. my*.* like in myGovernment.nl, whereas on the other hand government organizations need to publish information and their services. The addition of information by citizens should not only be relevant to other citizens, but also to government organizations thus supporting democracy. Information can be harvested by mechanisms like RSS, which is already available on many sites including blogs. Services available on these personal sites could be simple and composite services, in which case composition can also be made by other users with mechanisms like Yahoo pipes. One can envisage that a particular user has constructed a combined service that can be of use to other users. Well known examples are in government services like Wabo. Mathijsse and Wagenaar (2006) already indicated that such a networked government is required. Combination of services should imply more than a simple list of simple services. The underlying services should not be visible to end-users and thus the information and processes of the different services need to be integrated. Thus, intermediates will be created (Mathijsse and Wagenaar, 2006).

Besides tagging and user construction of services, search is also of importance. Of course, everyone is familiar with search engines like Google and Yahoo. One can have dedicated search engines that harvest information from websites including web services. These search engines can have different user interfaces, evolving into virtual environments. We see already the evolvement of Google to a three dimensional visualization (also with the dimension of time) where the result of services can be shown. It is easy to add ones own services in this environment, even with ones particular environment like a city. In this way, we see a new generation of web based service platforms evolving, in which one can add its own content and software. These service platforms are integrating all types of human interaction like email, chat, and voice (Klooster, 2007). Gaming engines are the basis of those new platforms, where one can have an avatar and communicate with others in those environments. These new platforms can be the future user interface of the Internet, supporting all types of business and human interactions. Integration with the real world is already taking place in the film industry with sensors on actors, in traffic by visualizing traffic jams in a virtual environment, and so on.

Basic questions that René would ask will be how to make optimal use of social tagging and communities in a service oriented environment like a government and combine these approaches with interactive virtual reality platforms to support democracy.

Conclusions and future research

Technically, a number of standards has emerged that still need to converge. Business wise, we see these technical standards more and more applied in terms of service offerings. Services, platforms, and functionality become available on the web. We see a shift from push to a pull with respect to integration. As more services become available and people are able to construct their specific applications with these services, the demand for new services will increase. The need to integrate is more and more driven by customers as they have the means to do it themselves. We also see a shift from contractual to transactional relations in such a pull environment, thus enabling the changes in organizational networks as Wagenaar (1997) predicted. Customers are getting used to switch between different sellers as switching costs become lower. Technology will also become available to persons to construct their gadgets and use them. Organizations like Google, Yahoo, and Amazon are driving these changes. The forces for integration depicted in figure 1 are still the same, but new technology and new global suppliers of service platforms on the web add a new dimension to integration with new independent players.

The issue of semantics in this new environment was already identified in the EDI era (Wagenaar, 1997). Persons are able to interpret semantics (if they can understand the language) and make the proper decisions. They form communities, interact with sellers, rate sellers, etc. Software applications are not yet able to perform these functions. In this respect we still have two challenges.

With René, I discussed several challenges with respect to IT in organizational networks. The firs challenge relates to service description and discovery. Current services are most often (technical) web services. The technical UDDI standard for service description and discovery is evolving in a standard that includes service semantics (WSMO: Web Service Modelling Ontology). From an architectural perspective (Lankhorst, 2005), these web services support business services. Thus, a proper way would be to find a business service. The result will also give the appropriate web service(s). One could envisage that a business service is the ontology for web services. In retail, a product catalogue is part of these business services. Government services can also be used to find the appropriate web services (Hofman, 2007). The second challenge is semantic mapping. Software applications need a clear defined semantics to operate and each application will have a different semantics. We can envisage different solutions to such a challenge:

— The previous mentioned open-EDI initiative, in which negotiation on semantics and processes of different applications per transaction was the objective, is one of the options. It still needs further research.

— A second solution is to store common semantics and processes in repositories and map application semantics to these agreed semantics. One could for instance envisage a transport or a supply chain reference model. These models should not only specify the semantics of information that organizations share, but also the interactions in case two organizations would like to do business according to that reference model. In case these organizations have existing software applications, they should map the semantics of a reference model to their internal semantics. The interactions could consist of business transaction patterns that could be implemented by an application. Workflow and integration patterns are already commonly applied (Hohpe et.al., (2004). Eventually, an application only needs to know trading partner communication protocols and URIs as configuration files.

— A final option is to construct software modules implementing a specific business application reference model. Externally, such a module should support the business transaction patterns. These business transactions patterns include finding the proper business services, an offering phase, and finally the delivery of a service by a supplier. Internally, business policies need to be implemented by rules to integrate these patterns. Examples of policies are supplier selection, offer negotiation, and business planning, e.g. for critical path analysis. An example of such a system with still limited functionality is already given by Hofman (1994). With the current technology state of integration software, it should be feasible to construct these modules and form business webs. One can even envisage that one's business services are also parameters of such a system.

One of the final challenges that I discussed with René, is the dynamics of business processes. To be able to interact in organizational networks, business rules representing business policies need to configure business processes. This field of research is still fresh, but will be one of the research issues for the coming years.

Concluding, concepts are available, the market seems to be ready, technology is available, but semantics need to be taken a step further. Additionally, also a mind shift has to be made. Many persons, especially ICT professionals, still like to construct clear specified systems with identifiable processes. Realizing these systems based on finding business services and configuring processes with rules is still for them a challenge.

Finally, I am grateful that I had a number of fruitful discussions with René. These discussions were on the application of ICT to solve business issues according an architectural framework and a possible contribution from my side to TBM.

References

ABZ, Assurantie Data Netwerk (ADN), www.abz.nl.
Belastingdienst, Sagitta Binnenbrengen, http://www.douane.nl/zakelijk/binnenbrengen/en/binnenbrengen.html.
Berners-Lee, T. & Hendler, J. & Lassila, O (2001). *The Semantic Web*, Scientific American.
BPMn (2006), *Business Process Modelling notation 1.0*, www.bpmn.org.
Bray, T., & Paoli, J. & Sperberg-McQueen, C.M. & Maler, E. (editors). *eXtensible Markup Language*, www.w3c.org.
Datex (2006). *Datex II User Guide, version 1.0*, www.datex2.eu.
EC – DG Taxud, Transit, http://www.douane.nl/zakelijk/vervoer/vervoer-11.html.
eTOM (2007). *Enhanced Telecommunications Operations Map , version 7.0*, www.tmforum.org.
EU (2006). *Directive 2006/123/EC of the European Parliament and of the Council on services in the internal market*, www.ec.europa.eu.
Erl, T. (2005). *Service Oriented architecture, concepts, technology, and design*, Prentice Hall.
Hofman W.J. (1994). *A conceptual model of a Business Transaction Management System*, Uitgeverij Tutein Nolthenius.
Hofman, W.J. (2003). *EDI, Webservices en ebMXL - interacties in organisatienetwerken*, Uitgeverij TuteinNolthenius.
Hofman, W.J. (2007). *eGov Transparancy: semantic web and service discovery*. Paper presented at the eGovernment Interoperability Campus.
Huemer, C. (2006). *UN/ECE Modelling Method in a nutshell*, www.unece.org/cefact/umm/umm—index.htm.
ISO 9735 (1987). *Electronic Data Interchange for Administration, Commerce and Transport (EDIFACT) – application syntax rules*.

Hohpe, G. & Woolf, B. (2004). *Enterprise Integration Patterns - designing, building, and deploying messaging solutions*, Addison-Wesley.
Katranuschkov, P. & Gehre, A. & Scherer R.J. (2003). An ontology framework to access IFC data, www.itcon.org.
Klooster, R. (2007). *Virtual Cities*, http://www.epractice.eu/cases/virtuocity.
Krämer, B.J. & Lin, K.J. & Narasimhan, P. eds. (2007). *Service Oriented Computing, ICSOC 2007*, Springer.
Lankhorst et.al. (2005). *Enterprise Architecture at work - modelling, communication, and analysis*, Springer.
Mathijsse, R. & Wagenaar, R.W. (2006). Schakelen tussen de wijk en de wereld, in *Digitaal Bestuur*, oktober 2006.
PortInfoLink, Rotterdam doorvoer Systeem (Rodos). http://www.portinfolink.com/content/producten/producten—melding—lading.asp.
OASIS (2006). *The framework for eBusiness*, www.oasis-open.org.
Tapscott, D & Williams, D (2006). *Wikinomics - How mass collaboration changes everything* Portfolio,
Vlist, ir. P. van der (1987). *Telematicanetwerken*, Uitgeverij Tutein Nolthenius.
Wabo (2006). *Wet algemene bepalingen omgevingsrecht*, www.omgevingsvergunning.vrom.nl.
Wagenaar, prof.dr. R.W. (1997). *De virtuele koopman, fictie of werkelijkheid*, Inaugurele rede bij de aanvaarding van het ambt van hoogleraar tele-informatica aan de faculteit der Economische Wetenschappen en Econometrie van de Vrije Universiteit van Amsterdam.

Abbreviations

BPEL	Business Process Execution Language
BPMn	Business Process Modelling notation
ebXML	Electronic Business XML
EC	European Commission
EDI	Electronic Data Interchange
Edifact	EDI for Administration, Commerce, and Transport
EU	European Union
MS	Messaging Service
RDF	Resource Description Framework
RSS	RDF Site Summary or Really Simple Syndication
SAML	Security Assertion Markup Language
SOA	Service Oriented Architecture
SOAP	Simple Object Access Protocol
UMM	UN/Edifact Modelling Method
UDDI	Uniform Description, Discovery Interface
UN	United Nations
URI	Uniform Resource Identifier
W3C	World Wide Web Consortium
WSDL	Web Services Definition Language
WSMO	Web Services Modelling Ontology
XML	eXtensible Markup Language
XSD	XML Schema Definition

Sonnet voor René Wagenaar

Professor was hij voor studenten
Researcher in zijn vakgebied
Organisator voor jong docenten
Filosofisch soms zijn lied
Data exchange, specialisatie
Realist en theoreet
Wijdse systeem integratie
Applicatie die er toe deed
Geweldig met hem te mogen verkeren
Een man waarmee te lachen viel
Nooit meer elkander kunnen inspireren
Al vroeg nam God immers zijn ziel
Als vriend heb ik je gekend
René je was een grootse vent

Jo van Nunen

> It is true that the ict-sector caused heavy losses on the world's stock markets. However, it did manage to lay the foundations for a networked world ...

From Civil Servant

Strength and weakness in networks

Lorike Hagdorn – van der Meijden

Abstract
In 1997, René Wagenaar gave his inaugural speech at the VU University. The content and his performance and presentation were impressive. René had been a colleague at the EUR for many years and I was very happy for him and Brenda that he was awarded for his work by this position at the VU. Ten years later, in 2007, I gave my inaugural speech at the same university, in the same great hall, at the same desk. Unfortunately René was not with us anymore. This chapter is based on my inaugural speech and hopefully René will enjoy it anyway. René's work on edi, modularization and shared service centres highly contributed to the development of business-networks. This chapter gives a future outlook to and related research topics on the strategic development of networks and how profit, planet and people can gain from these networks.

Introduction
This paper deals with networks of organisations or interorganisational networks. The points in the network are organisations, which are connected by relations. This complete network ensures that products and services are delivered to the customer. The relations in this network may be of different natures: purchase-sales relations, combined product development (such as the way in which Philips and Sara Lee, for instance, successfully developed the Senseo coffee machine), service relations, with carriers, for example, to actually get the Senseo machines to the shops.

In this paper I want to demonstrate that thinking in terms of chains has become absolutely inadequate. The reality consists of networks. Looking, thinking and working from a network perspective creates new insights which may benefit both science and practice.

I will illustrate this by means of practical examples, which show why it is both relevant and necessary to think and work in networks. I will then familiarise you with the progress made in science and share with you my vision as well as my questions with respect to strength and weakness in networks'.

CHAINS VERSUS NETWORKS

We will first look at some of the concepts that we will need for my argument.

1. Organisation: a unit acting as an independent entity that may consist of various organisational parts, such as Unilever, the Ministry of Justice, Rabo, the city of Amsterdam, Eneco, etc.

2. Network of organisations or interorganisational network: a coherent whole of organisations with various interrelationships pursuing the same goal: serving a market in the best possible manner. These are the so-called industrial networks (Hakansson, 1992). Dell, Nike, Cisco and the fast growing fashion chain Zara have even formed smart business networks (Vervest, 2005): networks of organisations that collectively continue to introduce new models, reacting to any market demand quickly and flexibly, thus creating rapid growth. All this is supported by work processes that are as simple as possible, modularized (Hoogeweegen, 1999), flexible, solution-oriented and enterprising employees, and very accurate ICT systems.

I would like to divide these interorganisational networks into three categories:

— the primary or production networks that ensure the actual sale, distribution and production of goods and services;

— the secondary or support networks in which the support activity for the primary networks takes place, such as research & development, marketing & communication, personnel department, management development, finance, ICT, standardisation;

— the tertiary or stakeholder networks in which relations are maintained with parties that are not directly active in the primary or secondary networks, but have an influence on them nevertheless, for instance national, regional and local politics, environmental organisations, branch associations, etc.

This paper mostly takes the perspective of the primary or production networks, where transportation, distribution and logistics play such an important role, and occasionally makes an excursion to the support and stakeholder networks.

3. The chain: a concept that has long been used in logistical or supply chains (the chain of logistical steps needed to get from raw material to end product. A more recent example is the chain thinking displayed by the government, such as the immigration chain, the criminal justice chain

and the safety chain (see also Wagenaar, 2002). Administrative processes, too, are more and more often treated as logistical chains, for example when switching to a different energy supplier or taking out a mortgage. A chain suggests straightforwardness, unequivocalness and security, in terms of the order of the processing steps as well as in terms of the parties that execute the processes to take the product, the alien or the file concerned to its final destination. When we look at a supply chain, the primary process bears a strong resemblance to a chain: from production to distribution to delivery. The supply chain is not always formed by regular parties. For example, that specific PC that you order from Dell often contains components from other suppliers than the PC with the same specifications that is delivered at your neighbour's door two days later. These same suppliers also deliver goods to Toshiba and Hewlett Packard, for example. What we see is not a supply chain, but a supply network, or rather: a demand network. The customer demands products and the network organises itself in a flexible way to meet this demand as precisely as possible.

Thinking in chains is a valuable model-based approach for designing or analysing the primary process of the steps that one product, alien or file passes through, and for making improvements on the basis of that. However, from the perspective of the cooperating organisations, the network approach is a much more realistic representation of reality, and is therefore preferable by far.

NETWORKS IN BROADER PERSPECTIVE

In addition, networks are not just about the relation with direct customers and direct suppliers, but about a *broader* network in which the customers' customers, the customers' other suppliers, the suppliers' suppliers, the suppliers' other customers, etc., are also included.

The proposition that I want to put forward here, and that I want to continue working on in the coming years is that the more organisations
— are aware of their role and position in this broader network,
— know more clearly which role/position they wish to fulfil in this broader network, and
— work more intensively on obtaining or retaining this position
the more successful they will be.

In this context I look at a successful organisation not only from a financial perspective, the profit, but also from the perspective of employees who need to be able to apply and develop themselves optimally. As a third component the care for our planet is a major success factor. The challenge that many organisations face is to find the balance between these three driving forces. It is my conviction that a broader view of the network and, on the basis of that, the execution of a conscious strategy will contribute to this substantially. The major challenge for the supply chain is not only to be active in terms of the logistical operation with suppliers and customers, but to look more broadly into the network and to act more strategically within it.

Strength and weakness in networks
In order to understand what a network strategy should involve, it is now time to focus on strength and weakness in networks. Strength is one of the major factors when it comes to entering into, or dissolving, relations in networks between organisations. Research that I recently undertook with one of my students among 68 supply chain managers into the factors that play a role in the loyalty between organisations, shows that strength is by far the most important factor, in comparison with reliability, competencies, switching costs, integrity and the number of alternative parties offered.
Strength and lack of it often lie close together. A nice example is the battle that Albert Heijn and Peijnenburg fought some years ago. Albert Heijn used its power to purchase the Peijnenburg cake at lower and lower prices. In its turn Peijenburg used the strength that its brand has with consumers and went as far as discontinuing to supply cake to Albert Heijn. The result was that Albert Heijn customers were not amused and even went to other supermarkets to buy their cake: every retailer's nightmare.
This shows how the direct supply chain relation between Albert Heijn and Peijnenburg requires a broader look into the network: in this case the relation that was built up in the secondary network between Peijnenburg and the consumer.
The lack of power in the network also became painfully visible when in mid-September 2007 a headline in the Financieel Dagblad (a major Dutch financial newspaper) read: "Lost sales underestimated, shops miss out on a third of their turnover'. A quarter of this, i.e. approximately 8%, is caused by empty shelves... representing a turnover value of 1.5 billion Euros...(see footnotes 1 and 2 and Boer&Croon, 2007). The result of short-sighted chain thinking? A tightly synchronised supply chain could be the obvious solu-

tion, but clearly this is not as easy as it sounds...! Piet van der Vlist's (2007) recent dissertation provides a solution approach that goes against the standard procedure. Shops usually place their orders as late as possible, so that the shelves just remain stocked. Van der Vlist shows that in the supply chain stock should be lying on the retailer's shelves as much as possible, where consumers can buy the products. This reversal asks for a *joint approach*, not only by the direct relation between supermarkets and distributors, but also by producers.

Another example of strength is the development in the music industry. Where Apple was once a supplier of PCs with a precocious operating system for enthusiasts, that fought against the power of Microsoft, Apple now is market leader with its Ipods, with which they turned the music business upside down. This market changed from a suppliers' market into a customer-driven market. It is not the music supplier, but the listener who decides at which moment he or she downloads a song. The medium 'cd' is nearly ready to join the single and LP in the museum. Apple's next coup, besides the music market, may be the telephony market with the Iphone. Here we see Apple's main strength: the development of user-friendly software and a beautiful design that it has mastered in the PC-business, in combination with strategic insight into its network. Apple has been able to give the lack of strength that it had long felt in the market a twist, particularly with regard to Microsoft, by using this strength to market a completely new product with suppliers and customers remaining partly the same. Apple created a *new production network*: a new style of music branch, thus creating itself a powerful position.

A third example is the world port of Rotterdam, where strength and lack of it form an important combined action, both for the individual parties within the port and for the port as a whole in its positioning in Europe and the rest of the world. After decades of fantastic growth in volumes, it now seems to have reached its limit due to restricted space, vulnerable accessibility and necessary environmental demands. This requires powerful innovations. Strong points of the port of Rotterdam are its natural location with good hinterland connections, the possibility to load and unload very deep-draught ships, particularly at Maasvlakte 2 in the near future, and its excellent customs and ICT facilities. When we look more deeply into the supply chain, or rather the network, to see what is going on there, then it becomes clear that the port's eventual customers, the producers, are contemplating supplying the mainland of Europe via several ports from both a cost and environmental perspective, and because of shorter turnaround time. For goods produced in the Far East that enter Europe through Rotterdam and are then transported to Eastern Europe, the route via ports such as Constanza on the Black Sea might become more attractive.

As far as the growth of transhipment is concerned, this constitutes a threat to Rotterdam. However, it also provides an opportunity to keep those goods that no longer physically come through the port of Rotterdam but via other European ports under the responsibility of the port of Rotterdam in terms of information supply and customs handling. This could then be a *new service* to the producers and other partners in the logistical chain: a potential new role in the supply chain, in which space, physical accessibility and CO_2 emission are no longer a restriction, but in which added value can be created. Rotterdam's strong position in the area of customs and ICT will help it to market such a new service.

Network strategy

Now that we have explored the (lack of) strength of networks in practice, I would like to run through the research questions with you that go with the proposition that was put forward earlier and that I hope to be working on in the years to come. The central theme in this context is: *How do organisations find their way on this playing field of strength and weakness in networks?*

Science is fast developing knowledge in the area of interorganisational networks, *but how far have these organisations themselves advanced, how aware are they of their role and position within the broader network?*

In a first research supply chain managers were asked how 'network-minded' they were. In other words, how familiar are they, not so much with their own customers and suppliers (we presume that they know these parties well) but with their suppliers' suppliers, their suppliers' other customers, and as well as with their customers' other suppliers and their customers' other customers. You will see in the middle that these managers know the most about their customers' suppliers and their suppliers' customers. These probably often constitute the competition. However, here too the information is limited to operational issues; there is no insight into the strategies of these parties. The category of the suppliers' suppliers is the great unknown.

We subsequently asked if they think that they have sufficient knowledge of this, or if they would like to know more and if there are plans to obtain such knowledge. It becomes clear that particularly on the customer side there is a need for more information and that there are plans to collect it.

Earlier research shows that the awareness of these supply chain managers with regard to the broader network in which they participate is quite low. I would like to expand this research and regularly repeat it to see how organisations develop and to enable organisations to emulate other organisations in this area.
The second question is: *which position should an organisation aspire to in the network?*
Various perspectives are relevant when it comes to making this choice:

a. The strategy of the individual organisation. This determines the orientation in the network. I like to make use of the three basic strategies as defined by Treacy and Wiersema (1993): customer intimacy, operational excellence and product leadership.

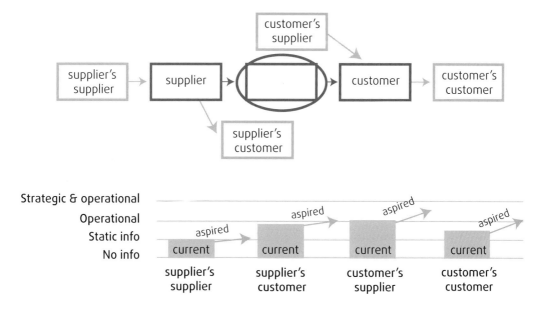

Figure 1. *Network-mindedness of supply chain managers – First indication*

When the organisation opts for the customer intimacy strategy, a close and excellent relationship with the customer is the first matter of importance, with the organisation fulfilling the individual customer's wishes as much as possible. This strategy features a wide range of products and much service and attention for the individual customer. Albert Heijn, for example, does this with its bonus card and gourmet club.

When an organisation adopts a customer intimacy strategy, it has a position close to the customer with many relations towards partners in the production network.

Organisations that adopt the operational excellence strategy choose to excel in the operational process, by realising the lowest possible costs against an acceptable price. The range of products is usually limited. Examples are Aldi and Zeeman.

Operational excellence aims to acquire a position in the primary network where the goal is to keep the costs as low as possible and where products are taken to the customer in the highest possible volumes. Organisations with this strategy feel very strongly about managing the supply chain and cooperating within it.

Organisations that adopt the product leadership strategy, such as Apple and Microsoft, always want to be the first to introduce new products and be the best in their category with their product or service. Characteristic qualities of such organisations are strong brand marketing and a great innovative capacity.

Product leadership has a different focus in the network. Constant innovation is a key requirement when employing this strategy. These organisations often cooperate with existing or new suppliers or with other partners. Michael Porter (1985) indicates that each organisation should adopt only one of these strategies, in order not to get 'stuck in the middle'. Treacy and Wiersema, however, state that organisations should adopt one of these strategies as their main strategy and truly excel in it and derive their competitive position from it, but that they should nevertheless employ the other two strategies at an acceptable threshold level.

When we discuss this matter from a network perspective, it takes on a different aspect: if one party applied itself to customer intimacy and fully dedicated itself to the contact with the customer and anticipated the customer's wishes, if the production parties concentrated on the operational excellence, and if a third category continuously focused on product innovations and improvements, then the network as a whole would encompass all three strategies on a high level. Is that realistic? To a certain extent it is. The port of Rotterdam actually is such a network. The forwarding agent is in touch with the network's customer and finds a tailor-made solution for transporting the goods from a to b across the world in constantly changing volumes, with different urgency levels, etc. The transhipment companies, transport companies, etc. ensure the operational excellence. The product leadership, the innovation process, could be spurred on, which is why universities, colleges and other knowledge institutions are asked to help. They do this from the secondary or supportive network.

When an individual organisation chooses a strategy, the individual strategies of the other parties in the network should be well known, in order to be able to assess what is needed in the network. This enables the organisation to take up a position that adds value for the network's customers and therefore for the network as a whole, and specifically for the organisation itself, which needs to be positioned.

b. The structure of the network, that is, the complete set of relations that makes up the network, from where the choice regarding the organisation's position can be made.

The literature recognises two kinds of positions in particular: bridging positions (Woolwock, 1998) and closed positions (Coleman, 1988).

A closed position is a position in the network where many parties are involved in many different relations with each other. In this 'small world' the parties know each other well. Together they work on the creation of the network as well as on its reputation. They call each other to account for bad performance (Baum, 2003; Kumar, 1998). The opposite situation is the bridging position, where the individual organisation bridges the gap between two groups of organisations that are not interrelated. Such a gap is called a 'structural hole'. The more mature networks become, the more intense the fight to close the 'structural holes' becomes. Finding bridging positions between unconnected parties turns out to be an interesting option (Burt, 1992). Apple did this brilliantly when it introduced the Ipod: the consumer and the musician were connected, but only by means of many intermediaries and with another product. Apple made the direct link and took up the bridging position. Apple thus created a unique position by actually orchestrating the network.

c. Once the strategy and the desired position within the structure have been determined, then the next question is: what kind of relationship should be maintained with the various parties, and in connection with this, what should the management role look like? Are they casual relationships, in which purchases/sales take place every now and then, or are they co-makership relationships, in which supplier and producer work closely together? Do the parties enter into research & development joint ventures? Which alliances are important and with which parties?
The positioning choice will probably differ between the primary, secondary and tertiary network. In any case these three networks will have to be taken into account both separately and in connection with each other when this positioning choice is made.

After determining the desired position, the next logical question is *How can the desired network position be obtained?*
The extent to which a network can be manipulated in view of the sphere of influence of one organisation is very limited. Particularly when other parties within the network have also adopted a conscious network strategy, various parties will aim for 'bridging positions', various parties will want to be in the driver's seat, etc. It is no sinecure for an organisation to realise its desired position, but there are a number of factors that will help the organisation to be successful.
Being familiar with the other parties' strategies within the network is the first condition for an organisation to see if its own ambition can be realised. Diederik van Liere (2007) introduced the term 'network horizon' to describe how far an organisation looks into the network. Fortunately he was able to demonstrate that there is a limit to the extent to which an effort should be made to collect this information: the horizon may be limited.
Acquiring a new position in the network will require an organisation to enter into relations with new parties, and possibly also to cut off relations with existing parties. A number of competencies will help to achieve this (Verduijn, 2004):
– First of all a well developed so-called Quick Connect Capability (Vervest, 2005), which ensures that within the primary network parties can quickly change parties in terms of work processes and the corresponding ICT. It is essential that the work processes are organised in a modular way and that the ICT is geared to these work processes.

In addition maintaining contacts with potential partners in the network will require constant attention, so that people know each other and relationships based on mutual trust have been developed.
– And that requires a flexible organisation with people who can look beyond the boundaries of their own organisation and who are always looking for new chances. The network organisation listed earlier seems to meet this profile (Volberda, 2004; Roobeek, 2005; Roose, 2005; Wintzen, 2007; and footnote 3).
It is a challenge to gain more in-depth knowledge of these factors and to find others that contribute to realising the desired network position.
When this position has been achieved, how can it be retained and when is it time to start striving for another position?
Other parties, too, are active in the network and the composition and structure of the network change all the time. A bridging position is particularly difficult to maintain. When other parties get in touch with each other directly, the organisation may even be sidelined (Burt, 2000).
It is therefore important to gain insight into the potential vulnerability, or reinforcement for that matter, created by changes in the network.

The most important research topic, finally, is: *Are organisations that consciously and actively work on their strategic positioning in the network more successful in the area of profit, people and planet?*
It is relatively easy to measure an organisation's success in the area of profit. I would like to expand on that by also measuring success in the area of planet (Guenster, 2005; and see footnote 4) and people, which will by no means be easy. Furthermore, demonstrating a relation between implementing and realising a network strategy and the success of an organisation in the area of people, planet and profit is quite an ambition, but very much a worthwhile one.
Based on René's famous 'EDI-game' of 'Port of Rotterdam-game', the business networking game has been developed, which demonstrates the impact and issues in developing a network, find the right network partners, developing shared service centres (even with competitors) and experiencing the power of fast ICT-connections in this network. I would have loved to cooperate with René on this topics.

[1] It concerns figures in the non-food retail (DIY, books, Electronics, fashion and sports). Financieel Dagblad 13 September 2007

[2] In food retail the figures are better (1 a 2%), but the margins are lower, so here, too, large improvements can be made. Sources:
Optimal Shelf Availability (2003), Report ECR-Europe, www.ecreurope.com
Corsten, D., T. Gruen (2004), Stock-Outs Cause Walkouts, *Harvard Business Review*, May 2004.

[3] Eckart Wintzen's BSO is a nice example of one of the first professional network organisations, in which the 'fission principle' continued to ensure the optimal format. As soon as a cell expanded into a unit with more than 60 employees, it would be divided into two new cells that would then go on independently. For this management concept he was recently (10 years after the fact) awarded a prize of the Koninklijk Instituut voor Ingenieurs (Royal Instituton of Engineers).

[4] See also the Dow Jones Sustainability Index www.sustainability-indixes.com.

References

Baum, J.A.C., Shipilov, A.V., & Rowley, T.J. (2003). Where Do Small Worlds Come From? *Industrial and Corporate Change*, 12(4), 697-725.
Boer & Croon (2007). *Het geld ligt op de winkelvloer*, uitgave Boer&Croon, Amsterdam
Burt R.S. (1992). *Structural Holes: The Social Structure of Competition*. Harvard University Press: Cambridge, MA.
Burt, R.S. (2000). The Network Structure of Social Capital, Research in Organizational Behaviour, Vol. 22, 345-423. New York, NY: Jai/Elsevier.
De Man, A.P. (2004). *The Network Economy*, Edward Elgar Publishing Massachusetts USA.
Guenster, N., J. Derwall, R. Bauer, & K. Koedijk (2005). *The economic Value of Eco Efficiency*, working paper, RSM Erasmus University, The Netherlands.
Hakansson, H., & Johanson, J. (1992). 'A model of industrial networks'. In: B. Axelsson & G. Easton, *Industrial Networks: a new view of reality*. New York: Wiley.
Hoogeweegen, M.R., Teunissen W.J.M., Vervest, P.H.M., & R.W. Wagenaar (1999). Modular Network Design: Using information and communication technology to allocate production tasks in a virtual organization, *Decision Sciences*, 30(4), 1073-1103.
Johansson, J., & Mattson, G. (1992). 'Network positions and strategic action' in: B. Axelsson & G. Easton, *Industrial Networks: a new view of reality*. New York: Wiley.
Kumar, K., Dissel, H.G. van, & Bielli, P. (1998). The Merchant of Prato revisited: towards a third rationality of information systems. MIS-Quarterly, 22(2), 199–226.
Liere, D.W. van (2007), *Network horizon and the dynamics of network positions*, Ph. D. Thesis, RSM Erasmus University, Rotterdam, The Netherlands.
Porter M. (1985). *Competitive Advantage*, New York: Macmillan
Roobeek, A. (2005). *Netwerklandschap*, Sdu publishers, The Hague, The Netherlands.
Roose, H. (2005). *Managen van een Netwerkorganisatie*, uitgeverij Maklu Antwerpen.
Treacy, M., & F. Wiersema (1993). Customer Intimacy and Other Value Disciplines, Harvard Business Review, 71(1), 84-93.

Verduijn, T. (2004). *Dynamism in supply networks,* Ph.D. Thesis TRAIL Research School The Netherlands.

Vervest, P.H.M., van Heck, E., Preiss, K., & Pau, L.F. (Eds) (2005). Smart Business Networks. Berlin, Germany: Springer.

Vlist, P. van der (2007). *Synchronizing the Retail Supply Chain,* Ph. D. Thesis, RSM Erasmus University, Rotterdam, The Netherlands.

Volberda, H. (2004). *De flexibele onderneming: strategieën voor succesvol concurreren,* Kluwer, Deventer.

Wagenaar, R. (2002). "De virtuele ambtenaar: naar een transparante overheid?", inaugural speech Technische Universiteit Delft.

Wintzen, E. (2007). *Eckart's Notes,* Eckart Wintzen together with Lemniscaat.

Woolcock M. (1998). Social capital and economic development: towards a theoretical synthesis and policy framework. *Theory and Society* 27, 151–208.

NEW FORMS OF ELECTRONIC SERVICES AND IMPLEMENTATION AIMED AT SOLVING SOCIAL BOTTLENECKS IMPLY THAT GOVERNMENT BECOME MORE TRANSPARENT AND TAKE ON THE ROLE OF DIRECTOR OR PARTICIPANT IN A VIRTUAL WEB OF PUBLIC-PRIVATE COOPERATION TO A GREATER EXTENT THAN IT HAS DONE BEFORE.

From *Civil Servant*

Transparency in Services Networks
Combining Choice and Obligation

Wil Janssen, Erwin Fielt, Marc Lankhorst

ABSTRACT

Transparency is an important issue in Internet-related interactions and transactions, both in a business setting and in electronic government. The issue of transparency has been one of the major points of discussion between René Wagenaar and the authors, both in Erwin Fielt's PhD research into intermediaries and in his cooperation with Wil Janssen and Marc Lankhorst on future e-government services.

Although the general assumption has been that transparency has increased thanks to the Internet, recent research indicates that transparency in e-business can be more a strategic design choice than an inevitable phenomenon. In an e-government setting, transparency to a certain extent is obligatory: people are entitled to know what information the government possesses, they have the right (or even obligation) to know the law, and so on. Having said that, the degree to which these obligations are supported by electronic services and associated government policies is limited, and there is a strategic element as well. In this chapter, we confront the strategic choices and obligations with respect to transparency in services in e-business and e-government, based on research that was conducted in the Netherlands with regard to electronic intermediaries on the one hand, and citizen information portals on the other. Despite the anticipated differences in the nature of the two application areas, there are interesting similarities and cross-sectoral lessons to be learned, in particular when it comes to public-private collaboration. René Wagenaar was also very interested in ways to organize this collaboration, as can be deduced from his many publications.

We argue that, with the growing integration between business services and government services, and the fading boundaries between public and private responsibilities from a user point of view, tension between design choices and obligations in transparency will increase in the near future, with unforeseen consequences.

INTRODUCTION

The Internet is almost synonymous with transparency, seemingly allowing us to obtain all the information we need, find and compare every product available, and almost see what is going on everywhere and all the time, and often for free. New services like Google Earth make every backyard visible to everybody. In services networks, such services can be combined with other information sources to help us find the nearest cobbler, or check out the latest crimes scenes.[1] Search engines seem to present anything we want to know effortlessly and objectively. Benkler (2006) speaks of the rise of the networked information economy, an economy that is built around information and communication over pervasive communication infrastructures. In such an economy, transparency is a crucial issue, both in the design of services as well as in regulation. Information can be gathered, filtered, and personalized, but it can also be manipulated, misused or misinterpreted. Search engines need not be objective. They can be manipulated by web pages, steered by information providers who pay for them (albeit usually in a way that is more or less transparent to the user). Information with regard to individual people may be private, outdated or inaccurate. All in all this makes transparency a complex issue when it comes to services.

Transparency refers to the visibility of information in a business network, in other words, the extent to which information is made available. This means that transparency can refer to information regarding transaction objects, people and organizational performance, as well as access rules and authorizations. Of course, transparency is not a new issue that is limited to, for example, the so-called Web 2.0 era (O'Reilly, 2005) or the Internet. The whole issue of transparency has to do with the different (informational) roles in the service network and the discussion regarding disintermediation and reintermediation. In the literature on electronic intermediaries, there is a lively debate going on about intermediation, disintermediation and reintermediation (Chircu & Kauffman, 2000; Giaglis, Klein, & O'Keefe, 2002). Intermediation refers to the entry of a new player as an intermediary, disintermediation to the exit of an existing intermediary, and reintermediation to the re-entry of a disintermediated player. Intermediaries can, for example, increase transparency by providing information to customers about the offerings of multiple suppliers and providing the functionality to compare these offerings.

Although the Internet makes information more easily available, this does not mean that information becomes more meaningful or less strategic in nature. Gathering, filtering, and 'reselling' information can have substantial added value and thus lead to interesting roles in value networks. Hagel and Rayport (1997) discuss 'infomediaries' who capture customer information to be used by selected third-party vendors. Amazon, for example, can no longer be regarded as a retailer. Instead, it is an information broker, linking many different portals, vendors, and users (who can also sell items) in an intelligent environment, allowing the company to exploit its intermediate position to generate new information that has strategic value to both buyers and sellers alike.

Not everything about transparency is controlled by organizations themselves. There is substantial and growing legislation concerning information transparency, aimed both at restricting transparency (such as privacy legislation) and at increasing it, such as Basel II and the Sarbanes-Oxley Act. The capital adequacy framework known as Basel II has defined requirements on the financial and operational risk management of banking organizations, with the aim of promoting stability in the financial world. The Basel II Framework imposes strict regulations on banks in terms of risk measurement and management, with wide-ranging implications for their organizational structure and IT systems. The Sarbanes-Oxley Act of 2002 was drawn up in the aftermath of the Enron scandal, to force companies to adopt good corporate governance practices and to make company executives personally accountable.

Transparency is not restricted to private organizations. It is just as strategically important to public institutions. In a democratic society, people have a right to know what their government knows about them. At the same time, information can be used to improve public services, for example by personalizing them, much like it is done in the private sector. Both, however, have been lacking until now, in almost every nation worldwide: it is difficult to access your own personal information stored by the government, and public services are usually of the 'one size fits all' kind. The boards of government institutions are becoming increasingly aware of and are trying to live up to their responsibility. In addition, there is a growing awareness that the use of the most efficient channel in communicating with customers can enhance the overall quality of service delivery, even in times of budget cuts (Scott, Golden, Hughes, 2004; cc:Egov 2007). This leads to the introduction of citizen-centric information portals, such as Denmark's Borger.dk (Denmark, 2007) and MijnOverheid.nl (PIP, 2007) in the Netherlands, which provide transparency of user data (profile) as well as of government services and performance.

The issue of transparency has been one of the major points of discussion between René Wagenaar and the authors of this chapter. During Erwin Fielt's PhD research, which was supervised by René Wagenaar and Wil Janssen, the strategic value of partial transparency became clear in the discussion regarding the Tapestria case, and it was reconfirmed in the other cases. Ultimately, the Tapestria e business service was not successful. We had several debates on whether or not the failure was caused, at least in part, by limited transparency. It was impossible to prove either way.
The issue of transparency in public services is also an essential element in the research project Burger- en Bedrijvendossier ('Citizen and Company Dossier'),[2] in which Delft University of Technology and Telematica Instituut co-operate, involving René Wagenaar, Wil Janssen and Marc Lankhorst. The lack of transparency in public services clearly annoyed René, and in B-dossier we worked on improving the perspective on public services, increasing transparency and empowering citizens, in line with the vision of the virtual civil servant.

The remainder of this chapter is organized as follows: in the next section, we take a closer look at what transparency actually involves in e-business and in e-government. From these observations, we arrive at a better understanding of transparency in general. We then look at the issues concerning the obligation and strategic choice in favour of transparency when the boundaries between public and private services start to blur. From these findings, we draw a number of conclusions on how transparency could evolve in the near future.

Transparency in E-Business
With regard to transparency, we can distinguish the following aspects (Fielt, Janssen, Faber & Wagenaar, 2007; Fielt 2006):
— Kind of information: what information and is made available in the business network, and in what form.
— Information flows and processing: the routes information takes through the business network, in particular the sources and destinations, and the information processing.

— Information rules: the rights, obligations and constraints with respect to providing, handling and accessing information.

As we have seen, transparency can refer to information regarding transaction objects, people and organizational performance, as well as access rules and authorizations. Moreover, transparency is also strongly related to trust, in that it reduces uncertainty by providing relevant information (Buuren, Strating & Faber, 2004). All this makes transparency an intricate issue in the design of services, and service networks.

Transparency in business networks can move into two directions: transparency with regard to suppliers and the supply of products to customers, to which we refer as 'supply transparency', and transparency regarding customers and demand for products from suppliers, to which we refer as 'demand transparency'. Intermediaries play a special role with respect to transparency, because they connect many customers to many suppliers. In this section, we draw upon research from Fielt (2006) into business-to-business intermediaries. If we want to have a better understanding of transparency, we need to take a closer look at how an intermediary deals with it. We start by looking at two case examples: Tapestria and SeaQuipment.

Tapestria, an electronic intermediary in the soft furnishing industry between 2001 and 2004, was a new initiative of Hunter Douglas, a large firm that was already active in the adjoining markets of window coverings and architectural products. The firm provided a web-purchasing service for interior fabrics to professional designers in the United States as well as and a sales service to European producers. Tapestria positioned itself as a managed marketplace: a mix between an electronic marketplace and a traditional wholesaler. Tapestria opted in favour of 'partial' transparency: creating transparency and non-transparency at the same time. Tapestria possessed information about designers and their purchasing behaviour (search, order), producers and their products, the prices of products, and logistics. It provided information to designers and producers about products and product prices, but not about the companies that made the products. Tapestria used its own brand instead of the producers' brands. Price information was only available to users with a full trade account. Tapestria did not provide producers information about designers either. To inform designers about products, it also provided product visualisation via the website, as well as supplying them with physical samples.

Another example is SeaQuipment, an electronic intermediary in the maritime industry. SeaQuipment was an initiative of the VNSI, the Netherlands' Shipbuilding Industry Association. SeaQuipment provides a web-catalogue to ship owners, shipyards and maritime suppliers. The web catalogue has a product structure developed by SeaQuipment. Anyone can look for information in the catalogue. Maritime sellers have to register and upload their products to the catalogue. SeaQuipment provides basic information about firms and products, but no price information, which is left to buyers and sellers themselves. Sellers are responsible for and have control over their own product and firm information (free text). Buyers are anonymous, and no registration is required. As a result, SeaQuipment and sellers know little about the buyers that use SeaQuipment. This means it is hard to judge the efficiency and effectiveness of SeaQuipment as a marketing tool.

When we relate these cases back to the different forms of transparency, we see that supply transparency requires intermediaries to make a strategic choice between a high level of transparency regarding suppliers and product supply, with greater opportunities to create value for customers, and a low level of transparency regarding suppliers and product supply, with greater opportunities to create value for intermediary and/or suppliers. When intermediaries want to create maximum transparency for the benefit of their customers, they make it easier for customers to gather information on and compare the products of different suppliers. When intermediaries want to create minimal transparency for the benefit of suppliers, they should not support product comparison. Intermediaries can also limit supply transparency to protect their own position. Tapestria's customers were unable to approach fabric manufacturers directly, because they did not know who these manufacturers were. One way to limit possible disadvantages for suppliers is to provide a higher level of supply transparency to a targeted group of customers than to other users, for example providing price-related information only to interior designers with a trade account in the case of Tapestria.

In conclusion, transparency is an important issue in business networks in general and for intermediaries in particular. On the one hand, there are competitive forces that favour a restriction on information sharing and a low level of transparency (e.g. price comparison), while on the other hand there are cooperative forces that encourage information sharing and promote transparency (e.g. just-in-time inventory management). Intermediaries have to make a strategic and balance the interests of their customers and suppliers, and of themselves with regard to supply and demand transparency.

Transparency in E-Government
As we argued in the introduction, there is a growing pressure to create a higher level of transparency in e-government. Not only should information be made available as a matter of principle, it should also be easy to access. Bovens (2003) argues that, in the modern networked information society, people not only have political and social rights, they have a right to information as well. This includes having access to rules, regulations, and policy information, as well as to personal information and basic registries. Access in this case not only refers to physical access, but also to accessibility (not making it too difficult or expensive to access for citizens) and clarity. In 2000, the Committee Franken (Franken, 2000) suggested incorporating these rights into the constitution, stating that 'everybody has the right to access government information (…). The government ensures the accessibility of government information.' This emphasizes the growing importance of transparency in government services. Government has a strategic choice in the way information is made accessible, either electronically or physically, in an integrated way (using portals), in a distributed way (through the various organizations), and so on. In other words, despite the fact that information is a right, there are many options.

Citizen-centric portals are an important way of accessing and integrating government information and services. We define a citizen-centric information portal as a way to present all information regarding citizens in a structured way, as a basis for effective, efficient and transparent electronic government services. There are two extremes when it comes to implementing this concept. At one extreme, all information is presented and disclosed in a uniform, transparent way, resulting in an unambiguous citizen record. This means that all government organizations have to share information regarding citizens and processes, and need to resolve possible ambiguities and inconsistencies (which does not imply that all this information has to be stored in a central place). It may even be necessary to change rules and regulations (e.g. in the definitions of crucial concepts like 'household' or 'income'). At the other extreme, hardly any information is shared, and citizens are faced with the inconsistencies, borders, and inabilities of different organizations to work together, which is pretty much par for the course at the moment.

A large survey conducted in the Netherlands concerning e-government services (Burger@Overheid.nl, 2006), indicated that 70% of the people regarded finding information as problematic by, while about 65% feel irritated by repeatedly having to provide information that they had already provided on earlier occasions. The most important outcomes of this study were:

— More than half of the respondents (57%) have a positive attitude towards citizen-centric information portals, with only 10% displaying a negative attitude.
— Advantages that were mentioned include one-time only data provision, speed, time-saving, working from home and having insight into the status of processes and agencies, i.e. transparency.
— Disadvantages that were mentioned primarily had to do with concern privacy and data volatility. Also, the lack of personal contact was seen as a disadvantage, as was the possibility of the misuse of information on the part of the government itself.
— 34% of all respondents would like to restrict the services to government organizations, whereas 39% would like to include other, non-commercial organizations, such as schools and hospitals.
— A large majority of respondents would like to know what information is known about them at the tax department (91%) and at their municipality (90%). Electronic patient records and social security agencies have high scores as well (63 – 72%).

The provision of e-government services in many ways resembles that of private services. Despite the differences between the public and private sectors that make a transition towards electronic services more difficult, government institutions are becoming increasingly aware of and try to live up to their responsibility to the country's citizen. The complexity of e-government service provisioning also becomes apparent from a requirements study on future e government services in the Netherlands (Derks & Lankhorst, 2006). Government management is a two-tiered affair, with a top level of elected politicians who ultimately answer to the voters, and a second level of professional administration. This makes the provision of government services more complicated, since the complexity of the interests that need to be balanced at the political level may conflict with an efficient and effective service delivery.

Currently, several countries are implementing citizen-centric portals that may help increase transparency in government services. In the Netherlands, the so-called Personal Internet Page (PIP, 2007) or 'MijnOverheid.nl' ('MyGovernment.nl') will be a key concept in this respect (Figure 1). Its roll-out is planned for 2008. It will allow citizens to access municipal and national government services, and access and correct their personal information. Its use is restricted to public organizations.

COMPLEXITY IN FADING BORDERS BETWEEN PUBLIC AND PRIVATE SERVICES

The question that now arises is what it is that we need to realize a full-blown demand-driven information portal for e-government services (Janssen & Zeef, 2006; Lankhorst & Derks, 2007). From the extensive user studies that have been carried out by, among others Velsen, Geest & Hedde (2007), we conclude that, in a next generation of citizen-centric information portals, boundaries between the public and the private sector are going to fade. In the eyes of individual citizens/customers, for example, there

Figure 1. MijnOverheid.nl (concept) (PIP, 2007)

is only a vague distinction between social security, health insurance and other financial services. Moreover, the privatization of government services, for instance as healthcare, contributes to the blurring of these boundaries, leading to new intricacies with regard to service transparency.

The fact that boundaries are fading does not mean that public and private services become totally similar or integrated. There are major differences between the two sectors. Van Dijk (2002) describes the role of political regulation, the fact that government is its own referee, its monopolistic position, and the fact that the government is a gigantic complex of organizations instead of a single entity, as dominant factors. Moreover, as Mintzberg (1996) has argued, our relationship with the government is much more complex than that between customer and supplier. When it comes to simple government products, e.g. a passport or driver's license, we can indeed see ourselves as mere customers. For more complex services, such as education or healthcare, which may require lengthy and intimate interactions, the label client would be more appropriate. What is most important, however, is our role as citizens: our rights with respect to the government far transcend those of customers and clients. We are entitled to being treated professionally, not because we pay for it (as customers would), but because a democratic government is 'of the people and for the people'. Of course, these rights come with strings attached: we are also subjects, obliged to pay taxes, obey the law, and in other ways respect the rules and regulations our government needs to impose to protect the rights and needs of others.

To provide for the needs of citizens in a genuine way, integration and cooperation across different public and private organizations is needed, especially at the lower levels. However, such integration is far from simple as Wagenaar (2006) has demonstrated with regard to the introduction of shared service centers. Things become more complex when they also involve the integration with private organizations. An example is healthcare: in the Netherlands, we have a mix of private health insurance and publicly provided benefits and facilities.

First of all, sharing information between different organizations is an important factor when it comes to providing user-friendly services. Within the Dutch government, a system of 'basic registries' is currently being set up, which will be the authoritative sources of specific types of information, examples of which are registries of civil status, addresses, buildings, vehicles (license numbers), etc. In the future, government institutions will be required to use these centralized registries to process these types of information. This should alleviate the problems citizens are currently experiencing with the fragmented nature of services, where they are asked to provide the same information over and over again to a variety of institutions. At the moment, citizens have little influence on the way 'their' information is used. Privacy laws sometimes limit the private use of data held by public administrations against the interests of citizens, who might benefit from sharing this information with others. In other cases, the boundaries are blurred, even though citizens would prefer it if a clear line were drawn. An example of this is the new 'BurgerServiceNummer' (citizen service number), which has been introduced in the Netherlands. This number, similar to the US social security number, will be used by virtually all government organizations to identify citizens. Although it was initially intended to be used only by government organizations, health insurers are now also given access to the information, while banks want to use it for fraud prevention purposes, and others are already knocking at the door as well. Allowing the private use of this number makes it possible to combine information in ways that are clearly not in the interest of citizens. And even if using the information in these ways is illegal, when the number is 'out there', such misuse often cannot be prevented and only punished afterwards, when the damage has already been done.

Sharing information is only a first step in providing integrated services that really serve people's needs. The next step is to coordinate the service delivery process. Again, healthcare services provide an example. In the Dutch context, the local (municipal) government plays a coordinating role in providing home care services to its citizens. This entails organizing the process of assessing which type of care a person is entitled to (although the assessment itself is carried out by another institution), helping with the selection of care providers, providing financial support, etc.

This example also shows that cooperation between public and private organizations is needed to meet people's needs. Home care organizations are private companies, who must work together with municipalities, doctors and others. Similar situations arise, for example, in social security, where public social security institutions work together with private intermediaries, public and private educational institutes, municipal organizations and others to help unemployed people find jobs. Such coordination is even more difficult to realize than merely exchanging information.

We need to realize the integration of sub-services of various parties into a single, composite service, in which the responsibilities are clearly assigned and people know what to expect from whom. Such an integrated service requires an integrated contract, which contains the rights and obligations of the parties involved. Combining public and private services in such a manner will be very complicated, especially when it comes to assigning rights, obligations and responsibilities. The difference between citizens (and their legal rights and obligations) and commercial clients (and their contractual agreements) will be difficult to reconcile in a single service offering.

The leading role of policy and legislation are typical of government services. The equivalent layers in private companies are business objectives, for instance creating shareholder value, and the strategies and business rules that are designed to realize these objectives. This means that there also has to be an agreement regarding the relationship between policy and legislation on the public side, and objectives and strategies and business rules on the private side. The fundamentally different relationships companies have with their customers compared to the ones citizens have with their government determine the choices these organizations make at these levels. Public organizations are bound by political and legal imperatives, while private organizations will evaluate the private-public collaboration from a business perspective where both cooperative and competitive forces play a role.

As a result, collaboration may be hard to realize, and providing clients with a transparent view on the various aspects of this cooperation at the levels discussed above may be even harder. This transparency is required to ensure the trust that is needed to make such cooperation successful in the long run.

Outlook: The evolution of transparency

We discussed the role of transparency in public and private services networks. The complexity of the cooperation between public and private organizations makes it very difficult to provide the clients of these organizations with a clear insight into what is happening with their personal information, who is accountable for the service being delivered, what the actual status of the delivery process is, etc. Such cooperation will only receive the necessary level of trust from clients involved if the transparency that is required can be provided. Within the Dutch government, the various agencies and institutions are relatively autonomous. Central control over the service delivery processes across multiple agencies is, therefore, difficult or even impossible to achieve. The complexity of this inter-agency cooperation has always been a keen interest of René Wagenaar, as expressed, for example, in his inaugural address (Wagenaar, 2002) on the 'virtual civil servant', and in his work on cross-agency business processes (Gortmaker, Janssen & Wagenaar, 2005; Gortmaker, Janssen & Wagenaar, 2006), and shared services in government (Wagenaar, 2006; Wagenaar et al., 2006).

Cooperation becomes even more complicated when private and public processes are combined, since different types of regulation apply to the relationship between companies and their customers than to that between citizens and government. Although contractual relationships through service-level agreements may to a certain extent help organize this cooperation, many of these processes require a much more complicated coordination structure than is provided by traditional service delivery. Often, long-running processes within multiple organizations need to be synchronized in various ways, while at the same time providing (partial) services to their clients.

Organizations are either obliged to provide transparency on the basis of relevant regulation, or they can use it as a strategic asset in service design. Both options are relevant in e business and e government, albeit in different ways. With the growing interaction between public and private services, the different roles transparency plays can lead to complex dilemmas. This is already true in the case of healthcare and municipal services. However, things will become more complicated. An example of this is road pricing (another topic in which René was interested; see also Vrancken & Wagenaar, 2005). In a private setting, it can be worthwhile to use information that has been gathered to provide interesting propositions to drivers regarding when and where to drive, etc. It can provide drivers insight into their driving behavior. At the same time, the information has a tremendous commercial value. When commercial service providers become involved, information can be used in a variety of ways, many of which are unlikely to serve the interests of the people to whom the information pertains, and some may even harm their privacy. Similar objections have been made with regard to the use of chip cards in public transport.

There may be negative side-effects, not only for citizens and customers. An additional complication is the resistance increased transparency and collaboration may encounter among the employees of public and private organizations. Traditional boundaries may break down, responsibilities are re-allocated, and an increased level of accountability will be required from the companies, government agencies and individuals involved. Vice versa, a lack of accountability stands in the way of the transparency needed to provide integrated e government services (Gortmaker, Janssen & Wagenaar, 2005), and even more so when public and private services are combined. Private parties will simply not accept a lack of accountability from government agencies if they need to work together on providing certain services. Again, trust and transparency are two sides of the same coin.

Moreover, implementation creates a number of dilemmas, such as centralized versus decentralized decision-making, and a radical or gradual introduction (Wagenaar, 2006). Choosing the wrong implementation strategy may hinder the introduction of new services and the acceptance of choices that have been made with regard to transparency. René described two extreme approaches: a 'big bang' approach and a 'soft pressure' approach, each with their own pros and cons. He proposed combining the two strategies, by using the 'big bang' in theory story and the 'soft pressure' in practice, and he warned us to be cautious with respect to the level of ambition and scope. This implies identifying quick wins where there is general agreement on the choices regarding transparency.

The future will bring an enormous amount of public and private services, glued together in mash-ups over the Internet. The boundaries between organizations will be penetrated by services that will exchange all kinds of information. On the one hand, this will benefit those who use the services, because the information can be used to personalize services. On the other hand, there will also be benefits for commercial and public service providers, who can exploit the bewildering amount of information available in various ways.

However, because the dangers of an unimpaired exchange of information are also enormous, the need for transparency will be bigger than ever: safeguards have to be in place to prevent any unauthorized use of information. At the same time, however, providing the transparency that is needed is reaching levels of complexity that are not matched by current technology or legislation, which means that there are many challenges ahead, not only for the virtual civil servant, but for all of us, challenges that we are sure René would have relished.

[1] Such as www.misdaadkaart.nl in the Netherlands.
[2] Please see b-dossier.telin.nl for more information. B-Dossier is a combined research initiative of the Telematica Instituut with partners from government and academia, including the Dutch Tax and Customs Administration, the Municipality of The Hague, SVB, UWV, ING, ICTU, the University of Twente, and Delft University of Technology. The project aims at supporting integrated, demand-driven electronic services by public and private organizations to citizens and companies.

REFERENCES

Bovens, M., (2003). *De digitale republiek. Democratie en rechtsstaat in de informatiemaatschappij.* Amsterdam: Amsterdam University Press [in Dutch].

Burger@Overheid.nl (2005). *Online communiceren met de overheid, nu en in de toekomst: een onderzoek onder het Publiekspanel van burger@overheid.* Netpanel [in Dutch].

Buuren, R. van, Strating, P. & Faber, E. (2004). A Theoretical Approach To Trust Services in eBusiness. In *Proceedings 17th Bled eCommerce Conference* (Bled 2004). Bled, Slovenia, June 21-23, 2004.

Chircu, A. M. & Kauffman, R. J. (2000). Reintermediation strategies in business-to-business electronic commerce. *International Journal of Electronic Commerce*, 4, 7-42.

Denmark (2007). Borger.dk. http://www.borger.dk, Accessed December 7, 2007.

Derks, W. L. A. & Lankhorst, M.M. (2006). *Definitie en conceptualisatie van het B-dossier.* Technical Report TI/RS/2006/013, Telematica Instituut, Enschede, The Netherlands [in Dutch].

Fielt, E. (2006). *Designing for acceptance: Exchange design for electronic intermediaries.* Telematica Instituut, Enschede, the Netherlands. Available at: https://doc.telin.nl/dsweb/Get/Document-66766/

Fielt, E., Janssen, W., Faber, E. & Wagenaar, R. (2007). Exchange Design Patterns for Electronic Intermediaries. In H. Österle, J. Schelp and R. Winter (Eds.), *Proceedings of the 15th European Conference on Information Systems* (ECIS2007) (pp. 155-166), St.Gallen, Switzerland.

Franken, H. (2007), *Rapport commissie grondrechten in het digitale tijdperk.* Available at http://www.ivir.nl/dossier/grondrechten/bronnen/rapport—gdt—5-00.pdf. Accessed December 7, 2007 [in Dutch].

Giaglis, G.M., Klein, S. & O'Keefe, R.M. (2002). The role of intermediaries in electronic marketplaces: Developing a contingency model. *Information Systems Journal*, 12, 231-246.

Gortmaker, J., Janssen, M.F.W.H.A., Wagenaar, R.W. (2005). Accountability of Electronic Cross-Agency Service-Delivery Processes. In M.A. Wimmer et al. (Eds), *EGOV 2005*, LNCS 3591, pp. 49-56. Springer-Verlag, Berlin, Heidelberg, 2005.

Gortmaker, J., Janssen, M.F.W.H.A. & Wagenaar, R.W. (2006). Coordinating Cross-agency Business Processes. In Ari-Veikko Anttiroiko & Matti Malkia (Eds.), *Encyclopedia of Digital Government*, pp. 237-243. IDEA Group, Hershey, Penn.

Hagel, J. & Rayport, J. F. (1997). The new infomediaries. *McKinsey Quarterly*, 54-70.

Janssen, W. & Zeef, P. (2006). Vision and Valuation of a Citizen-Centric Shared Information Portal. In *Proceedings 19th Bled E-Commerce Conference* (Bled 2006). Bled, Slovenia, June 5-7, 2006. Available at: http://www.bledconference.org/Proceedings.nsf/Proc2006Research?OpenPage

Lankhorst, M.M. & Derks, W., (2007). Towards a Service-Oriented Architecture for Demand-Driven e-Government. In *Proceedings 11th IEEE International EDOC Conference* (EDOC 2007), October 15-19, 2007, Annapolis, Maryland, USA. IEEE Press.

Mintzberg, H., (1996). Managing Government, Governing Management. *Harvard Business Review*, May-June, pp. 75-83.

O'Reilly, T. (2007). What is Web 2.0? http://www.oreillynet.com/pub/a/oreilly/tim/news/2005/09/30/what-is-web-20.html. Accessed December 7, 2007.

PIP (2007), Persoonlijke Internetpagina. http://pip.overheid.nl. Accessed December 7, 2007. [in Dutch]

Scott, M.,W. Golden, and M. Hughes (2004). A Click And Bricks Strategy For eGovernment. In: Yao Hua Tan et a. (Eds.), *Proceedings 17th Bled eCommerce Conference* (Bled 2004), Bled, Slovenia, June 21-24, 2004.

Cc:Egov (2007). A Handbook for Citizen-centric eGovernment. Available at: http://www.ccegov.eu/downloads/Handbook—Final—031207.pdf.

Van Dijk, J.A.G.M. (2002). e-Government. In: Bouwman, H., van Dijk, J.A.G.M., van den Hooff, B., and van de Wijngaert, L. (eds.), *ICT in Organisaties*. Boom, Amsterdam, The Netherlands [in Dutch].

Velsen, L. van, Geest, Th. van der, Hedde, M. ter (2007). Het B-dossier toegepast: gebruikersevaluatie van de Haagse WMO-portal. Technical Report TI/RS/2007/057, Telematica Instituut, Enschede, The Netherlands [in Dutch].

Vrancken, J.L.M. & Wagenaar, R.W. (2005). An Evolutionary Approach to Road Pricing. In *Proceedings of the 5th European Congress on Intelligent Transport Systems and Services (ITS)*, pp. 1-7. Hannover: ITS Europe.

Wagenaar, R.W. (2002). De virtuele ambtenaar: naar een transparante overheid? Inaugural lecture Delft University of Technology, Delft, The Netherlands [in Dutch].

Wagenaar, R.W. (2006). Governance of Shared Service Centers in Public Administration: Dilemmas and Trade-offs. In *Proceedings of the 8th International Conference on Electronic Commerce* (ICEC 2006), Fredericton, New Brunswick, Canada.

Wagenaar, R.W., Matthijsse, R., Bruijn, J.A. de, Voort, H.G. van der & Wendel de Joode, R. van (2006). Implementation of Shared Service Centres in Public Administration: Dilemmas and Trade-offs. In V.J.J.M. Bekkers et al. (Ed.), *Information and communication Technology and Public Innovation* (Innovation and the Public Sector, 12), pp. 141-158. IOS Press, Amsterdam.

NEW E-COMMERCE BUSINESS MODELS BY THEIR DIGITAL NATURE WERE EASY TO COPY BY OTHER PEOPLE. THE RESULT WAS A SITUATION WHEREBY INNOVATOR AND COPYCAT DRAGGED ONE ANOTHER INTO THE FINANCIAL ABYSS, BY SPENDING EVER-INCREASING AMOUNTS OF MONEY ON ADVERTISING AND COSTLY SOFTWARE IN AN ATTEMPT TO ATTRACT AND RETAIN CUSTOMERS.

From *Civil Servant*

The Virtual Merchant Is Searching for Profit
How Google Is Auctioning Keywords and Will Create New Business Models

Eric van Heck

Abstract

This article elaborates on the notion of the virtual merchant introduced by René in his inaugural address entitled 'The Virtual Merchant: Fiction or Reality'. Already in 1997 René made clear that the virtual merchant will become an important business model and he identified obstacles and opportunities with regard to the use of these virtual merchants in online trading. In this article we will illustrate with the example of Google how virtual merchants indeed became a dominant actor in the network of traders on the Internet. It shows that searching for profit – as always an important characteristic for merchants – in Google's case has to do with the innovative use of auctioning keywords. We will explain the main features of Google and show how Google is searching for other profit making business models. We discuss Google by taking René's view and discuss obstacles and opportunities. Finally, conclusions are formulated.

Introduction

For centuries searching for profit is a key driver for most organizations. A key element is that a company has to create value both for its suppliers and its customers. There are several ways to create such value. In this article we will explore how the virtual merchant concept introduced by René in his inaugural address (Wagenaar, 1997) indeed became reality. The key question we will address is: what are essential characteristics for successful virtual merchants and what are potential business models?

The objective of this article is to provide executives and researchers guidance in their evaluation of current or new business models. We will illustrate the concept developed by René by analyzing one of the most successful virtual merchants of our time: Google. Interesting about Google is that nowadays almost everybody is using Google as a search engine, but not that many people know exactly how it works and how Google is making money. In lectures with various audiences around the world – ranging from first year students in Rotterdam, to master students in Helsinki or executives in Jakarta – the question "When you are using Google are you searching the Internet?" was usually answered with the wrong answer. Most in the audience will answer with 'yes'. However, the answer is 'no': you are searching in a database of Google. It illustrates again how people use – but not understand – complex technologies.

Section 2 provides a comprehensive overview and understanding of virtual merchants and business models. Section 3 explains how Google works and provides a detailed explanation of the key word auction that Google uses for making money. Section 4 provides examples of evolving business models that Google is working on and shows how searching for profit is evolving over time. Section 5 discusses the characteristics, obstacles, and opportunities taken into account the view of René and a future outlook.

Virtual Merchants and Their Business Model
In his inaugural address René analyzed the parallel between the physical trading routes (like the ancient Silk Road that connected Europe with China) and the virtual trading routes at the electronic highway (at that time that term was used for the Internet). He was on of the first that recognized the importance of the virtual merchants that connect sellers with buyers (Wagenaar, 1997). His claim was that everybody – with small investments – could become a virtual merchant. The merchant could find new suppliers for potential buyers, could create or combine new products or services, or could deliver new ways of connecting buyers and sellers for example by introducing online auction concepts. The virtual merchant could be an interesting business model that is able to create benefits for all. Important aspect is the ability of the virtual merchant to create trust both for sellers and buyers.

The literature of business models exploded during the Internet hype of the 1990s. In general it is viewed that the term business model survived in the debate between academics and business people. It means that besides some confusion the concept business model is worthwhile both from an academic and a business perspective. We derive from several stream of research the core characteristics of business models.

A business model is explained by Gartner is the abstract pattern of mechanisms that a company uses to focus resources, create customer value and realize it (Raskino, 2007). In research executed by Lynda Applegate and the group at Harvard Business School the emphasis is also on value creation for all stakeholders involved. They state that 'a successful business model aligns an organization with its environment' (Applegate et al, 2007:26). Interesting is that business models related to the role of virtual merchant have evolved quickly the last decade. Processes among the main stakeholders (buyers, market maker, sellers) made new ways possible that could to create value for all (see for a detailed analysis and framework Kambil & van Heck, 2002). Work by the OpenGroup emphasized the architectural components of so-called boundaryless business models, see Solomon (2003).

How Google Use Auctions To Makes Money

In the beginning of developing the business model of Google the search and other technologies were not the problem, the problem was how to make money with a 'free' search engine. John Battelle (2005) presents very well in detail how this struggle for searching for profit evolved over time. The concept of auctioning keywords saved Google from bankruptcy. How is it working?

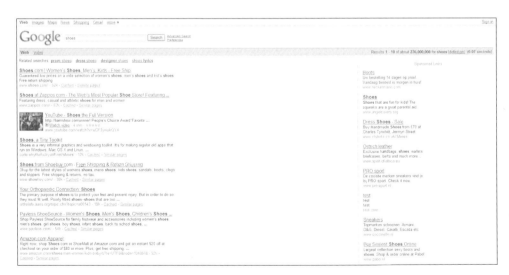

Figure 1, Example of the Google's search and auction results (sponsored links).

A user of Google is typing in a key word. Google provides the relevant (organic) links and the sponsored links. For example a user is looking for 'shoes'. Figure 1 shows the results. The organic links are on the left side, the sponsored links are at the right side. When users clicks on the sponsored link (for example the link 'Mens Designer Shoe Sale'), the user is sent to the advertiser's web page. The advertiser pays the search engine for sending the users to its web page.

Advertisers submit bids stating their maximum willingness to pay for a click. The ad with the highest bid (and in Google combined with the estimated click-through rate) is displayed at the top. When a user clicks on an ad in position K, the advertiser is charged by the search engine an amount equal to the next highest bid (in position K+1) plus a fixed small increment (1 dollar cent). For example, the highest bidder bids $1.50 and the second bidder bids $1.40. The highest bidder will be the number one but pays the second highest price plus 1 dollar cent (in our case $1.41). Google's key word auction therefore can be considered as a 'generalized second price auction'. Bidders can indicate a maximum budget and also can indicate for which locations in the world they have in interest.

Google Business Models

Google not only introduced a new way of making money but also a new way of developing innovations. It uses an open innovation laboratory where users are co-creating innovative business models. The innovation laboratory can be viewed and used at labs.google.com. We have analyzed four promising business models that are explained at Google Labs. The business models were analyzed for the EU sponsored project BeinGrid (Van Heck, 2006). Also during numerous student and executive sessions these business models were analyzed and discussed in detail. For each of the business models we have identified:

— Its core and its main stakeholders
— Its critical capabilities or resources
— Its value creation process
— Its pricing model
— Its strategic risks

	Google Music Trends	**Google Gmail**	**Google Docs & Spreadsheets**	**Google Earth**
Core business model and stakeholders	Stimulate digital music sales by showing trends; Google talk users; Google; Digital music sellers	Free Gmail to create community and services Google Gmail users; Google; Advertisers	Pay-per-use software Application Service Provision (ASP) Google users, Google	Location-based services Google Earth user; Google; Advertisers, Google Earth service provider
Capabilities business model	Information aggregation – spotting trends	Email communication and data storage; filtering techniques; sponsored links	Running software and storage Connection with Search, Gmail, and Google Talk	Location data and satellite imagery; Integration of advertising Customization to specific providers
Value creation	Stimulation of music selling; forecasting music demand; information aggregation; efficiency	Free Gmail use and storage; sponsored links; Efficiency and lock-in	No software installation at own server; Multi-user applications; combined with instant messaging; efficiency and lock-in	New services with digital map content; sponsored links; Novelty and complementarity
Pricing model	Free services for Google talk users Click-trough-rate to music sellers	Free services for Gmail users Key Word Auction	Pay per use; sponsored links	Membership; sponsored links

Table 1: Analysis of four business models developed by Google Labs

The first business model is Google Music Trends. The business model aggregates what Google Talk users are listening to. For specific music genres and countries one can create a ranking of music songs in terms of popularity. The second business model is Gmail. The free email program offered by Google provides the functionality to receive and send email but also offers advertisers to link to clients by using sponsored links. The type of sponsors is related to the content of the email communication. The third business model is Google Docs & Spreadsheets. It provides to users software. Google is tinkering here with its role of Application Software Provider (ASP) that delivers software as a service (SAAS) to the client. The fourth business model is Google Earth. This revolutionary model provides detailed localized information to the users. Combined with mobile technology it is able to offer mobile services.

From a business model perspective it is interesting to notice that each of the four business models has distinctive value creation opportunities. The dimensions provide an excellent basis for analyzing the key characteristics to identify the sustainability and viability of the business model.

With regard to the first business model the low quality of the service is problematic. The quality of the rankings is and the high competition provides evidence that there will a low potential to generate sufficient profit. The second business model faces stiff competition and the service itself will not be sufficient to generate sustainable profit over time. The third business model provides a new way of delivering software to customers. The ASP model has some risks but is worthwhile to develop knowledge and insight about the way customers (especially consumers and small and medium sized enterprises) will start to use the 'software as a service' services. The fourth business model combines location-based services with satellite imagery. Its potential is very high. In several courses students and executives could vote for the business model with the highest potential. Google Earth was always the winner.

Discussion and Future Outlook

Firstly, the Google example shows how the virtual merchant became reality as foreseen by René in his inaugural address. Indeed infrastructural, institutional, and economic barriers had to be taken. For a sustainable business model the introduction of the key word auction concept was a key innovation. The auction determines the value of keywords (the second price plus 1 dollar cent) and determines the allocation to the highest bidder. René would certainly try to make clear how users of Google (potential buyers and sellers) are eager to trust Google. He would claim that if Google was not trusted anymore the business model could easily be flawed. He would certainly make the point how far Google could go (from a technical point of view) in getting detailed consumer information and that it would lead to tensions related to privacy and security. He would stimulate governmental agencies to dive into the details how Google is operating and how it needs to be surveyed.

Secondly, the other new business models developed by Google show how virtual merchants continuously are searching for profit. We conclude that the Music Trend business model has a high risk of not generating profit. The Gmail model has a medium potential to become a viable business model due to its 'trust' component. Google Docs & Spreadsheets and Google Earth will have a high respectively very high potential as a viable business model. The combination of location-based technologies and services will open up new ways of connecting buyers to sellers. Mobile merchants could form the next wave of virtual merchants using mobile technologies to create value and profit.

Thirdly, it is clear that virtual merchants are reality and will become the routers in our packet-switched economy.

References
Applegate, Lynda, Robert D. Austin, F. Warren McFarlan (2007). *Corporate Information Strategy and Management, Text and Cases*, McGraw-Hill, Seventh Edition.
Battelle, John, (2005). *The Search, How Google and Its Rivals Rewrote the Rules of Business and Transformed Our Culture*, Nicolas Brealey Publishing, Boston/London.
Kambil Ajit & Eric van Heck, (2002). *Making Markets*, Harvard Business School Press, Boston.
Solomon, E., (2003). *Boundaryless Information Flow Reference Architecture; Six Example Boundaryless Business Models*, 38 pp., The Open Group, July 2003 (www.opengroup.org)
Raskino, M, (2007).*What "Business Model" Means and Why It Matters*, Gartner Research, 21 May 2007.
Van Heck, Eric, (2006). *Searching for Profit*, BeinGrid Presentation, RSM Erasmus University, November 16, 2006.
Wagenaar, Rene, (1997). "*De Virtuele Koopman: fictie of werkelijkheid*" (The Virtual Merchant: fiction or reality), Inaugural Address, Free University, Amsterdam.

PART 2

THE VIRTUAL CIVIL SERVANT

AS FAR AS PUBLIC SERVICE AND PUBLIC GOVERNMENT ARE CONCERNED, THE POSSIBILITIES ICT OFFERS TO ESTABLISH A MUCH MORE INTENSIVE AND PERSONAL CONTACT WITH CITIZENS AND COMPANIES IS LAGGING BEHIND.

From Civil Servant

Managing Change in e-Government: Policies and Strategies

Roland Traunmüller, Maria A. Wimmer and Gerti Orthofer

ABSTRACT

In recent years, there have been many changes in the areas of e-Government. In the first part of this paper, we describe the important role of the EU as policy developer, which provides guidance and incentives to the member countries. We use the Austrian e-Government Policy as an example. Next, we present the means the EU uses to shape the future, including Ministerial Conferences, the eEurope Award Competitions, Modinis Interoperability Recommendations and the Roadmap e-Government 2020. In the final section of this chapter, we focus on developing e-Government strategies and managing changes. Both these elements have a broad span – reaching from abstract concepts to down-to-earth advice.

e-Government as Driver in the Knowledge Society

The Lisbon strategy has given Europe a vision on the general development of the Knowledge Society, in which e-Government plays an essential part. The two elements are streamlining the machinery of Government on the one hand, and enabling economic growth through a modern Government. This means that e-Government is a driver influencing many parts of society: economics, employment, education, health, etc.

The EU defines e-Government as the use of information and communication technologies in public administrations with the aim of improving public services and democratic processes. There are several issues that deserve to be addressed at the European level: privacy, security, interoperability, etc. There are many reasons to urge in favour of a common e-Government policy. Cross-border activities are increasing – so customs, taxes and procurement will benefit. In addition, e-Government needs to pace progress at a European level, and learning from mutual experiences becomes a valid argument.

EU Policies on e-Government: The Beginning

The EU has established a vision and initiated strategies for the Knowledge/Information Society in general and e-Government in particular. As far as EU policy with regard to Information Society is concerned, the Lisbon agenda was the starting point. The initial phase started in 2000, when the EU launched two Action Plans, eEurope 2002 and eEurope 2005, which generated a positive momentum for the short-term development of the Information Society. In this phase, the main focus was on creating projects that could serve as pilots and showcases.

The terms e-Readiness and Availability marked the period between 2000 and 2005, with an emphasis on rapidly bringing public services online to show readiness and availability. To illustrate this, we discuss some relevant points regarding 'IT for Innovative Government'. The specific citations are from the IST Call 4 (CORDIS 2004):

— *Innovative ICT for democratic involvement, in particular e-Participation*: Research should address innovative tools and methods for fact-based policy development, agent technologies, intelligent formulation and enactment tools supporting the preparation of democratic decisions, scalable dialogue tools as well as new possibilities for interactivity in democratic processes.

— *Intelligent, inclusive and personalized e-Government services*: Research should focus on public service obligations of assuring privacy protection and public services that are provided for all. Citizen-centric, context-aware, intuitive and intelligent interfaces capable to serve every citizen individually. Seamless, personalized multi-device service delivery.

— *Adaptive and proactive e-Government support systems*: This means modeling of administrative processes by using of emerging ontologies and semantic web languages. Technologies support the legislative and policy development process such as intelligent tools to develop policy scenarios and to manage administrative processes and content. Public service requirements are: process transparency, preservation of diversity, multi-level governance, multilingualism, new services and new ways of service provision.

— *Secure pan-European e-Government*: Important themes are secure architectures, environments, information infrastructures, service dependability, and interoperability in public administrations across Europe. Therefore, a secure and interoperable implementation of pan-European e-Government is necessary, including the use of smart card technologies, biometrics and trusted services.

EU Policies on e-Government: 2010 and Beyond
In 2005, a policy adjustment was was decided based on the Kok report (European Commission 2004). The emphasis shifted from the creation of pilots and precursors towards the future development of high impact services and guidance by measurement. Under a new label – i2010 – plans were developed to create high impact services and progress measurement. The i2010 e-Government Action plan (European Commission, 2006) contains the following five points:
— *Inclusive e-Government – no citizen left behind*: Advancing inclusion through e-Government to ensure that, by 2010, all citizens benefit from trusted, innovative services and easy access for all.
— *Efficient and effective e-Government*: The goal is to receive high user satisfaction, transparency and accountability, a lighter administrative burden and efficiency gains.
— *High-impact services*: This means implementing key services for citizens and businesses. By 2010, 100% of public procurement will be available electronically, with 50% actual usage, with agreement on cooperation on further high-impact online citizen services.
— *Putting key enablers in place*: This enables citizens and businesses to benefit, by 2010, from convenient, secure and interoperable authenticated access across Europe to public services.
— *E-Participation*: Strengthening participation and democratic decision-making will result in the creation of tools for effective public debate and participation by 2010. Also, these benefits should be made tangible to citizens.

National Policies: Austria as an Example
In parallel to the EU activities, member states like Austria have developed national policies. In 2007, a benchmark study was carried out by Cap Gemini on behalf of the European Commission, to evaluate EU Online Services (20 basis services, 12 for citizens and 8 for enterprises, in 27 European Union states) and chart the progress of online public service delivery. In 2002, Austria ranked eleventh among the member states, and it managed to forge ahead continuously. Last year, Austria ranked first for the first time, and this year, the country was able to maintain its lead-

ing position. The goal and 'motto' of Austria in this respect is that public administration should become 'easier, faster and better'. That is why it is important to focus on the client's perspective, to increase the quality of the services and enhance people's trust in the administration. Furthermore, a modern and dynamic administration has competitive advantages for the business location. In the following paragraphs, we provide an outline of Austria's e-Government policy on the basis of official documents like www.ref.gv.at

Strategies are planned and coordinated from a central location, at the so called *Platform Digital Austria*. This Platform is responsible for identifying objectives and roadmaps, and it supports the elaboration, monitoring and implementation of e-Government projects. Furthermore, there is an *ICT Board and E-Cooperation Board* that is closely connected to the Platform Digital Austria and responsible for discussing and approving the results of the operational working groups.

Also, because of the federal structure of the Austrian state, planning the *collaboration* of the various actors in the area of e-Government is important to ensure the pursuit of shared objectives. The main actors in Austrian e-Government are the Federal Chancellery, the provinces and the associations of local authorities and municipalities. In practice, the Ministry of Finance is also an important player, being in charge of the federal ID computer center (Bundesrechenzentrum, BRZ). Voluntary cooperating bodies have been established in which provinces and local authorities participate:
— *E-Government Working Groups*: They are responsible for the implementation of e-Government strategies. To create synergy and interoperable solutions, working groups include representatives of the federal, regional and local authorities.
— *Austrian Association of Cities and Towns* (Österreichischer Städtebund): This organization represents the interests of large municipalities in Austria. It has set up some 30 technical committees to explore innovative measures and program adopted by the towns and communities, develop statements regarding new legislation and discuss the implementation of new policies.
— *Austrian Association of Municipalities* (Österreichischer Gemeindebund): This is the legal representation of the interests of smaller and medium-sized municipalities in Austria.

Interoperability is a key characteristic of the Austrian e-Government strategy. It is considered especially important because of the federal structure of the Austrian state. The provision of services by a large number of regional and local authorities on the one hand, and the provision of basic services to local and regional authorities by the central administration on the other, require the use of interoperable solutions. These solutions need to be planned and developed in a cooperative way, taking the requirements of stakeholders from various administrative levels into consideration.

Additional central themes in Austria's e-Government policy are the 'Design for all' principle and e-Inclusion. E-Inclusion is also a central goal at EU level, the aim being to reduce gaps in the use of ICT and to promote the use of ICT to overcome exclusion, and to improve economic performance, employment opportunities, the quality of life, social participation and cohesion. Help.gv.at, for example, is an information portal for citizens and businesses. It has also become the main transaction portal for local authorities. The underlying idea is that local authorities ought to have a one-stop-shop platform for e-Government services. Help.gv.at also supports processes within the administration, supporting the transfer of electronic forms to electronic record systems and automated procedures. One of the next steps in the development of Help.gv.at will be the exchange of information regarding local administrations and service.

Within this context, LDAP.gv.at is a central directory service, which eventually is intended to contain the information of the entire Austrian public administration (local authorities, regions, Federal Ministries, self-governing bodies, etc.). The specification LDAP.gv.at describes the data model of the administrative system (organization, organizational unit, personnel, user rights). LDAP.gv.at will serve as a central hub for the distribution of data.

The forms provided by help.gv.at use the Form Style Guide, which allows the use of standardized lay-out for web forms and is part of the overall strategic design. On the one hand, the consistent use of standardized allows offers the entire public administration to present a uniform image to the outside world. On the other hand, public administration has declared its intention to provide non-discriminatory access to its electronic services. Web forms are often the key to such open access. The Form Style Guide lays down minimum requirements. For example, Level A of the international WAI Guidelines has to be incorporated, and the W3C HTML/XHTML has been identified as the relevant standard.

Although Help.gv.at supports the view of the customer on the administration, the Portal Group is one result of the good cooperation between the federal, regional and local public administrations. The advantages are reduced expenditure for the user administration and simpler management of access rights as a result of single sign-on. The maintenance of many parallel directories is no longer necessary. The portal group is a link-up of administrative web portals for the joint use of the existing administrative back office resources and applications, for example official registers. The interconnected system enables participating organizations to use their own user administration to access the accessing applications of other administrative bodies.

A very helpful project is EDIAKTII, which defines a format for the communication between authorities, companies and citizens. This standard for electronic file exchange will be usable at all government levels as well as by business and citizens. In addition, it will be the standard for long-term archiving.

Shaping Directions

Although from a legal point of view, the EU has no direct influence on the administrations of the Member States, considerable influence is exerted in an indirect way to shape the direction of change. One example is the fact that the EU finances many multinational projects within the Framework Program, as well as dedicating many events and initiating special activities, for example in the following four areas:
— Ministerial Conferences
— The eEurope Award Competitions
— Modinis Interoperability Recommendations
— Roadmap e-Government 2020

Ministerial Conferences on e-Government

Ministerial Conferences on e-Government result in decisions regarding further steps and are often combined with exhibitions, for example the eEurope Awards presentations demonstrating the state of affairs. Such combined events took place in 2003 in Como, jointly organized by the EU and the Italian Presidency, in 2005 in Manchester, organized by the European Commission and the UK Presidency, and in 2007 in Lisbon jointly organized by the EU and the Portugal Presidency (Gieber et al, 2007).

The main aim of the Lisbon Conference was to show the progress that was made between 2005 and 2007 – in general terms as well as specifically in relation to the i2010 e-Government Action Plan, the foundation of which is a holistic approach based on three pillars:
— A single European information space
— Innovation and investment in research as well as inclusion
— Improved services and quality of life.

The question whether or not progress was made can be answered with a resounding yes. The Lisbon Conference showed the progress that was made in the previous two years. If look at the roll-out and adoption figures, for example, 2006 was quite an impressive year for the advanced member countries:
— Citizens: Basic services are available in 36 percent of all cases, and 24 percent of all citizens use at least some of them.
— Enterprises: Availability was at 68 percent, usage at 64 percent.

The eEurope Awards Competitions

Knowledge transfer aimed at building better e-Government solutions is on demand. All too often the wheel is reinvented – so using the experience of successful projects is required. Such collections of model project cases are known as good or best practice and can be seen as signposts for development. Award programs offer an effective way to identify high quality cases. For this reason, the European Commission launched a good practice awards program in 2001 within the framework of the e-Europe initiative.

The aim of the eEurope Awards for Innovation in e-Government is to promote the exchange of good practice and experience in the public sector across Europe. The initiative has proved successful and the biennial e-Government Awards (with the latest one in 2007 in Lisbon) have gained a high reputation. The aim of the Awards is to highlight and provide information about the efforts that have been made by a broad range of national, regional and local authorities. An independent panel of experts has identified model cases (which were selected for exhibition and presentation) designed to allow authorities all over Europe to benefit from each others' expertise (Gieber, 2007).

Various criteria were applied, such as innovation, relevance, transferability and impact. The following issues areas are considered relevant:
— An innovative and ambitious approach to tackling a serious problem
— High adoption rate and customer satisfaction
— Superior integration and collaboration of different systems and entities
— Creating successful public-private partnerships
— Compliance with significant e-Government-strategy goals
— Good implementation of a cross-border collaboration
— Exemplary project development and a sound engineering approach

Transferability is a special criterion. Projects have to provide a valuable and sufficiently detailed list of advice for others in e-Government. Furthermore, the underlying principles can be examined and adapted by others or used as inspiration and guiding principles. We want to emphasize that assessing transferability is not easy – such an assessment involves looking the supply side (what can be learned) as wall as the demand side (who can learn).

Impact and benefits are other relevant criteria that are also hard to assess. At a qualitative level, there are various features: accountability, openness, transparency, accessibility to services, provision of information for decision-makers, etc. At a quantitative level, the impact can be measured on the basis of adoption rates and user satisfaction, while the internal impact can be measured on the basis of resources, throughput and cost savings.

Modinis Interoperability Recommendations
In 2006, a study was conducted in the form of the Modinis Lot 2 report on 'Interoperability at Local and Regional Level', the main contributors being CERTH/ITI (Thessaloniki), EIPA (Maastricht) and ifib (Bremen) (2006). The underlying rationale behind the study was that the success of e-Government depends on its central claim of providing one-stop on-

line government, which involves providing a single access point to a large number of public services, regardless of government level and agency. The core problem is that there are many transactions and repositories are involved – data are brought together from various sources and distributed to several repositories, which means that achieving interoperability is crucially important.

The study focused on the current state of affairs in the member states, key success factors and main barriers, recommendations to different stakeholders, using status reports (questionnaires filled out and delivered by national experts) and selected examples of good practice cases in interoperability as input. In addition, the best cases of the Good Practice Framework were analyzed, identifying 18 cases as best cases in terms of interoperability, ranging from civil registration, e-forms exchange and land-registration to procurement and e-identification. The sample contained cases from all levels of government (local, regional and national) and also covered the various layers of interoperability. In addition, the study provided an analysis of existing technical literature and various national reports. Feedback from stakeholders and experts was organized during the process.

Below, we provide two examples from the report to illustrate the recommendations. To begin with, at EU level, several areas are addressed:
— *Legislation*: Promote harmonization in the administrative practice amongst member states; also promote intellectual property rights.
— *Policy/Management*: Internationalize the Interoperability discussion and promote a common terminology
— *Funding/Financial*: Support of Interoperability projects and research
— *Technical*: Create a European e-Government Interoperability infrastructure: e.g. portals classifying local authority services, documenting good practice and relevant experience.

The second example concerns recommendations that point to Policy and Management, including a number of proposals to the European Commission: establishing a portal dealing with Interoperability issues; enhancing interoperability research; and promoting a common terminology on e-Identity. Some of the suggestions aimed at the local and regional level include:

— Proposals range from compliance with national strategies to new ways of knowledge transfer.
— It is important to realize that interoperability is an investment in the future.
— Because innovative solutions are a strong point, knowledge transfer aimed at increasing quality is crucially important
— There is an emphasis on transforming organizational structures and developing awareness regarding cultural issues.

Roadmap e-Government 2020

Planning e-Government for the future requires an e-Government research agenda. An EU project was awarded to the University of Linz, and later transferred to Koblenz University (when the project leader Maria Wimmer became Professor in Koblenz). The project, which is called 'Road mapping e-Government 2020', involved nine partners and was completed this year. It focuses on at visions regarding European citizenship and innovative Government; it implies developing visionary e-Government scenarios for 2020 as well as a detailed research roadmap for the transformation process, the aim being to convert the EC Government landscape into a coherent community and contributing to the development of the EC into a leading knowledge society.

The methodology and results are described in detail in 'Roadmapping eGovernment Research: Visions and Measures towards Innovative Governments in 2020' (Codagnone and Wimmer, 2007). Below, we present a brief summary.
— *Taking stock*: The first step focused on describing the current state of e-Government research in Europe. This part investigates the main e-Government research programs as well as the relevant ongoing and completed research projects.
— *Building visions*: Regional workshops were conducted to evaluate potential research and implementation scenarios with regard to e-Government until 2020. The regional scenario-building workshops focused on potential scenarios and involved participants from the public, academic and industrial sectors. The different views that emerged from the various workshops we integrated into a holistic vision.
— *Gap analysis*: The aim here is to assess the differences between existing

and possible future outlooks regarding e-Government research, identifying gaps and discussing possible developments.
— *Detailed roadmap*: In this part, research challenges and actions are identified in response to emerging technical, organizational, social, economic and political trends. Again, the method was based on a series of regionally distributed workshops that created roadmap ideas and received feedback with regard to the roadmaps that had been developed.
— *Consolidation, compilation and dissemination*: The current state of affairs is summarized, describing potential future scenarios of governments and society by 2020 and providing a roadmap of research in e-Government for the period to come.

The results of the Roadmap 2020 study identify the following research themes as topics that urgently need to be pursued:
— Fostering trust in Government
— Semantic and cultural interoperability
— Information quality
— Assessing the value of IT in Government
— Citizen engagement and enhanced democratic principles
— Mission centricity
— New cyber infrastructure and building block industry
— Ontologies, intelligent information and knowledge management
— Governance of Public-Private-Civic Sector Relationships
— E-Government's role at regulating the virtual world
— Cross border activities and the need for governance capabilities
— E-Government in the context of an ageing population
— Data privacy and personal identification in e-Government and e-Participation service provision

Developing e-Government Strategies
Having a vision: Although developing and realizing e-Government strategies involves a number of issues, the entire process begins with a vision. Because e-Government is a transformation in the long term, what is need is an imagination that transcends the here and now. In practice, political priorities focus on producing results that are visible in the short term. To develop e-Government successfully, politicians need the courage to adopt a vision that goes beyond the immediate future.

Committed leadership: The implementation of e-Government requires a long-term commitment and a strong, dedicated and informed leadership. Government in the digital era means that the roles of public officials and citizens are to a large extent transformed.

Goals and criteria: Objectives should be realized in response to actual social and economic demands. There are high level objectives: offering services to citizens, promoting the economy, broadening participation, improving back office integration. These grand objectives have to be reformulated with people's everyday needs in mind. Thus, developing a well-defined and realistic set of goals and criteria is crucially important. Failure to do so means that social and economic demand will not be met.

Broaden planning: Make planning participative and taking different points of view into account. There are various possibilities: developing a mentoring structure, bringing in NGOs, creating public-private partnerships, etc. Because e-Government has to be built in a volatile and evolving environment, goals may need to be adjusted dynamically and plans may have to be altered. This requires a less technology-oriented approach that is open to change. In addition, collecting information about existing projects or initiatives and joining active networks is necessary.

Start on the ground: Although there has to be a vision, everything has to start at ground level. This means building on existing structures and resources, using existing infrastructure and premises, bringing together interested groups and active persons, etc. Starting on the ground also means paying attention to concrete details: precise cooperation agreements, sufficient allocation of budgets, well-defined work packages and milestones, etc.

Success Factors Guiding Development

There are certain success factors marking application development. They have to be carefully deliberated:

— *Holistic view*: Because looking at problems in isolation is often misleading, the connections between processes and their environment have to be taken into account. In other words, a holistic approach is required.

— *The right technology choice*: Technology should be in line with the underlying vision, rather than simply involve the installation of ready-made technical systems. Looking at problems from a purely technological perspective will not yield the balanced view that is needed.

— *A sound engineering approach*: This is indispensable: building suitable systems, looking for standards, usability and security.

— *Trust, security and privacy*: These aspects are crucially important, and safeguarding unimpeded communication is a must. The adoption of applications depends on the trust and confidence of citizens; they need to provide the same level of quality that people are accustomed to when dealing with traditional service channels.

— *Process-orientation and redesign*: Process focus is essential. This includes proceeding from a view on functions toward a view on interfaces. Interfaces have to be integrated, and no stand-alone solutions are to be allowed. In addition, evolutionary design is important and participation a must.

— *Using standards*: Standards are a driving force and yield substantial advantages from an organizational point of view. From a technical point of view, standards ensure a smooth exchange of information.

— *Reusable modules*: Using identical structures for identical processes improves comprehension and transparency. This is the case well for staff as well as for clients. Reusability allows for cost reduction and sustainability, which provides a valid argument.

— *State of the Art Tools*: There are several tools available, such as ARIS, ADONIS, Income, etc. Modeling has to be integrated: processes, data, information flow, roles, organizational units and resources

Managing Change

A compendium for managers: there has to be a major focus on change management and on how to handle implementation. Such a compendium should include clearly defined goals, look for endorsement from high ranks, communication with stakeholders and actors, give guidance to staff, generate the right mindset, and be aware of administrative culture.

The right mindset: Negative attitudes must be overcome: e.g. widespread fear of change, risk avoidance, self-centered behavior involving the shielding of information, bureaucratic attitudes. It is important to create the appropriate right mindset. Experience teaches us that focusing on limited, single-issue concepts is often a recipe for inertia.

Administrative culture: Change includes transforming organizational structures as well as developing awareness regarding cultural issues. Administrative culture is a factor that is often underestimated; managers need to understand administrative culture and create a climate for change.

Guidance for staff: Public employees need a better understanding of their place in the evolutionary process. There are a number of ways to achieve this: an exchange of experiences; transparency of (local) developments; lessons learnt. Adopting this approach will motivate people to innovate together and generate success more quickly. It is also important to learn from past mistakes. Change management also means empowering civil servants – for instance by setting up a qualification initiative designed to develop the necessary human resources.

Management qualification: In these kinds of projects, people frequently complain about a lack of leadership. Qualified management is essential to the success of any project. Managers need to be able to set priorities, be aware of innovation, have an interest in exchanging idea and be able to use management tools. In addition, they need to have the appropriate expertise and be able to manage projects in a disciplined way (sticking to tough demands of deliverables and schedules).

Involving the stakeholders: External and internal stakeholders have to be identified, and shared goals and a shared understanding of the task involved need to be established. There is a need for a win-win approach and stakeholders need to feel that the benefits are balanced. Stakeholder involvement can be organized in various ways (steering committee, advisory board, user group).

Actors and arenas: Keeping stakeholders on board is a continuous process. In any project, there are several arenas of negotiation, including as planning, design, implementation and maintenance. In each of these arenas several stakeholders may be involved as actors. All actors are embedded in different situations, and they are bound to have different policies, visions and attitudes. Such a divergence in standpoints is natural – even if it is not apparent at face value. It does mean, however, that stakeholder commitment has to be reaffirmed in every phase of a project.

Funding and partners: E-Government activities are expensive and the financial returns relatively limited. Funding projects is a demanding task, to which innovative solutions have to be applied. Public-private partnerships offer opportunities for funding and for the joint development of projects. Having said that, balancing the interests of private and public partners is difficult.

Counting benefits: Examples are performance-related efficiency and effectiveness, for instance providing a list of synergies between authorities and improving the service results: product and service improvement, quality of service, increased transparency and improved cooperation, not to forget cost reduction, saving of material expenses and time saving.

Change is pervasive: Managing change in e-Government ranges from abstract concepts to down-to-earth matters. In that sense, e-Government Research and Development is faced with a landscape in progr022; those involved can be proud to be part of that progress.

References

Communication from the commission to the council. The European Parliament. The economic and social committee and the committee of the regions (2002). *eEurope 2005 Action Plan*
http://ec.europa.eu/information_society/eeurope/2005/all_about/action_plan/index_en.htm.

Communication from the commission to the council, the European Parliament, The economic and social committee and the committee of the regions (2000). *eEurope 2002 Action Plan,*
http://ec.europa.eu/information_society/eeurope/2002/action_plan/pdf/actionplan_en.pdf.

European Commission (2004). *Facing the Challenge: The Lisbon Strategy for Growth and Employment.* Report of the High Level Group chaired by Wim Kok, Brussels: EC,
http://ec.europa.eu/growthandjobs/pdf/kok_report_en.pdf.

European Commission (2006). *i2010 eGovernment Action Plan: Accelerating eGovernment in Europe for the Benefit of All,* COM 173 final, Brussels: EC, http://ec.europa.eu/idabc/en/document/5763/254.

European Commission (2007). *The User Challenge. Benchmarking The Supply Of Online Public Services,* 7th Measurement, September 2007, Prepared by: Capgemini,
http://ec.europa.eu/information_society/eeurope/i2010/docs/benchmarking/egov_benchmark_2007.pdf.

Codagnone, C., & Wimmer M. A. (Eds.) (2007). Roadmapping *eGovernment Research. Visions and Measures towards Innovative Governments in 2020*, Results from the EC-funded Project eGovRTD2020. IST-2004-027139, ISBN: 978-88-95549-00-2, http://www.egovrtd2020.org/EGOVRTD2020/FinalBook.pdf.

Gieber H., Leitner, Ch., Orthofer, G., & Traunmüller, R. (2007). Taking Best Practice Forward, In: Chen H. et al (Eds.), *Digital Government: E-government Research, Case Studies, and Implementation.* Springer-Verlag New York Inc., ISBN 978-0387716107.

Tambouris, E., Tarabanis, K., Peristeras, V., & Liotas, N. (2006). *Study on Interoperability at Local and Regional Level, Interoperability Study.* http://www.egov-iop.ifib.de/index.html.

Cordis (2004). 2005-2006 Work Programme, 2.4.9 ICT research for innovative Government. http://cordis.europa.eu/ist/workprogramme/wp0506_en/2_4_9.htm

ORGANIZATIONS ARE FACED WITH THE CHALLENGE OF DESIGNING THE PROCESSES BEHIND THEIR WEBSITES IN SUCH A WAY THAT THE FOCUS IS ON THE CUSTOMER, SO AS TO INCREASE THEIR ABILITY TO RESPOND AND ACT 'REAL-TIME', AND REALIZE CONSIDERABLE SAVINGS IN TERMS OF OPERATIONAL COSTS.

From Civil Servant

ICT and new forms of inter-organizational public service provisioning

Arjan van Venrooij

Abstract

In 2002, René was a member of my promotion committee, and in relation to my promotion research he and I talked a lot about the role of ICT with regard to new forms of inter-organizational public service provisioning. This was one of the subjects in which René was particularly interested and about which he had far-reaching ideas. In this contribution, I begin by using four models to demonstrate the role of ICT in support of new forms of inter-organizational public service provisioning. Then I will look at the future by outlining some of the ideas René had about modular electronic service provisioning.

In the service models I describe, the focus is on the use of ICT, especially with the aim of streamlining the service chain. René, however, wanted to take things one step further. From a network point of view he showed me the potential of ICT when it comes to actual innovation of public service provisioning. René believed that with the current approach, which tends to focus on the use of ICT to support existing service provisioning, people fail to use the virtual channel to create and provide genuinely new services. According to René, new forms of electronic service provisioning and maintenance aimed at solving social bottlenecks imply a government that opens its windows in ways it has not done before, and that assumes the role of director or participant in a virtual electronic web of public-private cooperation.

Introduction

In 2002, René was a member of my promotion committee, and with regard to my promotion research he and I talked a lot about the role of ICT with regard to new forms of inter-organizational public service provisioning. This was one of the subjects in which René was particularly interested and about which he had far-reaching ideas. The talks we had were educational and inspiring. René seized the defense of my dissertation 'New forms of inter-organizational public service provisioning' (Van Venrooy, 2002) as an opportunity to extend our discussions and talks about the role of ICT in new forms of inter-organizational public service provisioning to a more 'public' platform. In my contribution, it is my pleasure to describe our talks and discussions on the basis of four organizational models regarding service provisioning in the public sector and the role of ICT in that respect. These models were developed by me within the framework of my promotion research, and then discussed extensively with René.

Within the models, the focus with regard to the use of ICT is on streamlining the service chain. René, however, wanted to take things one step further. From a network point of view he showed me the potential of ICT when it comes to actual innovation of public service provisioning, which is why I will finish my contribution by providing some of the images and ideas René was kind enough to share about this subject.

Public service provisioning and the role of ICT

Before discussing the four models regarding service provisioning in the public sector (Van Venrooy, 2002), I will introduce a pair of dimensions that are of interest to the organization of service provisioning, to wit centralization versus decentralization and standardization versus diversification.

Centralization versus decentralization

The Netherlands are a decentralized unitary state with territorial as well as functional government bodies. In accordance with this idea, tasks and responsibilities are placed on as low a level as possible within the public government framework (municipalities and provinces). The autonomy of decentralized government bodies has been under pressure for a long time. The national government assumes an increasingly regulatory attitude, and as a result lower-level government bodies have increasingly been responsible for implementing national regulations (co-government). This has resulted in a multiform system of tasks and authorities, which is reinforced by the functional decentralization that also involves government policy being developed and implemented horizontally. Needless to say, this affects service provisioning, and in time it has led to a patchwork of organizations providing government services and products.

The fact that the national legislator has become involved in a growing number of policy areas has not formally affected the municipal autonomy, and nor has it resulted in a centralization with regard to the implementation of policy. Services are primarily provided locally, in a decentralized way. One of the reasons why this is the case, is that the decentralized government bodies are physically closer to the country's citizens and businesses. The service provider (municipality) is located closer to the 'customer' (citizen). The system in which service provisioning based on co-government, (municipal) autonomy and central responsibility exist side by side leads to unclear authority structures (Commissie ICT and Overheid, in English: Committee ICT and Government, 2001). This committee argues in favor of abolishing the co-government figure. A significant argument is that physical proximity is becoming less and less important in today's network society. In a virtual world, the implementation of policy is no longer necessarily a matter of location. After all, the application and delivery of services takes place via networks (the Internet) rather than via physical channels. In other words, there is no need to burden municipalities with providing services in areas in which they are currently involved on the basis of the co-government principle. Consequently, virtual service provisioning can lead to centralization with regard to implementation.

The argument in favour of abolishing the co-government structure does not mean by definition that service provisioning ought to be centralized. A movement in the opposite direction, towards decentralization, is also possible. In fact, this means a return to system that formally exists in the Netherlands at the moment. In this option, the municipalities are given many of the authorities that they lost as a result of the co-government regulations.
On the basis of this discussion, we can argue that centralization versus decentralization is a dimension along which a (re)organization can be varied. In one extreme, the implementation of regulation is largely centralized, whereas in the other extreme it is to a large extent decentralized.

Standardization versus diversification
A second dimension along which service models can be developed is that of the standardization and rationalization of products, processes and (flows of) information versus diversification. This dimension can be divided into two (interwoven) elements, one of which has to do with the exchange of in-

formation between organization, while the other involves standardization of the application of regulation.

With regard to the exchange of information, the following applies. Government actions are based on legislation and regulation, in which it is explained under what circumstances citizens and business have certain rights and obligations. In many cases, the information that is needed to implement these rights and obligations is not clearly described, which is one of the reasons why such a host of (ICT) systems and databases is being used in everyday practice. This is one of the causes of the fragmentation we encounter in public service provisioning. The ICT applications that are being used in practice simply are unable to communicate with one another, which hinders the cooperation and integration of service provisioning. Standardization of data definitions and data exchange formats may increase the possibility of cooperation and integration. At this point, it should be pointed out that the standardization of information offers no guarantee that the information can in fact be interlinked. Whether or not government bodies have the authority to establish such a link is primarily a principal and political decision. Privacy legislation and the fact that the government can only use the information for the purpose for which it has been collected make it harder to develop new services by linking data (Commissie ICT en Overheid, 2001). However, by standardising data and the exchange of data, important conditions are being created for new possibilities.

When rules are being applied in practice, there is inevitably a certain degree of discretionary room for manoeuvre. There is a certain freedom to bend rules and facts to bring them closer together. This is necessary to avoid formalism, rigidity, social irrelevance, injustice and consequently loss of legitimacy, and emerges in part because the terms that are used in regulation can be accidentally vague, or because there is a difference between the rules and social reality. Discretionary room for manoeuvre limits the role that automated systems can play in support of decision-making. In addition, various government bodies and decision-makers (can) use their own guidelines to decide in individual cases. The diversity with regard to guidelines makes an equitable development of systems that are designed to support the decision-making process difficult.

Standardization of data and standardization of (decision-making) processes (rationalization) means that they have to be described more 'rigidly', making it possible to transfer tasks from back office experts towards front office staff or computers. This may help counter fragmentation in service provisioning. With regard to the application of regulation, the extreme options are uniform application versus responsive application of regulation. Responsive application involves much more tailor-made services, and as such this option is less suitable for automated implementation. From now on, we will refer to this sub-dimension as rationalization, to indicate a trend towards a more uniform implementation. Rationalization and standardization of (the exchange of) information go hand in hand. Rationalization is impossible without standardization and vice versa.

On the basis of the two dimensions outlined above, centralization versus decentralization and standardization versus diversification, it is possible to distinguish four service models that are decidedly different from each other, to wit the Autonomy Model, the Concentration Model, the Franchise Model and the Exchange Model. These extreme models should be seen as four different organizational arrangements with regard to public service provisioning. Based on the extreme models, René and I have discussed the question what choices can be made to tackle the core problem of fragmentation in public service provisioning, and what role ICT plays and can play in this respect. Below, I will describe the core of each model and the role of ICT.

Autonomy Model

In a way, the Autonomy Model is a return to the municipal autonomy that formally is the basis of the Dutch decentralized unitary state. In this model, the co-government figure is abolished. The autonomy model is based on the notion that it is best to deal with problems as closely as possible to the citizens and businesses involved. The municipality is the best available organization to do so. In the autonomy model, policies are in principle developed and implemented by the municipalities. Because of the short lines between those who govern and those who are governed, municipalities can provide the services that people and businesses need. In addition, the physical proximity is supposed to serve as an incentive to improve the quality of the service.

However, municipalities are not the only players. Many other parties provide services to citizens. The autonomy model is based on the notion of governance, where policy and service provisioning are not determined by an organization higher up in the government hierarchy, but where there is a network of actors that together shape the public sector. All these actors have their own interests and objectives. In this multi-actor network, consultation and negotiations result in government and implementation arrangements, which, due to the physical proximity between the governors and the governed, match the wishes of the governors. Citizens can use democratic control to insist on a reduction of fragmentation. The autonomy model implies a shift of resources from the national government towards municipality. It is given the means, through lump sum financing, and authority to implement integral policies, which makes it possible to reshape the existing service package (redefinition) and to improve efficiency on a local scale and increase the effectiveness of policy.

A shift in responsibilities towards the local level of government represents a multiform interpretation of the public sector. After all, there are over 400 municipalities. This not only affects the way the public sector is organized (the autonomy model in theory allows for as many arrangements as there are municipalities), it also influences areas like legal equality. Because local circumstances can be taken into account to a much greater extent than is currently possible, legal equality is no longer a nationally determined concept in which all citizens of the Netherlands are treated equally. Instead, they treated equally at a local level, while there may be differences at a national level. After all, the situation in East-Groningen is different from that in The Hague. In the autonomy model, this justifies the existence of different arrangements and regulations in the two areas. Having said that, it does not mean that it is every municipality for itself. Municipalities can decide to work together or use each others' facilities. They can also dispose of tasks or outsource them to organizations in the field. Whether or not this will happen depends on the local set-up.

Role of ICT
The autonomy model assumes the development of new forms of inter-organizational public service provisioning, which can be implemented at a local level without the need for major investments at a national level.

When we look at the practical examples of this model, we see that the investments that are needed to apply ICT in an innovative way are often large. During the implementation phase of the new service model, there are often major problems involving the existing ICT infrastructure, the so-called legacy systems. Traditionally, every service delivery process is supported separately by individual information systems, which often leads to problems when services need to be integrated to ensure a more customer-oriented service provisioning. Different information systems are used that are unable to communicate with one another. In addition, a direct online connection between the front office and the various implementing organizations is lacking, as a result of which front office employees often have insufficient insight into the status and progress of the service delivery processes within in the implementing organizations. In these local and regional initiatives, ICT is often a bottleneck rather than an enabler when it comes to new forms of public service provisioning. The necessary investments with regard to ICT often turn out to be too large for these relatively small-scale and fragmented initiatives, and the ICT knowledge is too small to allow for genuine innovation.

Inter-municipal cooperation in the area of ICT may offer the solution to this problem. Within the autonomy model, cooperation in the area of ICT also depends on the local situation. Some municipalities will decide to develop their own applications, while others will opt in favour of working together with other municipalities and/or organizations, for instance the province or healthcare of social service institutions. Examples of municipalities working together in the area of ICT are GovUnited and ANDEZ-2. The VNG (Association of Dutch Municipalities) and EGEM have conducted a survey into the cooperation with regard to ICT at the inter-municipal level (EGEM, 2007). Local authorities, decision-makers and ICT people from 458 municipalities were asked to share their experiences with regard to cooperation in the area of ICT. No fewer than three quarters (349) of all Dutch municipalities took part in the survey, 209 of which indicated that they were indeed working together with others. In all, 337 municipalities were listed as partners in cooperation. However, it is not easy for municipalities to work together when it comes to ICT. The lack of an administrative commitment and a shared vision, as well as differences in culture, are important reasons why this kind of cooperation often fails (EGEM, 2007).

CONCENTRATION MODEL

The concentration model is located at the other extreme of the (de)centralization dimension. The central idea behind this model is that, in an information society, it is no longer necessary to organize services at a geographical level. As a result of ICT, the physical distance between government on the one hand, and citizens and businesses on the other and between front-office and back-office becomes less relevant as an organizational criterion. Centralization can lead to economies of scale and fragmentation can be decreased by reducing the number of back-offices. After all, the number of parties involved will also be reduced.

The concentration model focuses primarily on the processes and administration. Within this model, the front-office only provides information, forms and applications. In addition, customers are supported in preparing applications up to filling forms. Evaluation, processing and feedback of the result to the customer involved are all carried out by the central back-office. Similar to the distinction being made in the IT world between a 'thin' and 'fat' clients and servers, this model contains what we could call a thin front-office and a fat back-office. Needless to say, this model is only feasible on a large scale when the products and services are organized in such a way that they can be processed (almost) completely automatically, which will reduce the discretionary room for manoeuvre with regard to policy.

In the concentration model, there is room for a multitude of front-offices that all serve as intake organizations for the central back-office, because all they have to do is provide information and possible help the customers involved fill in the paper (or online) forms. This means that the staff can be less highly qualified compared to a situation whereby individual staff members process the information themselves. The forms are sent to the central back-office.

Within the concentration model, the service providers are free to offer a product from the central back-office's product range. They are paid by the central back-office on the basis of the number of intakes they carry out. This way, the concentration model encourages the emergence of front-offices that provides services that are logically connected. Front-offices determine what services they will provide, and in that respect compete with other providers. As a result, the quality of service should improve and the level fragmentation should be reduced. In this model, the central back-offices are responsible for realising the nationwide coverage of their product range. This means they will have to negotiate with service providers at a local level in order to persuade them to offer their products.

Role of ICT
The concentration model is based on a strict separation between front-office and back-office. At a national level, the central back-office is accessible to the decentralized front-offices, the so-called contact points, which include the municipalities, via ICT. In this new service model, ICT is the enables of innovation, and the opportunities that it provides are optimally utilised. Electronic customer files and ICT applications are developed and managed at a centralized level, and are accessible at a decentralized level via secure network link-ups. In addition, there is an electronic exchange with the main suppliers of source information, including the GBA. Also, a large part of the service provisioning process will be automated. ICT applications will be developed at a national level, which is also where the main investments will be made. These investments involve considerable amounts of money that the municipalities will not be able to afford.

Franchise Model
The central idea behind the franchise model is standardization. In this model, products, data and work processes are standardised and rationalized in such a way that they can be provided by certified service providers in their entirety. In this model, the offer can refer to an individual product, but also to a complete product range (for instance organized on the basis of demand patterns). Because both the product range and the work processes have been standardised, it does not matter where implementation takes place. This applies to the front-office as well as the back-office. There is room for different back-office organizations servicing one or more front-offices or managing their own front-offices.

In the concentration model, the front-office does little more than pass on information to the back-office. In the franchise model, the front-office can carry out an important part of the service delivery process, including the assessment of applications. This transfer of authority towards the front-office is made possible by the far-reaching standardization and rationalization of processes. The question as to where (front-office or back-office) decisions are to be made is an issue about which front-offices and back-offices can negotiate and service level agreements can be made. The front-office organizations buy services from the back-office organizations, which will allow back-offices to compete with one another. The national government allocates a budget to front-office organizations with which to purchase services relating to the implementation with regard to specific policies. At a central level, the ministries will set the policies, design the work processes, certify back-offices and front-offices and monitor the quality of policy implementation.

Role of ICT
ICT also is an important enabler in the franchise model. Again, the existence of an electronic customer file is an important condition for the realization of the desired service delivery model. Through the development of ICT applications with electronic customer files, the service delivery process, including the transfer moments, have to run as smoothly as possible. This model also attempts to develop the ICT applications at a centralized level. Within the franchise model, uniformity with regard to the work processes is important for the operation of the centrally developed ICT infrastructure.

EXCHANGE MODEL
Although the central idea behind this model is also standardization, it does not involve a decisive say on the part of the central government with regard to the decision-making processes (application of regulation). This model focuses on standardising information between the various operational organizations (interconnectivity), and on increasing the interoperability of the computer programmes that are used in the various front-offices and back-offices.

At the moment, standardization is a slow process because of the involvement of a large number of relatively small parties, each with the power to demand a standard, or reluctant to run the risk of developing a standard that potentially has little chance of success. In this respect, the national government, being the major player that it is, can take the initiative and 'enforce' (the development of) standards by promoting (co-)funding.

One of the possible elements of this model is the development of a routing institute for various policy domains, similar to RINID in social security. This will enable an active interpretation and implementation of the standardization of information flows. The routing institute can serve as a junction of information flows that the various front-offices and back-offices within the relevant policy domain can (or must) join. The routing institute processes information requests from its member organizations and rout them to the relevant other organizations, whereby the requestor does not need to know who provides the relevant information.

Role of ICT
In the exchange model, the role of ICT is aimed especially at 'connecting' organizations via a routing institute. This means that organizations do not have to make several arrangements with regard to the exchange of information. Due to the use of a centralized ICT organization, the routing institute, and the standardization of information flows, the 'member' government bodies are able to exchange information with one another. The central ICT organization serves as a junction in the network of member organizations. This allows new organizations to join the existing network with running a great deal of risk.

Because in the exchange model, the role of ICT is above all aimed at developing and implementing exchange standards, the development of programmes is less risky. Standardization will open up the market to new entrants. It becomes possible to use the programmes that have been developed by others, which also makes it possible for those parties providing parts of individual modules, rather than complete solutions, to acquire a place in the market.

In the exchange model, it is the responsibility of the ministries to investigate the opportunities for standardization and the take the initiative and encourage the parties involved to adopt standardization via obligations (regulation) or subsidies. When formulating policy, ministries take the existing information infrastructures and architectures into account. This means that they will investigate how existing databases and data definitions can be used to implement new policies.

CONCLUSION
In this contribution I have used several (extreme) service delivery models to express some ideas and discussions surrounding the role of ICT with regard

to new forms of inter-organizational public service provisioning. The models reveal the 'two faces' of ICT. On the one hand, ICT is an enabler of new forms of public service provisioning, and far-reaching innovation can only be realized through an innovative application of ICT. On the other hand, it is difficult to utilise the new opportunities of ICT to their full potential, and ICT can be a bottleneck, in particular at a regional level in situations in which the service provisioning is are inter-organizational in nature.

With regard to the autonomy model, we have seen that many municipalities find it difficult to absorb all the new ICT developments that come their way, which makes it hard for them to utilise the opportunities of ICT their full potential. As a result, ICT becomes an important bottleneck. The existing legacy systems that are insufficiently connected to each other, a lack of knowledge, and a lack of capacity and resources are the main causes for this state of affairs. Cooperation between municipalities in the area of ICT seems a good solution, making it possible to realise economies of scale and bundle knowledge. However, realising that kind of cooperation appears to be difficult.

With regard to the concentration model, we have seen that a large-scale application of ICT and a concentration of its implementation yield economies of scale. Within this model, there are a limited number of back-offices (in principle one for each service or policy area) connected to a large variety of arrangement with regard to the front-offices. Virtual suppliers (for instance wonentotaal.nl, verhuizen.nl and verbouwen.nl) can also offer themselves as a channel for the back-office. Because the entire implementation will be centralized, the number of back-offices will be reduced to a very limited number for each product. This means that a large-scale application of ICT is required. The result of the centralization/concentration of the implementation of policy is that ministries will have to standardise policy and policy implementation and rationalise the work processes. Data definitions and exchange protocols are developed by ministries and, together with intake modules, will be made available to the front-offices acting on behalf of the central organization.

With regard to the franchise model, we have seen that the centralized rationalization of processes enables the use of ICT in the implementation (deciding on individual cases) of policy. The use of ICT makes it possible to connect products by integrating electronic forms and linking systems. Ministries not only develop policy, they will also have to translate regulation into databases and detailed assessment guidelines.

With regard to the exchange model, we have see that the use of a centralized ICT application, the router institute, and the standardization of the data flows makes it relatively easy for government organizations to exchange information. The router institute serves as a junction in a network of member organization. Although ICT is needed to connect the organizations within the network, the impact on the internal organization of the member organizations is limited.

The focus in the examples described above and in the service delivery models has primarily been on the use of ICT to streamline and optimise chains. René, however, wanted to take things one step further. Using a network perspective on service provisioning, he has shown me the potential of ICT for a genuine innovation of public service provisioning, which is why I will end my contribution with several images and ideas about this subject which René has shared with me, and which he presented, among other places, at the opening conference of the Center for Public Innovation (CPI), a cooperation of universities and the business community of which both of us were members (CPI, 2004).

Our sights on the future: modular electronic service delivery
René was of the opinion that chains are often rigid and inflexible with regard to new developments in their external environment. He made a comparison with the business community, where chains have become less important, and have to a large extent been replaced by (temporary) networks. This development is characterised by an ability to respond to changes in the environment in a much more flexible way. For that to be possible, however, the links between processes of the various partners in a network with regard to information processing need to be less specific. Instead, they need to be based on standardised interfaces and uniform data definitions. René believed that as a result of the existing approach, which focuses primarily on how ICT can be applied to support existing processes and structures, the government misses an opportunity to use the virtual channel to

offer genuinely new services. In his view, new forms of electronic service provisioning and maintenance aimed at solving social bottlenecks imply that government, more than ever before, open its windows and take on the role of director or participant in a virtual electronic web of public-private cooperation. Government will no longer be the only party that determines the shape and content of the service provisioning, which will more and more be the result of cooperation with third parties, and which will consequently also be subject to more frequent changes. In short, the demands that will be made with regard to the configuration of the service will be higher, in terms of customization, expandability, changes, reuse and costs. According to René, this requires a modular approach to the service, using components that each offer a clearly delineated functionality. This principle is very similar to what we see in the automobile industry, which for years has benefited from a modular approach in its production processes.

René viewed software as something that we find under the bonnet of the electronic service provisioning. He believed that, if we could manage to adopt a modular approach to this software, using components that can be assembled like car parts, it would be possible to create a unique level of flexibility. What he believed made it even more interesting is that open communication standards make it possible to access these software components, put them to work and even share them with other user organizations from afar. Within this context, René introduced the concept of web services to support the electronic public service provisioning and make it more flexible. René believed that the breakthrough of the Web and the associated protocols of HTTP and HTML, together with the availability of safe, fast and, above all, cheap connections to the Internet, make it possible to translate software components into workable applications 'on demand' in the form of web services.

The vision for the future that René outlined is that of a 'living infrastructure of software components' that will grow in number and quality, and perhaps even in the percentage of 'open source' applications.

REFERENCES

Commissie ICT en Overheid (2001). Burger en overheid in de informatiesamenleving. De noodzaak van institutionele innovatie. Den Haag

EGEM (2007). Vermenigvuldigen door delen, 11 stappen om te komen tot intergemeentelijke ICT-samenwerking. Een onderzoek door Zenc, in opdracht van EGEM en de VNG.

Venrooy, A. van. (2002). *Nieuwe vormen van interorganisationele publieke dienstverlening.* Eburon: Delft

Wagenaar, R.W. (2004). *Een Virtuele Regisseur van Flexibele Publiek-Private Netwerken.* In: Openingsbijeenkomst Center for Public Innovation. CPI: Rotterdam

ONE OF THE TOOLS TO ARRIVE AT A MORE ACHIEVEMENT-ORIENTED GOVERNMENT IS THE LARGE-SCALE AND SMART USE OF ICT.

From Civil Servant

In search of network government: discussion and future outlook

René Matthijsse

Abstract
An important restriction in the solution of social problems and the centralization of the citizen's demands in an increasingly complex and dynamic society is the departmentalization within government. Mutual cooperation between public organizations, as well as cooperation between public and private organizations, is required if departmentalization is to be countered. The Netherlands are ready for a network government. A transformation has to take place in three areas in order to create a network government step by step: cooperation between organizational networks, more attention to information management and different management mechanisms. In this contribution, I address some discussion themes to which professor René Wagenaar made a significant contribution.

Cooperative networking in the public sector
In solving social issues like education, healthcare and disaster management, close cooperation is required between various government organizations. Government needs to organize itself integrally around these social issues and pay more attention to demand management of public service provisioning to citizens and businesses. The public sector's current organization is still insufficiently flexible in the implementation of policy. Every government organization carries out its own specialization, reaching an optimum scale and operating within a familiar environment. The traditional reflexes of the classic government structure no longer function; there is a need for greater flexibility. This flexibility is created by new forms of formal and informal cooperation. In essence, a network government is characterized by cooperative structures between parties that are at the same time autonomous and mutually dependent, with the aim of establishing a kind of coordination of activities. Within a network approach to organizations, tasks, responsibilities and authorities between organiza-

tions are divided anew and the way tasks are coordinated is reorganized. Important questions in this respect are what are really the core activities of the organizations involved and what activities may be carried out better by others in the network or as a joint effort. Shared Service Centers, multi-channel customer contact centers and the outsourcing of activities to other public organizations or the private sector, are all manifestations of this new approach to organizing. The goals of this new approach are to increase the quality, and to find the optimum scale and efficiency. The public sector thus wants to respond adequately to social problems and questions from citizens.

The network government will consist of various units or modules that will cooperate with one another and with market parties. The mutual dependencies are high. The exact configuration will change continuously and be dependent on the social issue that needs to be resolved. These developments and initiatives require new governance arrangements. The organizations that are responsible for implementation play an important role in this respect. They opt in favor of a higher level of cooperation, albeit with a preference for maintaining their autonomy. Organizing and developing customer-oriented processes takes place under the management of the organizations responsible for implementation, possibly supported by procedures and legislation. This development process is based primarily on mutual trust and personal initiatives.

Tension between policy and service delivery

A network government cannot exist without governance. The way governance is implemented will, however, change drastically. Historically, policy departments manage organizations that responsible for implementation above all on the basis of how they function internally. After policy has been developed, it is determined in minute detail how and by whom it is to be implemented. Internal management ignores the fact that most expertise regarding the implementation itself is not located at the policy departments, but rather at the bodies that are responsible for implementation. To manage a flexible network government with autonomous parties, output management offers a better approach. The national government only determines what needs to be done, not how, which means it is not actively involved in the internal functioning of the departments. The policy-makers trust in the knowledge and expertise of the implementers, confident that the policies will be implemented as effectively and efficiently as possible. Output management thus creates the room to use this knowledge and expertise to realize innovation. This does not mean, however, that the implementers have all the freedom in the world to decide how they operate. The central government indicates the conditions and frameworks within which they carry out their duties, thus guaranteeing sound government. Nevertheless, it will not always be possible to apply this kind of output management precisely because output management of the network as a whole requires the use of the knowledge that is available at the level of implementation. In the case of entirely new policies or when the implementers have not yet managed to attain the necessary level of excellence, this knowledge is not or hardly available. If that is the case, the policy department will decide to keep a closer eye on the way policies are implemented. Developing a self-regulating network is a process involving all the partners in the network, with the aim of achieving a sufficiently high level of performance. It is to be expected that that the boundaries between the public and the private sectors will continue to fade. If this development continues, the role of policymakers will shift toward in which they assume the role of overseer and are responsible for setting the conditions. The more independent the networks are, the important it becomes to safeguard the principles of sound government in the implementation of policies. To bring policy and implementation in line is a fragile process. Although the partners in the chain are dependent from the point of view of customers, they are not dependent if we look at their original service delivery process in which historically existing bodies have merged together. Implementers sometimes become defensive of their own position in this discussion, or opt in favor of a more offensive approach. In these cases, performance measurement needs to be applied carefully and moderately, because it does not always fit in with the complexity of the implementation by professional organizations and it may lead to undesirable strategic behavior.

In this respect, the ministries struggle with their new role as managers at a distance. This role now needs to be carried out more on the basis of actual content rather than on a historical position. One of the problems here is the far-reaching separation in terms of responsibilities and authorities between policy and implementation. These are two different worlds, in which the policy cycle and implementation each have their own perspective and rhythm. A detailed prescription of how and by whom policies should be implemented, which is usually the case, hampers the implementers in their attempts to realize higher levels of specialization and improve the quality of their service delivery. It is as Galbraith and Mintzberg realized: flexibility is promoted by reorganizing cooperation, standardization of work processes and improvement of the exchange of information.

OPERATIONAL EFFECTIVENESS AND SHARED SERVICE CENTERS
Professors René Wagenaar and Hans Strikwerda were pioneers in the field of implementing shared service centers in public administration. Governments are looking for ways to improve the service provisioning to their citizens by using the Internet, while at the same time reducing the operational costs of back-office and ICT. The implementation of shared service centers (SSC's) is still claimed to be a valuable organizational redesign that will lead to less redundancy in operations, reductions in staff and a more concentrated knowledge accumulation. However, decision-making with regard to and the subsequent implementation of such SSC's are complex tasks that are fraught with the risk of failure. This is partly due to diverse expectations and interests among the actors involved. There are various scenarios one can think of when it comes to decision-making concerning and the implementation of SSC's. They lie in the spectrum from central top-down steering to bottom-up emergent process growth. René Wagenaar and the author have researched and proposed a framework for strategic choice that may be helpful in the search for a successful implementation strategy, and promote future empirical research in developing 'best practices'.

The implementation of SSC's has many more effects: government processes and information management become the subject of a systematic policy, the division of power and roles will shift, internal and external information relationships and organization structures will change, and specific knowledge and experience will accumulate within the organization. Consequently, SSC's can be considered important drivers towards innovation within the public sector.

As is the case with many other organizational change processes, the realization of the benefits SSCs may yield require careful management and clear leadership, if stakeholders are to be persuaded to participate and commit themselves to use the shared services. The introduction of a SSC is a critical strategic decision. It implies a long-term relationship between the SSC and its clients with considerable complexity and risks. The SSC can be viewed as a particular kind of outsourcing arrangement between many clients and one vendor, where classical outsourcing often concerns the relationship between one client and one or more vendors. Much can be learned from existing literature on outsourcing and experiences from existing SSC's. However, the number of documented cases regarding SSC's in public administration is very limited. It would appear that the views and opinions of those who are directly involved in the relevant decision-making differ considerable with regard to the need for and claimed benefits of SSC's in the public sector. However, these views are often not explicitly articulated, which may be part of the reason why the public sector decision-making processes involving SSC's are progressing at such a slow pace.

The governance and implementation of shared service centers can be seen as complicated organizational and technical interventions. A deep understanding of the administrative and organizational processes involved is a pre-condition for developing effective policies and for assessing the impact that the introduction of SSC's will have on the stakeholder organizations. Our findings indicate that the views and opinions among key public managers whether and how to introduce SSC's appear to vary greatly. The Dutch government has set clear objectives for the coming period towards a leaner and more effective public service system, and has developed a number of initiatives to build authentic data resources that have to be shared among all public agencies that deal with those data. The intention is to create a situation where citizens and companies have to provide their information only once, while public administrations use this information as a shared resource. This will turn out to be an essential driver for the further interoperability of public services and remove a major technological and semantic barrier with regard to the implementation of SSC's.

The main problem with many governments remains the lack of central authority and control. There is no simple equivalent to the hierarchical management structure we find in private companies. It has been suggested that, by initially selecting a limited number of basic services within an SSC that are in the interest of all actors involved, it is possible to build on a common platform for a further dynamic growth model in scope. In our opinion, the 'A momentum for a Big Bang' or the 'Big Bang as the story, soft pressure as the practice' strategies offer the best chances for a successful introduction of SSC's within public administration at this early stage.

INFORMATIZATION IN THE PUBLIC SECTOR REQUIRES POLICY SETTING
The government increasingly becomes an information-driven organization. Organizational infrastructure and information infrastructure will increasingly merge in a network government. As a result, information management becomes an administrative issue. The question if and how policy must be deployed can no longer be separated from the (im)possibilities of information technology that is needed to implement policies. Strategic information policy is an essential condition for improved cooperation within networks. This turns the area of informatization into a strategic issue for which the higher echelons within the government organization are responsible. This is a different situation from the one that existed in the past, when information policy was a consequence of government policy, of which it now has become a precondition and an integral part. Because information policy has become a vital element of the primary process of government, the risk of failure of information policy and the supporting ICT solutions has become that much more serious. In addition, the issues continuity and information security have become more than mere ICT matters. These issues have become an integral part of policy setting and implementation. The government has to say goodbye to fragmented solutions, and instead build a commonly shared information infrastructure. Standardization ought to be considered a strategic theme rather than a technical instrument. With regard to the information provisioning of the government, a network approach thus equals standardization and the development of shared basic provisions, which facilitate the sectoral and supra-sectoral information requirements. These are the data and services that are used by all government institutes, for which they all have a similar significance, regardless of the policy area.

In addition to steering from the central government, a need emerges for an information director or chief information officer per sector for the planning and organization of shared basic provisions. A lot of the information being used by organizations responsible for policy implementation is not supra-sectoral in nature. An information director facilitates the sector-specific and sector-wide information policy – including an unequivocal definition of information – ultimately to realize a better cooperation between networks. The most important role this information director plays is the proper allocation of the responsibilities with regard to information. The role of information director facilitates the sector-wide information policy in order to create a better cooperation with the information partners involved. This type of role develops the connection between administrative goals and information flows. Furthermore, there is a responsibility with regard to demand articulation and policy formation. The way the role of director is interpreted varies per sector, depending on the sector's level of organization, the maturity of the information policy and the degree of trust. The information director above all has to act as a bridge builder. He explains the interests of the various parties, helps people and organizations come together and makes sure that best practices are communicated within his own sector and to other sectors.

The way the role of information director is filled in will vary per sector. If a sector's information policy has a high level of maturity and there is a determining player within the chain, the information director can assume a dominant posture and also enforce changes at process level. However, if the level of maturity is low and the sector is characterized by a large degree of autonomy, the information director will play a facilitating role, and initially carry out only minor changes in technology. In addition, the information director can facilitate cooperation with the network through an improved supply of information and the creation of shared facilities. After all, this does not clash with the autonomy of the individual organizations.

ICT GOVERNANCE AS A CONTINUOUS PROCESS

In the coming years, we can expect 'a parade of misunderstandings and mistakes' when more and more information will have to be exchanged between organizations. There are two pressing problems that require our attention. First of all, there is insufficient coherence between the various sectoral developments and between the various information systems. Secondly, there is not enough steering, control and responsibility with regard to the intermediate stages that have been achieved and the intended final results. In the attempts to realize cooperation and integration, problems surrounding *stove piping* and *information hiding* emerge even more prominently than they did before. Often, the goals of individual organizations and their short-terms priorities prevail, at the expense of shared facilities. These have to be built up systematically and be available to be used by third parties, allowing for a greater social benefit. The digital service delivery by an electronic government still struggles with fragmentation and demands a clear direction.

Because of the increase in the number of implementation chains, it is important for ICT governance and ICT assurance to be put on the policy agenda at chain level. Issues like continuity and information security no longer fall exclusively within the ICT domain, but they are instead an integral part of policy setting and implementation. There is an urgent need for careful governance, with greater attention to risk management, more room for organizations responsible for implementation and a reduction of the demand for all kinds of certainties. ICT governance focuses on improving the value of ICT in realizing policy objectives, reducing the possible risks and improving coordination between processes and information provisioning. Chain governance goes further, and has to do with safeguarding the process with regard to policy setting, management and control and monitoring at chain level.

In the quest for integral solutions, there has often been an unsupervised cooperation as a result of a lack of concern steering. Introducing ICT governance forces the various links in the chain to pursue the same shared goal. This is a tricky process of looking for new organizational structures and other working methods. In addition, through strict steering, improvement often occurs in the often poor exchange of information and knowledge between the links within a chain. Furthermore, the information provisioning regarding the performance of the chain as a whole is reinforced. One of the main issues in this respect has to do with the question whether the information architecture is capable of responding to changing circumstances in the environment of the chain as a whole, or of one of the participants in that chain. This question is significant in a time of quickly changing legislation and regulation, for instance with the IRS, social security, police and the justice department. This requires an integral approach to issues, cooperation with partners in the chain, network governance and looking beyond the boundaries of one's own policy area.

PARTICIPATING LEADERSHIP

ICT governance is impossible without leadership. The exchange of information between government organizations is becoming increasingly multi-sectoral in nature. This allows organizations responsible for policy implementation and other organizations to operate as flexible links within the overall structure of an information system. This approach provides a meaningful foundation in structuring and shaping the provisioning and exchange of information. In fact, ICT governance to a large extent consists of properly allocating responsibilities in the area of information within a sector, promoting a vision, developing a sectoral information model and creating support and commitment.

Any organization in the public sector whose aim it is to cooperate needs an adequate and effective information infrastructure. Organization and information provisioning need to be brought in line and reach a certain level to enable intra-chain cooperation. However, for years, the public sector has been faced with islands of automation. The electronic government is still struggling with fragmentation. Often the objectives of the individual organizations and their short-term priorities prevail, at the expense of shared provisions that need to be built up systematically and be available for use by third parties, allowing for a greater social benefit. As long as government organizations continue to opt in favor of developing ICT in relative isolation, large-scale breakthroughs in services that really matter to businesses and private citizens are unlikely to occur.

In line with the attempts to realize better cooperation, government should opt more and more in favor of the development of an adequate information infrastructure for a shared use, and gradually say goodbye to fragmentation and high structural costs. Although the responsibility and autonomy of government departments will continue to be the starting point, mutual coordination and a focus on shared infrastructural provisions on the basis of unequivocal standards serve as markers on the course the government needs to follow with regard to automation, allowing organizations responsible for policy implementation and other organizations to operate as flexible links within the framework of a system. This kind of approach leads to meaningful solution scenarios with regard to structuring and shaping the supply of information between organizations and environment, building a bridge between the organizations that work together. By setting up a robust and stable information infrastructure, the government can respond to the social and administrative dynamics in continuously changing implementation arrangements. However, in practice, the development of an all-encompassing information infrastructure or a basic architecture for the entire digital government is not a feasible option, due to the large scale we encounter in the public sector. It is more pragmatic to talk about the desirable links based on unequivocal (semantic) standards between existing information systems and databases, each with their own functionalities and characteristics. This would imply a system of agreements with principles, models and standards. In some situations routing institutes may be needed as a shared facility and regional bodies for standardization and demand articulation.

Dissertation on ICT governance and control

What are the concrete issues that play a role in organizing new implementation arrangements and cooperation trajectories in the public sector, and in particular with regard to governance, organization and informatization? Earlier research by Venrooy (2002) and Matthijsse has shown that various management-related aspects play an important role in organizing and implementing new implementation arrangements, such as:

— *Political discussion and decision-making.* With the implementation of new implementation arrangements, political discussions and decision-making, with the influence exerted by the stakeholders involved, play an important role.

— Legislation and regulation. The formal authorities and responsibilities of public organizations have been laid down in legislation and regulation. As a result of desirable shifts in tasks and authorities, existing legislation and regulation often have to be adapted. Legislative trajectories need to move in parallel with change trajectories. In addition, privacy legislation plays an important role in the possibilities of new implementation arrangements.

— The *administrative aspects*. Distribution and alteration of tasks, responsibilities and authorities within and between organizations often lead to a shift in the existing roles and positions. Power and mutual competition play an important role in this respect.

— The *financial and economic aspects*. The existing financing structure of the public sector often poses as a restriction to change. Future costs and benefits are often difficult to visualize, and the perception among the organizations involved varies.

— The *(re)design of work processes*. Work processes within the organization and between organizations need to be (re)designed with adjustments in the organizational structure and allocation of the new tasks/functions of employees.

— The *data*. Data are the most important resource for the products and services of the government. To realize the new implementation arrangements, an exchange of data within and between organizations is often necessary. The quality of the data is a critical success factor. An additional factor is the power that organizations often derive from the management of databases.

— *The application of ICT*. ICT is an important enabler of new possibilities of organization, but it can also be an important hurdle, and the knowledge that is needed to be able to use the new opportunities is often considerable.

Implementation trajectories of new implementation arrangements are not limited to the integral design of processes and ICT. In these kinds of trajectories, the aspects distinguished above often play a role in a mutual combination and interaction. This produces a complex and dynamic process that poses considerable demands on the management of these kinds of implementation trajectories. For the benefit of research into the organization and implementation of new implementation arrangements and forms of cooperation in the public sector, with the guidance of Professor René Wagenaar a research project was initiated that resulted in a dissertation and various other publications.

The research framework has two dimensions, along the vertical axis the direction-related aspects that can be distinguished and, along the horizontal axis the project phasing that can be distinguished. On the basis of earlier research, the following direction-related aspects are central that (may) play a role in the governance of inter-organizational systems with networked organizations.

Accountability Item	Phases of development			
	Plan	Design	Build	Deploy
Policy Strategic	X	X		X
Financial economics	X	X	X	X
Organization	X	X		
Law and regulations		X	X	
Business processes		X	X	
Data and applications		X	X	
Information technology		X		
Social organization		X		X
Marketing and public relations	X	X	X	X
Project Organization		X	X	X

We consider these direction-related aspects as the steering controls for the organization and implementation of new implementation arrangements. The expectation is that these direction-related aspects have a different meaning and weight in the various phases of the organization and implementation process. The question is which of these aspects play a role in the various phases and how they affect one another. The framework gives us a context in our research into the organization and implementation of new implementation arrangements in the public sector. Also, the model is used by policy makers, project leaders and process managers as a tool for structuring and managing the necessary organization and implementation process.

Future outlook: major issues with regard to control and assurance
Control and responsibility have been relatively neglected. According to rough calculations, the government spends billions each year on ICT projects, most of which is not delivered successfully. A majority in the Dutch parliament demands a parliamentary inquiry into the waste of ICT funds by the government. The news about the ICT problems in the government and the recent report by the Court of Audit suggests that things are not going well. The government's ICT projects are too ambitious and too complex due to a combination of political, organizational and technical factors. As a result, it is hard to get the interoperability between government organizations and efficiency improvements in business management off the ground. Within the government, the processes of policy and implementation at the various organizations are increasingly interwoven in networks. The performance of organizations increasingly depends on the implementation processes in other organizations.

Parliament and government have no insight into the effects and feasibility of new rules that are being issued. If departments were to be transparent, bottlenecks would be visible at an early stage. In current thinking about governance, steering and responsibility are considered most important. Although the Minister has no line responsibility about the RWT's and ZBO's, he is the person managing them. To do so, he has two tools at his disposal. First of all, he issues guidelines with regard to how the various implementation agencies should work. In addition, he uses the ministries audit teams to verify whether these guidelines are being applied in practice. Thanks to these tools, the Minister definitely a grip on independent organizations. A wise Minister would, for example, issue a guideline stating that the management cycle within the organization must be closed, and he then monitors this. That way, he can be certain that the management of that organization continuously follows the cycle of plan, do, check and act. When that happens, the management can learn from any mistakes that are made, which will result in a reduction of the number of mistakes being made. Should the latter happen anyway, Parliament could ask the Minister what guidelines he has issued to the organization and whether he has made sure the guidelines were being observed. In today's politics, this is far from a reality. The necessary focus on the organization of control mechanisms for large ICT projects is often lacking. Usually, most of the attention goes to defining the guidelines. It is only when Ministers are being questioned by Parliament with regard to the fact that they have provided erroneous information that monitoring is given top priority.

The idea that all organizations responsible for implementation should work in exactly the same way is an illusion anyway. Every organization has its own origin, was founded at a different point in time and operates according to different guidelines. It is a patchwork that cannot possibly be standardized, although it can be monitored. Chain governance, the coordinated management and accountability of independent organizations with the public administration, is a difficult issue. A Minister whose monitoring mechanisms are up to speed need not worry about being attacked by Parliament on the basis of false information or futilities. Cabinet and Parliament can then work together on further improving the public administration. Improved steering and monitoring will also improve the often poor exchange of information and knowledge between the links in a chain. In addition, the availability of information regarding performance of the chain as a whole will improve. The information regarding the state of affairs of, for example, the implementation of large-scale ICT projects like Walvis and the police information systems are a good example of that.

REFERENCES

Atkinson, R.D. (2003). Network government for the digital age, Progressive Policy Institute, Policy Report, May 2003, www.ppionline.org

Beckers, V., van Duivenboden, H., and Thaens, M. (2006) Information and Communication Technology and Public Innovation, IOS Press,

Bergeron, B. P, (2003). Essentials of Shared Services, John Wiley & Sons, Inc., New Jersey.

Birkland, T.A. (2001). An Introduction To The Policy Process: Theories, Concepts, And Models Of Public Policy Making, M.E. Sharpe.

THE DESIGN OF AN ICT REFERENCE
ARCHITECTURE, THE AIM BEING
TO PRODUCE A CONCRETE AND
COHERENT VISION CONCERNING
THE ICT INFRASTRUCTURE NEEDED
BY THE ELECTRONIC GOVERNMENT...
THE MOST IMPORTANT RESULTS
ARE A DESCRIPTION OF A NUMBER
OF COMMON INTEGRATED
FUNCTIONS, MAKING IT POSSIBLE TO
ESTABLISH LINKS AT THE LEVEL OF
ELECTRONIC DATA EXCHANGE AND
AN UNAMBIGUOUS INTERPRETATION
USING XML DIAGRAMS.

From Civil Servant

New Government needs New Architectural Models

Norien Kuiper

ABSTRACT

As a student at the Faculty of Technology, Policy and Management, I had the pleasure to meet René Wagenaar during the evening lectures on ICT. The objective of this chapter is to stimulate cooperation by IT architects in multi-actor environments during the design phase to achieve certain benefits. The form of a debate was chosen, because René was eager to start a discussion. The debate is centered around the need for new architectural models for e-government, and how to arrive at these models. The plan is to cooperate with IT architects of multiple actors in the design phase using empty architectural frameworks as the point of departure. The debate starts with a stimulating proposition. Then two teams are discussing the merits of the plan. The teams themselves are judged by the jury. Subsequently the jury surprises everyone by coming up with another stimulating proposition related to René Wagenaar. Finally, an open question is put before the reader.

INTRODUCTION

E-government and architecture
Politicians and public managers have become increasingly dissatisfied with the returns obtained from e-government activities. IT development and maintenance costs are rising. Managing the costs has become a prime concern. Current e-government initiatives have a fragmented nature and are hardly coordinated. Consequently, there has been a plea for architectural models, tools and methods to improve this. Yet, there is a continuing discussion on how and in which direction this should proceed. René was one of the people involved in research concerning the need for architecture in the Dutch Government (Dool, Keller, Wagenaar, Hinfelaar, 2002).

Form: policy debate
In (http://members.home.nl/gp.broekema/debat10.htm) various forms of

debate are described like the parliamentary debate, the balloon debate and the chain debate. The form of a policy debate was chosen, because René worked at the Faculty of Technology, Policy and Management.

Who debates and where?
The policy debate takes place between two teams at the Faculty of Technology, Policy and Management. Each of the teams consists of a professor and a student. A new approach to fill the need for new architectural models within e-government is being discussed. Team Pro (professor Pro and student Pro of the Systems Engineering Department) is for the proposition, being debated. Team Contra (professor Contra and student Contra of the Policy and Management Department) is against the proposition, or has doubts. The jury determines which team wins the debate considering the line and the strength of argumentation and the debating rules as used in Delft (http:/www.delft.debatteert.nl/indexphp?page=page/wat.php). The debate is fictive, but to some extent based on real life.

Reading guide
This policy debate has four phases:
1. the setting up phase. In this phase the proposition for the debate is given. One speaker of each team gives an opinion;
2. the defence phase. In this phase a speaker of the Pro team tries to heal the holes. Then a speaker of the Contra team reacts on the proposition and the initial defence;
3. the conclusions phase. The first speakers of the Pro and Contra teams come up with their main conclusions;
4. the judgement phase. The jury designates the winner of the debate and makes a closing statement.
These phases will be used to structure the rest of this chapter.

Setting up

Professor Pro
What constitutes architecture and which types of models are necessary, is a recurring theme. Although there are many architectural efforts, there seems to be no silver bullet. René Wagenaar was one of the first to critically

discuss architecture and the role of models. Therefore, we use the following proposition as a starting point for the debate.

Proposition
New government needs new architectural models. The current single actor architectural models result in no cooperation at worst, or in low levels of cooperation at best.

The problem exists
Cooperation in IT is difficult to achieve in multi-actor environments, especially in the public sector. Often critical actors meet at a late stage in the IT production chain. For instance, they become involved at a point where IT implementations have been developed. Then the question that remains is whether the same IT implementation can be used by various actors.
In short, when actors use architectural models, they do so in a single actor mode. They act as if all IT will be done by a single actor (possibly assisted by external parties). No (or only a few) common pieces, will be done for all, or for groups of actors.

The problem is serious
By thinking of cooperation in IT in a late stage, actors miss cooperation in earlier phases of the IT production chain. In this way economies of scale cannot be achieved. More spending of public money on IT occurs to generalize the architectures developed, than would be the case with more cooperation early on in the design phase. In addition the time-to-market is extended. Sometimes IT solutions are delivered well after the intended political deadlines.

The problem is inherent in current policy
Current policy does not prescribe cooperation in IT, nor how to set up cooperation in IT. Sometimes IT implementations are used by groups of actors, because some higher management level has agreed to do so. The rationale of the need for collaboration is hardly known by the salient stakeholders. As a result, we seldom see that IT architects of multiple actors work together on architectural blueprints in a kind of collaborative design activity. In our opinion this is required to arrive at cooperation in the early stages of the IT production chain.

The plan is good
Our plan is to enable cooperation in IT by coming up with an empty framework and by making use of three domains, as shown in figure 1:
— the Common Domain. In this domain all IT will be done for all actors involved;
— the Group Domain. In this domain groups of actors will do IT together for all actors within the group;
— the Single Actor Domain. In this domain all IT will be done for a single actor.

We expect that convergence in IT, group feeling and the use of economies of scale are high in the Common Domain, medium in the Group Domain and low in the Single Actor Domain.

Layer n		
layer 1		

| Common Domain (all actors) | Group Domain (groups of actors) | Single Actors (one actor) |

«   »
Higher use of economics of sale   Lower use of economics of sale
More group feeling   Less group feeling
More convergence in IT   Less convergence in IT

Figure 1. *Empty framework for collaborative blueprint purpose*

Such an empty framework was described in the master thesis of Kuiper (2007) for cooperation in IT within the European Union. The European Union works with a Common Domain and a National Domain, which is effectively a Single Actor Domain. The option to do IT implementations for groups of Member States is not used, possibly because their conceptual model does not include a Group Domain. Many IT systems are implemented per Member State, so in the Single Actor Domain, even though the process descriptions are the same for all Member States. The result is lower use of economies of scale, less group feeling and less convergence in IT across Europe.

We expect that our empty framework can be used in all circumstances where cooperation in IT is relevant. Notable examples include:
— the use of the framework for e-government purposes, or
— the use of the framework as a basis for sourcing discussions.
We leave this framework entirely blank, unlike what IT architects usually do. Usually they fill in frameworks with standards, products, models and solutions. By leaving the framework empty, we facilitate discussions between architects of the various actors involved. We do not nail down these discussions upfront by coming up with a completed blueprint prepared by experts. Our plan is that architects of the various actors fill in the framework together. They decide together on how many layers they want to use, which standards are applicable, which models, and which industry solutions. Then the decision on what to do together, what to do in groups, and what to do alone, can be taken consciously and early on.
Our plan was inspired by discussions on process management (Bruijn, Ten Heuvelhof, In 't Veld, 2003), and by the Open Systems Interconnection Reference Model, see (ISO/IEC, 1994) and figure 2.

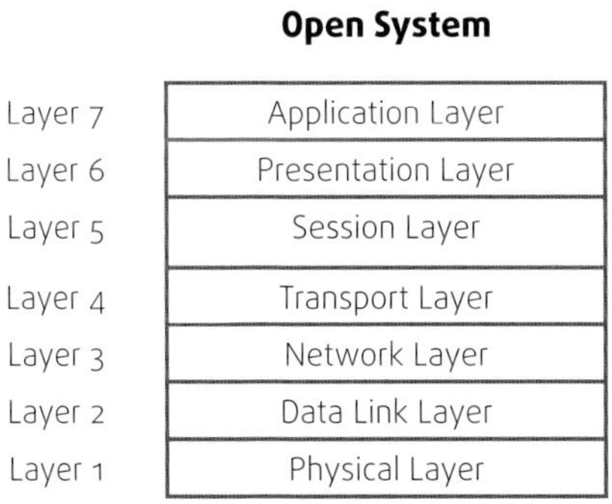

Open System

Layer 7	Application Layer
Layer 6	Presentation Layer
Layer 5	Session Layer
Layer 4	Transport Layer
Layer 3	Network Layer
Layer 2	Data Link Layer
Layer 1	Physical Layer

Figure 2. Open Systems Interconnection Reference Model (ISO/IEC, 1994)

In comparison to the Open Systems Interconnection Reference Model we can say the following. We added to our empty framework the notion of cooperation between actors by creating three layered stacks instead of just one. We propose the freedom of using the number of layers, that actors consider appropriate for the problem at hand. Often this will be less than the seven layers in figure 2. Furthermore, architects can use standards, industry solutions or made-to-measure software within these layers. It does not need not to be all standards, like in the OSI model.

The plan solves the problem
We believe that our plan and framework solve the problem of how to arrive at a technical fit with multiple actors early on in the IT production chain. It will enable the use of economies of scale and consequently reduce IT budgets across all actors involved. And here we mean budget reduction compared to the situation, where no cooperation in IT takes place.

Advantages outweigh disadvantages
The advantages of our plan are in summary:
— it is fairly simple. It will only take one workshop to explain our plan to IT architects, involved in multi-actor projects. Then the collaborative design activity can start;
— it will enable the use of economies of scale and consequently reduce IT budgets across all actors involved;
— it will reduce the time-to-market for new IT solutions due to the cooperation advantages;
— more convergence in IT will occur across actors over time;
— it will result in more group feeling between actors.
The disadvantage of our plan is:
— our proposition and plan need to be proven in practice.
We expect that the advantages will outweigh the disadvantage.

Professor Contra
We disagree with you, team Pro, in various ways.

The problem does not exist
We are not sure that the problem, you are trying to solve, is perceived as a general problem. The European Union, of course, is a very special environment, where politics, negotiations, trust and power determine to a large extent what happens. And that may not be the best thing from a systems engineering standpoint. So, yes, the problem may occur there. But does it occur elsewhere?

We think that cooperation in IT is in fact achieved in multi-actor environments. Look at the e-government movement in the Netherlands. In some cases actors have decided to develop and use certain generic IT components together, like DigiD for secure access to e-government applications.

The problem is not serious
We believe that IT is an expensive sector for other reasons. It is expensive, not because cooperation and economies of scale are missing. Instead the main cause is the dynamics of IT itself. Every three years another paradigm comes up. Now it is Service Oriented Architecture, but what will it be in 2011? What can you expect of actors in this sector given these dynamics? Cooperation or no cooperation, actors try to make the most of it. By the time they have finished a project, often the results are out of date already. That is a timing problem of quite a different magnitude than whether an IT-project runs some months late due to a lack of cooperation between actors.

The problem is not a consequence of current policy
We do not see the problem as a consequence of current policy. You cannot expect policy makers to prescribe cooperation in IT, nor to write down how to achieve it. Most of them have no background in IT at all. Perhaps they wanted to leave some room for initiatives such as yours. Moreover, cooperation needs time to get acquainted to each other. Consequently cooperation results in longer lead times.

The plan is not good
Your plan, team Pro, only addresses the technical fit of cooperation in IT, not the cultural fit of the actors involved. However, to be successful when cooperating, you need both a technical fit and a cultural fit (Child, Faulkner, Tallman, 2005). So, in our opinion, the plan does not address the entire problem of cooperation in IT.

The plan does not solve the problem
Cultural clashes are the most common reason cited for cooperation attempts to fail (Child, Faulkner, Tallman, 2005). Your model does not take that element into account. Cooperation initiated in this manner is bound to clash on cultural differences between actors, that were overlooked by

focusing on the technical aspects of IT with the domain model in figure 1. How are you going to handle that?

Advantages do not outweigh disadvantages
Our plea extends the advantages and disadvantages proposed by the proponent in several ways. We summarize it as follows.
Advantages of the plan:
— an advantage is using IT architecture to arrive at cooperative IT solutions early on in the design phase;
— there will be more support for cooperation in IT, since actors have designed the new architecture together.
Disadvantages of the plan:
— we are not sure that IT architects will understand what you mean with this empty model;
— IT architects work in different ways. Working methods and symbols may differ per actor. It will be quite a challenge to have architects of multiple actors working together to fill in the empty model;
— since IT architects hold strong opinions in general, there may be a long negotiation period needed to arrive at a filled in model. The time needed for negotiations increases the time-to-market of IT outweighing cooperation efficiencies.
We expect that the advantages do not outweigh the disadvantages in practice.

Defence

STUDENT PRO
We will now try to heal most of the holes, signalled by the Contra team.

Existing problem?
The problem does exist in various environments according to our experience. It is not specific to the European Union. Therefore we proposed our plan.

Plan incomplete?
It is true that our plan addresses only the technical fit. Cultural fit between cooperation partners can be addressed by using cultural profiles (e.g.

Child, Faulkner, Tallman, 2005; Deresky, 2002; Kuiper, 2007). A cultural profile is a composite picture on working environments, people's attitudes and norms of behaviour (Deresky, 2002). You can use cultural profiles for partner selection when cooperation is considered.

No understanding?
We will illustrate our plan by providing an example, that could come out of a collaborative design meeting of IT architects of multiple actors, as shown in figure 3. The example shows that an agreement was reached on the following aspects:
— the number of three layers used in the model, from bottom to top: network, middleware and application layers;
— using Internet and Common Communication Network / Common Systems Interface, CSN/CSI, at the network layer, message queueing at the middleware layer, and a search engine at the application layer for all actors in the Common Domain;
— using middleware such as database management systems and transaction processing systems at the middleware layer, and the corresponding applications at the application layer for groups of actors in the Group Domain, because of a high dependency on volumes;
— using a made-to-measure application at the application layer for single actors in the Single Actor Domain.

Search Engine	Database and Transaction Applications	Made-to-Measure Application
Message Queueing	Database Management Systems, Transaction Processing	
Internet, CSN/CSI		

Common Domain (all actors)	Group Domain (groups of actors)	Single Actors (one actor)
« ——————————————————————————————————— »		
Higher use of economics of sale More group feeling More convergence in IT		Lower use of economics of sale Less group feeling Less convergence in IT

Figure 3. Example of a filled in framework

More disadvantages?
We in the Pro team are optimistic about the advantages outweighing the disadvantages. IT architects are well-educated and often experienced people. So they will soon understand what we mean, certainly with workshops.

Different working methods?
Yes, the working methods differ per actor, but some forms of standardization exist, or are on their way (Torre, Lankhorst, Ter Doest, Campschroer, Arbab, 2006; Lankhorst, 2005). You can see our plan as a vehicle to further standardize working methods across actors by cooperation. For instance you can use landscape maps (Torre, Lankhorst, Ter Doest, Campschroer, Arbab, 2006) in the application layer of figure 3.

Long negotiation periods?
The time needed for negotiations to reach agreement on filled in models can be time-boxed. This is a common way to arrive at solutions quickly in the public sector.

Student Contra

We are impressed by your replies, team Pro, but we do note that you have not reacted to all our holes in your plan.

Experiences must be documented
So far, the evidence that the problem exists as a general problem is not substantial enough. One single case at the European Union is not sufficient to prove that we have a general problem here. You should document more experiences in a systematic and structured way. René Wagenaar would have asked whether your proposition is a proven theory or only a claim. We think it is a claim at this point in time.

Cultural fit insufficient
We are glad that you are aware of cultural aspects and want to use cultural profiles. But you forgot to mention communication training as another means to prevent cultural clashes (Hofstede, Pedersen, Hofstede, 2004).

Management unclear
Your example clarifies the plan and makes it more precise. It is a good ad-

dition to your empty framework. Nevertheless, it is not sufficient as it does not consider the management process in time.

Ending negotiations
Time-boxing is one way to end negotiations, but it is a blunt way. We prefer to use process management to design the decision making (Bruijn, Ten Heuvelhof, In 't Veld, 2003). Actors should decide beforehand on the level of agreement, that is being strived after for a model as depicted in figure 3:
— concensus (all actors agree);
— commitment (not all actors agree, but actors who disagree still commit themselves to the outcome), or
— tolerance (not all actors agree, and actors that disagree will not cooperate, but they will not hinder the other actors in reaching the outcome). Our experience in the Policy Department indicates, that too often people in the public sector strive after the highest level of agreement, consensus. Even when lower levels of agreement (commitment or tolerance) are perfectly acceptable, easier and faster to achieve. Time-to-market of IT solutions increases as a result of this extremely demanding way of decision making in the public sector.

Conclusions

PROFESSOR CONTRA
We had an interesting discussion with you on your plan. We now like to come up with our main conclusions.

Doubt
We welcome your plan, team Pro, but you have not yet convinced us. The plan may be too abstract. Your plan may help in certain cases, but you should not market it as if it is a necessity to move forward with cooperation in IT in multi-actor settings. Initiatives to cooperate in IT by higher management may work as well.

PROFESSOR PRO
Thank you, team Contra. Just some final remarks from our side.

Belief
We do see your points, team Contra, as a result of our debate. Certainly you have enriched our view. But we remain believers in our plan. We were able to address many of the weaknesses, signalled by you.

Future research
Still, we realize now more than ever, that our plan needs a test. We propose to give our plan a try here in an experimental setting, and see how far we can get with it. It could be combined with our trials on Collaborative Business Engineering, or your simulation games with process management (Bruijn, Ten Heuvelhof, In 't Veld, 2003). Perhaps we can convince you then.
We find our plan successful if:
— IT architects of multiple actors work together to fill in the framework. In this manner it will be a model owned and accepted by the actors involved, at the level of agreement they have decided upon upfront;
— based on the filled in framework, economies of scale are achieved;
— time-to-market of IT solutions decreases substantially for the cooperative solutions.

Judgement

THE JURY
Teams Pro and Contra, we found the debate interesting.

The winning team?
We noticed that you have not broken the Delft debating rules. We appreciate that. Taking everything into consideration we have come to a conclusion. The Contra team has been able to generate reasonable doubts on the plan of the Pro team. The Contra team has achieved this, even without an alternative plan or critical theory. Therefore we judge that the Contra team has won the debate. The Pro team can prove they are right by performing the experiments, as they suggested.

Exposure is important
Nevertheless, we welcome such early discussions on plans, that have not yet been tested in the scientific arena. It shows that the Pro team is willing

to expose itself to criticism and different opinions. There are not enough of such debates in our institutions. And that brings us to a new proposition, a variant on the initial proposition of the Pro team:

Another proposition
New government needs people like professor René Wagenaar to drive debates by making stimulating propositions and by posing critical questions.

People are crucial
See (Wagenaar, 2004) for some examples of what we mean. In our opinion, you can make architectural models in whatever way you like, but in the end people are the most important to make things work. We do like to conclude with a typical, open Wagenaar question: Reactions?

REFERENCES
Debatvormen. (2001). Retrieved January 13, 2008, from http://members.home.nl/gp.broekema/debat10.htm
Delft debatteert! Wat is debatteren? (2007). Retrieved January 13, 2008, from http://www.delft.debatteert.nl/indexphp?page=page/wat.php
Bruijn, J.A. de, Ten Heuvelhof, E.F. & In 't Veld, R. (2003). *Process Management – Why Project Management Fails in Complex Decision Making*. Deventer: Kluwer.
Child, J., Faulkner, D. & Tallman, S.B. (2005). *Cooperative Strategy*. Oxford: Oxford University Press.
Deresky, H. (2002). *International Management – Management across Borders and Cultures*. Upper Saddle River (New Jersey): Pearson Education Inc., Prentice Hall.
Dool, F. van de, Keller, W.J., Wagenaar, R.W. & Hinfelaar, J.A.F. (2002). *Architectuur Nederlandse Overheid. Samenhang en Samenwerking* (Report Ministry of Kingdom Relations and Interior). The Hague: Verdonck, Klooster & Associates.
Hofstede, G.J., Pedersen, P.B., Hofstede, G. (2004). *Werken met cultuurverschillen*. Amsterdam: Business Contact.
ISO/IEC. (1994). *Information Technology – Open Systems Interconnection – Basic Reference Model: The Basic Model*. Geneva: ISO/IEC.
Kuiper, E.J. (2007). *Convergence by Cooperation in IT – The EU's Customs and Fiscalis Programmes*. Master Thesis Delft University of Technology, Delft. Retrieved January 13, 2008, from http://www.itaide.org
Lankhorst, M. (2005). *Enterprise Architecture at Work*. Berlin, Heidelberg: Springer-Verlag.
Torre, L. van der, Lankhorst, M.M., Doest, H. ter, Campschroer, J., Arbab, F. (2006). Landscape Maps for Enterprise Architectures. In *Proceedings of the 18th Conference on Advanced Information Systems Engineering (CaiSE '06)*. Luxembourg.
Wagenaar, R. (2004). ICT en de nieuwe overheid. Presentation Delft University of Technology, Delft. Retrieved January 13, 2008, from http://www.ecp.nl/download/presentatie—R.—Wagenaar.pdf?PHPSESSID=fff3049e448e

THE USE OF THE INTERNET
OFFERS THE GOVERNMENT NEW
POSSIBILITIES TO DEEPEN ITS
RELATIONSHIP WITH ITS CITIZENS IN
A MORE INFORMATIVE, INTERACTIVE
AND CONSULTATIVE AS WELL AS
A MORE CARING AND EFFECTIVE
MANNER.

From Civil Servant

Navigating the bureaucratic maze: a messenger model for e-Government

Ronald Lee, Roger Bons, Elizabeth Dominguez, Kenneth Henry and Vu Nguyen

Abstract

This article pursues the direction set by Wagenaar and colleagues in the application of Web services composition methods for the integrated delivery of e-government services. Whereas Wagenaar et al address issues of web services orchestration among various governmental agencies, we here consider complementary issues from the client standpoint, in particular where the client's needs are exceptional and do not fit the assumptions of the available e-government processes. The proposal here is to provide 'on-the-fly re-engineering' to deliver a customized, integrated view of the procedure to the client, even though it may actually involve multiple separate back-office agencies.

Preface and dedication

In 1992, the Erasmus University Research Institute for Decision and Information Systems (EURIDIS) and the Information Management department of the Rotterdam School of Management defined a joined research project on electronic markets and artificial intelligence. This was the start of the cooperation between Ronald Lee, Rene Wagenaar and Roger Bons, which we recall with warm (indeed sometimes heated) memories of the brainstorming sessions and whiteboard discussions, joint conferences and projects for the European Union as well as the Port of Rotterdam. Lee's research in formal modeling and artificial intelligence in e-commerce and Wagenaar's research in inter-organisational relationships resulted in numerous joint publications (Bons, Lee, Wagenaar 1996; 1998; 1999; Bons, Lee, Wagenaar and Wrigley 1994; 1995; Lee, Bons Wagenaar 2001; Lee, Bons, Wagenaar, Wrigley 1994), including Bons' dissertation in 1997 (Bons, 1997). After that, we went our separate ways. Bons moved into the corporate world first to Philips in Eindhoven and New York, then to ING Group in Amsterdam; Wagenaar started his positions at the Free University in Amsterdam and later Technical University of Delft; and Lee moved to

Florida International University in Miami. Alas, we never managed to get back together to revisit the many discussions and explore the (new) interests we shared. We do however believe that the present article would have provoked interest and discussion from our friend and colleague, René Wagenaar.

Vaarwel, vriend.

Introduction: The red-tape problem

red tape, --n. (so-called from the red tape formerly used to tie up legal documents in England), bureaucratic procedure, especially as characterized by mechanical adherence to regulations, needless duplication of records, and the compilation of an excessive amount of extraneous information resulting in prolonged delay or inaction.

We have all had frustrations with bureaucracies. While dealing with a single bureaucracy can be bad enough, navigating among the requirements of several bureaucratic agencies is much worse. One important source of bureaucratic complexity is due to specialization of government activities in multiple agencies. Over time, these agencies evolve to service a wider variety of needs, and so develop a web of interactions with other agencies. As noted by Janssen, Gortmaker, and Wagenaar (2006, p. 44), 'Governmental services are increasingly organized around networks of agencies, as a set of interconnected nodes (e.g., Castells, 1996), and customer-oriented processes often bypass the boundaries of a single agency. ... Within public administrations, many different more-or-less autonomous agencies exist, each responsible for a certain set of tasks. Due to this fragmented nature of governments, the activities that make up a single governmental service, such as a building license, are often performed by different governmental agencies (Wimmer, 2002). As part of their historical heritage, agencies often are part of different hierarchies that are governed in isolation of each other. Cross-agency processes therefore need to rely on networking between stakeholders, with goodwill, mutual trust, and softer forms of governance mechanisms, such as service level agreements, instead of hierarchical control. Traditionally, the emphasis of public information managers has been on developing systems within the boundaries of a single organization or department without considering the need for interoperable systems and processes. This has resulted in a huge interoperability problem between governmental organizations because all agencies and departments have their own heterogeneous types of systems"

Solutions to these problems typically focus on the notion of 'one-stop shopping' or a 'single service window' to the collection of e-government services. As Wagenaar and colleagues point out, the technologies of service oriented architecture (SOA) and web services provide promise for this functionality. As they point out (Janssen, Gortmaker, and Wagenaar, 2006, p. 45)

"Web service orchestration is one of the most promising new technologies to support interoperability using process-driven application integration. Process-driven application integration is a relatively new paradigm for ensuring interoperability using a process model driving the flow of applications. Making agencies' internal processes accessible using Web services, and orchestrating the loosely coupled Web services using the process model, creates integrated cross-agency processes. In this way, dependencies between agency processes can be coordinated just by their external interface descriptions, without having to know the details of how these internal processes are performed."

However, the elegance of the technical solutions also has to contend with the realities of institutional territoriality and responsibilities. They continue (ibid p. 45):

"improving cross-agency business processes involves addressing many challenges outside the control of the managers of a single agency. A cross-agency process concerns the chained execution of tasks by different organizations that are responsible for these tasks and are often part of different hierarchies... The agencies work together in a loosely coupled structure, where the overall process performance depends on the weakest link in the chain. Many legal and organizational impediments exist because agencies are accountable and responsible for their roles and functions to the higher layers in the hierarchy, but not to the agencies involved in the cross-agency processes. Consequently, it is often unclear which agency is responsible for the whole cross-agency process – that is, managing the flow between agencies, monitoring service levels, and maintaining and improving the performance of the complete, end-to-end, cross-agency processes."

However, we note that cross-agency processes presently exist and are ubiquitous – but their responsibility lies with the client, rather than with any of the agencies. If there is a bug in the process, it is presently up to the client to locate and deal with it. On the other hand, this presupposes that there is sufficient transparency in the cross-agency process that the client is able to do this debugging. In some organizations, a special office, called an ombudsman (http://en.wikipedia.org/wiki/Ombudsman), is made available to help with cross-agency difficulties.

Challenge of this paper

A commonly cited goal for e-government is that citizens ought to have a single window or help desk for all their transactions. This is in contrast to the current situation where often the citizen must navigate a bureaucratic maze among different government agencies. On the other hand, the single window principle suggests that there would be an integration of the various back-office procedures by the multiple administrative agencies. In most cases, this presents a massive business process re-engineering challenge. But an even greater difficulty is political: these separate agencies have their own goals and responsibilities, reflected in the procedures they have developed. They are not willing to relinquish or compromise control of the design of procedures in the process of a government-wide integration.

Furthermore, regulations and procedures need to evolve to meet changing conditions. Each governmental agency has its own constituency to satisfy, and they need to adapt and adjust according to their own requirements. Adding the burden of a total integration effort among the various departments and agencies could paralyse their already limited adaptiveness. Thus, the apparent dilemma is this: from the client perspective what is desired is total integration; from the agency perspective what is desired is separate design and control of rules and procedures.

The solution we propose to this dilemma is a 'virtual integration' of these procedures. The novel approach taken in this project is to exploit artificial intelligence techniques to represent bureaucratic rules and procedures. Represented declaratively, bureaucratic rules and procedures, are not concealed in the black box of computer code, but made manageable by other (knowledge base) software tools.

In this paper we address the problem where a client must deal with the rules and procedures of several different agencies simultaneously to solve his/her problem. As discussed by Wagenaar and colleagues, the government agencies may have already invested in the re-engineering and integration of their cross-agency procedures using technologies such as web services orchestration. These solutions will focus on the more standard, high-volume processes. By contrast, our focus is on support for the more exceptional cases, that are not handled by the standard processes. In these cases, alternative combinations need to be explored. We refer to this as navigation. The focus here is on design of technology that can navigate process elements of the various agencies and synthesize a customized solution for the client; that is, 'on-the-fly' automatic generation of procedures for exceptional situations. Our perspective here is primarily client-centric; while inter-agency responsibilities and politics are important, they are outside our present scope.

Artificial intelligence and knowledge-based systems provide the principle reference technologies for the aspects of knowledge base extraction and abstraction and navigation and synthesis of procedural requirements.

These new capabilities provide not only for virtual integration of a single municipality or local government, but improved means for coordinating among the various levels of government: from municipality to local government to national government to, potentially, regional government such as the European Union, and other kinds of international governmental alliances (Lee and Dominguez, 2004).

This is especially advantageous for the distributed management of changes for procedures. Example: suppose that the EU issues a recommendation for all city governments that requires an additional check of previous residence for all new residency applications (e.g. due to higher levels of controls for terrorism). Using these methods, this would be a single procedure constituent that could be automatically distributed to all the (participating) cities in Europe. Rather than the usual weeks, or months, such change could be implemented, Europe-wide, in a matter of minutes.

Following the recommendations of Wagenaar and colleagues, our design is based on notions of components. Actually we incorporate two levels of components: one representational, as 'chunks' of procedures; the other implementational, as web services. First, procedures are decomposed into logical, re-usable components, which we call procedure constituents. These are utilized for procedure navigation and synthesis. The second sense of components include web services as developed for public administration (Feenstra, Janssen, Wagenaar, 2007).

Navigating among multiple agencies: messengers

Considering the challenge of citizen clients navigating the requirements of multiple agencies, there are several aspects:
— *discovery of requirements*; the client does not know what is required, and has some difficulty in finding out.
— *navigation among requirements*; in nasty cases, the standard solution is somehow frustrated; an alternative must be found. Sometimes, this is discovering flexibility within the requirements (e.g. fax, official copy); other times, it might be navigating around the bureaucracy (e.g. via Vienna).
— *transaction processing*; once a solution path is found, one actually performs the transaction.

We propose a 'messenger model' to help solve the problems of navigating among the requirements of multiple bureaucratic agencies. Our model makes use of a kind of computational agent, called messengers, which can visit, inquire, negotiate, and transact among agencies that offer a suitable electronic 'front desk', called a regime. An agency's regime is something like a Web site. However, whereas the content of a Web site is text and images, read by people, the content of a regime is rules and procedures, readable by messengers. Metaphorically, a (computational) messenger is like its human counterpart, a sort of errand boy, sent to do bureaucratic chores. It is sent to one agency, with a certain goal in mind. However, as seen from the scenario, this might require sub-goals, achieved through other agencies, indicated by referrals. (These referrals are network addresses, e.g. URL's.) When the messenger has pursued all the sub-goals, the various procedural requirements are gathered up together and presented back to the client for approval. Note: in fact, there might be multiple procedural solutions found; in which case the client selects one. If the various collected requirements allow for electronic documents, the messenger might then also perform the transaction on behalf of the client.

As mentioned earlier, we see the final version of this system as comprising two distinct kinds of functionality relating to procedures. This follows directly from the symbolic computing paradigm of artificial intelligence programming that allows the manipulation of representations both as data and as programs.

EXAMPLE SCENARIO: LABOR MOBILITY WITHIN EUROPE
The following scenario typifies inter-agency complexities as faced by individual citizens. The example we provide is condensed from several actual cases (names have been changed).

In the year 20xx, Professore Giuseppe Buratino, an Italian, moves to Holland, where he starts employment at Madurodam University. One of the first things he is told to do is visit the university personnel office, to

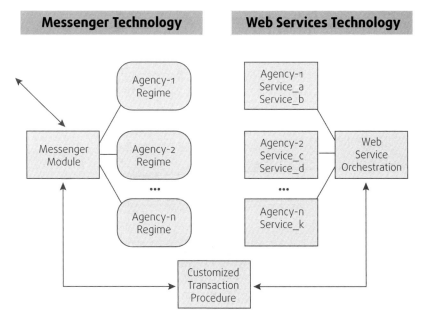

Figure 1. System Architecture

register himself in the university payroll system, as indicated in Figure 2a. (Little does he know that he is embarking on a voyage of discovery...) Once arriving at the university personnel office, he is told that in order to become registered for payroll, he must first obtain a so-called social-fiscal (SoFi) number. This is obtained from the Dutch Tax Office (Belasting Dienst), as indicated by Figure 2b. However, to obtain this, one must first be registered as an inhabitant of the municipality. Evidence of this is provided by a document known in Dutch as an 'uitreksel'. Roughly, it is an official voucher of the residence registration. This is obtained from the City Hall (Stadhuis), as indicated in Figure 2c. However, to obtain this, one must obtain a residency permit, known in Dutch as a 'vergunning tot verblijf'. This is obtained from the Immigration Office (Vreemdelingen Politie). This is shown in Figure 2d.

As a matter of fact, the simple set of diagrams presented here vastly oversimplifies the difficulties of this discovery process -- actually it takes Buratino the better part of two weeks. There were many mis-directions; for instance, he is originally told that he can obtain the SoFi number via mail. There is also confusion finding the correct office and desk (e.g. in City Hall), plus misunderstandings of language (e.g. 'uitreksel'). Also, there is of course waiting in lines, and multiple appointments (e.g. at the Vreemdelingen politie).

But these remarks are only about the discovery aspects. Actually transacting the procedure introduced further difficulties: because of the large number of refugees pouring in from central Asia, the waiting time for the interview has grown to more than four months! Since this was only the first of the four steps in getting registered for payroll, this means that Buratino might not be paid for nearly the first half year. The solution, in fact, was provided by the tolerance of the university. They agree to pay him on a provisional basis, until the SoFi number is obtained.

Our intention is that Prof Buratino would use a messenger to automate this discovery process. The messenger would act on behalf of Buratino to determine the appropriate administrative procedures to follow for his particular situation, also taking into account his particular preferences. For instance, he might be in a hurry, and willing to pay extra money to expedite

Figure 2a. Referral to Personnel Office

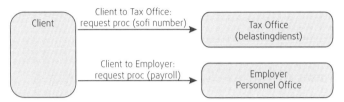

Figure 2b. Referral to Tax Office

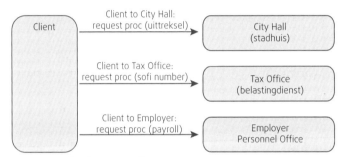

Figure 2c. Referral to City Hall

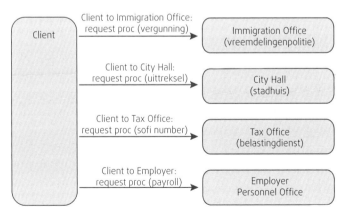

Figure 2d. Referral to Immigration Office

the process. On the other hand, maybe he can do his research thinking just as well when standing in line, and prefers to save money.

Thus, the client states his initial goal, and the messenger navigates among the various agencies to produce the procedure that needs to be followed. A messenger...
— is a transaction specific agent;
— navigates among administrative regimes;
— not a full-fleged agent; it has specific limitations of scope (may have to go back to home regime for further authorization or instructions)

The key to this messenger capability is that the relevant agencies present their various procedural requirements in a kind of electronic directory of services that can be understood by this computational messenger. We call these collected procedural requirements of each agency its 'regime'.

EXECUTING THE TRANSACTION: WEB SERVICES
The messenger provides the client with a plan of action for achieving their goal.
In this section we consider how that plan is actually executed, that is how the steps suggested by the messenger are translated and conveyed to the transaction processing systems of the respective administrative agencies.

Over the past few decades, business and administrative data processing has sought to reduce development costs by means of outsourcing and utilization of packaged software, such as Enterprise Resource Planning (ERP) systems, e.g. those of SAP and Oracle. However, a common difficulty with ERP packages is that they are based on standard business / process models, which are often difficult to adapt to the specialized needs of a particular organization. It is not uncommon that it is easier to adjust the organizational process to fit the software than the other way around. Perhaps more importantly, the resulting implementation is often very difficult to maintain and adjust in case of process change, which can also easily result in change-adverse behavior of the responsible IT department, limiting the organizations ability to quickly improve its processes when needed. Finally, integration with other applications (internal or external) is extremely cumbersome as well. This is particularly true of governmental agencies generally, and especially those at the regional and municipal levels.

These kinds of limited adaptability problems sorts of the integrated approaches have generated interest in so-called component based development, where systems are assembled from pre-defined building blocks. Of course the flexibility of this approach depends on the definitions of the components. As one might expect, greater flexibility would be provided by an open market for components. However, this raises the problem of inter-operability among the components. This has led to the notion of service oriented architectures (SOA) (Papazoglou & Georgakopoulos 2003). According to Feenstra, Jannsen, and Wagenaar (2007),

"The SOA paradigm focuses on building information systems by discovering, matching and integrating pre-developed services ... The basic idea of SOAs is to decompose a system into parts that are made accessible by services, to design these services individually and to construct new systems using these single services. SOA is a way of reorganizing a portfolio of previously siloed software applications and support infrastructure into an interconnected set of services, each accessible through standard interfaces and messaging protocols"

The technology of service oriented architectures is service oriented computing. This builds on earlier computing paradigms of modularity, object oriented designs, and component-based development. The computational services are components. Unlike the earlier paradigms, where modules are defined from the programming perspective, to reduce code redundancy, the modules of service oriented computing are defined from an application perspective, for which someone might charge for a single execution. An example might be authentication. Thus the 'granularity' of modules for services tends to be larger than for program modules. The most important advantage is the potential to share and re-use application developments among different administrative agencies. This is especially appropriate among regional and municipal administrations, that have similar applications needs.
The objection, of course, is that these application needs are similar, but also different. But that is exactly where the componentized structure of web services can benefit most: by acquiring web services from the external market for those aspects that are similar, complemented by in-house or local programming for those aspects that are different.

Beyond these advantages, web service architectures also provide the link between the symbolic model, synthesized by the AI-based Messenger software, and the production level transaction processing done by the administrative agencies.

Procedural knowledge bases: Regimes

Agencies are distinguished from one another based on what they are able to do. This is what is represented in the regime in a formal, computational way: what the agency is able to do.

Here we are concerned with the creation and maintenance of the procedural knowledge bases of each of the departments or agencies, what we have called 'regimes'. We assume that the principal input for creating regimes will be the existing procedures. These need to be converted into a formal specification. There are a variety of ways to accomplish this. For instance, many workflow tools provide a graphical interface, and can output a formal specification. This could be then be converted into a more standardized syntax for assimilation into the regime knowledge base. However, regimes are not merely the formalized collection of existing procedures. Rather, each procedure is decomposed into its logical parts, which we call procedural constituents. These procedural constituents may be re-used in various departments' procedures.

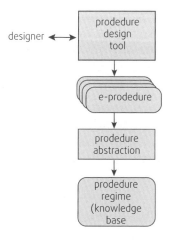

Figure 3. Formal specification and conversion of procedures to regime

We refer to this process of decomposing procedures into re-usable procedural constituents as decomposition. The initial creation of the regimes will thus involve the formal specification and subsequent conversion of the existing procedures, as illustrated in Figure 3.

In most cases, this will not be a single, one-time effort. Rather, procedures will need to be adapted based on client feedback and changing conditions. (For instance, procedures involving physical security of citizens are currently being reviewed and re-engineered after the terrorist bombings in the USA.) This same process of procedure abstraction and knowledge base assimilation can be used on a continuing basis, providing a kind of evolutionary knowledge engineering. To support evolutionary knowledge engineering we propose three techniques: inheritance of process (to compare different procedures using behavioral subclass/superclass relationships), procedure constraint grammars, and workflow mining.

Note: procedure (re-)designers should not need to modify the regime knowledge base directly. Our strategy is to have them create or modify complete procedure designs (e.g. via a graphical interface), and to let this be automatically decomposed and assimilated into the regime knowledge base.

Discussion and future outlook

As noted at the beginning, our purpose in this paper was to pursue extensions to the research work of René Wagenaar and colleagues in the application of Web services composition methods for the integrated delivery of e-government services. Wagenaar's group have addressed how web services orchestration can support the goals of having an integrated ('single window') view of government services that are actually distributed among various governmental agencies. While the technology makes this notion feasible, Wagenaar and his colleagues have considered the implications this has for organizational authority and responsibility among the agencies. Our focus here has been complementary in that we consider how web service technologies can be used from the standpoint of the citizen client, in particular where the client's needs are exceptional and do not fit the assumptions of the available e-government processes. The proposal here is to provide 'on-the-fly re-engineering' to deliver a customized, integrated view of the procedure to the client, even though this may actually involve numerous separate back-office scattered throughout multiple agencies.

The future outlook of this area of research may be regarded from the perspective of e-government technology development, but also from the perspective of how these emerging technologies might impact the ways governments govern.

In terms of e-government technologies, the area of automated composition of e-government web services has great promise. Not only will citizens have easier, faster access to government services, but it will be made easier to understand, also in multiple languages, with user-friendly explanations available. Another important research issue will be e-government transparency – the ability of clients to follow the progress of their transactions – which may sometimes be of long duration – but also to know why certain requirements are being made, and provided explanations behind government decisions that affect them.

The future outlook of service oriented computing for e-government may also be considered from the organizational standpoint. As organizational theorists have observed, organizational structures often emerge to accommodate information processing constraints. Service oriented computing will reduce these constraints and enable new forms of networked government organizations. At the same time, there are increasing trends towards inter-operability among governmental organizations, for instance in support of international trade alliances. Governments at present are largely defined in terms of geographical areas. The new era of e-government may address entirely different kinds of governance, on an international and even global scale.

REFERENCES

Aalst, W.M.P. van der (2000). Loosely coupled inter-organizational workflows: modeling and analyzing workflows crossing organizational boundaries , *Information and Management*, 37(2), 67-75.

Aalst, W.M.P. van der & Basten T. (2001). Inheritance of workflows: An approach to tackling problems related to change" *Theoretical Computer Science*.

Aalst, W.M.P. van der t & Jablonski S. (2000). Dealing with workflow change: Identification of issues and solutions. *International Journal of Computer Systems, Science, and Engineering*, 15(5): 267-276.

Bons, Roger W.H. (1997). *Designing Trustworthy Trade Procedures for Open Electronic Commerce*, PhD Dissertation, Euridis and Faculty of Business, Erasmus University.

Bons, R.W.H., Lee, R.M. & Wagenaar, R.W. (1996). "Obstacles for the development of open electronic commerce. *Proceedings of the Ninth International Conference on EDI: Electronic Commerce for Trade Efficiency* (pp. 191-202) Bled, Slovenia.

Bons, R.W.H., Lee, R.M. & Wagenaar, R.W. (1998). Designing trustworthy trade procedures for open electronic commerce. *International Journal of Electronic Commerce* 2(3), Special Issue, eds. D. Vogel and J. Gricar, pp. 61-83.

Bons, R.W.H., Lee, R.M., & Wagenaar, R.W. (1999). Computer-aided auditing of inter-organizational trade procedures, *Intelligent Systems in Accounting, Finance and Management*, Special Issue on Electronic Commerce, ed. Jae Kyu Lee, No. 8, pp. 25-44.

Bons, R.W.H., Lee, R.M., Wagenaar, R.W. & Wrigley, C.D. (1995). Modeling inter-organizational trade procedures using documentary Petri nets, *Proceedings of the HICSS-28 Conference*, (pp. 189-198), Hawaii, USA.

Bons, R.W.H., Lee, R.M., Wagenaar, R.W. & Wrigley, C.D. (1994). Computer-aided design of inter-organizational trade procedures, *Proceedings of the Seventh International Conference Electronic Commerce and Electronic Partnerships* (pp. 180-193). Bled, Slovenia.

Feenstra, R.W., Janssen, M., & Wagenaar, R.W. (2007). Evaluating web service composition methods: The need for including multi-actor elements. *Electronic Journal of e-Government* 5(2), pp 153 - 164, available online at www.ejeg.com

Janssen W., Gormaker J., & Wagenaar R.W. (2006). Web service orchestration in public administration: Challenges, roles and growth stages, *Journal of Information Systems Management*, 23 (2), pp. 44-55, www.informaworld.com/smpp/title content=g76843 3704 db=all

Lee, R.M. (1988). Bureaucracies as deontic systems", *ACM Transactions on Office Information Systems*, 6(2), pp. 87-108.

Lee, R.M. (1997). A messenger model for navigating among bureaucratic requirements, *Proceedings of the Hawaii International Conference on System Sciences*, Vol IV, pp. 468-477.

Lee, R.M. (1999). Bureaucracy made easy: e-procedures for global trade" *Global Networked Organizations: Twelfth International Bled Electronic Commerce Conference*, Bled, Slovenia, June 7 - 9.

Lee, R.M., Bons, R.W.H, & Wagenaar, R.W. (2001). Pattern-directed auditing of inter-organisational trade procedures, *Proceedings of the 1st IFIP Conference on eCommerce, eBusiness, and eGovernment*, Zurich, Switzerland, 4-5 October 2001.

Lee, R.M., Bons, R.W.H., Wrigley, C.D. & Wagenaar, R.W. (1994). "Automated design of electronic trade procedures using documentary Petri nets", *Proceedings Fourth International Conference on Dynamic Modeling and Information Systems*, Noordwijkerhout, , pp. 137-150.

Lee, R.M. & Dewitz, S. (1992). Facilitating international contracting: AI extensions to EDI, *International Information Systems*.

Lee, R.M. & Dominguez, E. (2004). ICT support for evolving harmonization of international alliances", *Digital Communities in a Networked Society: eCommerce, eGovernment and eBusiness*, eds M. Mendes, R. Suomi and C. Passos, Kluwer.

Papazoglou, M. P., & Georgakopoulos, D. (2003). Service-oriented computing: Introduction. I, 46(10), 24-28.

Wimmer, M.A. (2002). Integrated service modeling for online one-stop government. *International Journal of Electronic Markets, Special Issue on eGovernment*, 12(3): 1–8.

THE PROBLEM OF THE
UNAMBIGUOUS SEMANTIC
DESCRIPTION OF WEB SERVICES, IN
OTHER WORDS ESTABLISHING WHAT
EXACTLY IT IS THAT THE SERVICE
DOES, STILL NEEDS TO BE SOLVED. IN
ADDITION, THERE ARE SOME ISSUES
CONCERNING THE NECESSARY
SECURITY AND CONSISTENCY OF
THE WEB SERVICE ACTIVITIES AND
INFORMATION EXCHANGE.

From *Civil Servant*

Heidi: an electronic identity intermediary model in e-Government

Andreas Mitrakas

ABSTRACT

This paper presents a model that aims at easing typical shortcomings associated with operational requirements that often limit the way applications communicate with each other in electronic identity (eID) management. Heidi is an architecture that enables the smooth exchange of critical information in order to establish trust in an electronic identity management environment on the basis of a validation-centric model. Heidi builds on the concept of electronic intermediaries who act as shared e-Government services to facilitate application management that may also include certification authority-related services. Shared e-Government services have been deemed critical to the success of e-Government. Leveraging upon eIntermediaries is likely to bear fruit in terms of a further exploitation of infrastructures that have been developed in different contexts when information needs to be exchanged between discreet applications. In a broader perspective, leveraging upon shared e-Government service centers can greatly enhance the way e-Government services evolve when it comes to identity management

INTRODUCTION

The growing use of electronic identity technologies in daily transactions has highlighted the need for interoperability at the application level. The increasing availability and reliability of electronic applications has increased their use among citizens. Electronic identity management is used to identify and authenticate users in secure online transactions. Additionally, electronic identity management can support data confidentiality. As applications grow, in what are often perceived as isolated contexts, it is often necessary to ensure efficient application management by leveraging upon data sets generated in these isolated contexts. Furthermore, electronic identity is seen as an essential element with regard to securing and protecting certain information assets. In this chapter, we present a model that is designed to enhance interoperability in the use of electronic identities in electronic application environments for e-Government. The Hub eID Intermediary (Heidi) model aims at easing typical shortcomings associated with operational requirements that often limit the way applications communicate when relying on certificate management. The remainder of this chapter addresses the following areas: the dilemma of interoperability, some considerations regarding an eID model based on intermediaries, and Heidi, a model that enhances interoperability through a specific business process. The aim of this model is to enhance security and interoperability and alleviate the existing mistrust in linking eID management infrastructures.

The interoperability dilemma in eID management

Interoperability is the ability of products, systems, or business processes to work together to accomplish a shared task. Although interoperability is a technical issue, it typically serves organizational interests in that it provides a mechanism to interlink apparently fragmented infrastructures and systems that need to be combined to share a common objective. At a technical level, interoperability refers to the ability of software to exchange data via a common set of procedures, to read and write the same file formats and use the same protocols, and to ensure the accurate translation of data from one format to another. With regard to e-Government processes, interoperability has to do with the way information is used or exchanged in the various public administration agencies; which parties have access to certain types of data; how the information is presented to various types of end-users who may reside in different countries, etc. Factors that help determine the ability of a system to interoperate with other systems include the structure of a system, trade secrets and potential shortcomings in aligning with other systems. To contain such shortcomings, user communities and government agencies have set up their shared interoperability structures, for example e-GIF in the UK, SAGA in Germany, etc.). Finally, it is of critical importance to ensure that interoperability becomes a built-in feature of eID in e-Government, due to the interest these solutions present to small private sector service providers who do not necessarily want to face the costs in other solutions that are more expensive and less reliable.

The concept of shared e-government services centers has previously been researched by Janssen and Wagenaar, who have highlighted the case of isolated and unrelated computerized applications within a single public organization that overlap in function and content, resulting in isolated islands of technology. This reality apparently clashes with the concept of information systems that had been viewed as internal to public organizations (Janssen et al., 2004). Due to the authentication role that eID plays in e-Government transactions, eID interoperability has become closely linked to the provision of shared services in terms of the authentication and non-repudiation of public acts and systems usage. Such shared services can eventually help organizations solve their own specific integration problems and provide economies of scale, by sharing the standardized services among many participants. Service-oriented architectures can facilitate the orchestration of e-Government services and facilitate cross-agency processes (Gortmaker et Al., 2007).

In terms of an identity management that is largely based on certificate management through public key infrastructures (PKI), the lack of automated cross-certification services can be attributed to the inadequate standardization at the technical and operational levels. Such shortcomings are often reflected in certificate policies (CPs) and certificate practice statements (CPS), and they often reflect a legal divergence in the framework regarding electronic signatures. PKI certificates profiles often follow diverging approaches, limiting the ability of the relying party to make a positive comparison and thus to establish trust and equivalence levels. More specifically, although the CP structure is defined in existing standards like ETSI TS 101 456 (see also RFC 3039) or ETSI TS 101 042, there is still a significant gap in the standardization with regard to the way the CP requirements are implemented in the CA domain, for example with regard to the roles of the subjects involved, certification and registration requirements, etc.

The above-mentioned limitations pose restrictions, especially in the light of the absence of an appropriate regulatory certificate management framework that allows for the automated comparison of CPs and CPS in a meaningful way. As a consequence, automated cross-certification services are hindered and they often become obstacles to the secure electronic co-operation, information exchange and knowledge-sharing one might expect in an application context. Additionally, the general absence of interoperability architectures for e-Government exacerbates concerns regarding policy management. In this context, policy is needed to translate complex technical terms into service warranties. Generally speaking, several interoperability models exist, each with its own individual features that can be used to facilitate interoperability in e-Government certification services. The general distrust among e-Government actors in this area, , however, has thus far led to very limited results.

Although what has been described above refers to a general certificate management problem that affects all business sectors, there is a need for a sector-specific analysis, especially in the CP standardization part, where the dedicated requirements of the underlying user communities have to be taken into account, paying attention to their specific CP-related. In addition, application-specific constraints have to be properly analyzed and treated to determine whether they obstruct interoperability.

Automation and transparency in e-Government PKI needs to be made available in order to provide user-friendly and secure e-Government services to citizens in such a way that human processes are integrated into the relevant business model. Unified business models for e-Government implementations that address complex problems like liability and insurance are needed. Public Administrations should be able to make e-Government services available via their trusted service providers based on efficient Service Level Agreements (SLA). This is a proposed solution to contain start-up costs, service risks, non-effective usage, the use of outdated technologies and the cost of recruiting and training skilled people.

A risk must be highlighted here in terms of the overall split of opinion regarding what an interoperable eID model should look like. Most EU member states have taken diverging routes that show little resemblance to the models adopted by the industry when facing similar problems. The stakeholders in the eID are reluctant to allow identities to spill over identities, motivated by an inherent desire to control electronic identities much like they have been used to controlling physical identities of data subjects over time. Such examples include customer relations in the private sector and the reluctance to work together internationally with regard to citizen identity management in e-Government services (Cameron 2005). The shifting landscape from rigid IT structures towards web services that make it easy to connect services makes it necessary to add functionality to the electronic identity layer as well. The perspective of open grid services architecture (OGSA) and the shift towards Web 2.0 technologies raises the pressure to address eID interoperability models and to facilitate the need for e-Government services to interoperate with each other as well as with private sector services that citizens use when acting as consumers. As technology begins to thaw yet further, shared environments can help e-Government achieve its full potential.

It has been suggested (Estevez et al., 2007) that "Capturing infrastructure requirements: Most countries implementing e-government have developed national infrastructure projects that enable agencies to deliver local services more effectively. Infrastructure development involves many technical issues, such as: how the services are delivered, how the agencies connect to one another, and how they can tackle common problems (Authentication, secure transactions, etc.). Infrastructure development projects must be closely viewed with an eye on e-services opportunities. After identifying such opportunities, the common problems related to their development should be synthesized and analyzed." Identity management comes high on the list of pending issues for the successful implementation of e-Government services, due to the horizontal requirement of authentication in such an environment.

The eID middleman

Much of the work done with regard to eID infrastructure management is carried out through intermediaries. The principal, which in this case is a state agency, typically serves as registrar of requests for the issuing of eID credentials. Other tasks, such as the issuing itself, validation, token management, etc., are usually outsourced to several specialized service providers. The exacerbated role of electronic intermediaries is a feature in electronic transactions, which is a service-centered model. In eID, intermediaries have taken on a discreet role, thanks to the drive on the part of Public Administrations to outsource large portions of the electronic identity management to service providers. Public Administrations have, nevertheless, maintained core parts of activity for themselves exclusively. In Sweden, for example, the public sector also relies on identities that are issued by banks. In Belgium, a fully outsourced model has been used, while the Public Administration basically plays a role in the identification of citizens.

To date, eID intermediaries have provided the solid foundation that delivers discreet eID-related services that cover the issuing of credentials, time-stamping services, token management, etc. Major functions of an eID context that uses intermediaries in eID management include the following:
— Application owner: This is the e-Government agency that owns and controls the e-Government implementation that supports a smart card. The Application owner may assume additional roles in line with the operational model being used. The owner may be in charge of the identification part of the whole process that identifies entities to prepare them to receive their eID. Often, the public administration acts as registration authority (RA), which is a role associated with it in a public key infrastructure (PKI).
— Application service provider (ASP): typically an outsourced agent that carries out specific functions associated with an application at the request of the Application owner.
— E-Government liaison: in some cases the applications on offer may be supervised or even licensed through a registration scheme. Alternatively, in some cases an accreditation mechanism may be in place to ensure the integrity of the procedures in place and the features of systems in cases where several providers are used.
— Security services provider: This is an outsourced provider of security services that may additionally include certificate management services, etc. Usually, this role combines the roles of certification authority (CA) and validation authority (VA), carrying out discreet functions in a PKI.
— Token vendor: This is a role reserved for an outsourced provider of tokens. A typical vendor in this case makes the large quantities of tokens available, for instance the smart cards that are used as physical carriers of the electronic identity code.
— Additional roles, like dedicated network lines, can be further identified.

Heidi: A Hub eID Intermediary
In this section, we discuss a Hub eID Intermediary (Heidi) model. Heidi aims at easing typical shortcomings associated with operational requirements that often limit the way applications communicate with each other when relying on certificate management. Heidi is an architecture model

that aims at enhancing interoperability in an eID environment by using a validation-oriented approach. It builds on the concept of electronic intermediaries to facilitate application management, which may also include certification authority-related services. The architecture can remain neutral to the technology choices that are related to the management of the underlying application or the management of the certification authority.

Application-oriented solutions can enhance interoperability in specific operational environments. Especially in e-Government, this approach may bear fruit in terms of leveraging upon infrastructures that have been developed in different contexts and that need to interoperate, for instance in the case of electronic invoicing or electronic procurement, which are both areas where EU legislation has led to significant developments in terms of potential interoperability among the various actors in the member states. A policy framework can ensure that this approach becomes binding among its participants and that the technical, organizational and legal constraints of each approach are respected.

Heidi's background is associated with operational models in e-Government that focus on breaking away from a silo approach. In spite of the obvious benefits of a more individual approach, such as specialization and a greater potential to respect privacy rules, e-Government organizations do not necessarily have to stick to an approach that typically keeps them from offering cross-sector and cross-border services across the board (Eymeri 2001). Although operating in isolation and setting up silo-like constraints can be justified at a national level, in an EU-wide internal market a service-minded public administration implies opening up services to parties that do not necessarily reside in one single jurisdiction or member state. The shift towards e-Government warrants such a change in a way that interprets public interest as the need towards greater cooperation among public administrations for the purpose of enhancing services rendered within the EU.

It has been suggested (Feenstra et al., 2007) that "[d]uring the service composition process, a composition is realized by making use of the existing services provided by different service providers. During this process, decisions have to be made concerning which alternative service offerings to include in the composition. Different parties have often different requirements, opinions and interests, this will influence their choices made during the service selection process. The parties involved will vary in their opinion about the optimal composition." The selection of validation services that aim at becoming interoperable with Heidi requires specific attention.

Because Heidi aims at easing the shortcomings associated with limitations related to the way that applications communicate with each other, interoperability is focused on the ability on the part of the relying party to validate a certificate irrespective of the application framework that it operates in.

In figure 1, the policy framework is highlighted by referring to the certification practices statement (CPS). A certification authority typically uses policy in the form of a CPS to convey legally binding limitations to certificate users (subscribers and relying parties). A CPS is a statement of the practices that a CA employs in issuing certificates (ABA 1996). It is a com-

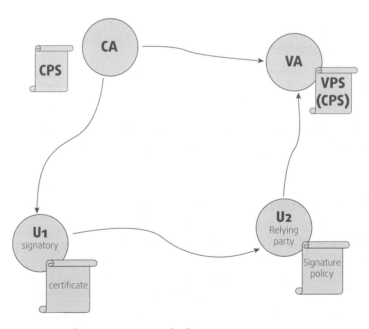

Figure 1. *Certificate management and policy set-up*

prehensive treatment of how the CA makes its services available and delimiting the domain of providing electronic signature services to subscribers and relying parties. A certificate policy (CP) is sometimes used together with a CPS to address the certification objectives of the CA implementation. While the CPS is typically seen as answering 'how' security objectives are met, the CP is the document in which these objectives are defined (ABA 2001; Mitrakas 2005b).

The relying party, on the other hand, may often rely on a signature policy, which describes the scope and use of such electronic signature, with a view of addressing the operational conditions of a given transaction context (ETSI 2002). A signature policy is a set of rules under which an electronic signature can be created and checked for validity (ETSI 2003). It determines when an electronic signature is valid within a given context, which may include a business transaction, a legal regime, a role assumed by the signing party, etc. In a broader perspective, a signature policy can be seen as a means to invoke trust and convey information in electronic commerce, by defining appropriately delimited trust conditions that address the perspective of the relying party within an electronic identity framework (Mitrakas 2005a).

Policy-mapping could be considered as an add-on service in the Heidi model used to rate trustworthiness based on the certificate policies of the participating issuing and validation authorities. Policy-mapping can be based on trust criteria. An automated policy-mapping tool can support the decision-making process of the relying party in making informed decisions with regard to the trustworthiness of the issuing authorities based on the criteria that relying parties find important (Batarfi et. al 2007; Backhouse et al. 2003).

Along these lines, the policy framework that prevails in the Heidi model includes the certificate policy of the issuing authority, which in this case is the certification authority. Additionally, a signature policy managed by the relying party sets out the conditions under which a certificate can be deemed valid and acceptable in a given application framework. In this model, the validation authority is seen as the appropriate trust-generating entity for the purpose of enhancing interoperability. The validation authority may in turn introduce its own validation requirements that could be enshrined in a discreet policy framework. In this model, the framework is known as validation policy statement, and it encompasses the validation content of standardized policy frameworks, for instance ETSI TS 101 456. A Validation Practice Statement could be used to describe the operational technical and legal constraints of the validation-oriented interoperability model. The fact that Heidi relies on its own policy framework provides warranties of non-interference with the operational environment defined by the participating issuing and validation authorities.

Validation centric interoperability

A validation-oriented interoperability model can be plotted along an overarching validation authority that includes a meta-directory that is typically based on validation data featured in the typical directory of a validation authority. The basic validation model based on an overarching validation authority can be illustrated as follows:

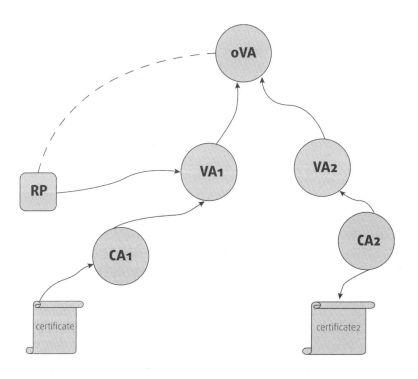

Figure 2. Validation-oriented interoperability through an overarching Validation Authority featuring a meta-directory

INTEROPERABILITY MANAGEMENT

The Heidi interoperability architecture for e-Government aims at making a framework available for secure interoperable e-Government information exchanges for multiple applications of e-Government organizations. A feature of Heidi is its cost-effectiveness, which may even appeal to small sized e-Government organizations (Mitrakas, 2007). The architecture meets the objectives for cost-effective and interoperable solutions that can be used among heterogeneous entities. Cost-effectiveness is focused on managing a meta-directory that projects data that have originally been produced in the context of local certification authorities.

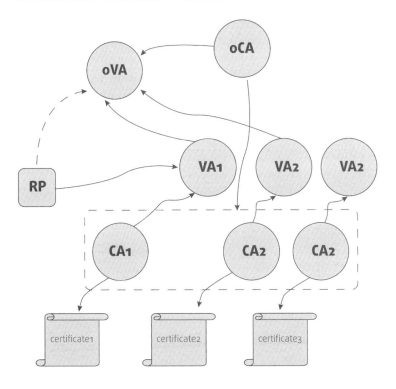

Figure 3. Validation-oriented interoperability through an overarching Certification Authority and a Validation Authority featuring a meta-directory

End-users like citizens, businesses and public administration organizations that are entitled to request services within the proposed infrastructure must register locally with the certificate service of their own administration. To facilitate the interactions among several public administrations, certificate services further need to trust each other by recognizing each other's top root so that they allow end-user to carry out transactions.

For the end-user certificate validation, an overarching Validation Authority (oVA) makes validation services available by redirecting certificate validation requests to the appropriate validation service of a local issuing authority. An oVA provides the end-user with the technical capability to check the certificate status in order to facilitate an application that relies on validation data. Therefore, the end-user, in its role as relying party, is able to access validation data, which can be transmitted using the prevailing protocols of a certificate revocation list (CRL) or the online status protocol (OCSP) (RFC3280 2002; RFC2560, 1999). Using a certificate trust list that is composed by a list of predefined and trusted CAs is a desirable add-on. Browsers and other applications have the ability to allow users to add other root certificates, in addition to the ones that are included by default, as needed. Thus, end-users can update the default lists of CA roots to match their individual requirements.

A potential risk associated with the oVA is that, by easing up root certificates that can take place within end-user applications, malicious actors could potentially exploit them to add false root certificates that can be further used to carry out bogus and fraudulent transactions. To overcome this problem, a list of trusted certification authorities is digitally signed by a dedicated Overarching Certification Authority (oCA), which is a mere technical facilitator, and is, as such, entrusted with the competence to set up a policy and technical framework to support the cross-border recognition of certificates issued by the various local certification authorities that service the small Public Administrations. An oCA can address the critical issue regarding the recognition of local certification authorities in a large number of contexts, being geographic, organizational, etc.

The system outlined above represents a basic interoperability model that can be used by public administrations in e-Government operations. The following section expands this basic concept by elaborating certain elements that are of interest to Public Administration with regard to the application environment in which interoperability is desired.

In addition to policy-mapping, setting up equivalence levels is a significant requirement that may have to be added at a later stage in order to ensure compliance with prevailing rules and to reconcile the differences with regard to the approach to voluntary accreditation conditions, in accordance with article 3.2 of Directive 99/93/EC regarding a Community framework of electronic signatures. To date, the degree of equivalence among accreditation schemes across the EU Member States is unclear, which may inhibit the use of certification services in cross-border transactions for Public Administration purposes. Using intermediaries is recommended to ensure equivalence levels that match prescribed criteria. Intermediaries could collect applicable policies in a repository as well as specify audit conditions and provide advance notice concerning the legal status of the scheme, or legal requirements under which a certificate has been issued or a root operates (Mitrakas et al. 1998). Policy-mapping tools based on decision support systems could be developed to facilitate the management of disparate policies of participating certification authorities.

The way operational requirements of an oCA are addressed also requires some attention. Based on current experience, whenever a new CA seeks recognition by the oCA, its name and root certificate have to be added to the master trust list signed by the oCA, and subsequently distributed to the relevant end-users. Distributing updated trust lists may involve scalability shortcomings if there are more than a small number of certification authorities used to propagate these lists. This problem could be addressed by setting up a single reference directory for certification authorities that want to include the root in a given trust list. By accessing the root directory of certification authorities, an end-user that transacts with public administration entities enhances its ability to establish the trustworthiness of the certification authorities issuing the certificate in question, because it can directly validate the certificate path online. The role of the oCA can be limited to providing the secure publication of the directory and ensuring the inclusion of a pointer to the directory by all trusted local CAs. Including certification authorities in a directory, however, is likely to require a classification mechanism for the certification authorities involved (ETSI TS 102 231, 2005).

An additional area of future attention could address policy frameworks related with the application layer in e-Government transactions. To respond to transparency requirements it is expected that online applications will become increasingly demanding in explaining to the end-user what they do and ultimately warranting the performance of the service. This requirement has been partially addressed through a combination of dedicated legislation and policy (e.g. CPS).

In e-Government it is still required to use policies at the application layer level, where the requirement for transparency in the transaction and accountability of the parties involved is more stringent than in electronic business (Mitrakas 2005a). Finally, specifying policies further to meet the needs of particular application areas, groups or organizations are additional expectations, for example in the area of e-Procurement. In e-Government it is expected that interoperability could be enhanced through best practices and standards regarding policy in specific vertical areas. Typical content for an application layer policy may include aspects associated with the kinds of underlying services involved, the profile of the providers that make these services available, architectural premises, disclosures with regard to data bases, personal data, validation services, as well as liability or warranty that may be offered to the end user. The scope of application layer policy is to contribute to the transparency of the application platform that might ultimately lead to trust and legal safety (Mitrakas 2005b).

Further standardization is a way to effect the desired changes needed to enhance interoperability in e-Government CA services. A set of overarching rules has yet to emerge and be accepted for this architecture to become fully operational. E-Government applications are likely to provide the additional drive, for example in the area of identity management, especially for areas like electronic invoicing and electronic public procurement (CWA 15236, 2005).

While interoperability remains a constant requirement for information society, e-Government applications need to also shift towards greater interoperability levels. Identity management is a key e-Government application that has the ability to render interoperability requirements possible across multiple functional applications such as e-Procurement and e-Invoicing, etc. A much needed improvement would be to strive for a policy framework that meets the requirements of law and associated applications.

CERTIFICATE VALIDATION THROUGH AN APPLICATION INTERMEDIARY

A critical success factor is the ability on the part of the Heidi model to feature validation data that addresses specific application contexts. An electronic intermediary in this case encompasses the certificate issuing function that is typically carried out by the CA. This feature supports the claim that the Heidi model increases efficiency due to a limitation of the required data associated with certificate validation. Heidi's validation-oriented approach relies on broadcasting known certificate validation data and focuses on where trust is created in an application framework that is supported by a PKI. The additional information that may have to be inserted concerns the additional certificate distribution point (CDP) of the oVA.

While more than a single application can be accommodated, operating in contexts enhances the scalability of this interoperability model. The basic validation model, with the use of an electronic intermediary, can be illustrated as follows:

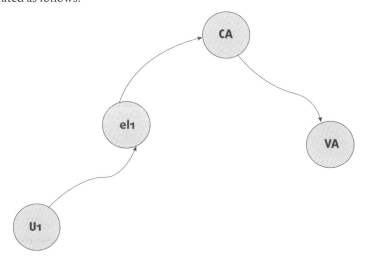

Figure 4. *Application intermediary (a)*

The basic usability of this model can further be enhanced through the involvement of several possible users that can be connected to the services of the electronic intermediary. The basic application model concept allows several end-users to use the electronic intermediary's services, as is illustrated in figure 5.

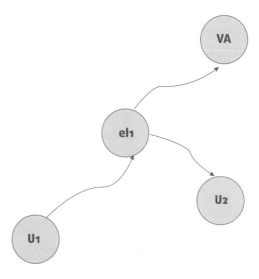

Figure 5. Application intermediary (b)

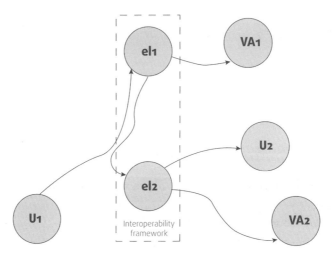

Figure 6. Application intermediary (c)

Further downstream, Heidi can be used in cases where several electronic intermediaries are used. In this case, the model allows interoperability to grow within the application framework made available through electronic intermediaries. Figure 6 illustrates the use of multiple electronic intermediaries.

The final extension of the application framework contains the full features of Heidi, complete with the overarching validation authority that uses a meta-directory to project certificate validation data produced at local level.

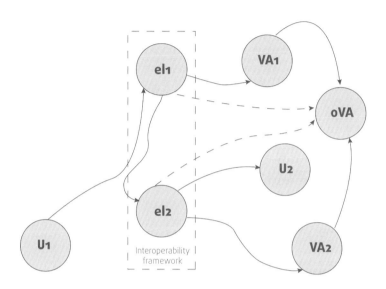

Figure 7: *Application intermediary (d) along with overarching validation*

Heidi can facilitate an application-oriented approach that ensures the validation of identity data and can accommodate an array of applications. By simplifying the certificate validation process, Heidi contributes to the interoperability of multiple applications. To propagate the Heidi model, more than one eID intermediaries could be set up in such a way as to facilitate discreet application contexts that share eID infrastructures in e-Government.

FURTHER STEPS
Policy-mapping is an optional step that may complement the basic model presented above. By adopting a flexible approach towards policy interoperability, the proposed model allows for an enhanced level of transactions in heterogeneous Public Administration services that require the validation of certificates and subsequently the management of identities of end-us-

ers. Mapping and reconciling policy frameworks in overlapping transactions may, however, threaten transactions, which are based on the use and acceptance of varying terms. A typical hard case may involve, for example, overlapping policy conditions, which apply to certificates issued by different certification authorities. The situation is exacerbated when certification authorities that do not have the means to recognize one another issue certificates that can be used in the same transaction environments (ETSI TS 102 231, 2005). Although such certificates may well be complementary to a transaction framework, the varying assurance levels they provide may threaten the reliability of the e-Government application environment as a whole (Mitrakas 2005b). Policies can play a significant role in terms of clarifying the operational framework of intermediaries acting in shared operational environments. Furthermore, a dedicated set of policy conditions associated with the provision of validation services would be beneficial. A validation practice statement can provide additional assurance to relying parties on secure path validation, validity time of certificates, etc. EU standardization is an opportunity that cannot be missed in this regard.

Conclusions

The Heidi model is a validation-oriented model that enhances interoperability in an eID environment. Additionally, Heidi builds on the concept of electronic intermediaries to facilitate application management that may also include certification authority-related services. This approach can be of use in e-Government applications that leverage upon electronic identity data. Heidi relies on certificate management to channel validation of certificates that at the end of the day provide the necessary assurance to relying. Cross-border transactions in e-Government can be facilitated through the Heidi model, thanks to the non-intrusive approach it adopts, which relies on known data that has merely to be broadcast further up stream to become useful at a cross-border level. Heidi leverages upon the concept of shared environments that are facilitated through an electronic intermediary. Further work on the policy aspects associated with certificate validation can enhance the Heidi model and underpin its practical use in terms of sharing e-Government resources.

Note: The views expressed in this chapter are strictly personal and they do not reflect in any way whatsoever the views of the author's employers past or present.

REFERENCES

American Bar Association (1996). *Digital Signature Guidelines.* Chicago

American Bar Association (2001). *PKI Assessment Guidelines.* Chicago

Gormaker, J., Janssen, M., Wagenaar, R., (2007). Requirements on cross-agency processes in eGovernment: the need for a reference model, in Mitrakas, A., Hengenveld, A., Polemi, D., Gamper, J., *Secure eGovernment web services,* IGI Publishing, Hershey.

Backhouse, J., Hsu, C., Baptista J., Tseng J., (2003). *The key to trust? Signalling quality in the PKI market,* Proceedings of the 11 European Conference on Information Systems (ECIS 2003), Naples

Batarfi, O., Marshall, L., (2007). *Conformance testing a set of criteria for assessing trust,* Journal of Computers, Vol., 2, No. 1.

Cameron, K., (2005) *The Laws of Identity,* Microsoft Corporation, Redwood

Eymeri, J., (2001), *The electronic identification of citizens and organisations in the European Union: State of Affairs,* 37th Meeting of the Directors-General of the Public Service of the Member States of the European Union, 26-27 November 2001, Bruges.

Estevez, E., Janowski, T., Ojo, A., (2007). *Planning for e-Government – A Service-Oriented Agency Survey,* United Nations University, UNU-IIST Report No. 361.

ETSI TS 101 456 V1.2.1 (2004). *Policy requirements for certification authorities issuing qualified certificates,* Sophia Antipolis.

ETSI TR 102 041 V1.1.1 (2002). *Signature Policies Report,* Sophia Antipolis.

ETSI TS 101 733 V1.5.1 (2003). *Electronic Signature Formats,* Sophia Antipolis.

ETSI TS 102 231 V1.2.1 (2005). *Provision of harmonized Trust Service Provider status information,* Sophia Antipolis.

ETSI TS 101 042 (2002). *Policy requirements for certification authorities issuing public key certificates,* Sophia Antipolis.

Feenstra, R. W., Janssen, M., Wagenaar, R. W. (2007). *Evaluating Web Service Composition Methods: the Need for Including Multi-Actor Elements,* The Electronic Journal of e-Government, Vol. 5 No. 2, pp. 153 – 164.

Janssen, M., Wagenaar, R. W., (2004). *Developing Generic Shared Services for e-Government,* Electronic Journal of e-Government, Vol. 2, no. 1, pp. 31-38.

Mitrakas, A., Hengenveld, A., Polemi, D., Gamper, J., (2007). Towards secure eGovernment, in Mitrakas, A., Hengenveld, A., Polemi, D., Gamper, J., *Secure eGovernment web services,* IGI Publishing, Hershey.

Mitrakas, A., (2005). Policy Frameworks for Secure Electronic Business, in Khosrow-Pour, M., (ed,), *Encyclopedia of Information Science and Technology, Volume I-V,* Idea Group Publishing, Hershey.

Mitrakas, A., (2005). Policy-driven signing frameworks in open electronic transactions, in *Soft Law constraints in eGovernment,* BILETA 2005 (British Irish Law Education & Technology Association), Belfast, 7 April 2005.

Mitrakas, A., Bos J., (1998). *The ICC ETERMS Repository to support Public Key Infrastructure,* Jurimetrics, Vol. 38, No. 3, Spring 1998.

RFC 3280 (2002), *Internet X.509 Public Key Infrastructure: Certificate and Certificate Revocation List (CRL) Profile* (obsoletes RFC 2459).

RFC 2560 (1999). *Internet X.509 Public Key Infrastructure: Online Certificate Status Protocol – OCSP.*

RFC 3647 (2003). *Internet X.509 Public Key Infrastructure – Certificate Policies and Certification Practices Framework* (obsoletes RFC 2527).

RFC 3039 (2001). *Internet X.509 Public Key Infrastructure - Qualified Certificates Profile.*

WITH THE CURRENT APPROACH FOCUSING MAINLY ON WAYS FOR ICT TO SUPPORT EXISTING SERVICES, GOVERNMENT RUNS THE RISK OF MISSING AN OPPORTUNITY TO USE THE VIRTUAL CHANNEL FOR GENUINE INNOVATION.

From *Civil Servant*

Let a Thousand Flowers Bloom for e-Government

Yao-Hua Tan and Helle Zinner Henriksen

ABSTRACT

The emergence of e-government has reinforced the need for robust inter-organizational information systems to streamline data-exchange in relation to Government-to-Business (G-to-B) e-government, where large amounts of data are exchanged on a regular basis. Streamlining and reducing the administrative burden is necessary to make companies competitive in the global economy. In this chapter, we elaborate on René's concept of Integrated Service Delivery in relation to G-to-B e-government. We discuss the concept on the basis of empirical experiences from a Living Lab in the ITAIDE-project, and conclude that user-driven innovation is the optimal way to develop the necessary robust inter-organizational information systems supporting Integrated Service Delivery.

INTRODUCTION

"One of the great challenges for European governments is solving the paradox of increasing security of international trade, while at the same time reducing the administrative overhead for commercial as well as public administration organization. It is vital to have timely information about business transactions. This information gathering is very costly for businesses and public administrations. Finding the right balance between control and cost of information gathering is the key to increase competitiveness of European businesses locally, nationally and internationally."

This paragraph served as the introduction to a workshop at the DEXA eGov conference in Krakow in 2006, where the ITAIDE project hosted a workshop with the theme 'New public-private partnerships between taxation and customs offices and businesses'.

The ITAIDE project, which is an acronym of *Information Technology for Adoption and Intelligent Design for E-Government*, aims at integrating and strengthening European research into innovative government by enhancing service offerings and disseminating good governance practices through increased security and controls, while employing intelligent software tools to reduce the administrative burden (see: www.itaide.org). The ITAIDE project addresses the issue of e-Customs, focusing on how customs documents and procedures can be digitized and redesigned and, in that context, which business-related and administrative challenges may be encountered.

Given the project's focus on innovation and inter-organizational collaboration, we found it obvious to invite René Wagenaar to give with a presentation at the workshop, because his academic interests very much included these aspects of Integrated Service (IS) research, and in particular because the concept of Web service orchestration supporting cross-agency processes in the public sector was among his most recent research interests (Janssen, Gortmaker, and Wagenaar, 2006).

René was generous enough to accept our invitation. When we heard about René's premature demise, we recalled the last time we met René at the ITAIDE workshop. As academics, we are witness to numerous presentations, most of which leave not much of an impression. As for René's presentation at the ITAIDE workshop, one slide remained etched in our memory: an image of a field of tulips in bloom. The slide was very colorful and quite unusual for a presentation at an academic conference. If we are to summarize our memory of René, it could be through the image of a field of tulips in blossom – colorful and with an unexpected twist with regard to the IS research agenda.

The goal of this chapter is to express the essence of the presentation René gave at the ITAIDE workshop. Based on the PowerPoint slides, the presentation is retold by the authors. Statements from René's PowerPoint presentation are shown in frames throughout the contribution. To develop the ideas further, we discuss the implications of the ideas brought up by René and elaborate on their current status.

René's focus at the ITAIDE workshop
The natural starting point for a workshop focusing on public-private partnerships is to define the public sector, including the tasks that one expects

to find there. There are numerous views on what e-government is and what its objective is. René chose to emphasize five attributes of e-government:

Objectives E-Government
— To improve Public Service Delivery (24/7)
— To reduce Administrative Burden (and thus the costs) to Citizens and Companies!
— To increase the Internal Productivity of the Public Agencies
— To improve Law Enforcement (with all citizens and companies being equal!)
— To increase the Participation of Citizens in Policy-Making

In particular the second bullet-point, which was also highlighted in the original PowerPoint presentation, was claimed to be of importance. IT investments can have many purposes and research often focuses on the benefits to adopters of IT. Even though reducing the administrative burden through IT implementation is crucially important, it is of equal importance to ensure that the customers benefit from IT implementation. In the case of e-government, customers are the citizens and companies that, at the end of the day, have to pay for the IT investments in the public sector. Although e-government research tends to be citizen-oriented (Scholl, 2005), given the more regular interaction between businesses and public sector, reducing the administrative burden is of greater value to businesses than it is to citizens, who interact with the public sector less frequently (Fountain and Osorio-Urzua, 2001). Taking that argument further, René posted a powerful statement against the afore-mentioned backdrop of tulips:

» *It is in the public interest to keep companies competitive in the global economy* «

The focus here is on how e-government supports the activities of businesses in the global marketplace. This perspective matches that of the ITAIDE project, which focuses on streamlining customs procedures to strengthen the competitive advantage of businesses. The statement stresses the view of government as a support unit for businesses – the Integrated Service Delivery concept is seen as key. However, there are hurdles in the development of Integrated Service Delivery:

Major Hurdles towards Integrated Service Delivery
—A lack of Interoperability between existing back-office systems (at the level of both legacy software systems and semantic data)
—A lack of overall Orchestration of agency processes to execute customer service requests
—Autonomy of public agencies (unwillingness to share data and systems)

The notion of IT as a way to streamline business processes is well-known in IS research, harking back to the EDI research of the 1980s, to which René also contributed (see, for example, Bons, Lee and Wagenaar, 1998; 1999 and Hoogeweegen, Streng and Wagenaar, 1998). The legacy of EDI research is stated explicitly when we refer to a lack of interoperability, which was and remains a major hurdle for businesses, and in particular government, which is relatively new to inter-organizational interaction involving businesses.

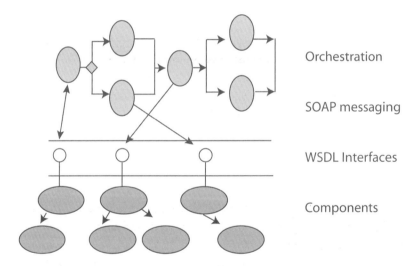

Figure 1. *Web Services allow for the modularization of software with standard interfaces*

The concept of integrated service delivery transcends the issue of interoperability, adding the concept of orchestration, which is necessary to fulfill service requests from citizens and businesses. The term orchestration refers to the development of a robust IT architecture based on modules and standard interfaces that support a seamless exchange of data. SOAP provides the messaging standards, while the Web Service Description

Language (WSDL) is used to specify web-services in a standardized way, making sure they can be interpreted by every software application (for further details see Janssen, Gortmaker, and Wagenaar, 2006). This kind of standardization and interoperability challenges the autonomy of the public agencies, which have a long tradition of maintaining rigid hierarchies and boundaries (often referred to as silos) that are difficult to transcend. At the same time, civil servants are expected to act fairly, responsively and honestly. All this means that realizing inter-organizational collaboration between public institutions and private businesses involves more than merely establishing a robust IT architecture.

Issues that have to be dealt with:
— Government-to-Business: SME's and Interoperability
— Cross Border Rule Re-engineering: Return on Investment
— Cross Border Security and Data Protection

Government support for SME's and interoperability are among the most urgent issues that need to be considered. In most economies, SME's represent the bulk of the business activities, both when it comes to generating value for society and the sheer number of businesses. SME's have implemented countless more or less advanced IT systems, and many have applied proprietary standards. One of the urgent issues is establishing systems that are flexible and that are capable of embracing this multiplicity.

It we return to the statement 'It is in the public interest to keep companies competitive in the global economy', we see that is stresses the importance of harmonizing and simplifying cross-border trade and customs regulations. To stay competitive in today's global economy, it is of the utmost importance to harmonize rules and regulations with regard to trade. The return on investment is the competitive advantage. Typically, the harmonization and simplification to which we refer is realized by re-engineering regulations. One of the objectives of ITAIDE is to develop the so-called e3-Control methodology for re-engineering trade and customs regulations, in particular by replacing paper-based by electronic customs procedures.

After 9/11, security has become an important issue. Again, to secure the growth of the global economy, it is of the highest importance to build robust information systems that can secure cross-border collaboration. The same applies to data protection. Today, storage capacity is virtually limitless. As we will demonstrate in the next section, collecting and storing data is no longer the issue – what is really important is handling and extracting the relevant information. However, the issue of data protection has become more transparent because data can easily be generated, copied and stored in various places.

Reflections on e-Customs
We will now position the results of the ITAIDE project with respect to René's views on e-government. The overall objectives of e-government as defined by René match those of the ITAIDE project, in particular with regard to the focus on reducing the administrative burden, which is very important to businesses that export their goods and therefore have to interact with government on a regular basis. The starting point for our reflection is the concept of Living Labs, which are used as empirical settings for the work in the ITAIDE project.

There are four Living Labs (LL) in the ITAIDE project, each involving different business segments and focusing on their interaction with customs in the various countries. The four LL's focus on the export of Beer (The Netherlands), Paper (Finland), Food (Denmark) and Pharmaceuticals (Ireland). The first two of these labs are almost completed. In this context we will focus on the lessons learned from the Beer LL.

One aspect that stands out with regard to these LL's is the difference between Government-to-Citizen and Government-to-Business electronic government. The most important differences between these two are the following.

I) The LL's can be used as test beds in an environment of e-government enforcement: the G-to-B interaction is regulated to a much higher degree than the G-to-C interaction. Whereas citizens are free to choose whether they want to use electronic instead of non-electronic government services, business do not have that choice. In the case of beer export, the brewery is obliged to provide relevant excise-related data to the government via an online system; the so-called Excise Movement Control System (EMCS).

II) Government-to-Citizen (G-to-C) interaction is more visible than Government-to-Business (G-to-B) interaction: the latter takes place on the basis of business routines that are invisible to the public. As a result, G-to-C figures much more prominently on the agenda, and since e-government is optional for citizens, e-government research is focused much more on G-to-C than on G-to-B, where the main research question is to determine on the basis of which key factors citizens decide to use e-government services, and how this choice can be influenced in a positive way.

However, given the role of businesses in the economy, the G-to-B aspects should not be overlooked. Furthermore, there are both traditional inter-organizational issues and new and interesting research challenges with regard to G-to-B side that have thus far been largely neglected by the academic community.

In his presentation, René mentioned three traditional inter-organizational issues, with reference to the major challenges facing integrated service delivery: a lack of interoperability, a lack of overall orchestration and the autonomy of public agencies. In the ITAIDE project, the concept of Living Labs is used as a tool to overcome these hurdles in an empirical setting. Different stakeholders involved in G-to-B e-government are brought together, with the aim of developing viable solutions.
Based on the results of the interaction with partners from the Beer LL, new customs procedures with regard to the export of beer, and in particular with regard to the payment of excises, have been developed. The partners involved were representatives from the largest Dutch brewery, the Dutch Customs & Excise authorities, IBM and academics from the ITAIDE consortium, who a;; contributed their knowledge and expertise to come up with new solutions.

The new solution in the Beer LL involves making paper customs documents obsolete by giving the Tax & Customs office direct access to the business ERP databases, to collect the data they need for the purposes of verification. The solution was piloted with a Tamper-Resistant Embedded Controller (TREC) electronic container seal and a service-oriented architecture for the exchange of data between the various actors in the beer supply chain, via the TREC device (brewery, carrier, Customs & Excise authorities, etc.). Figure 2 presents this solution, and it shows how a customs officer can check the content of the container without inspecting it physically. The TREC is mounted on containers that are loaded onto ships. It sends a signal (UCR) via a mobile or satellite network that can be used by customs officers to access the Directory Service via a web application, which provides access to the EPCIS database of BeerCo. This database contains the exact information from the logistics module of the ERP system of BeerCo about the contents of the container. Hence, without actually touching the container, the officer knows exactly what its contents are. For a more comprehensive presentation of the TREC devise and the service-oriented architecture, see Baida, Rukanova, Liu and Tan, 2007. This service-oriented architecture is a clear example of the Orchestration architecture presented in Figure 1, and it shows the immediate relevance of René's research to electronic customs. This service-oriented architecture was so successful in the BeerLL, that the Dutch Customs & Excise people are now considering using this architecture in various other IT projects that involve the exchange of data between various disparate departments within their organization.

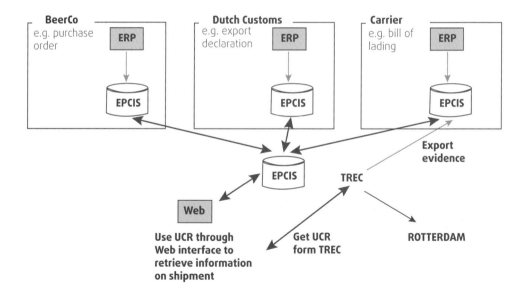

Figure 2. TREC devices and EPCIS databases used to share information and guarantee security and control (copied from (Baida, Rukanova, Liu and Tan 2007))

The TREC device has highlighted a strength of IT, namely the ability to redistribute control through transparency. In the above-mentioned case, the role of the government is very much a controlling one. Hence, one could expect e-taxation and e-customs solutions to be used to collect more data and to control businesses more intensely than is the case in the paper-based procedures. This is also consistent with research into the role of IT in controlling organizations, the argument being that IT makes it easier for one company to control another, because it can collect real-time data about the production processes of that other company (see, for example, Clemons, Row and Reddi, 1993). However, in the Beer LL the opposite appeared to be the case. Rather than using IT to collect more data, Customs and Excise collects far less information in the e-customs procedures.

The reason for this is that physical inspections are replaced by IT-audits. Instead of physically inspecting random trade transactions, the Customs & Excise people check the ERP system companies use to check their own operations internally, which involves a transformation from physical inspection towards system-based auditing. Typically, the internal control of a company is designed for management purposes and quality control. In the case of BeerCo, for example, quality control demands that data about each bottle of beer be stored in the ERP system of BeerCo, from the origin of the ingredients up to and including the final retail destination of the bottle. Clearly, if Customs and Excise officials have access to all this information, they have everything they need to carry out their duties. To some extent, this can be regarded as Customs & Excise 'outsourcing control' to businesses.

These empirical observations suggest that the hurdles mentioned by René are about to be overcome. As for the last hurdle 'Autonomy of public agencies', it is, however, not as a result of Customs & Excise opening up their systems, but of businesses opening up their ERP to Customs & Excise, allowing it to retrieve the information it needs. This suggests that the issue of orchestration is still partially open, in the sense that it is businesses that have to provide (access to) data rather than government improving its integrated service delivery via improved service to its customers (businesses). The issue of interoperability has so far not been highlighted, however, and back-office integration of data in government is still the exception rather than the rule (Henriksen and Damsgaard, 2007).

The concept of Living Labs has opened new ways to develop innovations. In the LL's, we have observed that, thus far, companies have played a more active role than citizens in the development of e-government. Observations among participants in the Beer LL demonstrated that businesses play an active role in redesigning relevant customs procedures. It appeared that businesses have greater expertise in simplifying procedures than Customs & Excise. This may be because public sector institutions are reluctant to change procedures (Andersen, 2004) or because innovation in the public sector is limited due to fear of failure (Moore, 2005). Also, it may simply be because businesses have to deal with government bureaucracy much more, and are consequently more aware of the desirability of looking for a simpler approach.

In the Beer LL the best design of e-customs procedures appeared when the design was carried out by IT developers, business representatives and Customs & Excise officials together. The idea of user-driven innovation is not new when it comes to developing commercial products and services (Von Hippel, 2005). Von Hippel calls this phenomenon democratization of innovation. It refers to an emerging process of user-centric innovation. where users provide a very necessary component to manufacturer innovation. Through empirical studies, Von Hippel demonstrates how user-driven innovation allows end-users to products for themselves. With the exception of a study involving an Australian library system, Von Hippel (2005) focuses on products for the consumer market, where end-users have a strong interest in the further development of the (primarily sports-related) products. However, based on our observations, the concept of user-driven innovation matches the activities that take place in ITAIDE's LL's.

As pointed out by Von Hippel (2005), two of the core problems in the innovation process are information asymmetry and sticky information, both of which can be overcome through the facilities provided in the LL's. Information asymmetry is overcome when Customs & Excise people are brought together with exporters struggling to report in the format required by the authorities. Another dimension that often causes problems when overcoming information asymmetry relates to IT. IS-related literature is rich in examples of IT developers finding it difficult to understand user requirements. By bringing IT developers together with businesses and Customs & Excise officials, with academics acting as interpreters, information asymmetry is minimized and the process of user-driven innovation has been initiated. The problem of sticky information, which in economics relates to the problem of the cost of moving information from where it is generated to where it is needed, also appears to be overcome during the interaction in the LL's.

Hence, this kind of co-design or user-driven innovation seems to be a typical feature of G-to-B electronic government as it has unfolded in the empirical setting of the ITAIDE LL's. One of the challenges facing researchers is to include all the parties within a supply chain to enable and facilitate this kind of co-design with regard to other government procedures.

However, some reflection is also necessary. Thus far, the obvious conclusion, that the e-customs procedures reduce costs for the businesses, turns out to be too overly simplistic. In the LL's, we observed that, although cost reduction is certainly a consideration, it is only a minor reason for businesses to make the transition from paper-based to e-customs procedures in cases where such a transition is still optional (cf. the above-mentioned statement about the enforcement mechanism government can apply to businesses). For businesses, long-term strategic considerations appeared to be much more important than cost-reduction. For example, in the BeerLL, the long-term strategic motivation for adopting the new e-customs procedures was that these procedures were redesigned to make them compliant with the requirements of the C-TPAT program of he US Customs (www.cbp.gov/xp/cgov/import/commercial—enforcement/ctpat/), thus preparing the brewery for further globalization. The C-TPAT program specifies requirements that importers to the US have to meet in order to benefit from a 'Green Lane' treatment at the US border, i.e. to qualify for reduced border inspections. Similar considerations also apply to the trade between the EU and China.

What the LL study shows is that, for some businesses, globalization plays an important role in their decision to adopt e-government services. Doing business at an international level implies having to comply with e-government services in other countries. Hence, it seems that, for businesses, the decision to adopt e-government services is determined more by strategic considerations than by simple costs/benefits calculations. There is a downside to this as well as an upside. The upside is that adopting e-government solutions does not always have to lead to saving money. The downside is that it requires a careful analysis of the international context of businesses to understand what drives them to adopt e-government solutions.

Conclusions and Further Research

It turned out that many of René's ideas are very relevant with regard to the e-government research that was conducted in ITAIDE. In particular the notion of the orchestration of web-services turned out to be very useful with regard to knowledge-sharing between separate government offices. In the BeerLL, this was implemented by combining the TREC with a service-oriented architecture, which made it possible to simplify trade and customs procedures considerably. Hence, orchestration could indeed contribute to the solution of the interoperability problem involving the back-office systems of public administrations, which René identified as one of the most fundamental challenges in e-government research. In this way, orchestration also helps develop Single Window solutions for e-government, where citizens and businesses only have to provide their data to the government once, and the Single Window makes sure that the data is distributed in the right format to the various relevant government agencies. Service-oriented architectures, and in general service orchestration, seems to be a promising are of further investigation in e-government research.

Furthermore, the results generated by ITAIDE support René's observation that the business perspective is as relevant as the citizen's perspective for e-government research. When it comes to developing new e-government service, there is virtually no collaborative co-design between government and citizens. However, in ITAIDE we found clear examples of collaborative co-design, and even cases of user-driven innovation, where businesses took the lead in designing new e-customs services. We were able to observe that, generally speaking, this user-driven innovation led to better results than when government developed the innovation by itself. Hence, it seems advisable to encourage user-driven e-government innovation for business-oriented as well as citizen-oriented projects. In future e-government research, it is important to investigate further which type of collaboration between government and businesses best fosters the co-design of e-government services.

Once more, we want to return to René's blossoming tulips and the accompanying text: 'It is in the public interest to keep companies competitive in the global economy ', and we would suggest that, based on our experiences in the living labs, the best way to place businesses in an optimal position in the global market is through user-driven innovation in a close collaboration between the public sector, IT providers and businesses.

REFERENCES

Andersen, K. V. (2004). E-government and Public Sector Process Rebuilding: Dilettantes, Wheel Barrows and Diamonds. Amsterdam: Kluwer Academic Press.

Baida, Z., Rukanova, B., Liu, J. and Tan, Y.H. (2007). Rethinking EU Trade Procedures – The Beer Living Lab, In M. Lynne Markus, J. Felix Hampe, J. Gricar, A. Pucihar, G. Lenart (eds.), Proceedings of the Bled Electronic Commerce Conference. Kranj : Faculty of Organizational Sciences.

Baida, Z., Liu, J. and Tan, Y.H. (2007). Design and Analysis of e-Government Control: the Green Corridor between Finland and Russia, In M. Lynne Markus, J. Felix Hampe, J. Gricar, A. Pucihar, G. Lenart (eds.), Proceedings of the Bled Electronic Commerce Conference. Kranj : Faculty of Organizational Sciences.

Bons, R.W.H., Lee, R.M. and Wagenaar, R.W. (1998). Designing trustworthy interorganizational trade procedures for open electronic commerce, *International Journal of Electronic Commerce*, 2(3), 61-83.

Bons, R.W.H., Lee, R.M. and Wagenaar, R.W. (1999). Computer-aided auditing of interorganizational trade procedures, *International Journal of Intelligent Systems in Accounting, Finance & Management*, 8(1), 25 – 44.

Clemons, E. K., Row, M. C. and Reddi, S. P. (1993). The Impact of Information Technology on the Organization of Economic Activity: The 'Move to the Middle' Hypothesis, Journal of Management Information Systems, 10(2), 9-35.

Fountain, J., & Osorio-Urzua, C. A. (2001). Public Sector: Early Stage of a Deep Transformation. In Litan, R. F. and Rivlin, A. M. (Eds.), The Economic Payoff from the Internet Revolution (pp. 235-268). Washington: Brookings Institution Press.

Henriksen, H. Z. and Damsgaard, J. (2007). Dawn of e-government - An institutional analysis of seven initiatives and their impact. Journal of Information Technology, 22(1), 13-23.

Hoogeweegen, M. J., Streng, R. J. and Wagenaar, R. W. (1998). A comprehensive approach to assess the value of EDI. Information & Management, 34(3), 117-127.

Janssen, Marijn, Gortmaker, Jeffrey and Wagenaar, René W. (2006).Web Service Orchestration in Public Administration: Challenges, Roles, and Growth Stages. Information Systems Management, 23(2), 44 – 55.

Moore, M. H. (2005). Break-through Innovations and Continuous Improvement: Two Different Models for Innovative Processes in the Public Sector. Public Money & Management, 25(1),43-50.

Scholl, H. J. (2005). Organizational Transformation Through E-Government: Myth or Reality? In M. Wimmer, R. Traunmüller, Gronlund, A. and Andersen, K. V. (eds.) Electronic Government, Proceedings of the 4th International DEXA EGOV Conference, Copenhagen.

Von Hippel, E. (2005). Democratizing Innovation. Cambridge, Mass.: MIT Press Ltd.

THE ENGINE OF ELECTRONIC
SERVICES IS SOFTWARE. IF WE COULD
DEVELOP SOFTWARE ON A MODULAR
BASIS USING COMPONENTS THAT
COULD BE LINKED LIKE LEGO,
WE WOULD BE ABLE TO ACHIEVE
AN UNPARALLELED LEVEL OF
FLEXIBILITY.

From Civil Servant

Rethinking Service-Oriented Government: is it really about services?

Nitesh Bharosa, Ralph Feenstra, Jeffrey Gortmaker,
Bram Klievink and Marijn Janssen

Abstract
Government service deliveryd systems need to be adapted to become customer-centric. Many of the discussions we had with René in the past dealt with innovative technologies aimed at creating a flexible, transparent and responsive government. Advances in Information and Communication Technology allow governments to rethink their information systems, organizational structure and strategies with regard to providing services. As such, we viewed technology as an instrument to help solve some of the problems facing society. Recurring issues were the e-government specificity of the research and the coherence of the service design for e-government research.

Introduction
Electronic government, or e-government, was one of the areas on which René focused as chair of the Information and Communication Technology section at Delft University of Technology, and it is an area that is still under development. One of the main challenge with regard to e-government is that initiatives are confronted with a highly fragmented organization landscape and ICT-architecture that has been vertically organized around departments, with little common horizontal functionality (Wagenaar & Janssen, 2002). At the time, no generic architecture was available to enable communication between front office and back office applications, among back office applications or with external systems. Applications were often monolithic application and imposed their own logic or business processes on organizations and lack the flexibility and adaptability required by today's dynamic environment. We expected that, in the long run, an architecture based on generic, standardized components would result into a more flexible provision of government services. Open, flexible architectures constructed of relatively small components should be reconfigurable to support a whole range of functions and in the end create more custom-

er-oriented products and services. Customers, in this context, are both citizens and businesses. Table 1 shows the starting point at the left side, the development in the middle and the resulting benefits on the right side.

From	To	Resulting in
Stove piped applications	Service-oriented	Flexibility
Integration	Assembly	Lower integration cost
Tightly coupled	Loosely coupled	Shorter development times
Build many times	Build once, reuse	Easier and cheaper maintenance
Designed to last	Designed for change	

Table 1. Overview of developments

It was in this light that the two PhD projects of Ralph Feenstra and Jeffrey Gortmaker were formulated. The former of these projects focused on designing new systems from existing ones, whereas the latter dealt with the orchestration of cross-agency processes. Over the years, we had many discussions with René about our research activities. We tried to meet once a week. Sometimes meetings were bilateral, while others were attended by all of us. After a couple of years, the next challenge was taken to come up with new research projects. The first research project to be formulated was that of Nitesh Bharosa. The basic idea was to translate the concept of orchestration to the domain of disaster management, where adaptation in real-time plays a major role. An opportunity arose when a new project was acquired, resulting in Bram Klievink's research, which is focused on the orchestration of public-private cooperation.

All these research projects were based on the premise that public administration can be shaped purposefully through designing technology and organization in relation to each other. Our discussion varied from research approaches and premises, to research needs, coherence between our research, and the vision for the future. A recurring theme was the use of innovative technology and the discussion on what makes e-government different from e-business research? What all these meetings had in common was that the scope of our research would be broadened, a vision on the future would be discussed and the meetings would take an unexpected direction and we would end up somewhere completely different from where we started. In this chapter, we discuss the scope of our research, the difference between our research and e-business, and our shared vision.

Research
The initial scope
Traditionally, the emphasis of public information managers has been on developing systems within the boundary of single organizations or departments, without taking the need for interoperable systems and processes into account. With the advent of web services, the technological threshold of creating interoperable systems has been lowered (Lim & Wen, 2003). As more systems can be accessed using web services, the emphasis of research is shifting towards the use of modular components and the coordination of web services invocations (Zhao & Cheng, 2005). Our research was not about building these technological systems, but aimed at shaping them within the context of government organizations that have to collaborate with each other to provide customer-centric services.

Cooperative, inter-organizational networks have become a common mechanism to deliver public services, and they are referred to as *Public Service Networks* (PSNs) (Provan & Milward, 2001). From an actor perspective, a PSN is a constellation of actors who have different interests and who use all kinds of information systems, but who depend on each other when it comes to effective service provisioning. Within PSNs, cross-organizational *business processes* can be carried out by public and/or private parties aimed at fulfilling customer demand by providing services or service bundles. From a systems perspective, a business process can be defined as a collection of tasks that transform a given set of inputs into a desired set of outputs. The tasks involved in a PSN primarily focus on processing information, and the inputs and outputs are informational in nature. Our approach to designing such a system begins with analyzing and understanding the businesses processes. This main reason for this is that business processes are both understandable by managers as well as ICT-persons. Furthermore, because business processes support service provisioning, which help to better understand and capture customer-orientation.

Participation in public service networks is not necessarily limited to public agencies. Parts of the ICT functions, and even entire business processes, can be outsourced to private organizations. The *hollow state* is a metaphor we have used in our research to describe the nature of the devolution of power and decentralization of services from central government towards subnational government levels and, by extension, third parties – non-profit agencies and private firms – who increasingly manage programs on behalf of the state (Brinton Milward & Provan, 2000). The hollow state focuses on orchestrating and steering rather than on performing administrative production processes. In our research, the state consists of many modules that are offered by public and private parties and can be composed in business processes, which in turn are orchestrated to enable customer-centric service provisioning.

Service-oriented government (SOG)
The concept of service-oriented government was introduced in analogy to the service-oriented enterprise (SOE). Enterprises can be decomposed into elements and organized by reconfiguring the various elements provided by a range of companies (Binder & Clegg, 2006). The elements can be invoked as services and they need to be orchestrated. Often, a core organization, referred to as the network manager or process director, coordinates these processes. Ideally, an SOE consist of organizations connected by services. These services are loosely coupled, which ideally makes it possible to create dynamic business processes and applications spanning organizations and heterogeneous information systems, which nevertheless offer the flexibility that is needed to adapt to changing circumstances quickly (Cherbakov, Galambos, Harishankar, Kalyana, & Rackman, 2005).
Nowadays, more and more government organizations adopt a service-oriented approach. The Dutch Government Reference Architecture (http://www.e-overheid.nl/atlas/referentiearchitectuur/) already states that all government organizations should adopt a service-oriented approach. From an architectural point of view, such an approach can be applied to all levels, including organization, business processes, applications and infrastructures. A service-oriented approach typically include infrastructure building blocks like DigiD, a national authentication facility, which can be accessed as services and included in business processes of other government organizations. These service provisioning organizations are typically organized as Shared Service Centers (SSC) (e.g. Janssen, Gortmaker, & Wagenaar, 2006). In fact, issues regarding decomposition, sourcing and orchestration issues lie at the heart of the SOG, because organizations first have to be decom-

posed into modules, after which should be decided how and who will carry out the specific tasks, and finally all the tasks have to be coordinated. The organizational structures of enterprises change due to the shift in focus towards in-house competences and the use of parts provided by other companies (Binder & Clegg, 2006). When an enterprise is modularized, its functions and activities are identified and assigned to modules, based on specific modularization principles. One such principle is that, at a business level responsibilities for business domains can be allocated, whereas within business domains the parties responsible for the various elements are free to design their own part (e.g. Versteeg & Bouwman, 2006). Organizations are aided in their service-oriented approach by service-oriented architectures (SOA), in which the contents of the modules are hidden and the environment is only exposed to the service interface (Fremantle, Weerawarana, & Khalaf, 2002), the idea being that the elements within the module can be altered without affecting the interface. In this way it should be easy to replace the modules, using a variety of sourcing options, without changing the interface. Modularization serves three purposes (Baldwin & Clark, 2000):
— making complexity manageable;
— enabling parallel work and improvement; and
— creating adaptivity to deal with uncertainty resulting in the need for changes.

Modularization and service orientation make it possible to integrate and disintegrate potential new business components efficiently and effectively, either by sharing modular components internally, or by outsourcing them. To adapt to changing circumstances, new partners, business services and supporting software modules can be plugged in or removed.
To date, few studies have looked at how loosely organized networks can be structured and managed effectively (Janssen, Gortmaker, & Wagenaar, 2006; Milward & Provan, 2003). Designing PSNs involves addressing many challenges that lie outside the control of individual organizations. Our design focus is on improving coordination in a network of agencies.

Coordination
Although we all have some idea what the term coordination refers to, a more precise understanding of what it means is often needed (Malone & Crowston, 1994). Coordination theory refers to the "(..) *theories about*

how coordination can occur in diverse kinds of systems" (Malone & Crowston, 1994). Although Malone and Crowston acknowledge that there are differences between types of systems (e.g. incentives, motivations and emotions are less important in computer systems than they are in human systems), they state that an inter-disciplinary coordination theory in which work from various fields is synthesized can be beneficial to each of these fields. Coordination theory can be applied to many kinds of systems, i.e. human, computational and biological (Malone & Crowston, 1994).

Malone and Crowston (1994) define coordination as '*managing the dependencies between activities*', the underlying notion being that of actors performing interdependent activities, possibly requiring or creating resources, to achieve goals (Malone & Crowston, 1994). The three main claims made by coordination theory are summarized by Crowston and Osborn (1994):
— Dependencies and mechanisms used to manage them are general in nature and can therefore be found in a variety of organizational settings;
— Often, several coordination mechanisms can be used to manage a dependency;
— Taken together, these claims suggest that alternative processes can be created by identifying the dependencies in a given process and by considering alternative coordination mechanism aimed at managing these dependencies.

Using the theoretical lens provided by coordination theory, web service orchestration can be viewed as the coordination of a sequence of web service invocations, i.e. managing the dependencies between a set of web services. Several coordination mechanisms can be used to manage the dependencies between the services, and alternative service compositions can be realized by applying different coordination mechanisms. Different compositions are likely to display different levels of performance in terms of the quality of service attributes (for example the speed, reliability, costs or scalability of a composition may vary).

Currently, many government organizations are in the process of making their information systems accessible by means of web services. Because web services are often developed in a bottom-up manner, the number of web services within individual enterprises is likely to grow enormously in years to come, which means there is a need for an overview of all web services, including those that have already been developed and those that are still under development. In short, there should be an overview of all the services, those that already exist and those that need to be developed, before functionalities or business processes can be bundled or sourced, and before a decision can be made as to which new services should be developed. Information technology portfolio management (ITPM) refers to the management of an IT-related portfolio of assets, similar to a financial portfolio, aimed at improving the performance of the portfolio by balancing risks and returns (Jeffery & Leliveld, 2004). In analogy to application portfolios, a service portfolio can be viewed as a management instrument that is used to support decision-making processes surrounding web-services. A service portfolio is more than a kind of catalogue of readily available services that can be reused by government organizations in designing new business processes and applications. Service portfolios provide the basis for developing a roadmap to the future. They also includes service evaluation metrics, descriptions of the characteristics of the required web services and service providers, context information, dependencies between services, monitoring and feedback mechanisms and decision support tools. Ultimately, a service portfolio can be used to automatically assemble new business process or help managers make decisions about whether to buy or source services, or to develop them in-house.

Coherence of the research projects
New systems and (business) processes can be designed by combining software components that can be accessed through web services provided by the service providers. Government organizations can act as service providers by providing information or functionality, an example of which is the authenticating service DigiD. New business processes aimed at service delivery can be composed by using these readily available services, after which it needs to be orchestrated. The basic promises of SOG seem to be a reduction in development and maintenance costs and the creation of flexibility by reusing components. One of the questions René would typically ask is whether these benefits are proven or whether they are merely based on claims. Because, in the case of SOG, few academic researchers have actually demonstrated the benefits, the benefits remain speculative.
Figure 1 shows the coherence of the concepts surrounding composition and orchestration. To the left, a number of services that are available in a service portfolio are depicted. These services can be provided by different organizations, i.e. service providers, and can have different levels of quality.

The service portfolio can be used to select a set of suitable services to create a new business process. To the right, the services are used to assemble and configure cross-organizational processes. The process manager can control and manage this cross-organizational process. It is exactly this process that students encounter in the practical course 'Design of innovative services and infrastructure'. Ralph Feenstra's research deals with composition, whereas Nitesh Bharosa, Jeffrey Gortmaker and Bram Klievink's research focuses on orchestration.

A *service composition* combines services on the basis of a certain composition pattern, to achieve a business goal or provide new service functions in general (Curbera, 2002). Service compositions may themselves become services, which turns composition into a recursive operation. During an online order process, for example, a composition can consist of a service that checks a customer's zip code as well as the delivery time of the goods that have been ordered. Ralph Feenstra's research deals with service compositions, in which services are selected and evaluated, and new services need to be developed for service compositions. To this end, a service portfolio, containing an overview of all (potential) services, can be created. The shaded balls

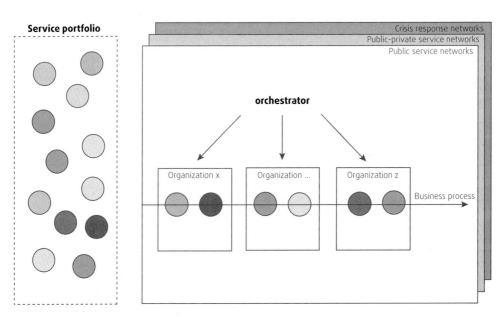

Figure 1. *Coherence among research projects*

in Figure 1 provide a graphical representation of the services. Composition processes face many technical and organizational hurdles.

In Jeffrey Gortmaker's research, an important requirement for cross-organizational business processes (supported by ICT in PSN) is the need for adaptability and accountability. As a technology, web service orchestration enables the creation of a chain of activities performed by independent agencies. The chain needs to be controlled, it needs to be able to adapt to changes in legislation, and organizations need to account for their actions. The aim is to support public agencies in taking up their role as process managers for accountable and adaptive cross-organizational business processes. Because there are many trade-offs that have to be made during the design process, there is a need for a reference architecture that indicates these trade-offs.

Nitesh Bharosa's research focuses on interagency disaster management, in which first responders need to react within a short time frame. Disaster response usually involves a large number of public and private organizations involved in geographically distributed operations, with a rapid need for coordinated control and decision making. The number of organizations involved, their information needs and the available information sources all tend to increase during a disaster, making things more complex and unpredictable. Bharosa's research aims at developing an information orchestration architecture that improves the adaptability of the disaster management network.

The collaboration among public and private organizations is the focus of Bram Klievink's research. Processes are not static and organizations need to be able to adapt to changing circumstances. In addition, many services do not only cross organizational boundaries within the public sector, but also transcend the boundaries between the public and the private sectors. The boundaries in question are subject to continuous change and may even be blurring. In addition, parties may be added to or removed from the network. Within this setting, there is a need for an architecture designed to manage and orchestrate the interactions among government and private organizations.

What is specific to Government?

A recurring question was how our research is different from that of others. One of the key elements in the discussions was the difference between the private and public sector. What differentiates e-government from e-business? The public and private sectors pursue different goals and operate within different settings. The public sector is concerned with societal and public values, which often have little to do with financial performance. Over time, we created a list containing the following elements specific to governments. To some degree the elements overlap, and they are often interrelated.

— *Equal access and rights*: Ideally, government provides equal access to their services and all citizens and businesses have the same rights. One aspect is that services should be accessible to all, including the disabled and people without Internet access. Not all people can be reached via the Internet, for instance the disabled or the elderly, and those who can be reached may suffer from information overload and lack the competences and skills to use the Internet to its fullest. The digital divide generally refers to the distinction between those with and without Internet access and computer skills. We preferred to speak of a social divide rather than a digital divide. The digital divide deals with the availability of broadband and Internet access, whereas the social divide refers to the knowledge and ability needed to use the Internet and other digital resources to one's advantage.

— *Transparency and accountability*: In our view, government should be transparent to its constituents. Government agencies should account for their actions or inactions. Transparency is a difficult concept, because actions designed to create transparency may have the opposite effect. Initially, publishing information on the Internet might result in a higher degree of transparency, but as the amount of information increased things became decidedly less transparent. Furthermore, information sources may be inconsistent or incomplete, which is one of the reasons behind the creation of accountable architectures.

— *Fragmented and complex landscape*: the government landscape is complex and consists of many agencies that vary in size, use all kinds of information systems and have different objectives that may either be complementary or conflicting in some regards. We frequently discussed the problems related to conflicting regulations and the ways ICT could be used to solve these problems.

— *Changes in law*. René worked together with Tom van Engers of the Leibniz Center for Law at the University of Amsterdam, on investigating the potential to adapt to changes in law and regulations. Research at the

Leibniz Center for Law is aimed at at automatically translating new laws and policies into the information systems of agencies. Politicians often make laws without understanding the consequences. Moreover, laws need to be interpreted. Politicians have limited insight into civil organizations and ICT, and they may not be interested in them at all. After all, their job is to represent constituents, not public organizations.

— *Lack of choice*. Customers have no choice in dealing with specific government organizations. In the Netherlands, a person can only renew his or her driver's license in the municipality in which he or she lives.

— *Knowledge of products needed*. Apart from having no choice, citizens and businesses are expected to know what the law demands from them. Citizens are expected to know that a driver's license is needed to drive on the road, tax forms have to be filed each year, etc. Although the government tries to inform people of their various legal obligations, at the end of the day it is the citizens and business who remain responsible.

— *No competitors*. Although in other countries government organizations compete with each other, for example when it comes to issuing providing driver's licenses, this is not the case in the Netherlands. As a result, there is no competition among government agencies with regard to aspects like price, speed of delivery, location and so on. As a result, there is little or no real motivation to innovate. There are no financial incentives (like shares or stock options). Furthermore, civil servants often fail to see the need to adopt new technologies, in part because it seems to apply that the approach they used in the past was the wrong one.

— *Who decides?* Decision-making power is divided among the national, regional and local levels, which all have their own political mechanisms. Elected politicians ought to make sure they take the needs of citizens and businesses into account. The relationship between government on the one hand, and citizens and businesses on the other, is different from the buyer-seller relationship that exists in the private sector. There are many relationships, which makes it difficult to determine who is responsible for what, and there is an inherent danger that decisions made at different levels may conflict. The lack of direct feedback mechanisms complicates matters even more. The feedback loop between citizens and government is often not a direct one, mediated as it is by a constellation of political parties, lobbyist, etc. Often, solutions are the negotiated outcome of a prolonged political process.

— *Time perspective*. Ideally government adopts a long-term perspective to guarantee a sustainable society. In practice, this often means that elected politicians operate within a four-year horizon.
— *Re-engineering*. Specialization and the allocation of functions among organizations are often determined by law. Because our democratic system is based on the separation of the legislative, judiciary and executive powers, it may not be possible to reorganize and restructure certain functions. Furthermore, this poses an even greater challenge in terms of coordinating the various departments. Service delivery requires complex collaboration across organizations.

In all, we managed to identify quite a list of problem areas. One of the differences between the private sector and the public sector is that a reduction in budget and resources often leads to increased competition in the private sector, whereas the public sector typically responds by increasing inter-organizational collaboration. Having said that, we believe the vision of creating an open, flexible and responsive architecture for customer-oriented service provisioning remains the same. At the end of our discussions, we often concluded that the public sector is more complex than the private sector, and that, as a result, many challenges need to be addressed in parallel. It is this complexity and the challenges it brings challenge that we like!

Vision on e-government

These unique elements influence the vision on e-government. Future research should match the unique characteristics of e-government and start with societal challenges to identify research needs. As public organizations vertically disintegrate and outsource services that were once produced internally, coordination with external organizations becomes increasingly important. René and Marijn Janssen cooperated in the eGovRTD2020 project, in particular in the scenario development part, together with Patrick van der Duin (www.egovrtd2020.org). This research was driven by the fact that many government-related planning activities only look at the short-term future, without investigating what e-government will look like in the long term (Bicking, Janssen, & Wimmer, 2006), and which research steps need to be taken to realize desirable futures and avoid undesirable ones. *Scenario building* has become an integral part of the innovation and policy-making process (Schwartz, 1991). The object of the scenario-method is to stimulate different perspectives or images of the future of a certain topic, in order to develop a better view on possible future directions. *Scenarios* can be defined as archetypical images of the future that often incorporate current realities. There are many different methods of scenario development (Bouwman & Duin, 2003; Glenn, 1999; Notten, .Rotmans, Asselt, & Rothman, 2003). Creativity and the involvement of subjective opinions by (possibly biased) humans are important ingredients in all scenario-methods. René was always a master at creative and 'out-of-the box' thinking, and he was deeply involved in the discussions and listened carefully to all the provocative ideas, as shown in the figure 2.

In a scenario-building workshop at the Group Decision Room of Delft University of Technology, scenarios were developed with government representatives, consultants and academics. In the scenario-building workshop, the participants were first asked to provide input with regards to social, political, economic and technological developments, using an elec-

Figure 2. Screenshot of the road-mapping session

tronic brainstorming tool. Participants were regularly asked to read each other's ideas, to stimulate the creation of new ideas. After 15 minutes this process was stopped and the participants were asked to explain their input. In addition, at this point they were given the opportunity to ask question regarding issues that were not clear to them.

After the initial round, the participants were asked to vote with regard to the impact/uncertainty of the various developments on a 10-points scale. The underlying idea was that some developments are more likely than others to actually occur, but when they do, their impact may be much higher. Different expectations may result in contradictory and alternative futures and thus lead to different scenarios. Developments with a major impact and a low level of uncertainty result in one type of future and need to be researched independently of the scenario chosen. Developments with a low impact (independent of their level of uncertainty) do not influence the future. Based on the scenarios developed by the participants, we were able to identify two key uncertainties:

1. *Confidence in technology*. When confidence is high, it is believed that technological developments will create new opportunities to solve social problems and issues regarding government operations. There still is much potential in technological development. When confidence is low, on the other hand, it is believed that the role of technology in solving problems is limited, and that further technological development will not result in innovations with regard to e-government.

2. *World order*. As we all know, the world is continuously changing, but it is highly uncertain which developments will turn out to be real determinants. On one end, the assumption is that the world order will be relatively stable – although changes may occur, they do not lead to large shifts in power distribution, affect the access to resources or lead to internal friction within Europe, while on the other end there is a belief in a dynamic, and possibly disturbing world order.

The two resulting variables are aspects that René would typically discuss, the technological aspect and the impact on society. Technology should be used intelligently, to accomplish the desired benefits and improve society. Several years before this project, René already cast a prophetic eye on the role of civil servants in his inaugural address at Delft University of Technology;

"The question that needs to be answered is: what can be done more and differently by the intelligent use of ICT? I suggest that we take another, more radical step. We have to give the civil servant a role that goes beyond more or less passively carrying out policy from behind a virtual counter. The same virtual civil servant can take on a more active role, namely that of virtual director in an integrated web of services, in which both commercial companies and public organizations are operating. More provocatively: perhaps it makes even more sense to outsource the role of director to a private party!" (René Wagenaar, 2002)

In his inaugural speech, René addressed this vision using the scenario of the future as shown in Table 2. In his vision, the virtual civil servant directs a network of public and private parties, while an event-driven architecture connects all their interactions. The coordination that is needed is supported by a platform that seamlessly integrates the information systems of various parties involved. Our research into composition and orchestration in the various domains is aimed at realizing this vision, using coordination theory as a basis for identifying specific requirements. Moreover, we began by looking at relative simple public service networks, gradually increasing

---

Friday morning, September 2009, 8.30 AM, control room Traffic Surveillance Service, city New York

On the digital map of the city an alarm lights up on 142nd Street, generated by an on-board computer of a car involved in a crash. A video-link is established immediately between Traffic Surveillance and the on-board computers of the cars involved in the collision. While a Traffic Surveillance employee is engaged in a video-conference with the drivers, the computer reads the 'black boxes' in the on-board computers, and analyzes and processes the data. The report is then displayed on an electronic screen in the police car that is closest to the incident, which will decide on the basis of the information whether or not assistance is needed, or whether a call to a towing service will suffice. A preliminary report listing the damaged parts is transmitted electronically to the Recycling Department of the Regional Environmental Control Service.
The drivers are requested permission for their personal data to be downloaded from the on-board computers, so as to be able to send a damage report to their insurance companies. With the drivers' approval this information will also be transmitted electronically.

After the data have been processed, they will be stored anonymously by the Service.

Table 2. The future as described in the Virtual Servant (René Wagenaar, 2002)

the complexity by including private partners and investigating real-time orchestration in crisis and disaster management.

This vision would ultimately result in a service-oriented government. Not only would the technical systems be built using service-oriented architectures and government organized as a service-oriented enterprise, government would also become service-oriented and customer-centric. In this way, technology facilities the needs and wants of society, the key term being 'services'.

THE FUTURE
It is, of course, extremely difficult to predict what the future will look like. Disruptive technologies or an unexpected event like 9/11 can alter the future in ways we cannot foresee. And on a more personal level, none of us could have foreseen René's passing away. After attending a workshop about the eGovRTD2020 project on Thursday morning, he went home ill on Thursday afternoon. On Friday, he informed us that everything was fine, and on Monday morning we were told that he passed away, which we initially could not believe.
The general view is that, in 2020, society will be different from what it is today, that the current difficulties in translating new technologies into government applications will in part have been resolved and that new challenges will have emerged. If we think in terms of cooperation within communities, solving the privacy problems and staying close to citizens seems to be the vision. The various government institutions need to realize that connectivity at a semantic level with other governments, but also with private parties, is of the utmost importance, and these are areas in which they all need to take responsibility with regard to the information society in general. It is expected that breakthroughs in e-government will not occur on the basis specific applications or disruptive technologies, but primarily as a result of changes in the relationship between government and its citizens.

René was always concerned about the value and limitations of research. What are the limitations? What can and cannot be proven? Adopting a service-oriented government to improve service delivery requires the disintegration of the public sector and the creation of new organizational frameworks. Because of the need for specialization, multiple agencies will be involved, and their interactions need to be coordinated. Coordination by a virtual civil service requires an event-driven architecture that integrates the efforts of public and private organizations, and needs to be based on a professional concern for the well-being of for the country's citizens and businesses. In order for SOG to happen, effective composition methods and orchestration are needed. The question remains whether SOG will be really service-driven and improve customer orientation. SOG is about creating an open and flexible architecture that can be reconfigured to meet customer expectations. Although it can be used to improve create a more customer-oriented government, that is by no means a foregone conclusion.

REFERENCES

Baldwin, C., & Clark, K. B. (2000). *Design Rules, Volume 1, The Power of Modularity.* Cambridge, MA: MIT Press.

Bicking, M., Janssen, M., & Wimmer, M. A. (2006). *Looking into the future: Scenarios for e-government in 2020.* Paper presented at the Sixth IFIP conference on e-Commerce, e-Business, and e-Government (I3E 2006), Turku, Finland.

Binder, M., & Clegg, B. (2006). Enterprise management: A new frontier for organisations. *International Journla of Production and Economics, 106*(2), 409-430

Bouwman, W. A. G. A., & Duin, P. A. v. d. (2003). Technological forecasting and scenarios matter: research into the use of information and communication technology in the home environment in 2010. *Foresight, 5*(4), 8-20.

Cherbakov, L., Galambos, G., Harishankar, R., Kalyana, S., & Rackman, G. (2005). Impact of service orientation at the business level. *IBM Systems Journal, 44*(4), 653-668.

Curbera, F. (2002). Unraveling the web services web: An introduction to SAP, WSDL, UDDI. *IEEE Internet Computing, 6*(2), 86-93.

Fremantle, P., Weerawarana, S., & Khalaf, R. (2002). Enterprise services. Examine the emerging les of web services and how it is integrated into existing enterprise infrastructures. *Communications of the ACM, 45*(20), 77-82.

Glenn, J. (1999). *Futures research methodology.* Washington: American Council for the United Nations University [on CD Rom: version 1.0].

Janssen, M., Gortmaker, J., & Wagenaar, R. W. (2006). Web service orchestration in public administration: Challenges, roles and growth stages. *Information Systems Management, 23*(2), 44-55.

Jeffery, M., & Leliveld, I. (2004). Best Practices in IT Portfolio Management. *MIT Sloan Management Review, 45*(3), 41-49.

Lim, B., & Wen, H. J. (2003). Web Services: An analysis of the technology, its benets and implementation difculties. *Information Systems Management, 20*(2), 49-57.

Malone, T. W., & Crowston, K. (1994). The interdisciplinary study of coordination. *ACM Computing Surveys, 26*(2), 87-119.

Milward, H. B., & Provan, K. G. (2000). Governing the hollow state. *Journal of Public Administration Research and Theory, 10*(2), 359-380.

Milward, H. B., & Provan, K. G. (2003). *Managing Networks Effectively.* Paper presented at the the 7th National Public Management Research Conference, Georgetown University.

Notten, P. W. F. v., .Rotmans, J., Asselt, M. B. A. v., & Rothman, D. S. (2003). An updated scenario typology. *Futures, 35*(5), 423-443.

Provan, K. G., & Milward, H. B. (2001). Do networks really work? A framework for evaluating public-sector organizational networks. *Public Administration Review, 61*(4), 414-424.

Schwartz, P. (1991). *The art of the long view.* Chichester: John Wiley & Sons.

Versteeg, G., & Bouwman, H. (2006). Business architecture: A new paradigm to relate business strategy to ICT *Information Systems Frontiers, 8*(2), 91-102.

Wagenaar, R., & Janssen, M. (2002). *Visualization of the Implications of a Component based ICT Architecture for Service Provisioning* Paper presented at the Proceedings of the 1st International Conference on Electronic Government, Dexa EGOV 2002, Aix-en-Provence, France, September 2-5, 2002.

Wagenaar, R. W. (2002). *The virtual civil servant: towards more transparancey in the public service?* . Delft: Inaugurall address, Delft University of Technology.

Zhao, J. L., & Cheng, H. K. (2005). Web services and process management: a union of convenience or a new area of research? *Decision Support Systems, 40*(1), 1-8.

es behelfsqualer / ...
Spurwegen

Ad-hoc nehmen (...
(hierarchie v. deren
             context aft an ...

Emergency Repair

Simulative - gaming

dennis gebruike
         ↓

PART 3

SOCIO-TECHNICAL DESIGN

THE MOST IMPORTANT RESULTS
ARE A DESCRIPTION OF A NUMBER
OF COMMON INTEGRATED
FUNCTIONS, MAKING IT POSSIBLE TO
ESTABLISH LINKS AT THE LEVEL OF
ELECTRONIC DATA EXCHANGE AND
AN UNAMBIGUOUS INTERPRETATION
USING XML DIAGRAMS

From *Virtual Servant*

Are Technology and Service Management compatible?
An imaginary dialogue with René Wagenaar.

Patrick Dewilde

Abstract
There is already more than enough technology, the problem is to put it to use for the benefit of mankind and the profit of service companies – that is the common wisdom in present day management circles. Technology is not able to contribute in substance to its own effective utilization, management science and technology must be totally divorced from each other if services are to become effective.

Would René Wagenaar have subscribed to this thesis? Judging from his actions the answer is a pertinent 'no'. René was closely connected to the ICT Delft Research Centre, he was a member of its management team and coordinating the activities of the Faculty of Technology, Policy and Management within the Centre. René fully subscribed to the general goals and strategy of the Centre, he and his staff participated in many multidisciplinary programs of the Centre and he contributed substantially to its set up. In René's view, technology and service science were complementary, each could strengthen the other. Bringing them together, improve the design and governance, rather than setting them apart would bring both to a higher level of performance. In his spirit, I want to develop this idea further, unfortunately without the help of René.

Rather than staying on a lofty theoretical level, let me illustrate the point by elaborating on two cases a little further: the emergence of 4G in telecommunication and the use of ICT for security and safety services. The fourth generation of telecommunications (4G) has been termed 'always seamlessly connected wherever you are at the best possible rate (connected anywhere, any time, anyhow)'. You get a feeling for it with what sometimes happens thanks to WiFi, one of the key technologies that could be termed 'pre-4G': when you walk in a hotel, you open your laptop (or your IPhone, no publicity intended here) and you are instantly on line – yes there are already quite a few enlightened hotels, Institutes, Universities and even cities, especially in the USA, where that is the case (unfortunately not our own overly centralized TU, even though some groups installed a system surreptitiously). But real 4G goes of course much further, it means effortless connection wherever you are, on the train, in your room, on the street, in your car, in your bathroom, wherever, whenever, together with seamless handover, few expenses and no effort to establish a connection. Needless to say that seems like a horror to service providers, it smacks of anarchy, no control on the customer's behavior, no milk cow for the company.

Not a horror for René, on the contrary. It took him no minute to see the potential for service provision in 4G environments, and to contribute a wealth of new ideas. Rather than being an anonymous agency asking money for clumsy services larded with unasked publicity, a good service provider would anticipate the customer's need, be present as a preferred partner when solicited and offer integrated solutions that take the customer's environment in consideration. In short, René would plead for new business models that understand the new technology and use it to profit. Needless to say, this way of thinking is so far ahead of normal business thinking, focused as it is on processes using proven technology, seemingly sturdy investments in frequency property and getting quick profits with as little new engineering as possible.

René would even go a step further. New services utilizing new technology would require even better technology which in turn would engender new services etc… Siamese twins, or better, the three visages of Vishnu: from expectation to serenity to anger, happily incorporating past experience, catering diligently for the present and working up to conquer the future with a vengeance. The good business architectures are those that can integrate technology to a new level of service quality and organization. The opportunities are there. René was fully conscious of them and working hard at incorporating them in his research program. In fact, when he joined our main 4G directed research program he uncovered a whole realm of new possibilities for business models and technological opportunities and was able to contribute directly to its effectiveness, inter-operability and orchestration. Taking all the recent mobile and internet technology in stride and working hard at developing new system science, or even better system design technology to take care of the new dynamic opportunities.

Another equally important case in point was the topic of safety and security. We are talking in this case about security provision by agencies such as police, firemen, port authorities or even safety management by local teams. Here the main idea was to explore the impact of our new insights in distributed intelligent agent technology and distributed computing for the security situation. The examples of poor functioning of standard telecommunications in emergency situations abound. In the 9/11 disaster, the firemen were ordered to go into the Trade Centre, exposing themselves to danger and blocking outgoing traffic. When the fireworks factory exploded in Enschede most if not all communication was blocked, and there also the security services went into wrong movements. The far away command post gauges the situation in a very different way than the local service workers. Because of communication congestion the situation awareness of the different players is often out of sync in the midst of the crisis, commands do not get through and the workers on the spot are left to their own devices. The two crisis cases just mentioned may seem extreme, but it is safe to say that the impact of the new paradigms in artificial intelligence and telecommunications on 'ubiquitous safety' has hardly been fully exploited. It must be possible to have the system provide much more pertinent information to all parties (the command centers, the leadership and the crisis workers), especially since all of them can be equipped with much more responsive mobile and ad hoc equipment that are functioning even when all normal systems are out.

All this cries for the development of much improved intelligence support. There is maybe no better field in which university research can have a large impact, because the issues are intellectually very challenging, the applications very direct and the field largely unexplored and untested. As member of the ICT Delft Research Centre Management Team, René took on himself the task of coordinating the 'Safety and Security' theme of the Centre. He propagated the insight that in security issues management and technology have to go hand in hand and all the major issues would involve close interaction between the two. Many 'old cows' have to be disposed of and fresh approaches initiated due to the unconventional nature both of the problem area and the technological possibilities. Remarkably enough, René had to discover that the establishment both at the university and the ministries were much more conservative than the service organizations such as the police corpses themselves, except maybe for the higher echelons. This may seem surprising, but it is due to the fact that in real crisis situations the command post is poorly accessible and the local crisis worker has to make decisions on his own more often than not out of pure necessity, so he/she wants to dispose of the best possible information.

This issue became one of the main challenges for René – as well as for ICT DRC – and we are missing René's engaging approach and optimism in adverse circumstances very much! Crisis management is a good issue for crisis management in Delft: breaking down well established prejudices on the value of technology on one side and the lack of appreciation for management problems on the other. Substantial progress had already been made by the creation of DECIS, a laboratory on distributed intelligence, by Thales, TU Delft, the University of Amsterdam and TNO, with security and safety as one of its vanguards. The plan was to consolidate efforts around DECIS, but that proved to be too much of a lofty goal, the centrifugal largely outnumbering the centripetal forces. The various security groups at TU Delft and beyond all have their own agendas, connections, idiosyncrasies and ideology. It turned out really hard to make some borscht out of such diversity! But failing the coordination, one is missing out on the opportunities. The art is to create a common substrate on which many initiatives may thrive. That is also what the best of our intelligence environments have achieved, a systemic approach that allows for freedom and diversity yet provides for transparent methods and bootstraps to the future. That is also how the internet was created, UNIX, TCP/IP, the web, WLAN and WiFi, in short all the things that made the brave modern world of global information exchange, distributed computing and open communication possible.

René clearly understood that that was also the way to go for new intelligent services and especially for security and safety. However, the challenges are enormous, but so are the potential rewards. An analysis shows that the key problem is with the formalization of intelligence. If human beings are largely superior to computers, it is especially in their ability to interpret and gauge a situation given adequate information. Modern computers at the other side are much better at, yes, computing, but also at information storage, communication, speed and interaction with equipment. A close interplay between humans and computers could provide for exactly the right mix of abilities that makes the distributed computing environment an extension of the human abilities to recognize and interpret, while providing key information to draw from and extending human's abilities to assemble it and share it with his/her peers, especially in critical situations. Impossible? René did not think so, and his views are shared by many of us who have made this theme our central challenge in the ICT Delft Research Centre to which René was so dedicated.

It is the task of University research to explore new avenues and think possibilities through, even to provide for the experimental grounds for further exploration. We form an institution that links past knowledge to the future, and develops new insights doing so. As a University of Technology, we are not only busy with understanding the 'what' of nature, but also, and most prominently, the 'how' to use nature to achieve a goal. The 'how' is not only technical, management and organizational issues play an equally important role. My personal thesis, and I am not sure René would have shared that point with me, is that the provision of sound methods of management is just as much a technological issue as is any use of nature or instruments. Intelligence translates into data and processes, human reasoning in neurons that fire and resonate on the warped surface of the cortex. Understanding how to design more effective systems using the potential of modern computers and communication is the key of our intelligence oriented research. 'Intelligence' is a theme for research that is just as central as 'energy' or 'health' or whatever other fashionable subject. Technology being the science of technical know-how and the latter being the skill or art used for a particular task, I believe that managing intelligence may indeed be the biggest intellectual challenge a technological university is facing.

René may or may not have agreed on the statements in the last paragraph, but I do know that he fully agreed on the thesis that our university research should focus on the discovery of new avenues, on developing management theory that incorporates and places modern technological developments and on creating environments in which free exploration of novel ideas is encouraged. We are not there to solve world's problem – that is a task for politicians – but to develop new insights and new knowledge. He was convinced that this could only be done in close cooperation with all the parties that can contribute, involving all relevant subjects, even the lowly technological ones, being creative in all of them and making sure that 'everything works together'.

René had the character of the 'universal man' of the Renaissance, and in being so he contributed substantially to the university ideal of our institution. We shall continue our system design and security research in line with his thoughts, ideas and our shared discussions and goals.

INSTITUTIONAL FACTORS REFER TO THE SYSTEM OF VERIFIABLE AND LEGALLY ENFORCEABLE AGREEMENTS AND GUARANTEES THAT ALLOW PARTIES TO SAFEGUARD THEMSELVES FROM RISKS IN CASE OF FRAUD, AS WELL AS COLLECTIVE APPLICATIONS THAT HELP REALIZE AS BROAD A PARTICIPATION AS POSSIBLE OF BOTH PRIVATE PERSONS AND BUSINESSES.

From Virtual Merchant

Exploring the public value of broadband

John Groenewegen and Rolf Künneke

ABSTRACT
René considered the Economics of Infrastructures an import complementary field of expertise to his research domain of ICT. Both authors had very stimulating discussions with him, especially about the possible pros and cons of the development of a ubiquitous broadband infrastructure in The Netherlands. This resulted in a joint project labeled 'Public value of Broadband' that is funded by the Next Generation Infrastructures Foundation. This chapter provides an outline of this project and an overview of different economic perspectives to public values. It appears that determining the public values of broadband is an issue of policy design rather than calculating costs and benefits.

INTRODUCTION
René was very much interested in the potential benefits of a ubiquitous broadband infrastructure to society. Some four years ago, the major Dutch telecom provider KPN launched a proposal to build a ubiquitous broadband infrastructure in The Netherlands. This would be a major investment that this company was not able to bear by its own. Obviously, KPN and other IC&T related firms would benefit by improved business opportunities and hence could expand their services to the customers. More bandwidth would for instance create better technical opportunities for content like pay tv, video on demand, and a broad variety of domotica applications [1]. However, rolling out broadband to all households in The Netherlands would be a major investment that is far beyond the financial possibilities of KPN.

Hence, governmental involvement was warranted, not only for direct financial reasons, but also because of the assumed significant social benefits of this project. There seemed to be a general public value in the development of a broadband infrastructure. Examples include the following. One element would be the wish to overcome the digital divide: in society all citizens should have equal access to information in order to have the same full opportunity to participate in the democratic process. Many local initiatives to build fiber optic networks and to promote city wide Wi-Fi are based on the objective to close the digital divide. A second element would be to facilitate socially desirable behavior of citizens. They will easier use online services of the municipality in the domain of health care (on-line access to medical services), education (on-line access to courses and education programs) and employment (visiting job search sites). A third element points to the macro level of a region or nation: the competitive advantage in a knowledge-based society is enhanced through the wide availability of broadband services

These social benefits are very complex, often indirect and difficult to quantify. Therefore René proposed a research program on the social benefits of broadband. Since this research project is not finalized yet, this chapter provides some background information about the economic perspective on public values related to the broadband infrastructure.

The chapter is structured as follows. First we provide an outline of the project (section 2). Section 3 elaborates the economic perspective on the notion of public value for the case of broadband. In section 4 some preliminary conclusions are drawn with respect to the question how to evaluate the public value of broadband from a government perspective.

Outline of the research program

The development of a high quality and ubiquitous broadband infrastructure is often perceived as a necessary precondition to develop a national leadership position in a networked, knowledge-based economy. This statement appeals to the intuition of many ICT users, politicians and the business community and is often accepted as common sense. However, apart from some theories and visionary exposé's on the general importance of broadband, there is a lack of research, in particular empirical, that evaluates and quantifies the social and economic added value of government supporting a broadband infrastructure. In 2004 a discussion had developed in The Netherlands on the desirability and necessity to support the development of a national glass fiber network that enables ubiquitous broadband access [2]. The investments are immense and a significant risk is taken, as a consequence stakeholders demand a national initiative with public and private involvement. The question, however, is whether such public participation can be legitimated. This question is dealt with from an economic perspective in section 3 below.

There are multiple options for realizing ubiquitous broadband, which differ with respect to the type of change pursued: discontinuous or incremental. The case of 'Delta Plan Glas' argues for discontinuous change by implementing an 'all fiber' based infrastructure, a leap forward with the aim of removing bandwidth as the constraining factor in the development of an information based, knowledge economy. The alternative is an incremental approach, continuously to extend the bandwidth limits of the existing, pluriform set of infrastructures. The feasibility and desirability of these options, or a mix thereof, are directly related to the prevailing market policies and the policy objective of establishing The Netherlands into a leading position in the information society [3,4].

Broadband and public value: an economic perspective

In the discussions with René we elaborated different economic perspectives on public value. The dominating one arises from neoclassical economics and in a sense minimizes the role of government in initiating and stimulating investments. That mainstream economic approach differs from the so-called institutional approach, in which public values and a pro-active role of government stand out. René showed a great interest in institutional economics, which seemed to be closer to the reality as he perceived it. In this paragraph first the neoclassical approach is discussed as a kind of benchmark for positioning government in infrastructures like broadband, and then institutional economics is discussed. Finally we will be able to identify two different paths of institutional change that could accommodate the development of a ubiquitous broadband infrastructure.

Neoclassical economics

Mainstream neoclassical economists start their analysis with an ideal market in which private actors exchange goods and services [5]. Assuming a set of preconditions, private benefits and costs are equal to the social benefits and costs. Under these circumstances all values are of an individual nature. Accordingly no public value exists in the sense that government should intervene. However, markets hardly ever function in that ideal way. Classical cases of market failure, involving natural monopolies, public goods and externalities, justify government intervention. Moreover, government is responsible for maintaining the rules of competition to eliminate market imperfections; that is to say, to eliminate distortions based on abuse of market power and collusion among suppliers. The assumption of potentially efficient markets and, consequently, a role for government to intervene only in cases of market failures and market imperfections, is known as the neoclassical approach. This approach has some serious limitations due to characteristics of infrastructures in general.

First, there is the issue of how to accomplish the construction of the physical infrastructure network. For broadband this means high capital investments and sunk costs into the new to build glass fiber networks, or alternatively the upgrading of existing telephone and cable networks. Under the conditions of the traditional neoclassical model, the basic question here is how to attract private investors? Their reaction is related to the is-

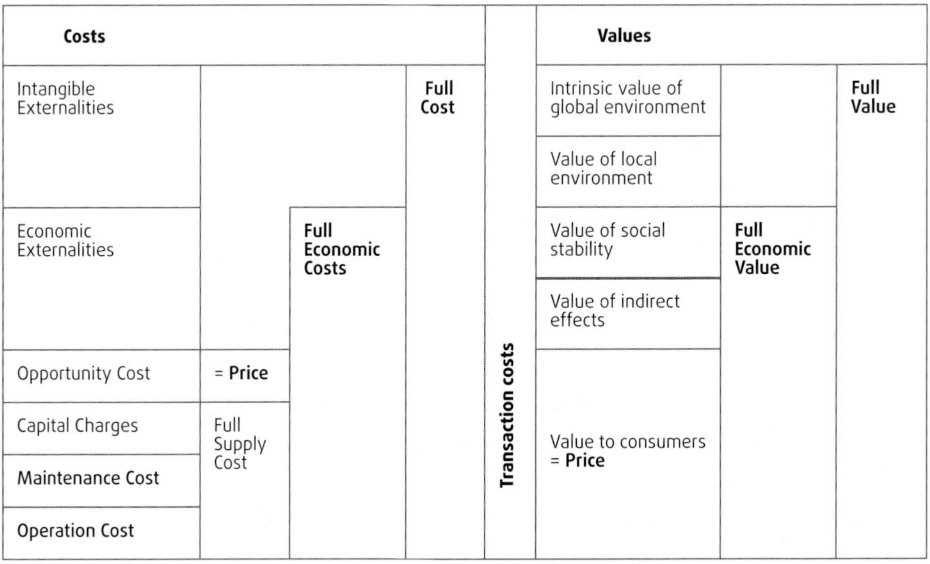

Costs				Values		
Intangible Externalities		Full Cost		Intrinsic value of global environment		Full Value
				Value of local environment		
Economic Externalities	Full Economic Costs			Value of social stability	Full Economic Value	
				Value of indirect effects		
Opportunity Cost	= Price		Transaction costs			
Capital Charges	Full Supply Cost			Value to consumers = Price		
Maintenance Cost						
Operation Cost						

Figure 1. Components of costs and values (adapted from Rogers, Bhatia, & Huber, 1998)

sue of the provision of services to the customers, and how to generate attractive profits.
Second, in the case of a ubiquitous broadband infrastructure services are offered by competing suppliers that make use of the same network. Under these conditions the regulation of access, price and quality, as well as the issue of unbundling vertically integrated firms arises.
Thirdly there are questions concerning the consumption of the services provided over the network. Is there a matter of public value involved in the sense that some services should be provided to all customers at a specific price (universal service)?

Having outlined the specific characteristics of infrastructures the question arises how markets in those infrastructures can cope with the efficient allocation of resources taking the 'real' cost and benefits into account. In other words: introducing markets into infrastructures, like broadband, poses the question which costs and benefits (or more in general: values) are registered by the price mechanism of the market, and which are external.

The framework of figure 1 distinguishes different components that constitute the costs (left) and the value (right) of a broadband infrastructure. The most left column of figure 1 specifies different cost components. Traditional mainstream economics defines the market equilibrium price as being equal to the opportunity costs. Under these conditions the direct costs are covered [6] plus an acceptable remuneration for the producers [7]. These opportunity costs equal the value, or utility, to the buyers as the users of the infrastructure. Hence, consumers are prepared to pay this price. Together, these components determine the price at which a producer would be willing to produce the broadband infrastructure and to supply it to other users for a market price. On the side of the individual user, it is shown that he is willing to pay a price equal to the value he attaches to the use of the infrastructure. Expectations about market prices drive decisions on investments in production and supply facilities and in consumers' appliances. Eventually, as is argued, the transaction(s) take place at the resulting equilibrium price, satisfying both producers and consumers. Principally, a neoclassical economist would argue that the state should secure a well functioning broadband market, solving occasional market failures and imperfections, like abuses of market power, via competition law.

Next to opportunity costs, economic externalities and intangible externalities have to be considered. Economic externalities are not included in the market price agreed upon by seller and buyer. Per definition, these values are 'external' to the price mechanism. However, these external effects have direct economic consequences for third parties that are not directly involved in the market transaction. Hence, their costs and benefits are influenced. A cost-benefit analysis would reveal and quantify these economic externalities to a certain extent in an objective way. Possible direct negative externalities of a ubiquitous broadband network would be the loss of economic value of the existing traditional telecom and central antenna networks. 'Intangible' externalities involve the individual and social costs that are not made explicit yet. These effects exist but are not subject to an economic cost-benefit analysis. The point is that in case of intangible externalities the economic decision makers simply have not incorporated the effects into their mind sets. These effects would first have to be made explicit and then an awaReness of their existence has to be created so they can become part of the decision making process.

— The right panel of Figure 1 shows the value to society of using broadband. Some of the total value is enjoyed directly by the consumers, in terms of useful services. Nevertheless, there are important indirect welfare effects associated with the use of broadband in enhancing the overall level of economic development and wellbeing in a society.

— Within the neoclassical context externalities are internalized by taxing or subsidizing the production or consumption of certain goods or services. For instance, investments in broadband networks might be subsidized if there are additional values to society. This assumes that a precise value can be calculated and imposed on production costs to arrive at the 'real' price. Typically neoclassical economics is mainly concerned with costs and benefits that can be quantified in one way or another.

The neoclassical approach is complemented by the so-called new institutional approach [8], which focuses on the question how transactions between individual actors can be best coordinated. Central is the idea that in case of externalities private actors will negotiate and conclude contracts that internalize the externalities. In the next paragraph we first discuss the new institutional economics (NIE) and proceed with another approach in institutional economics (Original Institutional Economics, OIE) which pays different attention to the question of the public value issue in markets like the one of broadband.

Institutional Economics
New institutional economics
Neoclassical economics assumes that markets function perfectly, i.e. the signaling function of prices is not disturbed and no transaction costs exist to coordinate the transactions. In the world of new institutional economics (NIE), however, actors are bounded in their rationality and can behave opportunistically. In coordinating transactions, moreover, actors have to protect themselves against potential opportunistic behavior of their business partners by making safeguards in contracts or by creating organizations that monitor and sanction. Investments and commercial deals are complicated by the presence of several categories of transaction costs. These are dependent on the attributes of individual transactions between buyers and sellers/investors in a specific market. Transactions costs include the direct costs of information gathering, the writing, monitoring and enforcing of contracts, plus the costs associated with the risk of ex ante investments having an ex post performance that is lower than anticipated. Then safeguards are installed to mitigate the consequences of contractual hazards of various types and of the costs associated with internal organization of the transactions. This has serious consequences for the extent to which transactions involving investments in broadband networks may materialize.

The institutional arrangements are private modes of governance. Like in NCE individual actors driven by utility or profit maximization create efficient modes of governance in negotiation with other actors. They exchange property rights through contracting as long as they can improve their position.

Private modes of governance will be efficient only when a government has established the right 'institutions of laws and regulations' (formal institutions). When the rules of the game are transparent, non-discriminatory and stable, the actors will have so-called 'institutional trust' in the enforcement mechanisms by public courts. At the same time government will have to apply the competition and corporation law so markets function efficiently. Also the reputation of negotiators becomes important for suppliers in this perspective. In many situations the internalization of externalities can be left to the private actors. Government only comes in when the externalities are of a highly complex nature. When a large number of actors is involved and when sources of externalities are diffuse, or when information is distributed rather asymmetric, the transaction costs of private internalization can become prohibitive. The costs of complex negotiations and monitoring rise significantly. Generally, when transactions or effects are complex, when contracts are incomplete because of lack of sufficient insight, and when the danger of opportunism cannot be eliminated at acceptable transaction costs, economists would identify a public value that warrants government intervention. The relevant questions than would be: What are these externalities? Who bears the costs and who profits from the benefits? Why are these costs and benefits not internalized? And, what can government do to internalize those externalities and at what costs? Note that the NIE perspective also implies that government should only produce the public value when social benefits exceed social costs. This is assumed to work well when information about costs and benefits is adequately transferred through prices.

In NIE also the public ordering of regulation and state owned enterprise is addressed: asset specificity and uncertainty can be such that the transaction costs for the private actors are too high to coordinate the transaction via hybrids or vertically integrated firms. In that case public ordering is warranted and differentiation between the type of public ordering should be made on the basis of transaction costs. It remains an economic exercise based on explicit well calculated costs and benefits. However, the third component in figure 1 raises an issue of determining the costs and benefits that demands a broader perspective, in which issues of public value are analyzed in relation to the responsibilities of the different actors, the risks, costs and benefits. Moreover, the issue of public value is then broader than the 'internalization of complex externalities' and concerns the societal valuation of issues that are not explicit and objective yet.

Original Institutional Economics
In the following we discuss the second approach in institutional economics that provides insights and concepts for such a broader analysis of questions like the public value of broadband. In the literature, different labels

are used such as the institutional, evolutionary perspective, or the Original Institutional Economics (OIE)[9]. The alternative approach starts out with heterogeneous actors, with preferences that are influenced by formal and informal institutions. It is argued that public values reflect preferences of groups in society about what constitutes the notion of welfare, in a given society and at a given time. Hence, social welfare is not considered to be a simple neutral aggregation of the outcome of all individual maximizing decisions, but a phenomenon that is identified, articulated, developed and operationalised in a socio-political process, within a specific society. Public values therefore differ through time and location. They do not result from a neutral selection mechanism in markets, but are the product of selection processes in highly politicized and institutionalized markets. OIE conceptualizes individuals, markets, institutions and public values differently than NCE and NIE. Commons[10] assumed human beings to be inherently self-interested, aiming to fulfill three 'fundamental wishes', namely equality, liberty and security. The first refers to the wish to be treated equally under similar circumstances, the second to the wish to be free of arbitrary decisions of superiors and the wish of security refers to the expectation that future disputes will be decided upon as was the case in the past. If these fundamental wishes are not fulfilled, individuals will invest in changing the 'rules of the game'

The actions of individuals are guided by the institutions: the so-called 'working rules' and customs. Institutions do not pre-determine individuals' actions, but 'frame' them in such a way that some room to maneuver is left. Within that space, individuals will try to influence other actors and take opportunities to change the rules according their own benefits. Individuals can impose their will upon others by means of persuasion (based on personality), coercion (economic power to withhold) and duress (the physical power of violence). The maximizing 'rational man' as we know him from mainstream economics is replaced by an 'institutionalized man' with satisfying behavior[11].

Only in very exceptional cases individuals are powerful enough to change the rules. Normally, individuals have to join forces, mobilize resources and organize pressure. Such collective action can lead to broader participation of more classes of people in adjusting the rules, thus constraining the actions of other groups in society. Institutions as 'collective action in control of individual action' are not 'neutrally efficient', nor are they always the reflection of the majority of a society.

OIE considers the embeddedness of individual actors as central to understand why they behave in a specific way. Actors have a cognitive structure, with which they perceive the reality of the world around them. Generally, this structure, which is shaped over time by their environment and experiences, will be shared by others. The concepts of embeddedness, mental maps and belief systems are important to understand path dependencies in the process of change. Obviously, also technological path dependencies, included in trajectories and regimes, influence the process of change.

Institutions allocate resources, benefits and burdens in the process of producing wealth. In mainstream economics, actors are supposed to select the most efficient scale of production, or the most efficient mode of governance from any given set of alternatives. The evolutionary perspective shows that these choices are 'pre-selected' within the actors' shared mental models, shaped over time by their environment and the social structures they join, in order to survive in a physical and social sense. Every group within which individuals interact and coordinate their actions towards common future ends is characterized by specific going concerns; a theoretical concept used by Commons to identify organizations at different levels. Going concerns can be located at different layers of an economic system: firms, regions, sectors, nation states and in international organizations at the supra-national level.

The approach of Original Institutional Economics addresses issues of public value from a much broader perspective, involving the shape of shared mental maps, experiences of learning, and the distribution of power via institutions. OIE is concerned with the way in which the infrastructure of broadband is framed as public value in the belief systems of individuals and groups. OIE also examines how these belief systems may collectively evolve towards societal and political pressures and how these pressures may drive political decision making and public and private strategy development. The OIE approach would focus on possible shifts in public values in relation to information provision in modern society.

TWO DIFFERENT PATHS OF INSTITUTIONAL CHANGE

Based on OIE, two main paths of institutional change seem to be relevant for the analysis of public values in broadband. The first path deals with the way in which uncertainty and risk perceptions in respect of future investments in broadband could be ascertained. This essentially involves the question which parties bear which risk at what costs and profits. Connecting responsibilities in investing in elements of the value chain with risk management involves the following steps: First, the main areas of responsibility and the particular uncertainties and risks associated should be identified; second, the responsibilities and associated risks should be assigned to the party best able to manage it; third, the right arrangement should be established to achieve this allocation of risks and responsibilities. It is obvious that there exists a wide variety of governance solutions. Bearing risk has a cost and the party bearing the risk will likely demand an adequate return. But allocating risk to a party, generally, gives the party an incentive to alter his behavior to minimize costs. Risk allocation therefore affects the parties' incentives to improve efficiency. Some parties are able to predict changes in relevant risk factors or can control the sensitivity of their business to the risk factor. Of course, some risks can not be controlled or anticipated and should be allocated to the party best able to diversify or absorb it.

A second path for institutional change deals with the representation of the cost-benefit calculation. This relates to the third component in figure 1, which was not addressed so far. Investments in broadband probably yield a much higher value to society as a whole than to the individual investors and users, representing a clear example of a positive externality and a public value. Yet, this income has not been made visible in the form of a cash flow, by the direct investors or by the consumers, so real incentives are lacking. Many positive and negative effects are external to today's markets and they will remain so, unless they are explicitly recognized as public values of importance and deliberately internalized and institutionalized in future market-systems. This obviously requires the incorporation of public values through a considerable public intervention. Government should translate these benefits into stimuli, constraints and prices, so that individual actors will begin to see these benefits as a reality. This is less far away from reality than it seems. Indeed, there are multiple examples of direct and indirect economic, environmental and social effects that were once fully external to market transactions, but that have been internalized as 'public values' into in today's economies. Labour relations, education and social security, as well as external safety rules, all constitute a rich case of public values in point. Of course, the extent and the particular manner of incorporation in 'the market' vary by country and culture. The nature of these differences and the consequences thereof are essentially an empirical issue in the context of OIE. There is no single or universal way in which 'the market' will reflect these public values.

SOME CONCLUSIONS

What are the public values of broadband? This question is extremely difficult to answer, as demonstrated in this chapter. There are different economic approaches to cope with this problem. Each of them addresses different categories of costs and benefits that would have to be operationalized and measured. Even costs and benefits that are not known yet should be taken into consideration. But what are these 'unknown unknowns'? How could we get some more understanding of the possible advantages of broadband, when we even cannot imagine them? Even if we would succeed to do this in one way or another, we could expect that different economic approaches result in different outcomes of the cost benefit analysis. In one case there might be a large social benefit, whereas other approaches would signal a negative result. Of course, we could always assume unknown future benefits that could legitimate investments in broadband infrastructures. But obviously this is of little help to derive at substantive and defendable policy decisions.

Determining the public value of broadband is simply a question of identifying and quantifying certain costs and benefits. Government has an important role to influence potential public benefits and to provide a suitable framework to realize them. Partly the public values will emerge through market processes. Consumers will favor certain services and be willing to pay a price that is higher than the opportunity costs of production. Besides, there might be some measurable external effects like higher productivity, and more employment that would add to economic welfare. Traditional cost benefit analyses often focus on these kinds of effects. However, our analysis stresses that public values for long-term investments like broadband, would be far beyond this limited approach. These public values are typically intangible and need to be fostered by government policy. Taking this perspective, the public values of broadband need to evolve by designing appropriate institutional arrangements. Hence determining the public values of broadband is an issue of policy design rather than calculating costs and benefits.

René initiated a very stimulating research project with a very complex socio-technical problem in which multiple actors are involved. It is one of the core issues in many infrastructure sectors. The possible rolling out of broadband is a fascinating example. We are looking forward to continue our work on this topic.

[1] Domotica refers to all electronic equipment in private homes that is used to monitor, program and/ or control residential services, including climate, security, light, telecommunication and information.
[2] An initiative by KPN, the incumbent operator, known as 'Delta Plan Glas'.
[3] The current market policy aims at competition between infrastructures.
[4] Objective of the Dutch government formulated by the Ministry of Economic Affairs, congruent with the objectives of the EU Action Plan eEurope 2005.
[5] (Douma & Schreuder, 2002)
[6] Direct costs include capital charges, maintenance costs, and operation costs.
[7] These would be the revenues that could have been reaped for instance if the capital had been put on a bank account, or invested otherwise
[8] (Oliver E. Williamson, 1998), (Oliver E.Williamson, 2000)
[9] (Rutherford, 1994)
[10] (Commons, 1934)
[11] The concept of satisfying behavior in economics is opposite to the concept of maximizing behavior and originates form (Simon, 1956)

References

Commons, J. R. (1934). *Institutional Economics: Its Place in Political Economy*. New York: MacMillan.
Douma, S., & Schreuder, H. (2002). *Economic Approaches to Organization* (3rd ed.): Prentice Hall.
Rogers, P., Bhatia, R., & Huber, A. (1998). *Water as a Social and Economic Good: How to Put the Principle into Practice*. Stockholm: Global Water Partnership.
Rutherford, M. (1994). *Institutions in Economics*. Cambridge: Cambridge University Press.
Simon, H. (1956). Rational Choice and the Structure of the Environment. *Psychological Review*, 63(2), 129-138.
Williamson, O. E. (1998). Transaction Cost Economics: How It Works, Where It Is Headed. *De Economist*, 146(1), 23-58.
Williamson, O. E. (2000). The New Institutional Economics: Taking Stock, Looking Ahead. *Journal of Economic Literature*, 38, 595-613.

IN MY VIEW, RELIABILITY, I.E.
THE UNRESTRICTED ELECTRONIC
TRANSFER AND GUARANTEED
DELIVERY OF MESSAGES TO THE
ADDRESSEE, IS CURRENTLY THE
INTERNET'S ACHILLES' HEEL.

From *Virtual Merchant*

Agent-based models for crisis management

Zofia Lukszo, Koen H. van Dam, Margot P.C. Weijnen, Gerard P.J. Dijkema

ABSTRACT
The agent-based modeling paradigm offers a flexible bottom-up modeling approach that can be used for a large range of applications. We illustrate the added value of the agent-based modeling paradigm over traditional numerical models by presenting two such applications – intermodal freight transport and an oil refinery supply chain. Subsequently, we discuss its merits for crisis management, more specifically for supporting decision-makers in dealing with situations of natural disasters and man-made crises. Agent-based models present a promising new modeling approach to support decision-makers in safeguarding critical infrastructure operation and protection in normal as well as crisis situations. It was René Wagenaar who brought the subject of crisis management to the Next Generation Infrastructures research agenda, and the discussion presented in this paper is largely inspired by the meetings we had with René to set up a joint research project on Information and Communication Technologies (ICT) enabled decision support for crisis management in critical infrastructures.

INTRODUCTION
Our society and economy have come to rely on services that depend on networked infrastructures. Through the interconnection and geographical expansion of local, regional and national networks during the past centuries and decades, continental and even global networks for energy, transport, telecommunication and information services have emerged, and new generations of global telecommunication and information infrastructure continue to emerge. Disruptive events such as terrorist attacks, computer virus epidemics and large-scale blackouts have, however, contributed to a renewed awareness of the critical role of infrastructures in our economies. A growing sense of vulnerability is prompting us to review the mechanisms through which we have hitherto ensured the reliability of infrastructures. The need safeguard critical infrastructure operations has created a demand

for novel modeling methods to analyze the behavior of critical infrastructures in normal and abnormal situations and identify measures for the adequate protection of critical infrastructure systems.

An infrastructure can be seen as a large integrated socio-technical system that is built from objects (sub-systems) linked together in a coherent system structure (Verwater-Lukszo and Bouwmans, 2005). The multitude and variety of nodes and links in these networks, as well as the multitude and variety of owners, operators, suppliers and users involved, have created an enormously complex system, the complexity of which is only growing with the recent developments of, for instance, market reform, vertical unbundling and privatization. The enhanced complexity of infrastructure systems controlled by distributed decision-makers is a serious barrier to diagnosing the causes of inadequate or inefficient infrastructure operation. Malfunctioning, outages and congestion imply substantial societal costs, hamper economic productivity and pose safety and security risks. More intelligent control of the existing infrastructure capacity is apparently needed to ensure the efficient and reliable operation of critical infrastructures. A solid foundation for such a control can be found in a systems engineering approach (Lukszo et al, 2006).

There is a serious need for models that can help decision-makers to analyze the risks in critical infrastructure operations and to assess possible solutions. Models can be used to support the search for innovative control concepts aimed at improving the performance of existing infrastructures during normal as well as critical operation. Recently, this new vein of research has gained momentum within the framework of crisis management in Information Technology and Telecommunication systems. When we talk about crises and crisis management we use the definition provided by H. Chen (2007):

"Crises are extreme events or disasters that cause significant disruption and put lives and property at risk. Such events or disasters could be caused by nature, e.g. flooding or humans, e.g. terrorism events. Crisis management encompasses activities ranging from immediate response and relief efforts to mitigation and preparedness that are aimed at reducing the impact of future events or disasters".

The remainder of this chapter is structured as follows. First, key concepts on agent-based modeling are introduced, including the use of ontologies and a generic framework. Next, various applications that have been made using this generic framework are presented, spanning a broad range of infrastructure domains. Finally, a discussion is launched on the possibilities and opportunities provided by this modeling paradigm to support crisis management.

Agent-Based Modeling
In this section, the agent-based modeling paradigm is introduced. After presenting a general description and some notes on guidelines for application of this paradigm, we address the use of a generic ontology and a generic framework.

Introduction
When modeling a system as complex as an Agent Based Model, one starts with modeling the actors in the system and then the system dependencies and interactions. A model of an actor or a group of actors (e.g. a community) is called an agent. An agent can be seen as a software entity that is autonomous, reactive, pro-active and capable of social interaction (Jennings, 2000). The behavior of an actor is formalized by using, for example, if-then rules: the so called behavioral rules.

Agents model the social part of the system, but they can interact in one way or another with one or more physical nodes. For example, an agent owns, operates or maintains a technology. Physical links, such as mass or energy flows, can only me made between physical nodes, while contracts and other social constructs can only exist between social nodes (i.e., two agents). Adding a number of individual agents (including technical components and their links) to create a multi-agent system leads to a model of a system without having to make system level behavior explicit; it emerges from the individual agents' actions (See Figure 1).

By modeling components rather than the entire system, the structure of the system is not pre-defined. Because agents can communicate and connect to other agents, various networks can be created by changing the behavioral rules, which makes it possible to test different set-ups of a control system (e.g., hierarchical or coordinated, see van Dam et al., 2004) in a simulated environment, and the agents' response to the emergent system behavior can be monitored. Furthermore, both technical and social changes (as discussed in the introduction) can easily be implemented in flexible simulation models. To summarize, the main advantage of building models in the bottom-up approach suggested here is that it creates a very flexible environment in which different experiments can be conducted.

If the system behavior is modeled explicitly, as is common in numerical approaches, for example, making changes in the model would require the modeler to adapt the system structure. Although that would make it possible to compare different configurations of the system, it is not clear how the most desirable situation can be obtained by influencing lower levels of the system. Agents (like the actors they represent) can exist at several hierarchical levels, for example if one actor supervises the activities of one or more other actors creating subsystems (van Dam and Lukszo, 2006).

Generally speaking, in many of today's infrastructure systems it is not possible for the problem owner to directly influence the whole system. For the model to be an effective support tool for the problem owner, it needs

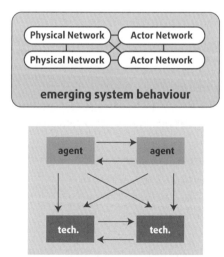

Figure 1. Although system behavior emerges from the models of actors (in relation to their physical components/technology), it is not modeled explicitly

to give insight in exactly how changes at lower levels impact the emerging system behavior. This way of modeling is close to how it works in the real world: the collective decisions made by more or less autonomous actors at various levels of a hierarchy together result in an overall system behavior.

Agent-based models, thanks to their bottom-up approach that models local behavior instead of system level behavior, provide a flexible way to carry out research with different scenarios and configurations of the system, including crisis situations. Furthermore, the actor-centric view allows visualization of, for example, negotiations.

Applicability
As a rule, multi-agent systems are applicable for (conceptual) modeling of complex systems if the following conditions are met (van Dam and Lukszo, 2006):
— The problem has a distributed character;
— The subsystems (agents) operate in a highly dynamic environment;
— Subsystems (agents) have to interact in a flexible way, where flexibility means reactivity, pro-activeness, cooperativeness and social ability.
Such models have already successfully been designed and implemented for various infrastructures, including transport, energy and industrial networks, as will be demonstrated in this paper.

Ontologies
In the Artificial Intelligence community, ontologies have been developed as a useful way of representing knowledge. Ontologies are formal descriptions of entities and their properties, relationships, constraints and behavior that are not only machine-readable but also machine-understandable. When two agents are communicating about certain concepts, we want to be sure that they give the same interpretation to the meaning and use of these concepts. Therefore, it is of the utmost important to unambiguously specify each concept and its meaning.

The meaning is stored not only in subclass-relationships ('is a ', e.g., apple is a fruit, red is a color) but also in property relationships ('has a ', e.g., fruit has a color). Ontologies contain explicit formal specifications of the terms in the domain and relations among them. In other words: it is a formal specification of a conceptualization (Gruber, 1993).

An instance is a single identifiable object within the limits of the scope of the model, belonging to a class that is formalized in the ontology. To use the fruit example, one can say that this one specific apple has a red color. In this view, a class is nothing more than a generalization of a number of instances that the modeler chose to put together. The class is abstract, whereas the instance is concrete.

Figure 2 shows a small fraction of an ontology for socio-technical systems, in which agents (social nodes) and physical systems (physical nodes) are both considered as nodes, with different properties. It shows, for example, that an Agent 'is a' Social Node and that it 'has a' Technology. The full ontology contains many formalized concepts, including different types of edges, properties, configurations, labels, etc. etc.

Ontologies are not only useful for communication between agents, but also for sharing knowledge between modelers, domain experts and users. No misunderstanding should be possible so a shared language is needed. Which concepts should play a role depends on the goals of the research and the problem owner should specify what type of questions should be answered by the simulation. To build an ontology, a knowledge engineer has to talk with domain experts to analyze the system and to make everything explicit. Key is describing concepts using already defined concepts, such as in the example used above. The knowledge rules (i.e., the decision-making rules) can then also be expressed in these formalized concepts.

When it comes to implementation of a model, ontologies are the basis of the class structure for object-oriented software implementation. The 'is-a' relationship is coded as the subclass relationship in class descriptions and the 'has-a' provides information on the properties of the class and the possible values (cf. the Java programming language).

Ontologies are even more powerful when they can be re-used so it is important to use a generic description as much as possible. This does not only make it possible to re-use domain and expert knowledge, but also to re-use source code. This is essential in the approach presented in the next section: by specifying a case study in previously formalized generic concepts previously implemented building blocks can be re-used. In other

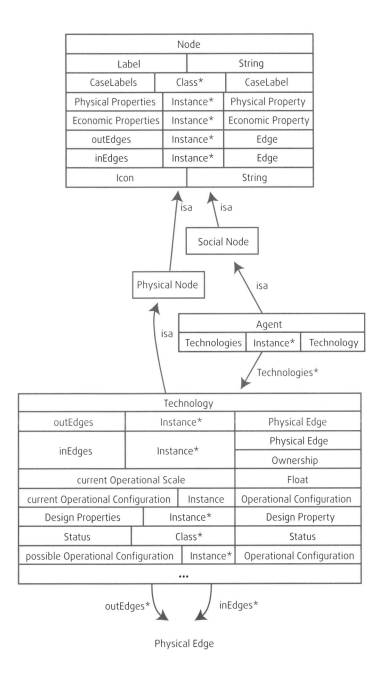

Figure 2. *A fragment of the ontology for socio-technical systems, showing the relationship between various classes of Nodes (Social and Physical) and some of their properties.*

words: ontologies facilitate re-use, sharing and interoperability of agent-based models.

Generic framework

A generic framework for modeling infrastructures has been developed, based on a growing number of case studies. This framework aims at supporting the modeler in quickly setting up new applications by re-using building blocks. These building blocks are generic components, consisting of source code with an interface supported by the generic ontology (van Dam and Lukszo, 2006). The goal is to deliver a generic approach to modeling infrastructures, both for the physical and the social components. This implies that the decision-making aspects also have to be in-

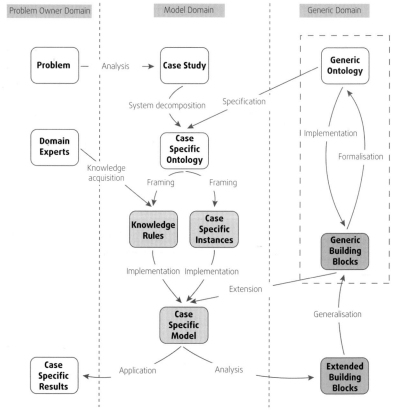

Figure 3. Application cycle for the re-use of ontologies and generic building blocks (based on Van Dam and Lukszo, 2006)

cluded in the model and that a generic approach to decision-making has to be found, in addition to a generic way of describing the physical reality.

Using the building blocks and approach described here, models of infrastructures can be built that provide insight into paths towards improved infrastructure control by demonstrating the effects of local decision-making on system level performance and by experimenting with different control strategies.

To develop an agent-based model, the following model building tasks are performed:
1. Conceptualize the problem in terms of actors and physical systems, including their relationships and properties. Distinguish the set of properties that will be variable in the model (i.e. the model parameters).
2. Visualize the interaction between model parameters in an influence diagram.
3. Extend the generic ontology with new abstract classes applicable to this case.
4. Create the model specification by creating concrete instances of the abstract classes from the ontology.
5. Implement the behavior of the agents, using generic components (e.g. searching for suppliers, determining a price, accepting contracts) and add new components.
6. Verify the model.
7. Validate the model.

After these tasks have been performed, the model is now ready for simulation. The following tasks have to be executed to use the model for simulations:
1. Formulate experiments: decide which model parameters to vary and which performance indicators to measure.
2. Decide on the values for the simulation parameters, (e.g., the number of simulation steps, random seed, etc.).
3. Execute the experiments.
4. Analyze the results.

Each new case study that is executed provides an opportunity to add new re-usable components to the library. This process is illustrated in Figure 3.

The ontology is stored in a Protégé (Gennari et al., 2003) knowledge base which can be changed without having to adjust the model source code, which functions independently. For physical components, possible in and out flows are defined, along with certain other properties. Furthermore, the ontology contains concepts such as 'transport contract' and 'physical flow' which are instantiated during the model run. This agent-based model is implemented in Java using the Repast agent simulation toolkit (North et. al, 2006).

Conclusion
Because of their bottom-up nature, agent-based models are suitable for simulating dynamic systems where the structure can or should change during a run, or where experiments with different configurations have to be performed. By making a strict distinction between social components (i.e., the actors) and physical components, and by formalizing this domain knowledge in an ontology, parts of the model can be re-used (e.g. re-using the model of a certain technology with a different agent, or re-using behavioral rules of one agent in another one, or even copy complete agents with their physical nodes into another model). The framework presented here supports the model developer in this process and makes it possible to build on earlier work.

Applications
Agent-based models have been applied to various infrastructure problems in a wide range of domains. Using the generic framework presented above, or at least the shared ontology for socio-technical systems, different models have been designed and implemented. This includes, for example, a model for CO_2 emission trading (Chappin et al., 2007), co-evolution of infrastructure and petrochemical clusters (Nikolic et al., 2008) and micro-combined heat and power generation (van Dam et al., 2008-1). Since a shared ontology is used, the agents from these models could, in theory, talk to one another. A bio-based power plant used in the CO_2 emission trading model, for example, can be included in the co-evolution of industry-infrastructure model. In the simulation, the agent representing the owner of this plant will interact with other agents, e.g. trade with them. Because they speak the same language, they can exchange meaningful information. Also, building blocks (i.e., source code) can be shared if they are written in a generic way.

Two applications that use this framework are presented in greater detail as illustrative examples: intermodal freight transport and a supply chain for an oil refinery.

Intermodal freight transport
Intermodal freight transportation is defined as a system that carries freight from origin to destination by using two or more transportation modes. In this system, hubs are one of the key elements that function as transferring points of freight between different modes. The location of hubs is a critical success factor in intermodal freight transportation and needs to be considered very carefully, as it has a direct and indirect impact on various stakeholders, including investors, policy-makers, infrastructure providers, hub operators, hub users and the community at large (Sirikijpanichkul and Ferreira, 2006).

The problem owner, in this case the government transport agency, has indicated that it needs greater insight into the relationships between the stakeholders to make a decision. Three steps can be identified on the path towards the development of a new freight hub in which tools can assist the problem owner:
— Generating possible solutions for the location of the freight hub;
— Evaluating the solutions for each stakeholder and the overall system level;
— Experimenting with different policies and measures to influence the decisions of the individual stakeholders

Steps two and three form an iterative process. A location can only be chosen after experimenting with different instruments to influence the actors. For each potential location, the situation should be analyzed and different scenarios played out before a judgment on the suitability of the hub location can be given. An agent-based model was developed for this purpose (Sirikijpanichkul et al., 2007) using the framework presented above.

During the simulation runs, the capital of each agent is measured and plotted in a graph. The main variable model parameter is the location of the intermodal freight hub. Three different locations for the hub are tested, with different effects on the actors (See Figure 4 for one such location scenario). When one of the actors loses money, compared to the initial situ-

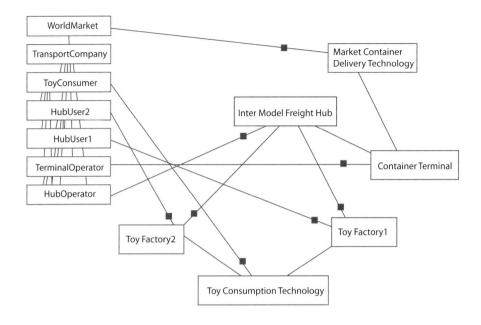

Figure 4. Geographical representation of the social and physical nodes of the intermodal freight hub model.

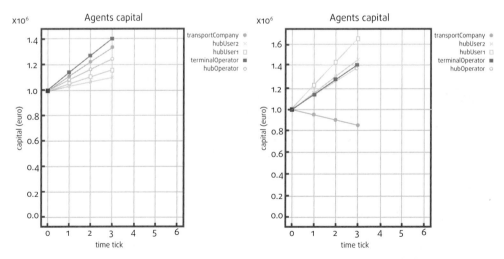

Figure 5. Different results in capital for different agents after varying the location of the intermodal freight hub

ation, experiments are conducted to identify measures that can reduce the losses and generate adequate incentives for all actors to agree with a certain proposed location.

The current model of the transport system incorporating an intermodal freight hub can be used to illustrate the different interests of various actors. By changing the location of the hub, it can be shown that some actors benefit while others loose (See Figure 5). Also, it is illustrated that simple measures to support actors who lose money can encourage them to support a hub location anyway.

To make realistic policy recommendations, a more realistic network representation is needed, together with more dynamic behavior of the actors. The future experiments can be defined to provide an additional layer for simulations that can be explored without having to make many changes to the modeled behavior. This means that all that is needed is a further extension of the ontology and the model specification in the knowledge base (and subsequent implementation of these additional components). No conceptual changes have to be made to the model.

Supply chain for an oil refinery

Supply chains are best thought of as socio-technical systems in which complex production technologies interact with distributed intelligent entities – each with their own dynamics, goals and desires. There is significant challenge in modeling such systems that function in dynamic, stochastic, socio-economic environments with intra- and inter-organizational complexity. Numerical modeling, traditionally the paradigm of choice in process systems engineering, could be adopted to represent such complex socio-technical systems. An alternative with complementary strengths is offered by agent-based models, which take an actor-centric perspective instead of the activity-based one. The actions of each agent and the interactions between the various agents are explicitly represented in such models, and the behavior of the entire system consequently emerges.

All the instances of the model components, i.e. the agents and all the technical components (e.g. refinery units, jetty, etc.) and their links (e.g. pipe-

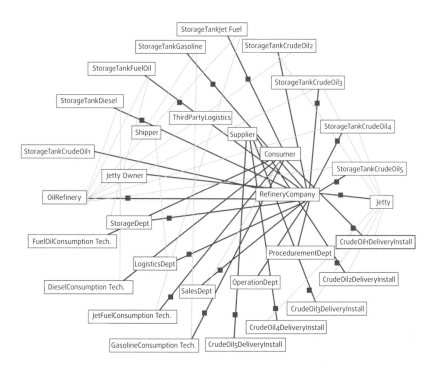

Figure 6. Screenshot of the supply chain model with agents (inner circle) and physical nodes (outer circle) as well as contracts and ownership relations (between agents, or between agents and physical nodes) and mass flows (between physical nodes).

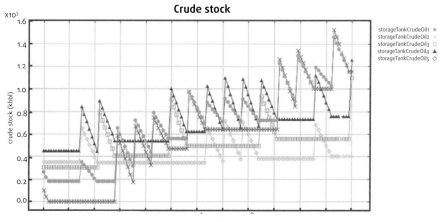

Figure 7. Base case for crude inventory levels from the agent-based model

line between the jetty and the crude storage tank) have been stored in a Protégé knowledge base, as mentioned before.

The agents in the model all act autonomously according to their own goals. A schedule is made so that some processes (e.g., procurement) only occur at certain intervals while others (e.g., production) are invoked in each time step of the model. Events such as the arrival of a crude carrier at the jetty are continuously monitored. Agent negotiations concerning trade and transport are formalized in contracts, providing a natural representation of their interrelations. The behavior of the agents was implanted once more using the framework described above, and re-using many building blocks from the intermodal freight hub case study. Figure 6 shows a screenshot of the agents, the technical components and their relationships.

Numerical models are the paradigm that is traditionally preferred for these types of systems. The agent-based model of the supply chain has been compared with a numerical model of the same system using the same assumptions. The result of this benchmarking exercise was that both modeling paradigms produce similar results and behavior (See Figure 7 for the crude inventory levels as generated by the agent-based model). Experiments confirm that the behavior of the two models is the same, validating the conjecture that the supply chain can be adequately described in both paradigms (van Dam et al., 2008-2).

Conclusion
It was demonstrated that similar results can be achieved using an agent-based model as with a numerical approach. However, each of the two modeling paradigms has its own advantages and disadvantages. Advantages of agent-based models lie mostly in the fact that relevant social interactions such as negotiation can more realistically be expressed in this paradigm, that re-use of model components is easier and that the model is much more transparent and easy-to-use for non-experts. Exactly these advantages make agent-based models a promising modeling paradigm for the support of decision-makers in situations of crisis management.

DISCUSSION

In this section, we draw extensively from several meetings the authors had with René Wagenaar while aiming to set up a joint research project on 'Agent-based models for crisis management' within the Next Generation Infrastructures program.

Crisis situations are often caused and/or aggravated by infrastructure failure and malfunctioning. Although a lot of the current research efforts on critical infrastructure protection was inspired by the terrorist attacks in New York, Madrid and London, natural disasters and other more mundane causes (e.g. technical failure, human mistakes, capacity overload) remain by far the most prominent causes of critical infrastructure failures. Instances of critical infrastructure failure in Europe over the past years include several large scale electricity black-outs and flooding of large areas; train accidents, tunnel fires, airport and airline strikes have taken their toll; on a more local scale, several regions suffered from drinking water contamination. Because today's infrastructures are in many ways interconnected and interdependent, the challenge of crisis management includes, besides imminent crisis relief and mitigation, the prevention of cascading failure across infrastructures. An example of multi-infrastructure failure is the case of Haaksbergen, November 2005, when electricity supply, road and railway traffic and mobile telecommunications all ground to a halt.

Agent-based models provide a promising avenue towards gaining deeper insight into the behavior of critical infrastructures in crisis situations. The cases presented in this paper has made it clear that the agent-based framework can be extended to underpin crisis management in critical infrastructures by playing out scenarios in which a crisis situation occurs. The first step is to formalize a generic description of such crisis scenarios, e.g. a flammable train load explosion, an airport strike, an electricity grid blackout, an airplane crash or a dike-burst. This generic description would then be expressed in the ontology. The second step is to add new behavioral rules to the agents to let them respond to and deal with these crisis scenarios, for example by deciding to buy crude from an emergency supplier, install emergency electricity generators, promptly decide on evacuation and evacuation routes, etc. The third step is to develop suitable representations of the information and insights generated which, for example, can be done by outplaying the scenarios with live players and decision-makers, respectively.

An attractive feature of agent-based models is that they provide a realistic context for training of decision-makers. Agent-based models enable visualization of negotiations, power distribution among decision-makers, institutions and social links that play a key role in crisis situations. The formal capturing of actor style and decision-making behavior through agents, makes it easy for the human decision-maker to identify with the model and suggest modifications if the model is not realistic enough in certain respects. Agent-based models thus provide a flexible test bed for crisis management allowing the decision-makers to play out a variety of 'what-if' scenarios. Even more importantly, agent-based models can support decision-makers during actual crisis situations by providing situation awareness support and visualization.

At a meta-level, this work would allow a deep analysis of the risks associated with the operation of critical infrastructures, for example risks originating from technical failure, from inappropriate decision-making and combinations thereof, eventually yielding much needed insight into the information processing capacity of actors, their decision-making and negotiations in crisis situations.

How would this materialize? Evidently, the success of such crisis management training and test bed facilities hinges on advanced information and telecommunication technology. Modern information systems allow for the collection of the massive amount of information generated during any disaster while it develops. Multiple sensors and actors involved in crises may 'feed' an agent-based system to elucidate patterns of decision-making. It may be clear that ICT will play a significant role by providing wireless communications channels, GIS data, tools for integrating different database systems needed for data sharing etc. To summarize, the agent-based modeling paradigm and ICT combined can provide much needed support for managing crisis situations, such as tools to support or effect coordination and cooperation, for example by task scheduling.

The development of an ICT-enabled, agent-based model supported test bed for crisis management requires a concerted knowledge effort of universities, industry, governmental organizations and first responder groups (e.g. fire brigade, police, ambulance services). The Next Generation Infrastructures (NGInfra) program is ready to support this collaborative effort. First steps will be made as a part of the ongoing research project 'Modeling the operation and evolution of infrastructure'.

The NGInfra-program is grateful to René Wagenaar for generously sharing his extensive knowledge and innovative research ambitions. Especially in the NGInfra-subprogram on 'Intelligent Infrastructures', we hope to see his crisis management research ambitions bear fruit. Our work on 'Intelligent Infrastructures' will certainly continue to benefit from René's inspiring ideas.

References

Chappin, E., G.P.J. Dijkema, K.H. van Dam, Z. Lukszo (2007), Modeling strategic and operational decision-making – an agent-based model of electricity producers, The European Simulation and Modelling Conference 2007, Malta, October 22-24, 2007.

Dam, K.H. van, J.A. Ottjes, G. Lodewijks, Z. Verwater-Lukszo, R. Wagenaar (2004), Intelligent Infrastructures: Distributed Intelligence in Transport System Control -- an Illustrative Example. Proceedings of the 2004 IEEE International Conference on Systems, Man and Cybernetics, October 10–13, 2004, the Hague, the Netherlands.

Dam, K.H. van, Z. Lukszo (2006), Modelling Energy and Transport Infrastructures as a Multi-Agent System using a Generic Ontology, Proceedings of the 2006 IEEE International Conference on Systems, Man, and Cybernetics, October 8--11, 2006, The Grand Hotel, Taipei, Taiwan.

Dam, K.H. van, M. Houwing, Z. Lukszo, I. Bouwmans, (2008-1), Agent-Based Control of Distributed Electricity Generation with Micro Combined Heat and Power -- Cross-Sectoral Learning for Process and Infrastructure Engineers, Journal of Computers and Chemical Engineering, Vol. 21, No. 1-2, pp. 205--217, January/February 2008.

Dam, K.H. van, A. Adhitya, R. Srinivasan, Z. Lukszo, (2008-2), Benchmarking numerical and agent-based models of an oil renery supply chain, 18th European Symposium on Computer Aided Process Engineering – ESCAPE 18, June 1-4, 2008, Lyon, France.

Gennari, J. H., M.A. Musen, R.W. Fergerson, W.E. Grosso, M. Crubezy, H. Eriksson, N.F. Noy, S.W. Tu, (2003), The evolution of Protege: an environment for knowledge-based systems development. In International Journal of Human-Computer Studies, 58 (1) p. 89-123

Gruber, T. R. A. (1993), Translation Approach to Portable Ontology Specification. Knowledge Acquisition, Vol. 5, pp. 199-220.
Chen, H., (2007), Presentation: Designing an Agenda for Scintific Research, International Workshop on Information and Communication Technology for Crisis Management, Delft University of Technology, June 2007.
Jennings, N.R. (2000), On Agent Based Software Engineering. Aritifcal Inteligence, Vol. 117 pp. 277-296.
Lukszo, Z, M.P.C. Weijnen, R. Negenborn, B. De Schutter, M. Ilic, (2006), Challenges for process system engineering in infrastructure operation and control, European Symposium on Computer Aided Process Engineering ESCAPE 16 – June 2006.
Nikolic, I., G.P.J. Dijkema, K.H. van Dam (2008), Understanding and shaping the evolution of sustainable large-scale socio-technical systems towards a framework for action oriented industrial ecology. In: M. Ruth and B. Davidsdottir (Eds.) The Dynamics of Regions and Networks in Industrial Ecosystems, Edward Elgar (In Press).
North, M.J., N.T. Collier, J.R. Vos (2006), Experiences Creating Three Implementations of the Repast Agent Modeling Toolkit, ACM Transactions on Modeling and Computer Simulation, 16(1), pp. 1-25, ACM, New York, USA.
Sirikijpanichkul, A., L. Ferreira (2006), Modelling Intermodal Freight Hub Location Decisions, Proceedings of the 2006 IEEE International Conference on Systems, Man, and Cybernetics, October 8--11, 2006, The Grand Hotel, Taipei, Taiwan.
Sirikijpanichkul, A., K.H. van Dam, L. Ferreira, Z. Lukszo, (2007) Optimizing the Location of Intermodal Freight Hubs: An Overview of the Agent Based Modelling Approach, J. of Transportation Systems Engineering & Information Technology, 7(4), 2007, pp 71-81.
Verwater-Lukszo, Z and I. Bouwmans (2005), Intelligent Complexity in Networked Infrastructures, pp. 2378-2383. In: Proceedings of the IEEE 2005 International Conference on Systems, Man & Cybernetics, Oct. 10-12, 2005.At: Waikoloa, Hawaii, USA.

THE WAY OF THINKING ABOUT
HOW TO DESIGN AN ARCHITECTURE
WITHIN THE ICT-SECTOR IS
FAR FROM FULLY DEVELOPED,
IN PARTICULAR WHEN THAT
ARCHITECTURE IS SUPPOSED TO
INCLUDE SEVERAL ORGANIZATIONS
AT ONCE.

From Civil Servant

Design and Evaluation of the Information Architecture Program

Paulien M. Herder, Uldrik E. Speerstra

ABSTRACT

In this chapter, we discuss the development, contents and initial evaluation of the Information Architecture specialization within the MSc program 'Systems Engineering, Policy Analysis and Management', in collaboration with the 'Computer Science' MSc program, both at Delft University of Technology. The first program educates multidisciplinary systems engineers with strong analyzing and complex system design skills. It was recognized that for students specializing in Information and Communication Technology, a closer collaboration with the Computer Science program would be fruitful, which resulted in a new curriculum on Information Architecture. This program was initiated and developed by René Wagenaar, Jan Dietz and a number of other colleagues with content-related and/or educational expertises and responsibilities. The authors of this paper, in their roles of Director of Education and Director of Innovations resepectively, collaborated with René in the design and management of the program. The objective of this chapter is to show the relevance and the attractiveness of the Information Architecture program by zooming in on its design and embeddedness and by discussing the results of the recent evaluation of the young program.

INTRODUCTION

Socio-technical systems are systems that consist of physical and social subsystems. Networked systems, such as water, energy, information and communication infrastructures, are prime examples of such socio-technical systems. Today, they are critical backbones of society. Many engineers are involved in their design and development and many other actors are concerned with their operation, management and governance.

In the design of new systems or the redesign or expansion of existing ones, one of the main challenges is to combine technical knowledge with managerial and operational knowledge, and to take the many uncertainties the system will face during its projected lifetime into account. Since these systems are deeply embedded in society, they are not only subject to rapid technological changes, but they also have to keep up with institutional and economic developments, such as deregulation, liberalization and changing market conditions.

Due to the limited possibilities to intervene directly in the established physical lay-out of large embedded systems, an important option is to ensure that the collective actions of players are steered towards a continued improvement of the system. This requires a breed of engineers with thorough technical expertise, combined with economic, organizational and managerial knowledge.

The department of Technology, Policy and Management (TPM) of Delft University of Technology offers a number of Master of Science (MSc) programs that combine the required engineering and social sciences. The department's mission is 'to make a significant contribution to sustainable solutions for societal problems in which technology plays an important role, by analyzing the structure and mechanisms of technical multi-actor systems and by developing strategies for the intervention, design and improvement of such systems'. This mission is reflected in the educational

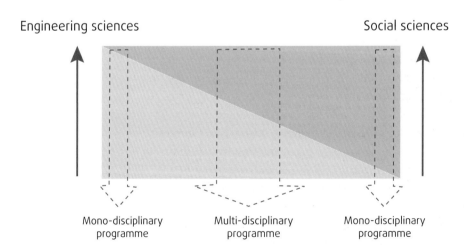

Figure 1. *The spectrum of mono- and multidisciplinary MSc programmes*

programs of the department, which all focus on technical multi-actor systems and are rooted in the two basic perspectives of the engineering and social sciences.

Depending on whether the emphasis is placed on the engineering sciences or on the social sciences, a spectrum of possible multi-disciplinary programs emerges, as depicted in figure 1.

Examples of purely engineering programs are chemical engineering, mechanical engineering, electrical engineering, civil engineering or computer science. Examples of relevant social science mono-disciplinary programs would comprise economics, public management, law, or management. The programs offered by the department of TPM are typically situated in the multi-disciplinary realm, in the center of figure 1. The current portfolio comprises three core Master programs: Systems Engineering, Policy Analysis and Management (SEPAM), Management of Technology (MoT) and Engineering and Policy Analysis (EPA). In addition, various specialization programs are offered in collaboration with other Delft departments and other universities, in the Netherlands and abroad. The rest of this paper focuses on an Information Architecture specialization, from the perspective of the SEPAM program.

Design of the program
The host program
Students in the Systems Engineering, Policy Analysis and Management (SEPAM) program are educated in a multidisciplinary environment, their curriculum providing a solid background in applied mathematics, systems engineering, policy analysis, organization and management, combined with essential knowledge of a selected technological application domain as well as the associated legislation, economics and public management in that domain. The generic objectives of the curriculum for SEPAM students are (Weijnen et al, 2001):
— ability to deal with a variety of complexities, including multiple stakeholders, uncertainty and multi-disciplinarity;
— versatility in systems and policy analysis, design and implementation;
— knowledge of systemic tools and techniques and their usage;
— substantive knowledge of a specific application domain.

The students can currently choose from the following technological application domains:
— Transport, Infrastructure and Logistics
— Energy, Water and Industry
— Information and Communication Technology
— Use and Development of Public Space

The complete curriculum takes five years to complete (i.e. three years for a Bachelor degree and two years for the ensuing Master degree) and concludes with a research thesis. It consists of theory courses (2/3 of the time), and projects (1/3 of the time) in which the acquired knowledge and skills must be applied to increasingly complex problems in small project groups. During the three-year Bachelor program, methods and techniques and basic knowledge are provided aimed at analyzing complex socio-technical systems in general and in particular on the domain chosen. For the two-year Master program the focus shifts towards the design, intervention and management of complex socio-technical systems.

Basic courses taught to students from all specializations, include among others:
— organization and management (public and private),
— mathematical modeling (continuous and discrete),
— research methods and data processing (quantitative and qualitative),
— analysis of complex problems (multi-objective and multi-actor),
— economy, law and policy (public and private), and
— design and management of policy and decision-making processes

In the SEPAM BSc and MSc program, theories, concepts, methods and techniques are taught in theory modules. The practical work within these courses is aimed at understanding and applying the concepts, methods and techniques separately in straightforward situations. The ultimate aim of the program is for students to be able to use the concepts and methods conveyed in the theory modules in more complex real life situations. For this purpose the program offers project modules, as this work form is particularly suitable for learning how to apply acquired knowledge.

The capstone project for the MSc program is the 'SEPAM design project', into which students can enroll only after they passed the larger part of the theory modules. The SEPAM design project involves a design assignment in which students apply all acquired theoretical knowledge on design and management methods, tools and principles for socio-technical systems to a realistic case in their application domain. Section 3 elaborates on this capstone project.

The room for free elective courses allows the students to cater the program to their individual needs. Some students decide to emphasize the business and management side of socio-technical system design, whereas others prefer to focus on in-depth technical and engineering courses. For students who want to emphasize their application domain specialization beyond the possibilities in their selection of free electives, but who do not want to lose sight of the multi-disciplinary context of the socio-technical systems, a collaborative engineering MSc program with a mono-disciplinary peer program is suitable. In such collaborative engineering programs, students from the contributing programs share crucial parts of the curriculum, while parts of the program will remain differentiated and geared towards the original program. The share of technical and engineering courses would increase from roughly 50% in SEPAM to around 70% in such collaborative engineering programs. Conversely, the share of social science

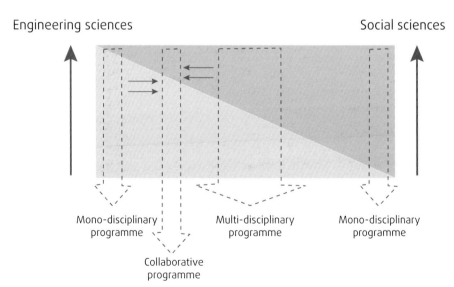

Figure 2. *The position of collaborative engineering programmes*

courses for students in the mono-disciplinary engineering partner would increase to roughly 20%-30%. This is depicted in Figure 2.

One of the strengths of this collaborative concept is that students encounter other disciplines, other conceptual frameworks and other ways of working during their education in stead of when they start working in regular jobs. Secondly, introducing other experts and disciplines to the program allows students greater flexibility, without compromising the overall quality of the program.

The Information Architecture program
A prime example of a successful collaborative engineering program is the Information Architecture (IA) program. From the SEPAM perspective, IA was built as a further specialization in the SEPAM program for students in the Information and Communication Technology application domain. In 2003, Professors Wagenaar and Dietz identified the need for such a program, both from the perspective of the job market and from a scientific research perspective. Increasingly, companies were searching engineers, with thorough technical knowledge, who would be able to deal with and act upon complex organizational and managerial situations. Indeed, the design and implementation of large-scale information systems and architectures, spanning multiple levels and sometimes even multiple organizations, required a whole new engineering consultant.

Scientific research, at the foundations of and feeding into the program, was conducted in the groups of professor Wagenaar and professor Dietz. Research into the design and management of information and communication services and infrastructures in a multi-actor context was executed by the group of Wagenaar. Mainly, research is being done concerning requirements analysis, and the design and management of information systems that span multiple organizations. Architecture concepts play a major role, with emphasis on transparency, adaptivity, reliability and complexity reduction through modularity. Dietz's research group specializes in the design of information systems, by analyzing, design, implementation and evaluation of automated information systems in organizations. The emphasis is on matching the system's functions to the needs of the organization.

After the idea for the Information Architecture program was born and the scientific foundations were laid, it was soon recognized that a collaborative engineering program, as set out in the previous section, would be the most appropriate format. The new program would be a combination of the SEPAM program and the Computer Science program, taught at the department of Electrical, Mathematical and Information Engineering. In that program, SEPAM students would be exposed to courses from Computer Science, while students from the Computer Science program follow courses on multidisciplinary and social sciences topics.

The program's shared goal is to educate engineers who 'are in command of an integral approach to business processes, information systems and information infrastructure (on company and intra-company levels) and who can manage projects in which these processes and systems are designed, developed, implemented and operated. The graduate has systematic knowledge of the missions and strategies of organizations and can relate these to the required information and communication technology.' (Speerstra, 2006) In addition to these application domain objectives, the SEPAM graduate would also fulfill the generic program objectives stated earlier.

Graduates from the Information Architecture program have the following core competences (Speerstra, 2006):
Design. The architect is capable of helping a client with the conceptual design of new business processes from existing ones, and of information systems that are needed in support of those processes. The architect is capable of designing application architectures from existing applications and components. Finally, the architect can develop formal models for verifying and validating the newly designed situation, and will make sure that the new systems link up with existing ones (legacy).
Engineering. The architect can assist the client in selecting the appropriate technologies for the desired applications, more specifically with regard to how applications of existing organizations can be coupled.
Management. The architect can organize and manage projects in which a new situation is being developed and implemented, including the migration to that new situation.
Advising. The architect can advise a client about the feasibility of proposed services and their organization, based on architecture (either existing or to

be developed) in which guidelines for the integral design of business processes and information technology support are laid down.

The resulting collaborative Information Architecture program outline is shown in Table 1. Students take a number of core courses in their original program, and in addition take key courses from the core of the partner program. For SEPAM students, this means that the application domain specialization, which is a regular part of the SEPAM program, is extended with courses from the Computer Science program. For Computer Science students, this means that basic courses on socio-technical system design, organization and management are required. The shared Information Architecture courses consist of new theory courses and the capstone design project. Finally, the students have some room for electives and finish their program with a final research Master thesis.

Capstone design project
Socio-technical system design

As set out in section 2.1, the capstone project for the SEPAM graduate is the 'SEPAM design project'. It is a design assignment in which students apply all the theoretical knowledge they have acquired with regard to design and management methods, tools and principles for socio-technical systems to a realistic case in their application domain.

The design of socio-technical systems differs fundamentally from that of technical system design in the majority of the general design process com-

Element	MSc SEPAM-IA (ec)	MSc CS-IA (ec)
Original programme basis	35	18
Specialization into partner programme	18	21
Information Architecture core (new)	18	18
Information Architecture design project	6	6
Electives	13	9
Research thesis	30	45
Total	120	120

Table 1. Information Architecture programme outline (ec = european credit = 28 study load hours).

ponents (Dym and Little, 2004; Maier and Rechtin, 2002). We will briefly illustrate these differences for the functional requirements, the objectives and constraints, the design space, and finally for the starting points of a design project (Herder et al., 2008).

Functional requirements: For a technical system design, this will be a straightforward description, e.g. 'the system must store data.' In a complex system design, the function will often be compounded, with different, contested, functions for the various actors involved. The system may also be 'distorted' upon implementation, i.e. it will not be used exactly in the way the designers intended. The more complex the system, and the greater the number of actors in the 'implementation field', the more likely it is that distortion will occur. Finally, given the socio-technical setting, the requirements are very often dynamic and change over time. Changing requirements are often fatal to proper project execution in conventional design settings, but designers of socio-technical systems must find ways to deal with this unavoidable phenomenon (Herder et al., 2008).

Objectives and constraints: The degree of complexity results in a massive number of objectives and constraints that the client and other actors can impose on the design. If the designer wishes to incorporate all these requirements, the system is very likely to suffer from over-specification, which precludes any real solutions, i.e. a realistic design. Moreover, the system designer will have to contend with conflicting objectives. The more complex the problem, the more difficult it will be to determine the 'solution space', let alone select the best design from the various options. Finally, in complex system design involving multiple stakeholders, it is rarely possible to define a stable and agreed upon set of design objectives and constraints. Instead, this set will again be contested and dynamic in nature.

Design space: Even in simple designs, the design space can quickly take on enormous proportions. For large socio-technical systems, the design space is practically unbounded. Other actors may also attempt to incorporate subsystems into the design space, or to ensure that they are excluded. It then falls to the designer to define and delineate the design space as best as possible. And, similar to the design requirements, the design space consists of a dynamic, contested set of variables.

Starting points: In complex system design, it is very difficult to find starting points for a design. The transplantation of models and design options is not simple and will indeed often be impossible precisely because these are systems embedded in a (dynamic) multi-actor field in a specific institutional context. Given the high degree of context sensitivity, the designer of a complex system will often have very few starting points.

The course objectives of the design project, therefore, imply that, on completion of the course, students are able to (Bockstael and Herder, 2006):
— choose suitable design methods and tools, taking into account the dynamic substantive and process characteristics of the socio-technical system and the multi-actor environment
— apply the chosen design methods and tools
— design a system taking into account technical, institutional and decision-making aspects.

Generally speaking, the students apply and integrate three main perspectives, which are rooted in three generic underlying design schools, into the design of these socio-technical systems (Bots, 2005; Bockstael and Herder, 2006):
— the technical perspective, which focuses on the physical artifact and its components, and on functional and technical system requirements, technological design choices, possibilities and limitations, resulting in a technologically feasible, robust, valid technical systems design (Dym and Little, 2004).
— the institutional perspective, which focuses on the organizational arrangements between the actors that will be involved in the design, implementation and operational phases of the system. This results in an institutional design that deals with the division of tasks, responsibilities, costs, benefits and risks. The knowledge to be applied here includes theories and approaches in the areas of institutional design, new institutional economics, evolutionary economics, and various regulation theories (De Jong et al, 2002; Ostrom 1990).
— the decision-making or process perspective, which focuses on how the systems and institutional design can be realized in a dynamic multi-actor setting. Process design and management principles should be applied in such a complex, multi-actor decision-making context. The resulting

decision process design deals with how stakeholders are involved, under which conditions, on which topics and which steps need to be taken. The knowledge applied here is a combination of systems architecting (Maier & Rechtin, 2002) and theory on process design and management (De Bruijn et al, 2002).

The three perspectives cannot be applied in isolation, because the ensuing designs interact and are strongly interrelated: specific technological choices affects which actors are involved and thus the options for institutional and process designs. Vice versa, preferences with regard to institutional arrangements affect the range of options for the technical system design.

The challenge facing students in the design project is vast. In the SEPAM-program, we provide the students with many concepts, methods and techniques to deal with design in the three main perspectives. There is, however, no off-the-shelf handbook for designing socio-technical, complex systems that explains how to link the technical, institutional and decision-making aspect. Moreover, the interaction and integration of these perspectives is highly context and case dependent. Therefore, this crucial design project posed a major implementation challenge to the program designers, and executing the project posed an equally daunting task to the students who enrolled in the Information Architecture collaborative engineering program.

Information Architecture Design Project

In the program's design, the Information Architecture design project required students to fix project teams of students with mixed backgrounds: students from SEPAM were to be combined into one team with students from Computer Science. Only then, full integration and mutual learning would occur, in stead of the worst case scenario of 'running two parallel programs which happen to have a large number of similar courses.' Real integration was therefore to be expected in the capstone design project.

As a real life design case study, interagency disaster response has been chosen in the second year of the program, being a major area of interest of René Wagenaar's research (Van den Berg and Bharosa, 2006, pp. 1): 'It involves multiple relief agencies, geographically distributed relief operations, and a rapid need for coordinated control and adaptive decision-making.

The effective mobilization of response to extreme events on a large scale requires the rapid search, exchange and absorption of valid information regarding sudden events, transmitted through a network of organizations that crosses disciplinary, organizational and jurisdictional boundaries. More specifically, the information systems used by the relief agencies are heterogeneous making it difficult to access and share information between the agencies. In addition, because of the complexity and unpredictability of the events during a disaster, there is need for rapid access to information beyond the police, fire department and ambulance data sources. For instance, information from hospitals, municipalities, or even private institutions may be required as well.'

The students enrolled in the Information Architecture program were required to deliver an appropriate and detailed information architecture, an institutional design for coordination and cooperation in case of crisis, and a process design which would indeed achieve such technical and institutional design. The case study exemplified the dynamic nature of requirements, objectives, constraints, and the design space, as explained in the previous section, mainly because of the inherent dynamic nature of crisis situations.

Each student group chose a specific type of disaster for their design project, ranging from a rapid outbreak of an infectious disease to terrorist attacks on the national holiday 'Queen's Day'. The students were coached by various staff members from both programs, and in weekly meetings René Wagenaar played the role of main supervisor with great enthusiasm.

The design project proved to be quite a challenge to the Information Architecture students for the technical and institutional design as well as the process design. Technically, the main challenge involved the heterogeneity of information systems in this domain. As each relief agency has different business processes and information needs, different information systems exist. Even though the students recognized the need for an overarching information architecture spanning the boundaries of the different relief agencies, they had some trouble in conceptualizing this need.

Another considerable challenge facing the students was the specification of the actor network and the ensuing institutional design and process design, especially because the set of actors involved is different for each type of disaster and the set is subject to change during the disaster's life.

Finally, the students realized that only little scientific literature on information systems for disaster management is available, thereby explicitly showing the relevance and timeliness of scientific research in this area, as initiated by René Wagenaar.

The final designs of the students groups were considered to be quite excellent. This may be explained partly by the composition of the groups. The SEPAM students had a strong background in process and institutional design, and the Computer Science students added to this their innovative solutions to purely technical information system problems. Putting students with different backgrounds but with enough in-depth knowledge of the other domain together in a group allowed them to complement each other's competences and skills, ultimately leading to excellent multidisciplinary designs.

EVALUATION OF THE INFORMATION ARCHITECTURE PROGRAM
After about two years of running the program, meaning that the first batch of students had almost graduated, the program was evaluated by a team consisting of its initial designers, including Professors René Wagenaar and Jan Dietz, of teachers, practitioners and students from the two founding programs. Using an informal evaluation protocol, in the form of a quick scan to see whether f the ambitions of the collaborative engineering program had been reached, the team assessed the program by means of an intensive half-day meeting and by conducting several interviews with teaching and research faculty of both departments. The following items were addressed at the program level:
— Job profiles
— Core competences
— Design and embeddedness of the program
— Outlook

In addition, various aspects concerning the individual courses, teachers and organization of the program have been evaluated, but these will not be discussed in this paper.

It was concluded that the integral approach of business processes and management on the one hand, and information services and infrastructures on the other, is relevant. The Information Architecture program meets a need that exists for Computer Science as well as for SEPAM students. The combination of the research groups headed by René Wagenaar and Jan Dietz respectively, which lay the scientific foundation of the program, had proven to be a valuable combination. The job profiles and core competences were evaluated and were recognized by practitioners as well by the students enrolled in the program.

The program initially suffered from small and larger conflicts with regard to practical issues like course schedules and study load. This was, however, mainly due to the highly constrained teaching schedules and available class rooms at the university. The actual design of the program, with basic and specialization courses and with new and shared Information Architecture courses, was evaluated positively. However, the core courses of Information Architecture had suffered from a lack of cohesion, which is a common problem with new courses and programs. The integrating design project, the programs capstone project, was evaluated positively, mainly for its challenging threefold design challenge.

Discussion and Outlook

In the final section of this paper, we will focus our attention on the outlook of the Information Architecture program. We will gradually zoom out from the specifics of the program itself to higher level reflections on the expansion of the program, and on further embedding of the Information Architecture knowledge and skills into other programs. In the wake of the evaluation meeting, we discussed these options with René in various settings. He was very eager to expand the program, to attract more students and to convey his ideas to more than just the regular SEPAM students. The outlook presented here therefore mainly represents ideas that were generated by René, in collaboration with the authors.

A number of relevant topics that should be taught to future students had already been identified in the evaluation meeting of the Information Architecture program, including failure rates, reliability theory, maintenance en compliance (Speerstra, 2006). Also, it was indicated that there was a need for more guest lectures and workshops by practitioners.

Given the relevance and the positive evaluation, and the ever-increasing enthusiasm of the faculty involved, it seems reasonable to try to attract more students to the program. Up till now, the Information Architecture program was most attractive for the Computer Science students, compared to the enrollment of SEPAM students. Relatively as well absolutely, the CS students outnumber the SEPAM students in the collaborative program. It may point to the fact that these types of programs have a high appeal to monodisciplinary students, whereas multidisciplinary students see less added value of such program, since they already are being educated in a multidisciplinary fashion. This observation, although congruent with observations in other similar mono- to multidisciplinary programs, has not been thoroughly examined yet.

To expose more students, and especially more SEPAM students, to the notions embodied in Information Architecture, a number of strategies need to be employed:
— enroll more students in the Computer Science and in the SEPAM programs
— draw more Bachelor students into the ICT application domain specialization, as they are eligible for the MSc Information Architecture program
— enroll more students with a higher-vocational background into this MSc program

Many ideas were generated to attract and enroll more students into both supporting programs, e.g. visiting high schools, visible events at student information fairs, and most importantly by critically assessing and improving the visibility of the ICT application domain in the generic courses of the SEPAM BSc program. By painstakingly going through all the courses, a number of possibilities were generated and followed up in the form of case studies, examples, and illustrations. It is expected that this increased visibility in the BSc program will lead to higher enrollment in the ICT application domain and later in the Information Architecture program, when SEPAM students are (also) convinced of the added value of this IA program over their regular SEPAM program.

The enrollment of students with a technical BSc degree from a higher vocational school is more difficult as these students are required to take at least a 30 ec minor program that prepares them for a university Master program. In addition, when mono-disciplinary students want to enroll in the multidisciplinary SEPAM program, they need further training in multidisciplinary BSc courses. This relatively high hurdle makes that vocational BSc students choose to enroll in the Computer Science program and take the Information Architecture program from there. Only recently, structural arrangements have been made with a number of vocational schools in the vicinity of the university with regard to enrollment in the SEPAM side of Information Architecture. These arrangements hold a promise for the envisaged larger numbers of enrollments in the program.

Finally, The Information Architecture notions would also be very relevant for at least one other multi-disciplinary program that is run at the department of Technology, Policy and Management: the Management of Technology (MoT) program. In it, students elect a specialization profile and Information Architecture was soon identified as a relevant profile for such students. Currently the MoT students merely touch upon the Information Architecture subjects in a generic design course. A specialization profile would comprise a set of courses covering in a nut shell the core ideas of Information Architecture. This idea for future expansion into another program even found its way abroad when an esteemed foreign institute showed interest in the program. Practical issues, however, hindered substantive and structural collaboration, but these initial contacts hold great promise for the future.

ACKNOWLEDGEMENT

The authors wish to thank Nitesh Bharosa, PhD researcher in the area of adaptive architectures for crisis management, for his analysis of the disaster management design projects that were executed by the students.

REFERENCES

Berg, J. van den, N. Bharosa (2006). *SPM4910 SEPAM Design Project Assignment, Assignment for students specializing in ICT,* Information systems for interagency disaster response, Delft University of Technology.

Bockstael-Bock, W., P.M. Herder (2006). Designing Complex Socio-Technical Systems – Experiences With Student Projects On Integrating Technical, Institutional And Decision Process Design, *Proceedings of International Design Conference DESIGN2006*, Dubrovnik, Croatia, May 15-18.

Bots, P. (2007). Design at the faculty of Technology, Policy and Management, *Journal of Design Research* 5 (3), 382 – 396.

Bruijn, J.A. de, P.M. Herder, H. Priemus (2005). Systems and Actors, *Proceedings of Foundations of Engineering Systems*, University Council on Engineering Systems, Georgia University of Technology, Atlanta, USA, December 14th.

Bruijn , J.A. de, Ten Heuvelhof, E. ten, Veld, R. in 't (2002). *Process Management, why project management fails in complex decision making processes*, Kluwer Academic London, Great Britain.

Dym, C.L., Little, P. (2004). *Engineering Design: A Project-Based Introduction*, John Wiley & Sons, Inc., USA.

Herder, P.M., I. Bouwmans, G.P.J. Dijkema, R.M. Stikkelman, M.P.C. Weijnen (2008). Designing Infrastructures from a Complex Systems Perspective, *Journal of Design Research* 7 (1).

Jong, M. de., K. Lalenis & K. Mamadouh (Eds.) (2002). *The theory and practice of institutional transplantation. Experiences with transfer of policy institutions.* Boston/Dordrecht: Kluwer Academic Publishers.

Maier, M.W., Rechting, E. (2002). *The Art of Systems Architecting*, CRC Press, Boca Raton, USA.

Ostrom, E., *Governing the Commons: The Evolution of Institutions for Collective Action* (1990). Cambridge, MA: Cambridge University Press, USA.

Speerstra, U.E. (2006). *Evaluatie Masterprogramma Information Architecture* (in Dutch), Delft University of Technology.

Weijnen M.P.C., P.M. Herder, W.A.H. Thissen (2001). Bringing knowledge management down to earth: knowledge sharing in education, research and industry, *International Journal of Technology, Policy and Management* 1 (2) 174-194.

THE BY NOW DEFUNCT DUTCH CABINET IN ITS STRATEGIC AGREEMENT LAST SUMMER STATED IT WANTED TO MOVE TOWARD AN ACHIEVEMENT-ORIENTED GOVERNMENT. THE MAIN THEMES IN THIS RESPECT ARE PUBLIC ORDER AND SAFETY, IMMIGRATION AND NATURALIZATION, CARE AND EDUCATION.

From *Civil Servant*

Infectious diseases and ICT
Rapid interaction by intertwining technology and institutions

Eric Bun, Tim de Koning, Ton Monasso, Pim Veldhoven, Alex Verheij

ABSTRACT

Because infectious diseases can spread rapidly and have a highly disruptive effect on society, an appropriate and swift reaction is crucially important. In the Netherlands, the current approach to fighting infectious diseases consists mainly of protocols and scripts. Important institutional arrangements between relevant actors are as yet ill-defined, and in particular the technological architecture involved is outdated and has many drawbacks.

In this chapter, we present the results of the analysis of existing systems and arrangements aimed at coping with infectious diseases and the design of solutions to existing deficiencies. This analysis and design were part of an educational project supervised by René. This type of crisis management was one of René's primary points of interest, as it involves complex interactions between technology and the related institutional arrangements.

Based on the shortcomings in the present situation, we specify the requirements of a solution and related institutions to improve the current state of affairs with regard to crisis management. We have designed two combinations of information systems and institutions that satisfy these requirements. The first of these, the Disease Notification System (DNS), focuses on the lack of efficiency and standardization between general practitioners and the system they use to record their disease reports. Secondly, the Decision Facilitation and Empowerment System (D-FES), aims at improving the existing suboptimal decision-making structure in times of crisis. This system filters input from various sources. The implementation of these systems is expected to enable a more rapid and appropriate response to outbreaks of infectious diseases, preventing potential disruptions of Dutch society.

INTRODUCTION

In our modern, open society, where there are many direct and indirect physical contacts between large numbers of people, often in many places and over a great distance, we are vulnerable to infectious diseases. Such diseases can spread very rapidly. Moreover, there is not only the risk of diseases spreading naturally, but there is also the danger of terrorist attacks or scientific mistakes leading to an outbreak. The success in treating infectious diseases and preventing them from spreading to a large extent depends on the speed with which the infections are detected, the institutional arrangements regarding the gathering of and response to relevant information, and on the information regarding the network, the disease and the disease-spreading characteristics.

As this chapter will show, the current system designed to fight infectious diseases, which consists of actors and technology, mainly involves protocols and scripts. Important institutional arrangements are lacking, however, and the relationships between relevant actors in times of crisis are ill-defined. In addition, the existing technological architecture is outdated and has many drawbacks. The reporting process between general practitioners and public organizations suffers from the absence of unambiguous human communication protocols, which causes delays in time and inconsistency. In case of an outbreak of an infectious disease, it is of great importance for responsible authorities to react adequately and proactively, and for a clear mitigation strategy aimed at controlling the outbreak to be in place.

The many drawbacks of the existing institutional and technological system can have major consequences when an outbreak of infectious disease occurs, and it poses a problem to the government organizations responsible for handling such an outbreak. Because these kinds of outbreaks are rare, these systems will not be used often. However, it is of great importance to have systems in place to minimize the damage if and when an outbreak does occur, all the more so because it will have a major impact on sectors like communication, energy and transportation.

The goal of this chapter is to identify the requirements of the technological and institutional system needed to prevent and respond to an outbreak of an infectious disease, and to use these requirements to design an improved response system. To identify the requirements, we begin by analysing the status quo (as per January 2007), based on desk research and interviews with a diverse group of experts. Next, we identify a framework within which these requirements have to be met. The requirements and framework provide a starting point for the design of two systems aimed at reducing the existing problems outlined above.

The research underlying this chapter has been based on a study project supervised by René Wagenaar. The topic of the problem analysis and designs closely relates to René's own interests in the areas of crisis management, and IT and design. Crisis management is a very clear example of the way in which ICT can be beneficial to society. The starting point is a genuine and technology-independent social problem: how can we guarantee a maximum of risk control and consequently safeguard the health and safety of citizens? Many reports, including the influential report of the Adviescommissie Coördinatie ICT Rampenbestrijding (2005), have identified communication as one of the crucial links in crisis management – one that often malfunctions. Whenever communication is a problem, ICT is likely to offer solutions, although it usually involved more than simply digging a cable and transmitting information. Communication as part of a decision-making process is a human affair, and one in which technology can play a facilitating role. Although technology itself may play a modest role, its existence can force institutions to change. As our case will show, major improvements probably do not involve setting up new information systems, but rather reallocating responsibilities. At the same time, demands for changed institutions may lead to the introduction of new technology, an example of which is the centralization of information, which is impossible without technology supporting the collection, aggregation and adequate representation of the information involved. The interaction between technology and institutions was at the heart both of René's interest in this area and of the project.

In the next section, we provide a brief outline of our methodology, including the theories we used, after which we explore the problem (section three) and formulate the relevant design challenges (section four). This results in two solutions to two separate but to some extent related problems: the Disease Notification System (section five) and the Decision Facilitation and Empowerment System (section six). We conclude with a discussion and reflection.

Methodology
This chapter is an extract of our report for the SEPAM Design Project (Bun, de Koning, Monasso, Veldhoven, & Verheij, 2006), one of the key courses in the largest master program at the faculty of Technology, Policy and Management at Delft University of Technology. For the design project, a typical TPM approach is used. Information systems cannot be designed without simultaneously taking institutions into account. The technological perspective describes the hardware, software and communication chains, whereas the institutional design has to do with the way responsibilities are distributed among the actors involved. The interaction between technologies and institutions is described clearly by structuration theory and by actor-network theory. For an overview of these theories, see Hanseth & Monteiro (1998).

It is impossible to implement new technologies, or adaptations in current systems, without thinking through the institutional consequences (Groenewegen, 2005; Hanseth & Monteiro, 1998). In a less passive way, changing institutions could help the functioning of technology. In this report, we consider technology and institutions to be of equal importance. However, institutional changes are often related to the technological system. An institutional design will deal with issues like the arrangements between actors, the way their relationships are regulated, the allocation of tasks and responsibilities, and the costs, benefits and risks involved.

In this chapter, we define institutions as 'system[s] of rules that structure the course of actions that a set of actors may choose' (Scharpf, 1997). This definition has a good fit with our focus on socio-technical systems, in which the primary focus is on actor interactions around and involving technology. It is also broad enough not to restrict creativity in our exploration of the solution framework.

In this chapter, we focus on structuration theory, because it has regularly been applied to the analysis of IT systems. Although it does not provide much prescriptive guidance (I. J. Cohen, 1989), it points at the necessity of having an integrated design, and it provides the analytical tools needed to investigate and think about the interactions at a general level. We use a framework (Groenewegen, 2005) originating from the field of institutional (heterodox) economics to check the coherence of technology and institutions. This model is an extension of Williamson's classic model (2000) on institutional change, of which technology is an integral part. Because this model, which is shown in Figure 1, consists of many relationships, we focus on the ones that may be most useful in our design: technology and formal institutions, technology and actors, technology and institutional arrangements and, finally, formal institutions and institutional arrangements. These relationships are displayed in bold. The reason we have decided to select these relationships is that it is easier for the people responsible – the central government – to steer on technology, formal institutions and institutional arrangements within a reasonable time scope.

A second theoretical strand we use in this chapter is Transaction Cost Economics (TCE), which draws a fundamental distinction between governance structures like firms on the one hand, and contracts on the other. The purpose is to explain governance structures that match specific types of transactions in such a way that transactions can be coordinated at minimal costs. The cost involved in the kind of outbreak discussed here directly relates to money, time and effort it takes to contain the outbreak. The two

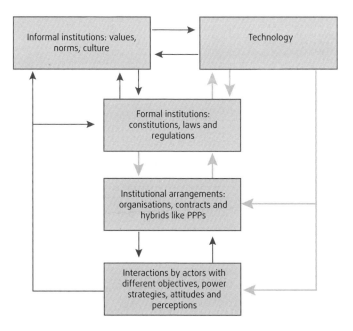

Figure 1 Model for institutional analysis (Groenewegen, 2005). The bold arrows indicate the relationships used in this institutional analysis

extremes of governance structures are market and hierarchy (Williamson, 1998). Factors that determine the costs, which in turn determine the place on this continuum, are asset specificity, frequency of contact and uncertainty, which are in fact determined by the following key characteristics: bounded rationality, opportunistic behaviour, a-symmetric information, and environmental complexity and uncertainty (Groenewegen, 1995). Asset specificity is the most important explanatory variable: "Transaction cost economics maintains that the principal factor that is responsible for transaction cost differences among transactions is variations in asset specificity." (Riordan, 1985)

PROBLEM DESCRIPTION

In this section, we describe two problems we identified earlier. We begin by analyzing the collection of information on individual outbreaks, and incorporate the results of that analysis in designing an improved IT system. Secondly, we examine the decision-making process at the managerial and political level and the inherent quest for information, and propose a new IT system design.

Collection of information on individual infections

In the Netherlands, there are many organizations involved in combating the outbreak of an infectious disease. To this end, many IT systems are in place to support information-sharing and decision-making processes. The current technical architecture of these systems reveals a complex infrastructure with a multitude of relatively fragmented IT systems (Bökkerink, 2006; Van Dijk, 2006). These systems can – in theory – perform much better when they are linked, aligned and supported by non-ambiguous IT governance. In the current situation, the general practitioner is the first actor who actively collects data about infectious diseases. If an infectious disease has been identified, the general practitioner submits a report in OSIRIS, an IT system. Accordingly, a GGD (municipal health service) worker forwards the relevant information to the National Health Inspection and the National Institute for Public Health and the Environment (RIVM), who can in turn decide to approve the report or send their recommendations back to the GGD. In case the report is approved, it will be marked as official and forwarded to the decision-makers involved. All these transactions are electronically handled by OSIRIS.

Although OSIRIS stores fairly detailed information about reported incidents, there are some drawbacks. General practitioners can use OSIRIS to report incidents, but in practice the most frequently used means of communication are still the telephone and regular mail (Jacobi, 2006). Obviously, these archaic communication means lack consistency, metadata and speed, and are more vulnerable to mistakes cause by human interpretation. Another problem is the depth of the information provided. More information about the situation of the patient and the symptoms could be very useful in determining the exact type of disease and for fundamental research on diseases. The third problem of these systems is that they are not directly connected to international databases. There are contacts with the European Center for Disease Prevention and Control (ECDC) and the World Health Organization (WHO), however connecting to the databases of these organizations is difficult and initiatives are focused on specific types of diseases (Jacobi, 2006).

Crisis decision-making

The escalation procedure is used to describe the essence of the command transfer system during crises (Ministry of the Interior and Kingdom Relations, 2004). As long as a problem does not supersede the local or regional level, the command is ultimately in the hands of mayors. Of course, in an operational sense, command is exercized by police and medical officers. If the problem cannot be handled at the regional level and has national implications, departmental crisis centers residing under various ministries dealing with public safety become involved. The departmental centers are physical locations with coordination facilities, where teams of civil servants are responsible for coordination, with the ultimate command being in the hands of the respective ministers. If the problem exceeds the policy area of an individual ministry, the national crisis control center (NCC) becomes the new crisis control headquarters. Ultimately, command is in the hands of a team of ministers, with at least the minister of the Interior taking part, and in the case of a terrorist threat the minister of Justice as well. When it comes to combating infectious diseases, a slightly different structure is used. The institutional structure described above does not contribute to the speed of the process when an outbreak occurs, while the lack of consistency with regard to the reports of general practitioners reduces the speed even more.

In situations where the institutional setting, the interactions and the informational requirements are all very much subject to change and where future developments are highly uncertain, the process designed to contain the outbreak is ambiguous. In times of crisis, things have to be clear and unambiguous, and reports have to be logged for the purposes of accountability. At the moment, none of these criteria have been met.

The challenge

Based on our analysis of the different phases in an outbreak, we have concluded that the two phases (information collection on individual diseases and crisis decision-making) have different requirements with respect to the information that is required, the actors that need to be involved and the technology that is most appropriate to contain specific outbreaks. Furthermore, each phase, from recognition to controlling the disease, should be taken into account when designing a decision support IT system. Below, we discuss the main shortcomings of the current technical, institutional and process-related arrangements, and thereby identify the high-level requirements of the system being designed.

Collecting information

To identify appropriate and efficient measures aimed at preventing an outbreak of an infectious disease, information is a crucial aspect in the initial phases of the outbreak. Information about the characteristics of the disease, such as its incubation period and infection threshold, are obtained from GGD disease reports and lab results. Although this first step is crucial in determining the scope of the disease and possible intervention measures, the current system has many shortcomings (Jacobi, 2006). First of all, when general practitioners recognize certain symptoms among their patients, they are obliged to inform the GGD. This information is transferred by means of regular mail or fax, which causes a substantial delay. The same applies to communication between the Ministry of Internal Affairs and local government organizations (Bökkerink, 2006). On the other hand, when the information has been examined in a lab, the results are transferred to the GGD. Because, at the moment, the lab data, the GGD reports and the information management system (OSIRIS) are not linked, it takes a long time to find the information that is needed and arrive at conclusions on the basis of this information.

Standardization is another issue, with the labs, the GGD and OSIRIS all using different data standards and formats (Jacobi 2006). Although many of the organizations involved, for instance hospitals, have standardized their internal documentation, these standards remain proprietary or incompatible with those in use by other organizations. When information is exchanged, the format of the information is not designed to help contain the outbreak of a disease, as a result of which finding the relevant information can be difficult, as these documents tend to grow very large. Although many types of information are gathered and stored, finding the right information can be very difficult, due to the different formats and the lack of a database to filter the information. Information filtering is also very desirable in the various phases of an outbreak. Based on previous experiences, it is possible to determine what kind of information is required, but currently the information is not being filtered with respect to its relevance to each specific stage. However, when an outbreak is detected, people are highly unlikely to use standardized protocols, because the real crisis situation is always different from any scenarios that have been constructed beforehand.

If we assess the current situation based on the list of success factors for management information systems identified in a large meta-literature study conducted by DeLone & McLean (1992), we see that most success factors, including clarity, format, appearance, accuracy, precision, completeness, currency and timeliness, which all contribute to information quality, are not accounted for in our case. At the database level, the redundant databases, the system reliability and human factors may pose problems.

Decision-making
When an outbreak is detected, the characteristics of the network, in combination with the disease characteristics described above, to a large extent determine the effectiveness of any intervention measures. The effect of a measure will depend on the accuracy and completeness of information being presented. Since decisions are made based on the information that is available, it is often the case that in the early phases, when little information is in fact available, decisions have to be based on existing protocols and hypotheses about future scenario's (Bökkerink, 2006). There is a paradox with respect to the timeliness and the validity of information. There is a tension between the information that has been verified and updated

information about a situation that is highly relevant but that has not yet been verified (Van der Brugge & Kemp, 2006). More specifically, because information often comes from parties at a decentralized level, once this information reaches the coordination structures at a national level, it may already be outdated. Another drawback of the decentralized system is that the interpretation and analysis of information are influenced by individual perceptions and experiences. This could result in a situation where different local authorities execute different strategies to contain the disease. Because local governments to a large extent have the authority to execute their own policy, it is difficult to impose a single coherent national policy (Van der Brugge & Kemp, 2006).

Another shortcoming with regard to decision-making is that information from various parties cannot be used appropriately in the OMT (Outbreak Management Team), IBT (Interdepartmental Policy Team) or IMT (Interdepartmental Management Team), because the information is too technical, information is delivered too late and there are too many formats (Bökkerink, 2006). This is caused by the fact that in many cases it is unclear which party has what information at its disposal. Although at the moment there are many parties who can deliver the same types of information, a centralized aggregation and filtering of information is highly desirable (Van der Brugge & Kemp, 2006).

Although many protocols, white papers and guidelines have been published on crisis situations (Jacobi, 2006; Ministry of the Interior and Kingdom Relations, 2002, 2004), as yet no unequivocal system has been designed in which both information and agreements regarding the sharing and authorization of information have been integrated. On the other hand, in the current National Handbook on Decision-Making during a Crisis, the national government has no absolute authority in the decision-making process (Ministry of the Interior and Kingdom Relations, 2002). In many cases the fact that a consensus has to be reached before action can be taken dramatically reduces the speed of the process (Bökkerink, 2006). In addition, decision-making at a global level and on a local scale are interdependent. Because strategic choices are influenced by choices made at a local level and vice versa, there is an increased need for coordination, especially when time is of the essence. After a crisis has occurred, an evaluation takes place on the basis of a specified protocol, the Evaluation Guideline. However, the results of these evaluations are poorly documented and not communicated well to the persons responsible, both at a national and at an international level. Although information is shared at an international level, the focus is on evaluating the containment strategies (Jacobi, 2006). It is in particular the status and position of certain functionaries, for instance mayors, that makes effective feedback difficult. As a result, not much is learned from crises that occur.

Although our analysis encompasses the entire outbreak cycle (from recognition to control), including all the necessary steps, from information gathering to data evaluation, a system supporting all activities involved would pose severe problems in terms of implementation and management, which is why we focus on the critical aspects in the outbreak cycle, where the main problems currently reside and there have been no initiatives to improve the existing technical systems. From the interviews we conducted with several experts within the RIVM and the Ministries of Internal Affairs (Bökkerink, 2006; Jacobi, 2006; Van der Brugge & Kemp, 2006) it has become clear, that the perception is that critical aspects occur in the early stages of an outbreak. Furthermore, the interviewees felt that the collection and exchange of data form the basis of sound analysis and decision-making. Following DeLone & McLean again (1992), we observe that almost none of the management information system success criteria have been met.

Based on literature and interviews, we found that the bottlenecks and shortcomings in the two phases we identified are very problematic, and no solutions are under development yet. This is why we propose two alternatives to tackle the process-oriented data collection and data exchange problems of general practitioners and the more technical problems due to a lack of intelligence within the system.

Disease Notification System

The first alternative, which we call the Disease Notification System (DNS), solves the efficiency and standardization problems that exist between the general practitioner and OSIRIS. General practitioners and lab workers use the DNS through Web Services, which is an extension of the Electronic Patient File (EPF). When they provide the symptoms of an individual patient via the appropriate application form, this information is analyzed by the Disease Classification System (a part of the DNS), which determines the level of importance in relation to a possible disease outbreak, and notifies the general practitioner or lab worker accordingly. This way, all the relevant information is immediately available online to all relevant parties, and the GGD worker can immediately process the information in OSIRIS, rather than of organizing and storing all the incoming data manually. To use these Web Services, a Service-Oriented Architecture (SOA) has to be implemented to manage the interfaces designed to ensure interoperability of the EPF with legacy systems. Using the DNS, the crucial time it takes to determine the likelihood of a possible outbreak is reduced significantly, and information is stored in a standardized and efficient way.

For the institutional design of DNS, we have used technology, formal institutions and institutional arrangements. Technology's main role lies in enforcing certain procedures within a given time frame. Compliance with these procedures can be monitored in detail. With regard to formal institutions, there is one norm that is particular important for the distribution and storage of patient data, namely the NEN 7510 norm regarding information security in the healthcare sector. Another formal aspect that has to be accounted for is the allocation of responsibilities. Institutional arrangements focus on the relationship between general practitioners and the system with regard to three variables: frequency, uncertainty and asset specificity. Both the frequency of communication between general practitioners and the system and the level of uncertainty are low, while the asset specificity is high. Based on the scores regarding the variables, Williamson's framework suggests a hierarchy. Changing the relationships themselves to achieve a hierarchical configuration would prove difficult, since many independent organizations are involved. Therefore, we suggest an intermediate form which leaves more room for diversity, but still counters the risk of exploitative behaviour. Relational contracting, a combination of semi-market contracts and the development of enduring trust relationships can be used for this purpose (Williamson, 2002).

The relationship between actors and technology in Groenewegen's model is particularly interesting and problematic here. The primary goal of general practitioners is supposed to be care for individual patients, based on the Hippocratic oath. Their contribution to the early warning system for outbreaks does not directly contribute to that goal, which means that they often see this type of informational obligation as an unwanted administrative burden, keeping them away from their primary concern (a point raised in a discussion with René). A somewhat related concern on the side of the doctors is that confidential information about their patients will be shared with other doctors or, even worse, non-medical staff. Confidence in technical solutions or fundamental choices (such as the anonymization of patient data) aimed at the prevention of this exchange is far from obvious. In our design, we try to overcome these barriers by using an information infrastructure that is already under development, the EPF. Although its implementation is problematic as well, practitioners (representatives) are heavily involved in its design and implementation. Another measure may be the legal enforcement of the obligation to provide information. However, without very invasive measures, it is hard to check for compliance, which means that it may be more useful to increase awareness by explaining the importance of this system. An attractive way of doing so is by providing feedback on the information that has been collected. Doctors may want to know which of their colleagues have similar patients. This information could be exchanged without revealing any sensitive data.

The DNS primarily consists of server-side software modules that are accessed through a secure channel by lab workers and general practitioners. The advantage of a centralized architecture is that the practitioners' IT systems, which are very different, as well as hard to manage and secure, require only minor adaptations. Physical security and a secure configuration can be better guaranteed and updates can be installed much more quickly. The financial structures can also be simpler, as only a limited number of organizations need to be paid to implement the system.
This secure channel already exists and only a small portion of server side hardware has to be installed on which to run our software modules. Because this system will be linked to the existing EPF, practitioners and lab workers will only have a small additional module on the client side through which relevant information is submitted, replacing traditional paper-based communication. Authentication and authorization (not shown in the figure) can be based on the existing infrastructures as well. Figure 2 presents an overview of the DNS. As the required data content,

format and lay-out will be consistent will traditional communication, lab workers and general practitioners will not require training other than a general and well-written briefing. Nevertheless, support must be provided in case of system problems of a technical or semantic nature.

Decision Facilitation and Empowerment System

To solve the second problem (suboptimal decision-making in times of crisis) we propose a second alternative, named the Decision Facilitation and Empowerment System (D-FES), which filters the input from various organizations and adds meta-data. The meta-data are used to connect different information types and aggregate a packet of related information. Furthermore, the meta-data are used to determine which information is relevant for which decision-making body, i.e. operational or strategic. Hence, information is not only standardized, but it is also filtered on the basis of its relevance. On the other hand, the D-FES creates a clear responsibility structure and protocol, while at the same time facilitating organizational learning. XML is the standard format in which information and meta-data are stored, as this is (becoming) the industry standard and has the highest level of flexibility with regard to future changes. It can also deal quite well with many different source systems, as XML messages can easily be transformed into different templates. D-FES generates PowerPoint

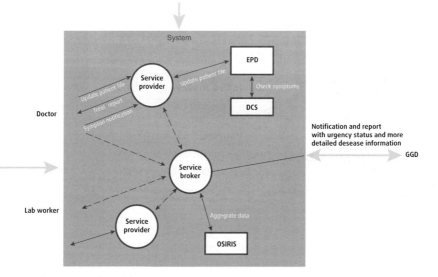

Figure 2 Overview of the DNS

slides that can be used to structure a meeting between decision-makers. This software tool is used because it is concise and enforces some structure, but not too much. To integrate the various information flows we have used a Service Oriented Architecture. Again, this provides the highest flexibility when it comes to re-using the information in different settings and adapting the system when needed. Figure 3 shows an overview of D-FES.

For the institutional design, we looked again at frequency, uncertainty and asset specificity to match these characteristics with a governance mechanism from an administrative and from an operational perspective. With regard to the administration of D-FES, the frequency and asset specificity are low, while uncertainty is high, which matches with trilateral governance, since this suits best the diversity found in the actors and systems using D-FES. In the case of the operation of D-FES, the frequency is very low, while asset specificity is very high and uncertainty can be neglected. Williamson's framework clearly suggests a hierarchy here, due to the fact that decisions may need to be enforced. We propose deconnecting the organizational and the informational structure to make it possible to bypass regular bureaucratic structures for exchanging information. Therefore, a

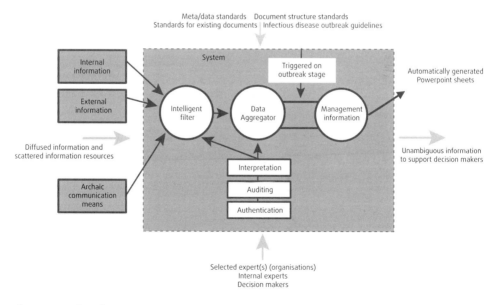

Figure 3 Overview of D-FES

Crisis Information Officer (CIO) will be installed that reports directly to the decision-making bodies. Figure 4 shows the relationship between important actors and the CIO.

Structuration theory reminds us of an important design awareness. Whereas we try to influence organizational structures (micro-social environments) by technology, it may also work the other way around and, in the same causal direction, have unwanted consequences. Following Giddens (F. Cohen, 1997) and Orlikowski (1991), the mutual relationship can be described from three perspectives (modalities): interpretive schemes, resources and norms. Within this terminology, interpretive schemes formalise and encode the existing stock of knowledge. Resources reinforce themselves through the positive feedback loop of controlling organizational focus. Finally, norms, especially when coded in technology, ensure that people act in conventional ways and determine priorities, criteria and other policies. In other words, an IT system can create a reality of its own as it shapes structures, while at the same time being shaped by them. In our case, we have to be very cautious in applying an IT system as the only possible approach. The system should bring semantics and the perceptions and approaches of individuals together, as this kind of coherence is precisely what is lacking in the current system. However, if the system does flatten creativity, responsibility and flexibility, new problems may be reduced. As now crisis is completely predictable, neither can its information structures be preformatted. A continuous reassessment of the way the system functions and interacts with the organizational structures is necessary. Our appointment of information liaison officers who can communicate through a variety of media, and the choice in favour of a human explanation of the data by the chief information officer (the decision-making expert) is also a measure that ensures structures do not become too rigid. Bouwman et al. (2005) discuss media richness theory as an analytical tool to assess the use of ICT in organizations. This theory suggests that not all media are equally suited to handle all communication tasks. When there is a need for information equivocality (similar understanding and perceptions) and not only for a large quantity of facts, rich media are more suitable. To some extent, rich media provide instant feedback, multiple cues, the ability to use natural language and the possibility to maintain a personal focus. The fact-based system we propose is a very thin medium in this sense, which suggests its use should only be supportive and not replace richer media channels like face-to-face communication.

Discussion and reflection

The two IT systems presented in this chapter can operate independently from each other. The power of their combination is that the information process needed for effective decision-making is improved in all the phases of an outbreak. Information from the DNS will not directly be used in crisis situations, but can prevent the process from escalating. The many differences between architectural choices of both systems remind us that there is no standard approach when it comes to designing systems that are aligned with their organizational and problem-related context. In René's perception, the problem context in terms of its actors, systems and processes should be the starting point in designing an appropriate system to contain outbreaks of infectious diseases. René especially emphasized the importance of conducting interviews with relevant stakeholders, and he explicitly required that the processes be designed in a way that they take into account possible resistance, for instance of general practitioners, in adopting their daily operations to the proposed solutions.

An effective response to outbreaks of infectious diseases increasingly depends on the interaction between multiple parties using a broad spectrum of ICT solutions. In this chapter, we used an approach based on this insight to create a more holistic design. This approach consists of a technological design laying down ICT solutions, and a design for the institutional

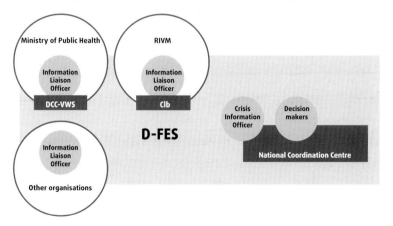

Figure 4 Position of the Crisis Information Officer

arrangements. The interaction between technology and institutions lay at the heart of René's curiosity. The fact that, although technology itself may play a modest role, its existence can force institutions to change and reallocate existing responsibilities, provides a window of opportunity to improve safety by means of ICT.

Although Groenewegen's framework indicated some relationships that were in need of investigation, it did not provide any substantial analytical tools. There is a need to 'feed' the framework with other theories and to operationalize them further. Because the framework is so flexible, it provides little guidance in a design process. The detailing of all relationships may suffer from eclecticism, which is a strength and a weakness at the same time. It is a strength because it enables the researcher-designer to adopt an interdisciplinary perspective. Its weakness lies in the possibility to shop selectively from the theoretical assortment and not enforcing enough focus to check for coherence with regard to all perspectives that have been applied. We have tried to reduce that danger by applying structuration theory, which operates at the crossroads of Groenewegen's elements. However, we did not investigate all the relationships with the same depth, which may have introduced a bias in our recommendations and considerations with regard to the relationship between technology and the people who are supposed to use it. Our theoretical understanding of IT systems may benefit from a more rigid, validated and parsimonious adaptation of Groenewegen's framework. Nevertheless, the outcomes of our research are still of a rather abstract nature. A further specification of the design choices down to the level of requirements will provide greater guidance for policy-makers. A continuous movement between abstract and more practical levels of analysis can feed our theoretical understanding as well. With regard to DFES, this may involve a careful analysis of a real or simulated crisis situation (which may already have been transcribed in the past), which feeds an improved version of our design, for instance by examining the exact types of information needed. The system can then be compared, in an experimental setting, with the 'traditional' approach to information gathering, as a way of validating our arguments and assessing effectiveness. With regard to DNS, insights from the Electronic Patient File may be used to improve our design. The designs are highly context and time dependent, but the method of analysis can be repeated from time to time, building on already existing insights.

References

Adviescommissie Coördinatie ICT Rampenbestrijding. (2005). De Vrijblijvendheid Voorbij.
Bökkerink, M. (2006). Transcript interview with Marc Bökkerink - Ministry of Internal Affairs and Kingdom Relations, Department Central Preparation. The Hague.
Bouwman, H., van Dijk, J., van de Wijngaert, L., & Van Den Hooff, B. (2005). Information Communication Technology in Organizations: Adoption, Implementation, Use and Effects: Sage Publications.
Bun, E., de Koning, T., Monasso, T., Veldhoven, P., & Verheij, A. (2006). Spread the information. TU Delft.
Cohen, F. (1997). Information system attacks: A preliminary classification scheme. Computers and Security, 16(1), 29-46.
Cohen, I. J. (1989). Structuration theory : Anthony Giddens and the constitution of social life. Basingstoke: Macmillan.
DeLone, W. H., & McLean, E. R. (1992). Information Systems Success: The Quest for the Dependent Variable. Information Systems Research, 3(1), 60-95.
Groenewegen, J. (1995). Transaction cost economics; an introduction. Unpublished Chapter in reader. Delft University of Technology.
Groenewegen, J. (2005). Designing Markets in Infrastructures: from Blueprint to Learning. Delft: Delft University of Technology.
Hanseth, O., & Monteiro, E. (1998). Understanding Information Infrastructure. University of Oslo.
Jacobi, A. (2006). Transcript interview met André Jacobi - LCI. Bilthoven.
Ministry of the Interior and Kingdom Relations. (2002). Nationaal Handboek Crisisbesluitvorming. The Hague: Ministry of the Interior and Kingdom Relations.
Ministry of the Interior and Kingdom Relations. (2004). Beleidsplan Crisisbeheersing 2004-2007. Den Haag: Ministry of the Interior and Kingdom Relations.
Orlikowski, W. J., & Robey, D. (1991). Information technology and the structuring of organizations (Vol. 2, pp. 143-169).
Riordan, N. H. (1985). Asset Specificity and economic organization. International Journal of Industrial Organization, 3(1985), 365-378.
Scharpf, F. W. (1997). Games Real Actors Play: Actor-Centered Institutionalism in Policy Research. Boulder: Westview Press.
Van der Brugge, M., & Kemp, M. (2006). Transcript interview with Matthijs van der Brugge and Michiel Kemp - Ministry of Internal Affairs, National Coordination Centre. The Hague.
Van Dijk, I. (2006). Transcript interview with Irene van Dijk - RIVM. Bilthoven.
Williamson, O. E. (1998). Transaction cost economics: how it works, where it is headed. The Economist, 1(1998), 146.
Williamson, O. E. (2000). The new institutional economics: Taking stock, looking ahead. Journal of Economic Literature, 38(3), 595-613.
Williamson, O. E. (2002). The Theory of the Firm as Governance Structure: From Choice to Contract. Journal of Economic Perspectives, 16(3), 171-195.

Part IV

Let a thousand flowers bloom

TO A CERTAIN EXTENT THIS GAP IS CAUSED BY THE MOBILE TELECOMMUNICATION TECHNOLOGY REQUIRED, WHICH HAS NOT BEEN SUFFICIENTLY DEVELOPED AS YET... MORE STRINGENT DEMANDS WILL BE MADE CONCERNING THE CONFIGURATION OF SERVICES IN TERMS OF TAILORING, EXPANDABILITY, ALTERATIONS, RE-USE AND COSTS. THIS SUGGESTS A MODULAR APPROACH TO SERVICES THAT WILL CONSIST OF COMPONENTS WITH CLEARLY DELINEATED FUNCTIONALITIES.

From *Civil Servant*

Strategy and business models: mobile telecommunication

Harry Bouwman, Mark de Reuver and Guadalupe Flores Hernández

Abstract

In many aspects, René was highly interested in discussing strategies and business models. These are also the core areas of our research, which lies in the domain of business models for mobile Internet services. We consider business models to be a blueprint for a service to be delivered, involving design choices and trade-offs in the service, technological, organizational and financial domain. Nowadays, strategic choices are often implemented in business models, mainly impacting design choices in the service and organizational domain. Specifically, choices on how to govern mobile service innovation that transcends the borders of single organizations are important here. However, technology as an enabler often impacts both strategies and business models. This is illustrated by the emergence of mobile web services that enable content providers to authenticate, bill and localize users without relying on network operators. Next steps in our research will be in the area of service innovation and design, focusing on marketing tools to support service design; service bundle composition; and embedding of services in (inter)organizational processes. Business modeling will remain an important area, as future research will include testing our business model approach in practice for its robustness and validity.

René loved strategy days. Discussions about the direction in which the Information and Communication Technology section of the Technology, Policy and Management Faculty ought to move were important to René. What are the research subjects that will important in the near future? How can we profile ourselves? What is our focus? What are the relevant scientific and practical questions? These are examples of the questions René liked to pose, during strategy days, but also during encounters in the university's corridors. Every year, at some point there would be a strategy day. About six months later, René would once again become a little restless, and the next strategy would appear on the horizon.

René had also been interested in strategic issues during the time he worked for KPN Research. What were the choices KPN Research had to make to cope with the challenges posed by the Internet? In his inaugural address at Delft University of Technology, 'The Virtual Civil Servant', he indicated that 'the telecom operators have overplayed their hand and are now forced to depreciate goodwill and frequency licenses'. Following Michael Porter, René looked for a possible explanation for the problems facing Telecom Operators as a result of the emergence of the Internet and the subsequent response from the financial markets in the fact that the virtual nature of the Business Models involved makes them easy to copy.

We shared an interest in strategy and business models, two concepts that are frequently confused. Whereas René's interest in these concepts in relation to information and communication technology was more general in nature, our research focuses on mobile Internet. In his research together with Peter Vervest, Martijn Hoogewegen et al. (see contribution in this volume), and later also in his inaugural address at the Free University of Amsterdam, René emphasized the fact that businesses operate in networks of suppliers, customers, logistical and financial service providers, and sub-contractors for specific applications. In the mobile Internet domain, the relationships between the actors involved, and the question as to how these relationships should be managed, play an important role. Governance is a key concept in that respect, one to which we will return later.

Under the influence of new technologies, and in particular web-services, we see that the balance between the various parties within the Mobile Value Network is slowly shifting. The translation of web-services towards the mobile domain affects the strategic positioning of the actors involved, as well as the way existing business models are being applied and redefined. Mobile Internet is the third subject on which we shared a common interest.

The objective of this chapter is to clarify the relationship between strategy and business models, and to show that, although business models do not change, as a result of technological innovations, strategies may, which is why in this chapter we investigate the relationship between business models and strategy, in particular in relation to the behavior of actors in the mobile domain. We begin by discussing different views on the main concepts, strategy and business models, after which we briefly discuss mobile web-services, i.e. technological innovation that we expect to have an impact in the mobile domain, and address the implications with regard to the strategy and business models of actors operating in the Mobile Internet web. We close by providing an outlook on future research.

Strategy and Business models

There is much confusion about the concepts of strategy and business models, which can be attributed to the different traditions from which these concepts originated. Business Strategy has a long tradition, both in practical and in conceptual terms. Publications on the concept of strategy go back to the 1960's. Although strategy was originally a military concept, the work by Mintzberg and Porter, among others, became leading in business or corporate strategy approaches. Corporate strategy has to do with an organization's basic direction for the future: its purpose (and the plans and actions to achieve that purpose), its ambitions, its resources and the way it interacts with the world in which it operates (Lynch, 2003). Strategy deals with strategic positions, i.e. an organization's environment, expectations and purposes, resources and capabilities, strategic choices and strategy implementation. When it comes to strategy, there are various schools of thought, like planning, entrepreneurial, cognitive school etc., as well as many strategy perspectives, like industrial organization (Porter), resource-based view (Barney), process perspective (Mintzberg, and followers in the ICT-domain like Kaplan, Henderson & Venkatraman, Ciborra)

The business model concept comes from a different tradition. In the 1970's, the concept of business model was used to describe and map business processes and information and communication patterns within a company for the purpose of building an IT-system (Konczal, 1975; Stähler 2001). Hedman and Kalling (2003) rightfully point out that the relevant literature on business models is dominated by descriptions of 'specific' empirically identified business models. Sometimes the concept is used to describe co-ordination mechanism in economic processes i.e. markets or hierarchies, or to discuss intermediation or disintermediation trends (Tapscott et al, 2000; Mahadevan, 2000). In other studies, the implementation of a specific market model (Hawkins, 2002), for example the electronic auction, is discussed in terms of business models (Timmers, 1998). Very often only one aspect is emphasized, for example the B2C-model for the retail sector (Roussel et al. 2000; Lee, 2001), or B2C and B2B are discussed (Alt & Zimmermann, 2001). Recently, business models have been related to peer-to-peer file sharing services (Hughes et al, 2007). Clearly, as a result of the breakthrough of the Internet, business models have been the subject of increased interest. The concept of business models was originally used in the Information Systems domain. Conceptualization was more or less driven by the need to describe organizational and/or transactional processes with the use of BPMN (Business Process Modelling Notation), Unified Modelling Language (UML), an object-oriented modelling language, or Integration Definition Function Modelling- family (IDEF).

The Business Model has managed to establish itself in scientific research in a short period of time and can be considered multi-disciplinary in nature. Disciplines like information systems, innovation studies, economics, e-business and marketing have rapidly adopted the concept of business models.

Business models defined

In our view, *"a business model is a blueprint for a service to be delivered, describing the service definition and the intended value for the target group, the sources of revenue, and providing an architecture for the service delivery, including a description of the resources required, and the organizational and financial arrangements between the involved business actors, including a description of their roles and the division of costs and revenues among the business actors"* (Haaker et al, 2006) It is clear that, in our definition, the concept of service and its various components takes on a central position, as does the assumption that services cannot and will not be delivered by a single organization or company, but that a number of companies have to work together, enabled by Internet technology, in creating and delivering the services.

Basically, business models are about the components that have to be discussed, designed, catered and put in place to deliver a service to end-users. It is more about ontology: an explicit (and often formalized) specification of a (shared) conceptualization (Gruber, 1995; Borst 1997) of the components or elements, relationships, vocabulary and semantics of the core object (Pigneur, 2004) The fact that this conceptualization is shared means

that common concepts can and have to be communicated between the actors involved. Afuah and Tucci (2001) see business models as a system of components (value, revenue sources, price, related activities, implementation, capabilities and sustainability), relationships and interrelated technology, while Mahadevan (2000) emphasizes value creation, revenues and logistics. Osterwalder and Pigneur (2002) discuss four basic elements:
— product innovation and the implicit value proposition;
— customer management, including the description of the target customer, channels, customer relations;
— infrastructure management, the capabilities and resources, value configuration, web or network and partnerships;
— financial aspects, the revenue models, cost structure and profit.

The number of components mentioned varies between four and eight. In all, twenty four different items are mentioned (Morris et al., 2005). Shafer et al. (2005) offer an overview based on twelve core publications, concluding that the core components can be summarized in terms of strategic choices, value creation, value networks and the capturing of value. The strategic choices have to do with customers (target, market scope), value proposition, capabilities and competencies, revenues and pricing, competitors, output (offering), strategy, branding, differentiation and mission. We focus on customer value and the organizational, technical and financial arrangements needed to provide a service that offers added value to the customers and providers of the services.

Strategies are increasingly being implemented into business models. Nowadays, many business ventures have a limited interest in formulating strategies; instead, they formulate business models (Hedman and Kalling 2003). Strategies, and consequently business models, to a large extent determine the processes that lie at the basis of the business case: the concrete operational implementation of the business strategy in a model. The business model is given shape by answering questions with regard to customer needs, the way the services are provided, the availability and the way in which the necessary technical, financial and human resources and capabilities are put in place, the way processes are defined, etc., Information and communication technology, i.e. Internet and mobile technologies, play an increasingly important role, not only in the organizational processes (back office) but also in the channels (front office) that are needed to deliver products and services to their end-users.

We want to illustrate how strategies are implemented in business models by comparing the business model of a gourmet restaurant and that of McDonald's. The basic business models are closely related. Customer value is generated by offering food and drinks at a specific price to customers. To provide this service to customers, a building and space are needed where the food and drinks can be served or collected (in the case of self service). There has to be a fully equipped kitchen to prepare and serve the food and drinks. Trained staff is needed to execute tasks, both in preparing the food and in serving customers. The level of training can be minimal, as is the case with McDonald's, or it can be very extensive. There have to be tables and seats, etc. Defining the target market (reach and scope), as well as marketing (branding), are is necessary for both types of restaurants. The strategic decisions have to do with the kind of restaurant one wants to be: a high volume, small margin, low quality, cheap, fast food restaurant like

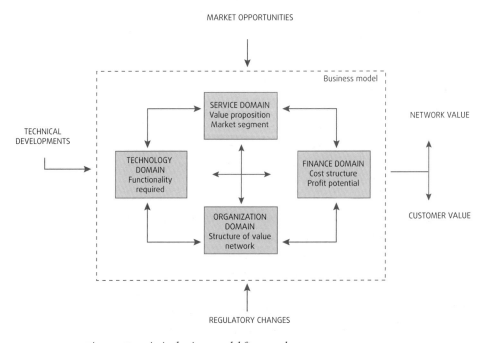

Figure 1: Descriptive business model framework

McDonald's, which uses marketing aimed at kids, or a small volume, high margin gourmet restaurant, with high quality cooking and highly trained and qualified staff, and a marketing strategy that is based on word-of-mouth. Typically, the topics that were mentioned with regard to strategic choices before by Shafer et al. are the ones that are most susceptible to strategy, and they are most directly related to the service to be offered. We will discuss how these topics are related to our model for analyzing and designing business models.

STOF-MODEL AND STRATEGY

Most of the strategic issues mentioned by Shafer et al. are included in our STOF model (for an extensive description of the model and its background, see Bouwman et al. 2008, and figure 1), as the *service domain*. The service domain contains a description of the value proposition (added value of a service offering) and the market segment at which the offering is targeted. Our model also contains three additional domains, i.e. a *technology domain*: a description of the technical functionality required to realize the service offering; an *organizational domain*: a description of the structure of the multi-actor value network needed to create and distribute the service offering, and to describe the focal firm's position within this value network, and a *financial* domain: a description of the way a value network intends to generate revenues from a particular service offering and of the way risks, investments and revenues are divided among the various actors in a value network. Competition, regulation and technology are viewed as external drivers in relation to our core model. As far as the external analysis of competitive forces is concerned, Porter's approach to strategy formulation (Porter, 1985) is helpful in making strategic decisions. Next, we provide a brief discussion of the STOF-model.

The central concept in the *service domain* is 'value': the perceived benefits and total costs (or sacrifice) to customers in target markets of (obtaining) a product or service. The service offering must be considered better, and perceived as delivering the desired satisfaction more effectively and efficiently than competing services. The key concept in this respect is customer or user experience. In many cases, the customer value that is envisaged in the initial idea for a service has little to do with the way customers assess the actual value, which to a large extent depends on the customers' personal or consumption-related context, which is why we introduce the related concepts of intended value and delivered value on the side of the provider, and perceived value on the side of consumers. These added concepts allow us to compare the different perspectives on the added value of a service. As we have mentioned earlier, the service concept is most sensitive to strategic decisions. Choices related to the implementation of the common strategy of the actors involved are leading in the service domain.

One of the central concepts in the *technology domain* is 'functionality', which can be defined as 'the things a system or application can do' for its end-users. Another core concept in the technology domain is 'technical architecture'. A technical architecture describes the fundamental organization of a technical system, which is needed by the firms in the value network to deliver the intended customer value of the service that is defined in the service domain. Important components of a technical architecture are applications, devices, access networks, service platforms and backbone infrastructure. Typically, the technology domain is more operational than strategic in nature, although specific technological choices may result in a strategic collaboration between the actors involved. However, this kind of collaboration is a core element of the organizational domain

Central concepts in the *organizational domain* have to do with the resources and capabilities that have to be available within the organization or organizational environment. Although the resource-based approach (Barney 1991) assumes that resources and capabilities should be organized internally, we observe that organizations do not control all the resources, in particular in the mobile and wireless services domains. In their analysis of business models, Hedman & Kalling (2003), conclude that economic value is ultimately determined by a firm's ability to trade and absorb ICT-resources, to align (and embed) them with other resources, to integrate them into activities and manage those activities in such a way as to create a proposition at uniquely low costs or with unique qualities in relation to the industry in which the company operates. Because collaboration, in-sourcing and network formation are possible strategies to obtain the necessary resources (Pfeffer & Salancik, 1978), organizations increasingly work together in value networks to deliver customer value (Madehevan, 2000;Miller & Lessard, 2000).

Within a value network which uses the (mobile) Internet, the main questions are related to access to critical resources, such as access
— to the Internet access network and backbone and/or mobile infrastructure,
— to content, i.e. to content developers, aggregators and hosting providers, to software and application platforms,
— to customers, customer data, billing, customer support and customer management, and
— based on the type of service, access to the providers of specific technology-related services, for instance mobile, location or positioning applications

The actors involved in the value network provide access to these critical resources. Like the other actors involved, customers are co-creators of value. In particular web 2.0 services can play a role in this respect.

Depending on the competitive environment, industry sector and the operating risks involved, specific actors contribute key assets, which in the case of mobile services refers to most of the technological and marketing-related resources, in the creation of value, and a different configuration of actors is likely to result, with some actors taking on structural, integrative roles in the alliance, and others taking on supporting, facilitating roles (Hawkins, 2003). With regard to cooperation, an important issue is network governance. It is possible to distinguish three aspects of value network governance. First of all, the basic rules for participating in the value network have to be determined. Secondly, it is necessary to monitor the extent to which the actors in the value network obey those rules. However, the primary decision that has to be made is who 'governs' or is the 'center of gravity' of the network, and in what way their legitimacy within the network is established. We expect that such legitimacy is closely related to access to and dependence on critical resources. Moreover, we expect that governance mechanisms partly depend on the stage of service innovation, i.e. development, roll-out and commercialization. These questions are related to De Reuver's PhD project, of which René was co-supervisor.

The decision to collaborate is strategic in nature. Strategic networks, such as traditional strategic alliances, joint ventures, and long term supplier relationships, or more modern Internet technology-enabled value webs, networks, nets or inter-organizational systems, are all sources of network value. The decision to participate and contribute has long-term consequences. According to Tapscott (2001), networks in which all the participants focus on their core competences are more flexible, innovative, cost-effective and profitable than traditional vertically integrated companies. Tapscott stresses that it is specifically the use of Internet technology that makes it possible to organize business differently in a more networked fashion, thanks to the economies of scale associated with the Internet. Search, coordination, contracting and other transaction costs are reduced considerably.

The core concepts in the *financial domain*, the financial arrangements, have to do with investment decisions, revenue models and revenue-sharing arrangements. Financial methods are aimed at average cost-effectiveness, net cash worth and internal return (Demkes, 1999; Renkema, 1996). Some methods go beyond the purely financial considerations, for example real option theory, a more detailed elaboration on the net cash worth concept that puts an explicit value on managerial flexibility to respond to future developments (Demkes, 1999; Renkema, 1996). Generally speaking, the cost side is reasonably well charted. As far as the revenue side is concerned, which from our point of view includes realizing cost reductions, but also long term advantages that stem from intangibles, existing literature is less uniform (Low & Cohen Kalafut, 2002). An important question is how investments are arranged within complex value networks. Investment decisions weigh the interests of the actors involved and take the mutual benefits of multiple organizations into account. Organizations that are connected through intended relationships and interdependencies consider risk sharing, solving common problems, and acquiring access to complementary knowledge to be major motivators for collective investments. Inter-organizational investments require explicit articulation and collective agreement with regard to the terms of investment and timing (Miller & Lessard, 2000). The share of each of the participants and the corresponding partnership ratio must be defined. The success of these arrangements depends on whether or not the role of each member within the terms of the institutional framework is clearly defined (Miller & Lessard, 2000). Although there is a clear connection between organizational and financial arrangements, there are few strategic implications.

We can conclude that strategic implications are of key importance in the service and organizational domains, and that they are less important in the technology and financial domain. This does not mean that technology, specifically as a driver, cannot have strategic consequences. In the next sections we briefly discuss the emergence of mobile web-services, and its strategic implications, while the business models of the core actors remain almost the same. The mobile web-services case is illustrative.

Mobile web-services and implications for telecom operators and mobile services providers

Web-services technology and their underlying service-oriented architecture have enhanced flexibility and interoperability in service development in the fixed Internet and traditional IT world. Mobile web-services (MWS), the topic of Flores' thesis, offer important opportunities with regard to providing generic service elements, like charging, authentication, authorization, accounting, context information and billing (Pashtan, 2005). Typically, these generic services are needed to access customers and customer data, or to provide billing opportunities. Moreover, mobile web-services are an extension of the more generic web-services that are used by service and content providers. MWS can enable 'anytime, anywhere, on any device and network' access to services, both for customers and for service and content providers (Farley and Capp, 2005). Because web-services technology allows for a seamless integration of existing applications, a wide variety of innovative services and service bundles can be made available and be presented as a single integrated business function (Farley and Capp, 2005). As such, the technology can compete with IP Multimedia Subsystem (IMS), a standard originating from the telecommunications domain. Currently, operators are implementing IP Multimedia Subsystem (IMS), a standard capable of providing similar generic service elements (Cuevas et al., 2006, UMTS Forum, 2003). However, there are serious differences between the two technologies. IMS is an add-on to the operators' core network, and since the operators host all generic service elements, their position will be strengthened. Content providers will have to negotiate and adhere to the operators' requirements with regard to using the services. By contrast, MWS can be hosted by any party, and they may well be used by content providers to open the de facto walled gardens that are currently present in mobile business. For example, offering standard MWS could solve existing issues involving billing and authentication, areas that are often mentioned by content providers as limiting true innovativeness in mobile data services (e.g., Jaokar and Fish, 2004). In a broader perspective, the competition between IMS and MWS can thus be interpreted as a traditional clash between the open Internet world and the more closed telecommunications sector. While IMS strengthens the operators' strategic position, MWS can be offered by any business actor and may therefore be used by content and service providers to disrupt the industry's existing structure.

Although we are aware that web-services are platform and language independent, we are of the opinion that the discussion regarding MWS is relevant, because the mobile context implies various specific constraints and opportunities. For example, the processing capacity of mobile devices is typically insufficient for XML messages (Limbu et al., 2004), data rates and network reliability pose challenges, and the existing session-oriented principles of mobile networks are incompatible with the asynchronous nature of web-services technology (Levenshteyn and Fikouras, 2006). In addition, authentication is different in mobile telecommunications compared to the fixed Internet, as it is SIM card-based, and personalization and privacy are more prominent issues, because mobile devices can more easily be related to persons. Finally, we see specific design considerations regarding the location of intelligence (i.e. in the network or in the mobile device) (Gehlen and Pham, 2004), the architecture used to implement MWS (i.e. opting in favour of a proprietary architecture, OMA's open architecture, or a mixed IMS / MWS architecture), and the server-client model (i.e. thin client versus thick client model). To take full advantage of the potential of MWS, it is important to develop an architecture that is based on standard technologies and protocols (XML, SOAP, UDDI, WSDL) and that uses Internet transport protocols (HTML, HTTPS, SMTP). Such architecture would define the building blocks and standard protocols used in MWS transmission. One of the design choices that has to be made has to do with the question whether to build proprietary solutions, for instance the ones that have been developed by Nokia and Vodafone (Nokia & Sun, 2004) or to opt in favor of open solutions, for instance the Open Mobile Alliance MWS architecture. Content and service providers may favor open solutions, because interoperability may generate value all around. Moreover, consumers would not feel locked in to a company and they would have access to a wider service offer. However, large companies may very well decide in favor of proprietary solutions (especially with regard to the technical architecture), keeping in mind that they already control a large portion of the market that they are reluctant to share.

Future outlook

What are the implications for future research and practice? In a recent contribution to a book, we started to work out some ideas about the impact of mobile web-services together with René (Bouwman & Wagenaar, 2006). We focused on mobile web-services, specifically on the role these services could play in service bundling. We found that, like in the government web-services research case (see the contribution by Janssen et al. in this book), orchestration was a key issue. We also looked at the possibility to use fuzzy logic as an alternative to orchestration, as discussed in the contribution by Carlsson and Walden. It may be clear that René was extremely interested in these topics. Our research will continue to focus on service innovation and design, in particular with regard to mobile services, with specific attention to service bundles and how they have to be composed and managed. We are aware that, when designing mobile services, a number of practical and theoretical implementation problems arise that need closer research. The first has to do with the support of the service design with more practical marketing type of tools, the second with the way bundles of services can be composed (as discussed before), and the third with the embedding of services in the existing business processes of the organizations involved, i.e. the processes of the provider of the service, as well as of the organization that makes use of these services.

Business modelling remains an important area. From an academic point of view, it is important to test our business model approach in terms of robustness and predictive validity.

References

Afuah, A. & C. Tucci (2001). Internet Business Models and Strategies. Boston: McGraw-Hill, Irwin

Alt, R. & H. Zimmerman (2001). Introduction to special Section – Business Models. Electronic Markets, Vol 11, issue 1, pp. 3-9.

Barney, J. R. (1991). Firm Resources and Structural Competitive Advantage. Journal of Management. Vol 17: 99-120.

Borst P. (1997). Construction of Engineering Ontologies for Knowledge Sharing and Re-use. Twente University PhD-thesis.

Bouwman, H. & R. Wagenaar (2006). Mobile service bundles, mobile service compositions and the role of fuzzy logic. In: P. Walden, R. Fuller & J. Carlsson (eds). Expanding the Limits of the Possible. Turku. pp. 145-159

Bouwman, H., T Haaker, H. De Vos (eds) (2008). Mobile service innovation and business models. Springer

Cuevas, A., Moreno, J. I., Vidales, P. & Einsiedler, H. (2006). The IMS Service Platform: A solution for Next-Generation Network Operators to be more then bit pipes. IEEE Communications Magazine. Sept 2006 75-8

Demkes, R. (1999). COMET: A comprehensive methodology for supporting telematics investment decisions. Enschede: Telematica Instituut

Farley, P. & Capp, M. (2005). Mobile Web-services. BT Technology Journal, 23.

Gehlen, G. & Pham, L. (2004). Mobile Web-services for Peer-to-Peer applications. IEEE 2004. Available at http://ieeexplore.ieee.org/iel5/9640/30469/01405210.pdf?arnumber=1405210.

Gruber, T.R. (1995). Towards principles for the design of ontologies sed for knowledge sharing. International Journal of Human Computer Studies. Vol. 43, pp. 907-928.

Haaker, T., E. Faber & H. Bouwman (2006). Customer and network value of 3G+mobile services. An holistic approach to balance requirements and strategic interests. Journal of Mobile Commerce , Vol. 4, no. 6, pp. 645- 661

Hawkins, R. (2002). The Phantom of the Marketplace: Searching for New E-commerce Business models. Communication & Strategies Vol 46, issue 2, pp. 297-329.

Hawkins, R. (2003). Looking beyond the .com bubble: exploring the form and function of business models in the electronic marketplace (pp. 65-82). In: B. Preissl, H. Bouwman & C. Steinfeld (eds). Elife after the Dot.com bust. Berlin; Springer Verlag.

Hedman, J. & T. Kalling (2003). The business model concept: theoretical underpinnings and empirical illustrations. European Journal of Information Systems 12, 49-59.

Hughes, J., K. R. Lang, & R. Vragov (2007). An analytical framework for evaluating peer-to-peer business models. Electronic Commerce Research and Applications. Vol, pp.

Jaokar, A. & Fish, T. (2004). Open Gardens. The innovator's guide to the Mobile data industry., Futuretex London. November 2004.

Konczal, E. (1975). Models are ᴛ Managers, not for Mathematicians. Journal os System Management. Vol 26, no. 2, p. 12.

Lee, C-S. (2001). An analytical framework for evaluating e-commerce business models and strategies. Internet Research: Electronic Networking Applications and Policy, Volume 11, Number 4, 2001 , pp. 349-359

Levenshteijn, R. & Fikouras, I. (2006). Mobile services interworking for IMS and XML Web-services. IEEE Communications Magazine. Sept 2006.

www.306.ibm.com/software/solutions/webservices/pdf/WSFL.pdf.

Limbu, D. K., Wah, L. E. & Yushi, C. (2004). Wireless Web-services clients development. Using Web-services standards and J2ME technology. Information Technology Standards Committee. Available at http://www.itsc.org.sg/synthesis/2004/4—J2ME.pdf.

Low, J. & P. Cohen Kalafut (2002). Invisible Advantage. How Intangibles are driving Business Performance. Cambridge (Ma) Persues Publishing

Lynch, R. (2003). Corporate Strategy. Harlow: Prentice Hall/Financial Times.

Mahadevan, B. (2000). Business models for internet- Based E-commerce. California Management Review. Vol. 42, No.4, pp. 55-69

Miller, R. & D. Lessard (2000). The Strategic Management of Large Engineering Projects. Shaping Institutions, Risks and Governance. Boston: MIT Press

Morris, M., M. Schindehutte, & J. Allen (2005). The entrepreneur's business model: towards a uni̇ed perspective. Journal of Business Research. Vol. 58, pp. 726-735

Nokia & Sun (2004). Deploying Mobile Web-services Using Liberty Alliance's Identity Web-services Framework (Id-Wsf).

Pashtan, A. (2005). Mobile Web-services. Cambridge, UK: Cambridge University Press.

Pfeffer, J. & G. Salancik (1978). The external control of Organizations. A resource Dependence Perspective. New York: Harper & Row, Publishers.

Pigneur, Y, (2004). An ontology for m-Business Models. Conceptual Modelling - ER 2002: 21st International Conference on Conceptual Modelling Tampere, Finland, October 7-11, 2002. Proceedings. . Lecture Notes in Computer Science. Vol 2503/2002, p. 3-6.

Porter, M. E. (1985). Competitive Advantage: Creating and Sustaining Superior Performance. New York

Porter, M.E. (2001). Strategy and the Internet. Harvard Business Review. March, 63-76.

Renkema, T. (1996). Investeren in de informatie-infrastructuur. Richtlijnen voor besluitvorming in organisaties. Deventer: Kluwer Bedrijfsinformatie

Roussel, A., Daum, A., Flint, D., & Riseley, M. (2000). B2C web business models: Winners and losers.Gartner Group Research

Shafer, S.M., H. J. Smith & J.C. Linder (2005). The Power of Business Models. Business Horizons, Vol. 48, pp. 199-207.

Stähler,P. (2001). Gesellschäftmodellen in der digitalen Ökonomie: Merkmale, Strategien und Auswirkungen. Köln: Josef Eul Verlag.

Tapscott, D., Lowi, A., Ticoll, D. (2000). Digital Capital – Harnessing the Power of Business Webs, Harvard Business School Press, Boston.

Tapscott, D. (2001). Rethinking Strategy in an Networked World (or Why Michael Porter is wrong about the Internet). Strategy * Business. Issue 24, vol. 3, pp. 34-41.

UMTS FORUM (2003). Strategic Considerations for IMS - the 3G Evolution.

Wagenaar, R. (2002). De virtuele Mabtenaar, naar een transparante overheid. Inaugurele Oratie, TU Delft, Technologie, Bleiod en Management.

WHEN WE SHIFT THE FOCUS TO MAN AS A 'NETWORKER' AND USER OF NEW ICT-TECHNOLOGY, WE CANNOT HELP BUT NOTICE THE PERVASIVENESS AND SPEED WITH WHICH NEW COMMUNICATION SERVICES SUCH AS E-MAIL AND MOBILE TELEPHONY HAVE COME TO CONTROL OUR LIVES.

From *Civil Servant*

Smart Adaptive Mobile Life Enhancements

Christer Carlsson and Pirkko Walden

René was a dear friend and an inspiring colleague and co-worker. We worked first together on methods and tools for building foresights on the development in communication technologies in a project called Imagine 21, which was funded in the EU-IST Program. This was later followed by joint work in a proposal called SmartAMLETS, which generated a series of spin-off projects both at IAMSR and at TU Delft. René had a key role in both projects and his ability to combine inspiring visions and practical, down-to-earth model building and project planning was an asset for all of us in the hectic days of conceiving and building the visionary and progressive SmartAMLETS project. René is deeply missed at IAMSR and by us who had the privilege of knowing and working with René. May he rest in peace.

The SmartAMLETS

The *SmartAMLETS* vision is that the routines of everyday life can be supported with smart and adaptive mobile technologies in such a way that actors who have to perform in a mobile life context will show enhanced planning and decision making capabilities.

Mobile life support is offered through 3G and mobile Internet based services and the use of mobile phones is growing and becoming the actual communication standard for large groups of people in their everyday lives; the present estimate is that there will be around 4 billion mobile phone users by the end of 2009. The basic challenge for advanced mobile technology and sets of new mobile services is to understand how and why people adopt or do not adopt mobile services. In a series of studies of the Finnish consumer markets (carried out by IAMSR every year 2002-7) we have found that the relationship between technology adoption and the adoption of mobile services based on that technology is asynchronous, i.e. the adoption processes are different – the adoption processes can even be explained from different conceptual frameworks. A partial explanation can be found through the insights which are formulated in the so-called *Braudel Rule*. This rule was introduced in the *Freedom Economy* by Keen-Mackintosh (2001) and it states that "... freedom becomes value when it changes (actually 'expands' in the original, French version; the difference is significant) the limits of the possible in the structure of everyday routines"; when this rule is applied to mobile services we could paraphrase it in the following way "... mobile services become mobile value services when they offer the possibility to expand the limits of the possible in the structure of everyday routines". This is a simple and effective way to formulate some guidelines for understanding which mobile services will create value and which mobile services will not make any difference. When applied to mobile service markets it may help us explain why some heavily promoted mobile services have failed, and why the SMS has been a success even if it was not advertised at all in the beginning – it was not even understood to be a mobile service.

René expressed an insight similar to the *Braudel Rule* when we worked on the visions that we believed would guide the development of telecommunication technologies in the 21st century: "we can follow up on the technology road maps – we can even formulate some of these road maps – but we cannot predict what is going to be a valuable technology for future users or in what way that value will be created".

In the following we will use some case material from the construction industry to give substance to the visions of mobile value services. This material was originally collected for one of the focus stories of the *Smart AMLETS* proposal.

MOBILE LIFE SUPPORT IN THE CONSTRUCTION INDUSTRY

The Finnish construction industry[1] is fragmented and is characterized by fierce competition which has made it difficult – and in some cases impossible – to build trust and long-term relationships among the actors. This is contrary to Finnish tradition that competitors in most industries can work together from time to time and benefit from good personal relationships. Fragmentation has led to poor communication and inefficient information practices among construction partners, which has contributed to – and even to some extent created – fragmented and poorly coordinated supply chains.

The Finnish construction industry faces a number of challenges: a need for supply chain management, growing and quickly changing information flows and a growing demand for customization of building projects. These challenges force construction companies to change and adapt their business processes to rather rapidly changing customer demands – the customers being the prospective house owners. A customer driven demand is moving the construction business away from large-scale, crowded and systematically planned housing areas to small-scale, spacious and flexible, more individually designed housing areas. This development is challenging for the construction industry as it has lived and flourished on the economies of scale. Nevertheless, flexible and advanced companies can turn the challenges into a growing, profitable business if they can develop and adapt their supply and information channels according to the demands of new groups of customers who want something else than what the industry has been used to produce and deliver.

A typical construction project in the private sector includes groups of actors, all of which have rather diverse objectives, different visions and wishes for the project, and very different levels of background knowledge and insight:

1. The primary construction company
2. Subcontractors for modules and services
3. Suppliers of building material
4. Logistics companies (transporting services for suppliers)
5. Public service agencies for building permits, inspection, water, power, telecom, etc.
6. Primary customers ((prospective, actual) house owners)
7. 'Secondary customers' (friends, relatives) who may have an influence on the primary customer's decision making process
8. Other actors (banks, insurance companies) which can decide key aspects of the construction project

The typical phases of a construction project include the following phases:
1. Planning, building permits, insurance and pre-construction work (construction company)
2. Marketing (construction company or sub-contractor)
3. Sales (construction company, sub-contractor or sales company)
4. Actual building, including tailoring and adaptation to customer needs and demands (construction company)
5. Landscaping (construction company or sub-contractor)

6. Delivery (construction company)
7. Choice of public service providers (power, gas, water, telecom, etc.)

These design stages are not naturally linear or of the waterfall-type, but include many rounds of iteration, especially in the latter parts and in the parts where the customer is involved. In Finland there is a tradition that a house owner 'builds' at least one house in his/her lifetime, which ex-plains the rather active involvement of the house owner. The increased role of customer involvement in building projects creates new challenges for all the actors. The customers' visions, wishes and demands may vary greatly as well as their level of activity (despite the Finnish tradition): some like their projects handled with as little personal effort as possible, some want to be an integral and active part of the project, even carrying out part of the construction work themselves.

Let us now turn to actual problems and challenges as the may emerge during a construction project for small, privately-owned houses.

In a typical construction project the communication is mainly face-to-face (or over phone) and relies heavily on paper documentation in all phases of the project. Since the small houses market is turning toward customization (thus changing the process from 'accept the plans, we build it' to 'here are the plans, we will adapt them as needed when you decide what you really want') there is a need for cost-effective multi-channel communication as face-to-face meetings are time-consuming, difficult to organize when many parties are involved and difficult to change when schedules change for the parties involved. Customers are not – and should not – be totally immersed in the project, they have their own lives to live. However, customers should be easy to contact in order to get their approval of necessary changes in plans; customers should be able to easily contact the constructor (or sub-contractors) to inform about changing needs, unstructured wishes (MMS to constructor 'I saw this kitchen, can you build or get me something like this') or if they have changed their minds about already agreed solutions. At some point this degree of flexibility and adaptation will become a strain on the resources of the construction company and decisions will have to be made if wanted changes can be carried out and if they make sense at all to carry out.

In the next section we will provide material from an actual project, which here will be summarized and simplified in order to save space. We have a medium-size constructing company BTB Ltd which is launching a new small-housing area that includes 10 detached houses and 3 small blocks with 6 apartments each. The houses will all be paid for before construction begins and they will be customizable according to customers' preferences. There are relatively little economies of scale available because of the customization but the project needs a full-blown information and supply chain infrastructure so that it can be run effectively and according to the specific customer demands.

There are three key challenges to be met by the information and supply chain infrastructure.

— *Logistics*: basic ('bulk') material should be delivered according to specifications and on time; material for customization and the customers' special requests must be coordinated with the main stream of building material.

— *Information flows*: customers, planners and builders must be able to have almost seamless communication (when questions/problems arise they will quite often stop that part of the project).

— *Customers*: most customers are getting their first (and only) house and have no experience with building projects; how could modern information and communication technology help the customer and save time and effort for all actors involved in the construction project? The constructor could possibly build competitive advantages by supporting effective and innovative dialogues with customers on the building project so that the customers will experience a learning process when they work out their visions and wishes on their future house. More advanced and experienced customers could participate in the process of finding and negotiating with sub-contractors.

Let us get some more details on the actors and the activities involved in the mobile life context.

Family Aaltonen has purchased a detached house. They want to be involved with the project and they want to customize their house with minor changes in plans but with major changes in materials and appliances. Thus, they need to be in constant touch with both the constructor and with several sub-contractors. This is their first experience with a building project and they rely heavily on the experience and knowledge of friends and relatives for opinions and for assistance in making their dream house come true.

Jaakko Eskelinen is an assistant project manager who works for the constructor; his primary responsibility is to coordinate plan changes, to order all basic materials and to monitor all actual on-site work.

Pirjo Peltonen runs her own small company; she is an electrician with three co-workers, and the primary sub-contractor for in-house electricity-related work. She needs to be aware (and able to quickly communicate with co-workers) of changes to basic plans and to coordinate her own work with other actors in the building project.

Antti Virtanen works with one of the key suppliers for the project which is contracted to deliver interior materials and appliances. His primary role is to help customers to choose from different materials and appliances in such a way that these will fit the overall design of the house, to order those delivered to the building site in time for the appropriate phase of the project and to carry out all modifications needed to fulfill wishes and new visions.

Typical mobile life support routines and technologies

The most effective way to make the building project work out as expected is to build an adaptive and effective infrastructure for mobile communication between all actors for real-time problem solving [mobile phones, smart phones, camera phones, PDAs, communicators, etc.].

It is often not well understood that this will require a good multi-channel platform to provide an effective infrastructure and database backup for the applications. The design can be of the type shown in Fig.1 where the necessary modules and their interaction is shown (this was in fact a prototype which was expected to become a market standard at the time for the *SmartAMLETS* proposal). The leftmost interface modules to support connectivity and the interface modules between B2B Integration, B2E integration and M2M Integration and the Service Management complex are the multi-agent *smart amlets*, software modules we planned to design, develop and implement in the *SmartAMLETS* project.

The mobile communication support for construction projects needs access to data sources for backup information, for storing data, for access to drawings, for access to details on construction solutions and for memos on agreed solutions. There is also a need for ad hoc access to data to illustrate 'new ideas and innovations' which have been introduced by the Aaltonen family. The communication is facilitated by camera phones for trouble shooting and decision making 'on the move' if parts of the building project become bottlenecks. The logistics of the building site and the delivery of material can be simplified with 'context-aware' mobile support for suppliers so that they are aware of where to deliver, when to deliver and also where & when to deliver after changes in plans.

PROPOSED SmartAMLETS IMPROVEMENTS
We proposed that the *SmartAMLETS* system will provide smart, adaptive technologies for en-hancing mobile life. This is rather easily said but we need to work out the functionality of the proposed solutions.
— What are smart improvements? Smart improvements in mobile life provide data, information (and even knowledge) at the moment when needed, appropriate for the place where needed and in the form most suitable for the purpose.
— What are adaptive enhancements? Adaptive enhancements activate the services and the sup-port which are most effective (productive, appropriate) in a changing context or situation.
— Steps in mobile life enhancements. Support which is context-aware; the context triggers smart support; changes in the context trigger adaptive enhancements.

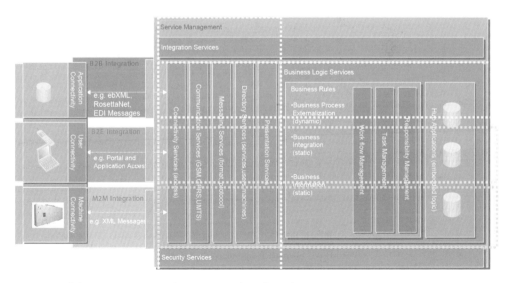

Figure 1 *Mobile communications infrastructure used as a basis for SmartAMLETS*

Some of the functions needed to carry out the *SmartAMLETS* agenda exist as software compo-nents and modules but it is required that they are combined through effective interface software to form an integrated support system for mobile life (as demonstrated in the construction indus-try).

Mobile Life: everyday activities, routines after implementing *SmartAMLETS*
Erkki Aaltonen is on a business trip and receives a message on his Nokia E90 at the airport ask-ing about bathroom plans. The plan changes are included, so he goes to an airport lounge, logs in to the *SmartAMLETS* webservice, views changes and sends back a message with proposed im-provements. Meanwhile, Anna Aaltonen, his wife, receives a message that there are new mes-sages at the *SmartAMLETS* visions and innovations corner for her. She checks the messages and finds out that a friend has seen a new idea in a magazine and sends a link to that. Antti Virtanen is responding to her question about kitchen plans and is asking for further information. There is also a message to all house purchasers in the region in the *SmartAMLETS* generic message area informing buyers about offers from 3 power supply companies. Jaakko Eskelinen has configured a number of customer information modules in the *SmartAMLETS* system with a partial reuse of information obtained from previous projects. He has updated profiles to include current participants and is acting as an information middle-man between the actors. Once the system is up and running he is able to concentrate on actual on-site work as the actors are communicating directly with each other.
Antti Virtanen is happy - instead of having to meet with each one of his 28 customers to start the project he is able to use profiles from previous projects to publish what is available as possible solutions in the *SmartAMLETS* system. Thus, when he meets with customers for the first time everybody is more prepared and the planning meetings can make faster progress. Since the pro-files are context-aware, he is able to use simple parameters in predicting further preferences (ar-tistic, novel, economical...) as the building project is progressing.
Pirjo Peltonen receives information from the *SmartAMLETS* system about planned installations which makes it possible for her to plan the power supply solutions. She can communicate with her co-workers and customers (through MMS) about final details as she is updated through the *SmartAMLETS* about plans and changes for each house-building project as soon as they are made by Antti Virtanen.

The mobile life processes as described here are more or less beneficial for people leading hectic lives but still wanting 'to build their own house' and for the constructors and sub-contractors who make it possible. There are, however, downsides to this mobile life: (i) the time span for planning and problem solving gets shorter, which may have an impact on quality; (ii) work al-ready done is made obsolete, which will raise costs; (iii) quick reactions 'on the move' may be based on partial data and fractional thinking ('making fast and bad decisions'). The mobile life processes, nevertheless, will probably have a significant impact on how the construction industry develops its business models and how its customers may both convey their visions and partici-pate in their own house-building projects. This creates added value to both constructors and their customers – how this value is formed and how the value processes will reshape the business are topics for research projects to come.

Context and use scenarios for SmartAMLETS

Let us work out the *SmartAMLETS* support and use in one more level of detail. There are inter-face modules to support mobile users and inter-face modules for B2B, B2C and M2M communi-cation; there are interface modules to give access to data sources for back-up information, for storing data, for access to drawings, for access to details on construction solutions and for memos on agreed solutions; there are interface modules for ad hoc access to data to illustrate 'new ideas and innovations'; there are interface modules for camera phones for trouble shooting and decision making 'on the move' if parts of the building project become bottlenecks; there are interface modules for 'context-aware' mobile support for suppliers so that they are aware of where to deliver, when to deliver and also where & when to deliver after changes in plans. These interface modules are the *smart amlets*, which form a multi-agent system to be implemented as part of the multi-channel architecture shown in Fiure 1. When these software modules are in place they will enable the B2B, B2C and M2M communications, which again will make it possible for the actors in the house-building project to handle many aspects of it in ways which have not been possible until we get the technology for mobile life in place:

Customers and end-users [the Aaltonen family]
— Problem-solving and decision making in real time

— Discussions and negotiations with builders without face-to-face meetings (avoiding travel)
— Explanations with illustrations, pictures from data sources to communicate ideas to builders
— Virtual teaming with family, friends, experts to provide ideas and support when needed
— Trouble-shooting with camera phones

Service providers and agents [application support for Pirjo Peltonen and Antti Virtanen]
— Suppliers of building material get orders through mobile phones (simplifying logistics)
— Specifications can be checked with advanced mobile phones (simplifying logistics)
— Details and components can be shown with mobile camera phones
— Location can be shown and explained with camera phones and GPS
— Delivery confirmed and accepted with mobile sign-off (simplifying logistics)
— Information on delivery to multi-channel database (simplifying logistics)

Constructor [Jakko Eskelinen]
— Constructor can communicate with customers for trouble-shooting, problem-solving and fast decision making
— Constructor can order material and components from various suppliers and get delivery times and order confirmations
— Constructor can trace deliveries and offer logistical assistance
— Constructor can sign off delivery and start payment
— Constructor updates multi-channel database with information on delivery
— Constructor can access supplier alternatives for material, components

The user scenarios build on some specific ideas about business models to connect constructors, suppliers and planners with planning authorities, logistics providers and customers. The business models build on the notions of *out-tasking* and *in-sourcing* proposed by Peter Keen in Freedom Economy (2001). An extension of these business models include value networks of specialists and advisers for problem solving and trouble shooting; the idea of value networks is actually an extension of the value chain model but offers more flexibility for including actors which may provide innovative value operations.

The scenario we are proposing assumes that the constructor uses contractor-building principles: contracting with networks of service providers with the equipment needed at the right place at the right moment of the project – the constructor does not need to own any building equipment nor hire any workers as all resources are owned and operated by the service providers. This has the added benefit for the constructor to free up operating capital. The information infrastructure built by the *SmartAMLETS* is a key resource for contractor building and as the mobile infrastructure built by the *SmartAMLETS* can be re-used numerous times it will give the constructor competitive advantages.

The implementation of the *SmartAMLETS* infrastructure follows a straight-forward development process with iterations over both existing and innovative solutions:

— Innovations [smart solutions on mobile platforms with personalization, localization, interpretation, context awareness]
— Systems engineering [agent support systems & multi-channel hub solutions]
— Business process (re-)engineering [out-tasking and in-sourcing]
— Product, process, system design [state-of-the-art, specific methods (QFD, Six Sigma)]
— Prototyping, user interaction & evaluation [actions research approach]
— Dynamic design of evolutionary applications [models and methods developed by TUDelft]

With these elements in place we can briefly return to and update the Mobile Life storyline to include the technology solutions [in italics in the following]:

Erkki Aaltonen on his business trip uses a Nokia E90 [*smart phone with SmartAMLETS*] which can handle the links sent by his wife [*agents retrieve, summarize material*]. Antti Virtanen is responding to questions about kitchen plans and is asking further information [*relevant material copied, re-routed*] through a Nokia E90. The *SmartAMLETS* message area [*material summarized, personalized, sent*] distributes offers from 3 power supply companies which can be handled with any smart mobile phone.

Jaakko Eskelinen configured customer information with a partial reuse of information obtained from previous projects [*loading SmartAMLETS software*]. The profiles include current participants [*personalization*] and provide interfaces between the actors [*agent support for localization, context awareness of operations*], which allows the actors to communicate directly with each other. Antti Virtanen uses [context-aware] profiles from previous projects [*personalization*] to publish available solutions in the SmartAMLETS message area [*summarize with agent support according to personal profiles*].

Pirjo Peltonen receives information from SmartAMLETS message area [*summarized and connected through the multi-channel hub*] and communicates with her co-workers and customers [MMS] about final details; she uses input from Antti Virtanen [*summaries by agents, links to data sources on multi-channel hub; updates through personalization, context-awareness*] which she gets from the SmartAMLETS message area.

Expected impact and results of the SmartAMLETS

With the help of the details we now have introduced it is possible to get a view of the *enhanced mobile life for customers and end-users* which could be produced with the SmartAMLETS.

SmartAMLETS will offer a state-of-the-art and easy access to information and communication, since it connects previously separate groups. SmartAMLETS will also offer time-savings and increased productivity, both by eased information flows and the use of generic and adaptable customer profiles.

From a customer perspective, SmartAMLETS will help with information overload and the anxieties with a complex and expensive house-building project by allowing easy, personalized access to information and communication. Other key benefits come from time-savings and better customer service.

The professionals involved in a house-building project will benefit from an *increased productivity of working time*.

Builders save time in communication with customers, suppliers and planners as they have (i) updated, summarized information available in real time, (ii) planning support available in real time, (iii) supplier information available in real time; orders and logistics are handled in real time.

Problem solving and trouble shooting can be handled without the need for face-to-face meetings as deliveries are traced, checked and accepted with the support system.

New ideas, innovations and requests for new material, components, etc. are included without time-consuming meetings.

Both customers and the professionals will benefit from *decreased fragmentation of everyday activities*.

Customers can respond to problems, questions, changes of plans at a place and time which is convenient as (i) customers' response is supported with facts through the multi-channel hub, and (ii) new ideas, innovations, changes, etc can be supported with facts, pictures, sketches and plans without lengthy searches in databases.

Constructors can simplify routines to reduce fragmentation as (i) suppliers can plan activities in real-time and reduce fragmentation, and (ii) planners can provide input when needed and plan this beforehand.

Value-added networks will reduce overall fragmentation per project for all actors involved as the needed input from out-tasking or in-sourcing partners is readily available whenever needed; this will eliminate the need for lengthy search and negotiation processes when specialised input is needed.

Last but not least there is a qualitative aspect to the support from the *SmartAMLETS* system in terms of *social impact, group benefits and individual development.*

Increased mobility and the ability to use multiple communication channels will enhance the users' know how and skill levels; services are largely device independent and will be available to most mobile phone users.

Increased communication between participants is made possible with the *SmartAMLETS* system, which allows a previously impossible connecting of documents and people (relatives, friends, suppliers, builders...); this again opens up new ways of working in cooperating teams.

SmartAMLETS delivers adaptive, enhanced multi-channel management which connects participants. This is especially important from a customer perspective as customers cannot be 100% committed to the house-building project as they have work and family responsibilities.

Conclusion

Even if the *SmartAMLETS* was an innovative and progressive proposal it was eventually not approved for funding by the EU-IST program. Key elements of the technology are now being re-used in a project aiming at *knowledge mobilisation*, which is implementing fuzzy ontology as part of the semantic web; then this ontology forms the infrastructure for distributed knowledge support which is context-aware, time dependent and personalized; the support is activated with questions of the type *what should I know now?* - and will be relevant for the time, place and cognitive profiles of the users. The knowledge is available through a multi-agent system which is activated and/or run with smart mobile phones. In this way the innovations we created for the *SmartAMLETS* continue to live and are developed further as we can use new technology.

Over the last two years a few others of the *SmartAMLETS* ideas have found practical forms and been implemented as mobile value services [*MobiTour, MobiFish, MobiGuide, MobiBlog, MobiBooking*] in the Åland and Åboland archipelagos. These services are now being turned into practical services for travelers and tourists in the archipelago and are being commercialized by some local small companies.

Thus, part of the *SmartAMLETS* will benefit the archipelago – it is a coincidence that one of the planning meetings of the project was organized in the Åboland archipelago. This snapshot shows the IAMSR and Delft members of the *SmartAMLETS* core group in the spring 2005; the jokes, the laughs and the relaxation after a long day of hard work is a fitting final tribute to René.edge support which is context-aware, time dependent and personalized; the support is activated with questions of the type *what should I know now?* - and will be relevant for the time, place and cognitive profiles of the users. The knowledge is available through a multi-agent system which is activated and/or run with smart mobile phones. In this way the innovations we created for the *SmartAMLETS* continue to live and are developed further as we can use new technology.

Over the last two years a few others of the *SmartAMLETS* ideas have found practical forms and been implemented as mobile value services [*MobiTour, MobiFish, MobiGuide, MobiBlog, MobiBooking*] in the Åland and Åboland archipelagos. These services are now being turned into practical services for travelers and tourists in the archipelago and are being commercialized by some local small companies.

Thus, part of the *SmartAMLETS* will benefit the archipelago – it is a coincidence that one of the planning meetings of the project was organized in the Åboland archipelago. This snapshot shows the IAMSR and Delft members of the *SmartAMLETS* core group in the spring 2005; the jokes, the laughs and the relaxation after a long day of hard work is a fitting final tribute to René.

---

[1] Dr Jussi Puhakainen, Turku School of Economics, was a co-author on an early version of this material and contributed the insight from the construction industry

THESE SERVICES APPEAL TO A BASIC HUMAN NEED, NAMELY COMMUNICATION, AND THEY HAVE BECOME VITAL TOOLS IN OUR DAILY ACTIVITIES.

From *Civil Servant*

Does Service Innovation require more than ICT?

Els van de Kar and Bart Nieuwenhuis

Abstract

This paper focuses on innovations in the services industry, an area to which René Wagenaar dedicated an important part of his scientific and industrial life. In this paper, we present the results of a project we discussed with René during the set-up phase, at the end of 2006. This project provides a match with his ideas on ICT-driven service innovations, the domain in which René cooperated with Bart at KPN Research and with Els at Delft University of technology. René fully agreed with the observation that the Dutch economy has become a true service economy, along with almost all the other Western economies. In this paper, we discuss the results of an explorative feasibility study for a center for service innovation. The study identifies obstacles to innovation in Dutch service companies. The results of the study are used as input to determine the agenda of the intended center. The study exists of desk research as well as interviews and workshops with innovation managers of major service providing companies in the Netherlands. This paper presents the results of this feasibility study using a service innovation framework.

Introduction

Throughout his career, René's has always found himself on the crossroads of business and science. Bart Nieuwenhuis cooperated with René at KPN Research, and later Els van de Kar and René worked together at the TPM Faculty of Delft University of Technology. Both authors of this paper René's fascination with the development of innovations using new technologies. This paper focuses mainly on the innovation process in service-providing companies in the Netherlands. Today, more than 70% of the country's GDP comes from the service economy, while more than 80% of our work force is employed in the services sector. This implies that it is difficult to realize economic growth in the Netherlands without increasing productivity in service companies.

On the one hand, we believe that information and communication technology (ICT) creates enormous possibilities for service innovation, while on the other hand the same service innovation is hindered by a range of non-technological factors that are often underestimated. The Directorate for Science, Technology and Industry of the OECD[1] reports very favorable conditions for the Netherlands: in June 2007, 33.5% of the Dutch had access to broadband Internet connections. With the exception of Denmark, no other country in the world has such a high level of broadband Internet penetration. However, as will become clear in the following sections, thus far this excellent starting point has failed to lead to a faster growth in productivity growth as a result of ICT-based service innovations.

One of the possible reasons for this paradoxical situation is that today's public innovation programs are mainly industrial or technology-driven in nature. Studies indicate that R&D expenditure is much higher in the industrial sector than it is in the service sector (OECD, 2007) p.22). The same is true when it comes to public funding of innovation programs. This is one of the motives behind the EXSER initiative aimed at developing a center for service innovation in the Netherlands. The objective of this initiative is to set up a multidisciplinary, private-public cooperation between service-providing companies and the research community in the Netherlands. In this paper, we present the results of the EXSER feasibility study, i.e. the results of the interviews and workshops involving service-providing companies on the possible added value of a collaboration between the Dutch academic and business communities.

The outline of this paper is as follows. We begin by discussing the economic background of our study, after which we present a service innovation framework we used to structure the information we collected during interviews and workshops involving over thirty companies, on the basis of which we have identified a number of service innovation themes. Finally, we present our conclusions.

Bart discussed the first ideas for EXSER with René at a dinner in Den Haag in November 2006. René was very enthusiastic about the initiative. In the same period, Els discussed her future plans with René. René recognized a perfect match and introduced the authors to each other. Unfortunately, the three of us were never meant to work together on EXSER.

Economic background

In this section, we discuss the economic background of the Dutch services sector. The productivity growth of the Netherlands, as in many other western economies, depends on service innovation-driven productivity growth in the service sector. We first present labor productivity growth figures in general, after which we discuss the relationship between ICT and service innovation. Table 1 gives an overview of the average annual productivity growth (EU, 2006, p26).

Average annual labor productivity	1990-1995	1995-2000	2000-2005	2005
The Netherlands	1.3	1.5	1.3	1.8
EU-25	2.2	2.0	1.3	1.1
United States	1.3	2.0	2.2	1.8

Table 1 Average annual labor productivity between 1990-2005

Productivity growth may be generated either by the industrial sector or by the service sector. Figure 1 shows the contribution of the service sector to the overall productivity growth (value added per person employed (percentage points)) from 1990 to 2002 (OECD, 2005). The diagram shows that, although the service sector does contribute to productivity growth, it does so a much lesser extent and its contribution is not proportional to its relative size.

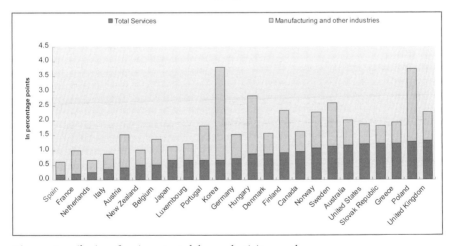

Figure 1 Contribution of service sector to labor productivity growth 1990-2002

To analyze the differences between countries, we can also look at the total factor productivity (TFP) growth figures. TFP measures the excess of the actual growth of output over the growth attributed to growth related to labor and capital inputs. TFP relates to growth resulting from 'real' innovation in terms of alternative ways of working and using new opportunities offered by technology. Table 2 shows that, during the first two 5-year periods, the Netherlands followed the US, but that in the third 5-year period TFP growth experienced a serious down-turn (EU, 2006, p29).

TFP growth 1990 -2005	1990-1995	1995-2000	2000-2005
Netherlands	0.9	1.5	0.7
EU-25	1.3	1.2	0.4
United States	1.0	1.5	1.2

Table 2 TPF Growth 1990-2005

With regard to ICT-driven labor productivity growth, economists assume that there are three major drivers: capital deepening, technological progress and ICT usage.

— ICT investments between 1995 and 2004 make up 0.4 percentage points of GDP per capita growth in the Netherlands (EU, 2006, p135), less than the US (0.8 percentage points) and about equal to the EU-15 (0.5 percentage points).
— The impact of technological progress (lower prices for ICT products) can be measured by looking at the contribution of the ICT sector to the aggregated labor productivity. From 2000 to 2003, the average annual labor productivity growth percentage was 1.1% for the EU-15 and 3.6% for the USA (EU, 2006, p. 136). This large difference is mainly due to the contribution of market services, i.e., 0.1% for the EU15 and 2.0% for the US.
— The third way ICT may have an impact on productivity growth is through a more effective use of ICT. Research confirms that TFP growth (as indicated in Table 2) relates to the use of ICT (Pilat, 2006), while other studies confirm the positive impact ICT has firm performance[2].

To summary, the services industry is important to the economic growth of the Netherlands. The above-mentioned figures show that productivity growth in the service sector lags behind in comparison to the industrial sector. Research in various countries suggests that the use of ICT may have a positive impact on TPF growth. If we look at TPF growth at a macro level, the performance of the Dutch service sector is above EU-15 average, although neither the Netherlands nor the EU-15 as a whole would seem to benefit sufficiently from ICT, compared to the US. Based on the above-mentioned figures, we conclude that it is especially the companies in the service sector that could benefit from a more effective use of ICT.

These developments have triggered Dutch and European policy-makers into investigating how service companies deal with service innovation and to what extent they benefit from the opportunities provided by ICT. This has been the subject of study in the EU-initiated RENESER project. The RENESER report concludes that the amount of service innovation initiatives in service companies is widely underestimated (Hertog & others, 2006). The innovation monitor of The Bridge looks at the status of product and service innovation among Dutch companies. It is also reported that managers are increasingly aware of the importance of service innovation (Brouwer, Burg, & Kuiper, 2007).

Services and service innovation

There are several definitions to define the concept of service, e.g. by (Kotler, 1997), (Grönroos, 2001). Existing definitions refer to specific characteristics of a service, e.g., the intangibility of the service, the interaction between producer and consumer when the service is created, the fact that a service cannot be stored after production to be delivered at a later time, and the fact that it is difficult to guarantee the quality of a service in advance. More recent studies focus more in the differences between processes involved in the provision of services on the one hand, and those involved in the manufacturing of products on the other. The differences turn out to be smaller than it appears. (Johnson, Menor, Roth, & Chase, 2000) argue that the distinction between service provisioning and manufacturing is blurred, while (Vermeulen & van der Aa, 2003) show that product development and service development have many aspects in common[3].

This connects to industrial companies that complement their physical production facilities with additional services provisioning. Companies increasingly use these services to create added value because of their need to cope with growing competition from countries like India and China. Examples are IBM, which moved from being a computer manufacturer towards being a service provider. Other examples are Nokia, which developed from a device manufacturer into a mobile service provider, Philips, which started providing healthcare services in addition to consumer electronics, and Xerox and Océ, which started offering document services in addition to copying machines. In fact, we see a continuum, with on one end product manufacturing complemented by some services, and on the other end companies that only provide intangible services (e.g. the financial sector).

After discussing services at a more general level, we now move on to service innovation. A framework is needed to structure the information obtained from our feasibility study. During a literature scan we conducted, we found the following models and frameworks relevant for service innovation:

— Berkhout et al. present the cycle innovation model, which visualizes the 'circle of change', linking changes in science to business, and technology to the marketplace (Berkhout & van der Duin, 2007).
— Faber et al. present the STOF model, which shows the business model elements of services (Faber et al., 2003).
— The Service Systems Engineering research program model of the TPM Faculty, in which René participated (unpublished). This model highlights the system service perspective. This model was later adapted in the Designing Mobile Service System book (Van de Kar & Verbraeck, 2007).
— Johnson et al. present the New Service Design (NSD) Process Cycle (Johnson et al., 2000). They also add the NSD-innovation matrix, which accounts for the role of customer contact in the service delivery system.
— The four dimension service innovation framework of Hertog, Broersma, & Ark (2003) for structuring service innovation activities, consisting of the following four dimensions: new service concept, new client interface, technological options, and new service delivery system.

The model suggested by Berkhout & van der Duin (2007) focuses exclusively on innovation, whereas Faber et al. (2003) focus on services and their business models, and the SSE models (Van de Kar & Verbraeck, 2007) approach considers services from a system perspective. Johnson et al. (2000) emphasize that service process design and service innovation must be inextricably linked during New Service Design (NSD). They argue that service designers should be concerned with the management of the NSD process, the NSS project and the NSD program. We have adopted the 4D framework suggested by Hertog et al. (2003), which was introduced to describe and analyze service innovations, and to map and characterize various service innovations, and extended it for our purposes.

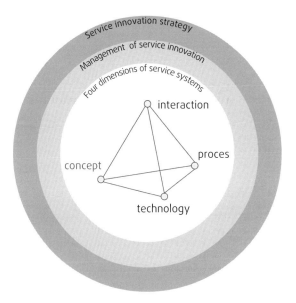

The inner circle of the framework shows the four dimensions of a service system. A service innovation requires changes in multiple dimensions, which have an impact on one another and between which relationships exist. The dimensions are:
— *Concept*: the essence of a service, which expresses how to create value for its users. This requires knowledge of customer wants and needs, and of the characteristics of other existing services.
— *Interaction*: the way in which the customer and the service provider communicate. (Communication may be active, for example in a shop, or passive, for example when the customer reads an advertisement).
— *Process*: the underlying business processes in which service delivery is prepared.
— *Technology*: the technology involved which supports and links the concept, interaction and processes.
The inner circle of the framework is used to identify areas of interest with regard to a particular service innovation. It also demonstrates the multidisciplinary nature of service innovations and indicates the type of expertise

that is needed to tackle the problems that are encountered during the execution of innovation processes.

The middle circle reflects the management issues needed to conduct service innovation processes in an organization. A company needs qualified personnel and access to specific management skills to conduct innovation processes effectively and efficiently.

The outer circle reflects a company's service innovation strategies. Some companies choose to engage in multiple innovation projects at an early stage, whereas others prefer to innovate through the acquisition of start-up companies.

The feasibility study

The feasibility study has identified innovation-related obstacles among Dutch service companies. The results are input to determine the agenda of the targeted center. The study is a combination of desk research and interviews and workshops involving innovation managers of major service companies in the Netherlands.

We have selected companies based on their sector, geographical location (Northern part of the Randstad[4]), revenues, number of employees, strategic empowerment, R&D effort, and their position in the value web. We decided not to involve more than one company from any given sector since, at this stage, since a possible competitive element may have had a negative

Advertising (2x)	Publishing
Distribution	Radio & TV
Energy	Retail (branch organization)
Entertainment	Retail Banking
Facility Management	Transportation rail
Home Care Services	Transportation air
Hospital	Business IT Total consulting (2x)
Housing	Telecom
HRM Services (2x)	Document Systems
Insurance	Electronics
Leasing	Engineering Services
Pension Services	

Table 3 Overview of companies participating in feasibility study

impact on the open communication we had in mind. Table 3 provides an overview of the sectors from which the companies were selected.

Findings

In this section, we provide an overview of the issues addressed by companies participating in the feasibility study. In the interviews we looked at how companies deal with innovation and how they develop their innovation plans for years to come. We also collected views on subjects that could be addressed by a service innovation center. We structured the information we obtained by formulating themes positioned in the circles and dimensions shown in Figure 2, and discussed the themes in a final workshop (see Appendix for the list of themes that were discussed).

Service innovation strategies

A wide range of service innovation strategies has been presented. At one end, we see companies that carry out various innovative projects internally. Within these companies, innovation begins at a very early stage of the life cycle, after which it is further developed into new business. The companies involved start from scratch and actively invite people to come up with new ideas. At the other side of the spectrum, we find companies that develop no new services themselves. Their innovation strategy is based mainly on the acquisition of innovative (start-up) companies (at a high price).

Which service innovation strategy companies opt for is influenced by European regulations. Some companies mentioned the impact of the Directive of Services, the goal of which is to achieve a genuine internal market in services, by removing legal and administrative barriers, with the aim of providing greater legal security and enabling cross-border service provisioning. Some companies transfer service concepts successfully from one country to another, which is a strategy that requires special attention to cultural differences and legal difference.

Generally speaking, service companies have little or no experience with pre-competitive, cooperative R&D. Some companies are afraid that anti-trust legislation could inhibit closer intimate cooperation. This applies, for example, to the construction sector.

Furthermore, service innovation strategies also depend on the other factors that determine a company's strategic management, e.g. profit or non-profit, national or international orientation.

Service innovation management
Generally speaking, service companies lack a centralized R&D or innovation-oriented organization. Innovation projects are conducted at different organizational departments and units. It is in only a small number of cases that staff members are dedicated to corporate service innovation management. The following issues were mentioned by our interviewees:
— One issue relates to the management style: bottom-up or top-down. Some companies are gradually moving towards a more top-down management style? Which aspects of service innovation should be organized at a central level? How can innovation be organized in such a way that it does not frustrate the creativity of people?
— Some interviewees indicate a desire to gain greater insight into the way innovation is adopted by customers. How can that be achieved? How can customers become more involved in the innovation process?
— Companies are also interested in the financial management of innovations. Generally speaking, service companies do not explicitly allocate substantial amounts of money to innovation projects. This applies in particular to companies that are listed at the stock exchange. Companies are looking for new revenue models, for instance based on intellectual property rights.
— All companies indicate that there are obstacles with regard to finding qualified personnel. How can we deal with scarcity on the labor market? Service innovation requires HRM policies, as well as education and career paths for service innovators.

Service system innovation
In this section, we discuss the four different dimensions of specific service systems and the themes mentioned earlier as being relevant to service innovation.

Service Concept
Service companies in the industrial and service sectors have clear ideas regarding the targets they want to reach in next three to five years. When they feel a need to do so, companies employ the services of management consultants and strategic advisors to define these targets more clearly. Although many companies realize that technologies like the Internet and mobile phones will enable new innovations, they expect true innovations to come from the market. The service providers state that they need to

invest if they are to follow proactively market trends, preferably a little in advance of the rest of the market. Examples of such trends are increased individualization, the multi-cultural society, the ageing population, digital living, mobility, globalization and global warming.

Several companies believe that customer needs are changing as a result of these trends. Banking and insurance companies, for example, are moving from 'one size fits all' toward 'tailor made', focusing on ever smaller market segments.

Service Interaction

In most cases, service innovation will change the way companies interact with their customers. Interviewees confirm the importance of this dimension.

Service providers interact with customer during the presales, sales and after sales phases. Companies are developing strategies to use multiple channels, e.g., shops, personal visits, call centers, the Internet and mobile Internet. Self-service concepts are emerging, i.e. retail and finance companies provide services that are available to people over the Internet. Also, cross-media strategies are being developed.

Service Process

Generally speaking, service innovation requires the modification of existing processes and the introduction of new processes, to provide customers with information, distribution and the billing of services across media. Some companies operate as links in a complex value chain. Consequently, process renewal requires discussions with other partners in the value chain, examples of which can be found in the retail sector.

Service Technologies

Obviously, ICT developments, especially those that are related to the Internet, play an important role in service innovations. The company representatives we interviewed indicated that they find it difficult to tackle technological issues due to a lack of qualified people.

The advantages that were mentioned with regard to new technologies like fiber, mobile and wireless networks, and new web technologies are: unlimited bandwidth, video/avatar call centers, sustainable digital storage, and new approaches to user interaction.

To deal with higher levels of individualization, companies apply technologies aimed at processing high volumes of customer data used to interact with people in their personal environment; to reach customers directly, in their living rooms or cars.

Security technologies are used to protect user privacy. New technologies also enable, for instance, integral systems designed to guide people through checkpoints at public transportation gateways quickly and efficiently, and luggage handling systems at airports.

Discussion

In the first half of 2007, we had the opportunity to discuss service innovation with leading companies in the Netherlands during a number of bilateral interviews and two workshops. The main objective of the project was to explore the feasibility of EXSER rather than to reach scientific conclusions. The results can be summarized as follows:

— First of all, companies in the services industry have hardly any form of centralized R&D or innovation organization. Interesting exceptions are companies that have moved from manufacturing towards service provisioning.

— Secondly, service companies spend more on service innovation one might expect on the basis of national statistics. Companies confirm that service innovation is performed by various units and departments within the company, in some cases initiated on the basis of observed customers needs; in others on the basis of technological developments, e.g. the Internet and mobile phones.

— Thirdly, service companies are not well-connected to the knowledge infrastructure of the Netherlands, i.e. academic and other research organizations, with the exception of large companies participating in national and international cooperation projects. Medium-sized and smaller companies are, however, less fortunate in this respect. If they are at all connected to the knowledge infrastructure, they are either connected to a person or research group within their own sector (finance, insurance, media or transport) or to technology-related organizations like TNO or the Telematica Institute.

In fact, these three observations confirm earlier results of RESENER (Hertog & others, 2006), albeit with some added Dutch flavor.

The feasibility study also yielded a number of new observations:

— Almost every company indicates that the innovation process is hampered by a lack of qualified personnel. Obviously, expertise related to the

product or service of the company is available, but expertise in other fields or technology-related knowledge is difficult to mobilize. In fact, companies are in desperate need of multidisciplinary teams or, even better, multidisciplinary employees able to carry out the necessary innovation projects.
— The service companies perceive service innovation management as the most important potential added value a service innovation center has to offer. Most companies are satisfied with their service innovation strategy based on their market research into important customer and supplier needs. Most service companies know where they want to be within three to five years, but they are looking for the roads to reach their intended destination.

Conclusions

ICT developments will undoubtedly play an important role in the innovations that are carried out by service companies in the Netherlands. The feasibility study confirms that productivity growth can be achieved by service companies. In this paper, we have presented a service innovation framework based on the 4-dimension model published by Hertog et al. (2003), and we used that framework to present the results of interviews and workshops involving 29 service companies. We conclude that service companies have strategic goals that are derived from targets based on social trends and developments, customer needs that require different interaction processes, and the need to continuously improve their organizations. In fact, companies indicate that these changes are interrelated and that a multidisciplinary approach is needed.

The challenges with regard to service innovation have to do with the way innovation should be organized within a company, the relationship with other companies in the same value chain, the relationship with (academic) research organizations and the success in acquiring qualified teams with multidisciplinary knowledge and skills capable of managing the four service innovation dimensions. We feel that our findings provide sufficient motivation to continue working on the creation of a center for service innovation 'EXSER'.

Epilogue

The start of EXSER depends on the readiness of public and private organizations to fund the business plan. Generally speaking, we expect national and international innovation programs on service innovation to emerge in the years to come. We very much regret it that René Wagenaar, with his multidisciplinary knowledge and skills in the areas of Physics, Economics and ICT, will not be part of that development. We know he would have loved it.

Acknowledgements

The authors want to thank Peter van Eijk, Pim den Hertog, Bram Kaashoek, Caroline van Lieshout and Jeroen Segers, who participated in the EXSER project. In addition, we want to express our gratitude to the representatives of the companies for their cooperation, and Harry Bouwman for his extensive review. Finally, we are grateful to 'Almere Kennisstad' (main sponsor) and Océ Technologies (co-sponsor) for funding the project.

1 See: http://www.oecd.org/sti/ict/broadband.
2 More references can be found in (EU, 2006).
3 The terms service design, service innovation and service development are usually considered separately in NSD (Johnson et al., 2000). Service innovation is often referred to as the outcome of service development. In this paper, we focus on service innovation, including the service innovation process, and treat service design and development as a part of service innovation.
4 The Randstad is the western part of the Netherlands and its economic center. The northern part of the Randstad includes (parts of) the Provinces of North Holland, Flevoland and Utrecht.

References

Berkhout, A. J., & van der Duin, P. A. (2007). New ways of innovation: an application of the cyclic innovation model to the mobile telecom industry. *Int. J. Technology Management, 40,*(4), 294-309.

Brouwer, P., Burg, W. v. d., & Kuiper, J. (2007). *innovation monitor 07/08*: The Bridge business innovators, member of Twynstra Gudde.

EU. (2006). *The European competitiveness report 2006, Communication from the Commission COM (2006) 697 final, Commission staff working document SEC(2006) 1467/2.*

Faber, E., Ballon, P., Bouwman, H., Haaker, T., Rietkerk, O., & Steen, M. (2003). *Designing business models for mobile ICT services.* Paper presented at the 16th Bled Electronic Commerce Conference eTransformation, Bled, Slovenia.

Grönroos, C. (2001). *Service Management and Marketing. A customer relationship management approach* (2nd ed.). Chichester: Wiley.

Hertog, P. d., Broersma, L., & Ark, B. v. (2003). On the soft side of innovation: service innovation and its policy implication. *De Economist, 151,* 433-452.

Hertog, P. d., & others. (2006). *RENESER Project: Research and Development Needs of Business Related Service Firms*. Utrecht: Dialogic innovatie & interactie (coordinator), Fraunhofer Institut für Arbeitswirtschaft und Organisation, PREST/CRIC/IoIR University of Manchester, Servilab / Alcala University.

Johnson, S. P., Menor, L. J., Roth, A. V., & Chase, R. B. (2000). A Critical Evaluation of the New Service Development Process. In J. A. Fitzsimmons & M. J. Fitzsimmons (Eds.), *New service development: Creating memorable experiences* (pp. 1-27). Thousand Oaks: Sage Publications, Inc.

Kotler, P. (1997). *Marketing management; analysis, planning, implementation, and control* (9th edition ed.). Upper Saddle River: Prentice Hall.

OECD. (2005). *Enhancing the Performance of the Service Sector.* .

OECD. (2007). *Key figures 2007 on Science Technology and Innovation*, EU DG RTD/C03.

Pilat, D. (2006). De economische effecten van ICT. *ESB Dossier, 91*

Van de Kar, E. A. M., & Verbraeck, A. (2007). *Designing Mobile Service Systems*. Amsterdam: IOS Press.

Vermeulen, P., & van der Aa, W. (2003). Organizing Innovation in Services. In J. Tidd & F. M. Hull (Eds.), *Service Innovation* (Vol. 9, pp. 35-53). London: Imperial College Press.

Appendix

Original list of themes on which workshop participants voted during the final workshop in September 2007. The themes marked * have a higher priority, according to the participants.

Outer circle: service innovation strategy
- export innovative services*
- service innovation life cycle and associated strategies
- innovation strategies from formally industrial companies
- regulation of service sectors (International/European regulation)
- innovation in non-profit sectors

Middle circle: management of service innovation
- creation of an innovative corporate culture *
- financial management: how to finance service innovation *
- co-creation
- innovation adoption
- user-centered design, and design focused on specific target groups
- dealing with scarcity on the labor market: HRM policies
- education and career paths for service innovators
- professionalism of service innovation processes (creative/structural; project-based/ innovative; central/decentralized)
- strategic cooperation with partners
- new business models
- patentees of services

Inner circle: service system
Service concepts, translation of following trends into value propositions
- Sharp rise in the ageing population*
- Digital Living*

- Mobility*
- Individualization (Personalization)
- Globalization
- Multi-cultural society
- Global warming

(Customer) Interaction*
- Databases with (detailed) customer data and privacy*
- Customer Loyalty
- Multi-channelling (sales)
- Cross-medial service offerings (various messages via different channels, in total complementary)
- Self-service (for example in the financial retailing and in hospitals)
- Anytime, anywhere
- Interaction with people in their personal setting (reaching the customer in their living room)

Organizational issues and business processes
- Cooperation with partners*
- Standardization of information exchange in the value network*
- Paying (billing of cashing)
- IPR in value network
- Human Capital (skills of people)
- Purchase of the knowledge that is required from other actors (possibility of patents being involved)
- Matching one's own internal front office and back office processes with the internal processes of partners
- Dealing with different company cultures when cooperating

(Enabling) Technology*
- Possibilities of large bandwidth (streaming video)*
- User interaction through new web opportunities (weblogs, social networks, virtual worlds)*
- Video/avatar call center
- Sustainable digital storage

IT IS ONLY WHEN THE AVERAGE CONSUMER AND SUPPLIER HAVE GATHERED SUFFICIENT EXPERIENCE AT A LOCAL LEVEL WITH INTERACTIVE ELECTRONIC CONTACT, AND DEVELOPED THE REQUITED LEVEL OF TRUST, THAT THEY MAY BE EXPECTED TO ENTER THE BIG CYBER ROAD.

From Civil Merchant

Next generation ICT users: inspiration and challenges for policy-makers

Jolien Ubacht

"René has died during his skiing holidays". A year after receiving this devastating news, I still find it hard to believe. The past few months of his life were so full of energy and inspiration for the future of our ICT research group at Delft University of Technology, a future that changed dramatically on that fateful day in February 2007.

The invitation to write a contribution to this commemorative book made me reflect on the last discussions René and I had. These discussions revolved around the societal changes that are evoked by ICT innovation and, more specifically, around the changing role of end-users of ICT in the age of digital communications, end-users who are no longer end-users, but who have become pro-active contributors to innovation, creators of electronic content, co-owners of communication networks, etc. This topic was inspired by a request from the Ministry of Economic Affairs to our Technology, Policy and Management Faculty, to write a reflection on their policy framework for the electronic communications sector for the years to come.

Although this area of ICT research was not on René's list of top priorities, he was enthusiastic and he encouraged me to explore the issue. We had interesting discussions on the implications of the changing role of ICT 'end'-users. We had come across a topic that intrigued us both, a topic that held the promise of new perspectives on possible research tracks in the field of ICT.

René did not live to see the final results of the TPM reflection for the Ministry of Economic Affairs. The essay that was co-authored by many TPM-colleagues was published in July 2007, five months after his death (Lemstra, 2007). However, our discussions on the topic of ICT users have continued to inspire me throughout the year and subsequent publications and research will follow. I therefore want to dedicate this adapted version of my contribution to the essay on the role of ICT end-users, in fond memory of the last discussions René and I had.

Abstract

When end-users[1] have access to high quality ICT-resources and have the skills to handle them, their innovative power to create new content or share their knowledge is amazing. This end-user creativity is not new, but thanks to the ever decreasing threshold to enter the virtual domains of the Internet, the scale at which these activities take place is growing fast, spurred by the rise of Web 2.0 applications. The joint activities of these 'end'-users are gaining momentum, which makes it interesting to explore the challenges for policy-makers in the positive sense: How can we fully benefit from the innovative power of end-user creativity? We challenge policy-makers to shift their focus and to reconsider the formerly passive role of the end-user. They will see opportunities to take full advantage of this trend by providing users with optimal conditions to explore these bottom-up initiatives. This requires them to consider the role of education and innovation policy and the networked cooperation between policy-makers in various domains. Also, we discuss the issue of governance of end-user owned network components.

Next generation ICT

As a result of the falling costs of digital equipment like photo cameras, multimedia PC's and mobile telephones, the high level of domestication of information and communication technologies (ICT), the availability of Internet access and the growth of skills in individuals with regard to using them, the threshold to enter the virtual domains of the Internet, and to start playing other roles in society via that access, has drastically lowered over the past decades.

End-users increasingly transcend their traditional role as recipients of information and media products and services at the end of the (digital) value chain, and assume a more active role. They use ICT for their own purposes or deploy their own ICT resources for others to be used, for instance in peer-to-peer (P2P) networks. In addition, by collecting, modifying and publishing electronic content, end-users venture into domains that hitherto were controlled by professionals, like journalists, photographers and organizations such as broadcasting and network companies. Also, they enter into direct economic relationships with other end-users, which turns them in private entrepreneurs in virtual and non-virtual worlds in which they trade information, services, physical and electronic goods, usually in person-to-person (p2p) transactions (for instance via eBay). And they are (in)directly becoming competitors of existing network operators because they themselves control elements of the network (for instance via private investments in the roll-out of a fibre-optic local loop or in setting up Wi-Fi networks).

These developments are not new, but the scale at which they take place is growing fast. The election of the Internet user as 'person of the year 2006' by Time Magazine was clearly inspired by this trend. If the joint activities of these 'end'-users reach a certain momentum, this may have consequences for policy issues, or it may make it possible to exploit innovative opportunities on the basis of these activities.

We begin by taking a closer look at what kinds of things end-users do when they use the possibilities offered by (new) information and communication technology.

NEXT GENERATION ICT END-USERS

What kinds of things do end-users do when they combine access to good ICT-resources with the skills needed to handle them? In Table 1, we provide an overview of conventional and new end-user activities. We follow the common classification of information, communication, entertainment and transaction as categories of functionalities in the ICT and media domain. If we look at the 'new activities' of end-users in Table 1, what are they doing differently than before?

First of all, it becomes clear that the new activities require *a proactive attitude* in dealing with information and media. End-users move from being passive consumers of information and entertainment (the well-know couch potato) towards a more active attitude in terms of providing information (for instance making websites), looking for information (for example downloading television programs) and creating digital media products (for example making a video and publishing it on YouTube). Searching for media products via the Internet rather than consuming pre-programmed program requires a different lifestyle.

A second striking aspect is that ICT enables end-users to *enter virtual worlds* (such as Second Life or electronic multi-user games) or *virtual markets* to establish a link between the services/products they wish to trade and people who are interested in buying them (such as eBay). ICT has made it easier and cheaper to take part in these worlds and markets. *Interactivity* is the key element here.

	Conventional activities	**New activities**
Information	Accessing digital sources (for instance via websites) Submitting data via paper forms that are then digitised (for instance by local governments)	Blogging Contributing to public wiki's Making websites for personal and commercial purposes Publishing their own digital information (for instance photographs via Flickr) Discussion via digital forums (for instance del.iciou.us) Open Software Development Digital submission of data and making appointments
Communication	Telephony via telephone, cable and wireless networks operated by public or private network operators	Privately built and operated fibre-optic and WiFi networks with or without open access to third parties (Mobile) grid computing Wiki's in learning environments and with organisations for knowledge sharing Web-based social networking (Cyworld; Hyves, LinkedIn) Voice over IP-telephony Online communities
Entertainment	Mass medium: television and radio programmes via conventional public and private broadcasting companies Cinema Video rental stores CD's, videos, DVD's	User-generated content (for instance via MySpace and YouTube) Interactive television programmes Mobile entertainment (for instance Podcasts, I-Pod, mobile television) Direct distribution of self-created music Internet television Media Centres Individual choice of digital offering Determining the time of broadcast (for instance after missing a show) Avatar in Second Life Multi-user online games (for instance World of Warcraft)
Transaction	Visiting a physical store Value chains with intermediaries Banking transactions via paper mail Payments with bank cards or credit cards	Virtual entrepreneurship (for instance in Second Life) Micro-entrepreneurship Person-to-person trade (for example via eBay) Online shopping (for instance buying books via Amazon.com) Digital banking, online payments Direct sale of digital products (for instance music directly from maker to buyer) Online sale of houses

Table 1. *A shift in the activities of end-users*

We also see examples where *participation in society* and exploiting one's own talents via virtual channels is encouraged. Adri, a housewife in her sixties, who never managed to finish secondary education, can still engage in economic activities and make money doing what she is good at, making children's clothing and selling them via the Internet. Mohammed, who does not do too well in school, can deploy his talents in a different way by digital micro-entrepreneurship. The personal benefits are not only economic in nature, and there are also serious social advantages. If we look at the *motivation* for participation via ICT, we notice that this is not purely economic in nature, but that other kinds of motivations also play a role, for example contributing to a joint product (like Wikipedia) or the joint development of open source software in response to the dominance of commercial products like those sold by Microsoft. These voluntary contributions to a common good yield personal satisfaction, sometimes a feeling of belonging to a group, or a satisfaction in sharing your knowledge with others, be them familiar as members of a social network or unfamiliar in larger, more anonymous digital surroundings. *Virtual social interaction* is an important motivation that operates on many levels, from local (neighbourhood sites) to international, or with regard to specific target groups. ICT users look for others like themselves via the Internet, to exchange information, e.g. to share experiences in the purchase of a product, ask and give advice, engage in cultural expression, to see and to be seen.

A specific aspect of this social interaction is the striking *blurring of the boundaries between public and private spaces*. Where 'older' generations of users are at times reluctant to provide information via social networking sites, youngsters have no such reservations and are happy to provide all their private information (Mangold, 2006; Nussbaum, 2007). To them, exposure is a motivation to be active in the 'market of attention', perhaps without being able to realize all the later consequences of what they do today. The fact that end-users can also own technical components in a network that has public access potentials, such as WiFi networks, is also an example of blurring boundaries between organizational and citizen ownership and management of infrastructures.

End-users *enter domains that previously were reserved for professionals or private and public organizations*. They are active in content creation, collecting and publishing news in ways that were hitherto the domain of organizations like public and commercial broadcasting companies and network operators, and of professionals like journalists and program makers. In addition, *they themselves replace or ignore the functions of intermediaries* like real estate agents, by negotiating directly with the buyers of their goods and services.

In Box 1, we present an overview of these aspects.
Although, as end-users, they play the role of 'recipient' of information, communication, entertainment and transaction (services), at the same time they also play the role of sender and even designer of these kinds of services. They become nodes in a network of information processing, in some cases for financial gain, but often for different kinds of reasons.

Intermezzo
This is the moment when René would say "nice overview, but where is the practical relevance? What are the effects and who should be interested in them?" Thus, challenging me to take the next step: bridging academic research and practical relevance, which was René's personal specialty. In the essay, I introduced personal stories to reinforce the image of the shift in the roles of end-users. During our last section strategy day, shortly before his death, René challenged the ICT section members to write such persona's to discover what type of students we wanted to address with our courses on ICT. This proved an inspiring activity and yielded a good impression of the students we expected to choose the ICT domain within the Faculty's teaching program. René and I shared a passion for visualisation; the whiteboard

---

» Proactive attitude
» Entering virtual worlds
» Entering virtual markets
» Interactivity
» Participating in society without school/formal diplomas, based on personal talents
» Motivation not only economic in nature, but also with a social orientation
» Virtual social interaction
» Blurring of boundaries between public and private spaces
» Blurring of boundaries between organizational and citizen ownership/management of infrastructures
» Entering professional domains, blurring or ignoring of functions of intermediaries

---

Box 1 *What is different? New aspects of ICT end-user behavior.*

in his office would always be filled with schemes, figures or matrixes after our discussions.

MEETING THE CONSEQUENCES

The next step, then, is translating these end-user trends into inspiration and challenges for policy-makers.

This translation can be made in two directions. Policy-makers can look at the negative consequences of these end-user initiatives and try to combat them, or they can look for ways to benefit from end-users' motivation and creativity and encourage them. An example of the former direction is the news stories surrounding new forms of child labour in digital worlds. Children who play games until they are exhausted in the hope of winning digital products that can then be sold for hard cash on digital auction sites (Doorn, 2006). Or the clampdown on illegal downloads that violate property rights. Or political questions about virtual sex with minors in the world of Second Life (Tweede Kamer der Staten-Generaal, 2007).

Because the Policy Framework for Electronic Communication (MinEZ, 2006) already paid attention to these negative consequences, I chose to look at potential positive effects of the initiatives of ICT end-users. If we look at the types of activities described above based on the assumption that a scale-up takes place, what are the potentials of this trend in terms of innovation, education, policy and governance?

ATTRIBUTE	The ICT driven technological revolution	
Phasing	Installation phase	Deployment phase
Timing Technology	BEFORE AND DURING THE BUBBLE Invention and early adoption	AFTER THE BUBBLE Broad deployment and use
Financing	Financial capital	Industrial capital
ICT use	**Transitions** Automation → Informatization → Business processes web enabled	
ICT solutions	Stand alone → Networked	
Focus Scope of ICT issues and solution	Technology-centric → User-centric National → Global	
Focus of learning	About ICT → Working with ICT → Innovating with ICT	

Table 3. Attributes of the current technological revolution

CONSEQUENCES FOR INNOVATION POLICY

We begin by looking for inspiration from the end-user initiatives for innovation policy. In the full essay, we used the trend that is represented in Table 3, in which Lemstra visualizes the shifting paradigms in business use of ICT that are driven by the ICT revolution (Lemstra, 2006, p. 243).

Table 3 shows the ICT-driven revolution translated into the consequences for the ICT sector and for the business side of ICT use. We extrapolate these consequences towards the individual ICT user. What innovative force emerges from these end-user initiatives? How can we benefit from the knowledge and experiences of end-users with regard to economic activities? Can we use these initiatives on a bigger scale in a broader context of the service sector that uses ICT, in the way it is currently done by the program makers who use user-generated content as inspiration for their own media products?

On the other hand, the question may be how we can create policy frameworks that allow end-users to fully benefit from ICT opportunities. Or create space and creativity, for example for alternative entrepreneurship at a micro-level, within existing frameworks that are currently focused on large and medium-sized companies.

The cross-fertilisation between existing sectors and this new trend of ICT user initiatives can also provide inspiration for new forms of business. In this context, the end-user represents a flow of new activity at micro-level. As micro-entrepreneurs, users become acquainted with and explore the boundaries of entrepreneurship, creating new ICT applications and services from a very pragmatic perspective. If we are able to blur the boundaries between entities that gather information and entities that need information to create added value, this will lead to new forms of knowledge valorisation. This may mean that in various policy domains attention has to be paid to the question as to how to create room for these initiatives to flourish. Not in the sense of 'how can we tax these new initiatives', but more in terms of how we can encourage these trends in order to generate new forms of business from the bottom up, unencumbered by legislation and regulation that may nip these innovative contributions in the bud. In other words: how can policy be used to stimulate the positive contributions of these kinds of initiatives, in order to bring them into existing sectors and bring about change and to ensure that new types of business cases can be economically successful and lead to innovation. Mobile network operators, for example, in their search for content and new applications that will generate more traffic on their networks (Wilson, 2006), are looking for multimedia content on mobile video and television, including user activities on YouTube.

The message to innovation policy-makers is this: explore and facilitate end-user initiatives so as not to miss opportunities for inspiration. This requires room, inspiration, letting go of existing prejudices and speaking the language of the ICT end-users. In terms of Christopher Hood's Tools of Government, we call this the optimal use of the detectors the Ministry has at its disposal to pick up signals in society (Hood, 1983). First get a good feel and understanding of the trend, before translating it into (desired chances in) policy.

Consequences for economic regulation

As far as end-users are concerned, ICT lowers the threshold to various markets. These are not always economic markets in terms of supply and demand, in which the market entrants are motivated solely by financial gain. Attention markets, where the exposure of knowledge or details of a person's private life are central, are very popular, not only popular amongst youngsters that put their whole private lives on line. These are person-2-person attention markets.

This approach to supply and demand is different from the more classical and formal channels, like public and private broadcasting companies, newspapers or cinema, or the audio material published by the music industry. It requires a different way of thinking. The question amongst policy-makers on 'how we should deal with this type of market' refers less to 'how should we organise this market' than it does to how they could allow this creativity in society, and how policy-makers should respond in a dynamic manner.

An example is the popularity of bands that publish their music via websites like YouTube, MySpace or ElectroBell. These bands circumvent the formal framework of the music industry and yet manage to reach a wide audience, with its own way of looking for interesting content. It is an audience that does not consume information and media via the packaged content of the formal channels, where a gatekeeper determines what is and is not sent to the end-users via the common transmission channels.

It is an audience that actively looks for direct sources of information and media content via the Internet, and that determines what it does and does not want to see. These skilled information gatherers, whose numbers are growing dramatically, no longer buy CD's, but instead make their own package of individual songs. They choose dynamically and creatively. This in turn requires a dynamic and creative response by governments, one that goes beyond the question 'how can we protect the property rights of the content creators'. A growing number of content creators opt in favour of the Creative Commons concept, a more flexible way of regulating intellectual property rights. The policy question that can be asked is whether the Creative Commons should be an extension of the current laws and regulations concerning property rights.

Consequences for education policy

In her book Technological revolutions and financial capital, Perez argues that technological revolutions lead to various tensions in society, including "[tensions] in capabilities, between those that are trained to participate in the new technologies and those whose skills become increasingly obsolete" (2002). If we look at the ICT users, we see new forms of learning, information gathering and (re-)processing, an example of which is the success of universities who make their educational material available online. But we also see forms where the knowledge and information not only comes from the teachers, but from the learning individuals instead. This can be compared to new forms of knowledge management within organizations, where the use of Wiki's encourages people to share knowledge. Or, in a broader sense, the use of Web 2.0 as a global participation network, where there is not only interaction between individuals, but also between individuals and companies (Wilson, 2006). These constructions allow individual users to contribute to the design of the products and services of companies and government organizations, or to play the role of editor, for example in setting up the interactive alternative to the Yellow Pages for companies: YelloYello.com. With YelloYello, individuals award stars to the listed companies and share their experiences in dealing with companies. Earlier we used the example of Mohammed that shows the discrepancy between Mohammed the educational underachiever and the same Mohammed who, according to his friends, is a great digital micro-entrepreneur. If he does manage to go far, it is because of his curiosity to become a virtual success and his intrinsic motivation to learn new things. How can this intrinsic curiosity be encouraged and be allowed to flourish in society? A question that shows the relevance of this end-user trend for the Ministry of Educational Affairs: should new skills be taught to next generation ICT users?

Consequences for governance
Under the heading of 'governance', new questions arise concerning the management of infrastructural components that are no longer managed by a central entity. For example: is the initiative of Wireless Leiden, a wireless network that is the result of connecting individual private WiFi hotspots an organization or is it something else? Should it obey the telecommunication legislation or does that not apply here, because there is no public network operator? We are dealing with an emergent development here, a bottom-up initiative by individuals who are not driven by economic considerations, but by pragmatic and idealist objectives (Vree, 2003).

Vree describes emergent infrastructures as follows:
A situation whereby "(…) a large-scale infrastructure is formed by many small private investments that in most cases were needed anyway for other purposes. Cars and ships are more and more equipped with ICT. Even a fraction of that equipment is enough for the melting process of local networks (…). It is a kind of symbiosis, in which a piece of the capacity of the already present ICT technology is used for the common good."
"(…) By Inversion of Infrastructure I wish above all to emphasize that investments occur inversely, not from the top down, but from the bottom up. It is not the government that invests primarily, but citizens and companies. The administrative demands of this inversion are different. The words organising, building or implementing that we see in the classical approach could be replaced by 'bringing about', 'making happen' or 'creating optimal conditions for growth'" (2003, p. 11).

Vree sees in all this a paradigm shift with the following characteristics:
— bottom-up investments by users;
— small heterogeneous networks that are connected to larger networks;
— the use of existing ICT for unpredicted purposes;
— user-driven development of infrastructures with a framework of common interest;
— self-organizing, flexible network development at the level of components and subsystems.

It is clear that this raises questions with regard to governance. We deliberately use the term governance, because it is broader than legislation and regulation initiated and implemented by formal government bodies. It also means that governments may have to lean on or even trust forms of self-regulation, because existing frameworks are challenged by these creative bottom-up initiatives. In addition, regulation through technical means (software) also has to be explored rigorously. We come back to this in the next section.

Consequences for cooperation in the policy domain
The ICT end-user trends address trans-sectoral domains that belong to several Ministries and thus require networked cooperation between them.
The innovation belongs to the Ministry of Economic Affairs, but the Ministry for Education, Culture and Science is involved for the user-generated content (broadcasting company files) and for questions regarding new forms of learning. These two examples show that there is a point where both Ministries need to come together: e-learning to lay the foundation for future labour participation (Mohammed) or to increase the unused potential of individual persons (Adri). Ostrom uses the term action arena, where actors communicate with each other and where specific rules apply (the action rules, for instance the rules regarding access to the action arena) (Ostrom, Gardner et al. 1994, p. 29). To study new phenomena it may be interesting to organise the action arena in such a way as to invite the actors involved in the new trend to the action arena. In our case this means inviting proactive and creative ICT users to enter into a dialogue with policy-makers with the intention to explore potential benefits and to make an inventory of hindrances that individuals encounter to fully benefit from the newly available ICT functionalities.
This allows the Ministry to keep a close watch on the speed with which changes take place. What is striking about this change trajectory is the emergent nature of the activities in question. This is not a centralized (top-down) process, but a highly individualized (bottom-up) trend. Does this fit in with existing policy frameworks? Is the trend incorporated into existing frameworks or are other environmental factors in play? Is there enough flexibility in institutional frameworks, in the policy processes, instruments and terminology to formulate a response to these questions?

To conclude, a remark about the mode of governance. In light of the emergent nature of the ICT user initiatives and the fact that many of these activities take place over the Internet, it is not always possible to make sure that formal legislation and regulation apply or, more importantly, are effective. If formal legislation and regulation fail to address end-user activities in full, can private, alternative modes of governance, through self-regulation or other kinds of coordination mechanisms, like technical standards, generate a new balance? After all, creative problems ask for creative solutions, especially when existing solutions can no longer be used effectively because it is no longer possible to control the object of policy.

Intermezzo
"So now what?" René would say, "You have sketched the end-user trends, you have pictured the challenges for policy-makers, what is your next step? Is this a one off exercise or can we do more"? Never easily satisfied, René would formulate the next challenge: going from trend to practical relevance and now towards a research track. Preferably a funded research track...

FUTURE OUTLOOK
The role of the ICT end-user as an active, creating person yields visions of a new type of resource in many ways. The years 2006 an 2007 have brought us many books that explore the consequences and possibilities of end-user power. Books like Wikinomics: How Mass Collaboration Changes Everything by Don Tapscott and Anthony D. Williams, The Wealth of Networks: How Social Production Transforms Markets and Freedom by Yochai Benkler, to Infotopia How Many Minds Produce Knowledge by Cass R. Sunstein and many, many more. What they have in common is that they envision the end-user trend to become a common pool of resources in many areas of application. In answer to the challenge to 'do more', I suggest that academic research should be carried out to benefit fully from these new resources and in order to do so, we have to start with basic research into questions such as:
— Which institutional framework is required to take full advantage of the innovative power and creativity of ICT end-users?
— What is the connection between ICT user activities and innovation/markets?

— How can we visualize the value creation of informal economic processes and markets that sprout from the activities of ICT end-users, in a quantitative manner?

— What types of end-user participation in innovation processes can we discern and which types of participation works best in which innovation process?

— What inspiration do ICT user trends provide for policy implementation and the design of alternative regulatory arrangements to deal with negative consequences of ICT use? In other words: what role can ICT end-users play in regulatory arrangements, with special attention to their motivation to contribute to common good principles?

— Which roles for (end-user) technology in the design of policy arrangements/frameworks?

— Which issues surrounding reliability, privacy, intellectual property rights, financial stimulation measures (micro-credit, vouchers), etc., from the point of view of the various (possible) functions and roles of ICT end-users should we address?

In short: the intention is to become familiar with ICT users in their various functions; see what they need, what they can contribute to innovation and markets, map problems they may run into and come up with creative policy options to address those problems. But above all to come up with solid academic research that yields insight into the ICT end-user practices by the design of models and guidelines for processes of innovation and education that work.

Finale

The ultimate challenge is to find resources for such academic research tracks. René had the drive, the creativity and the convincing power to interest others to take up this challenge ....

---

1 Although in a strict sense the end-user is no 'end' user anymore as s/he is no longer 'merely' the receiver of media content and information at the end of a services value chain or 'merely' the user of ICT infrastructures, we choose to use the concept for its signaling function in mainstream language.

References

Doorn, J. (2006). *Kinderarbeid in World of Warcraft (Child labour in World of Warcraft)*. Retrieved April 4, 2007 from http://www.webwereld.nl/articles/43274/-kinderarbeid-in-world-of-warcraft-.html.

Hood, C.C. (1983). *Tools of Government*. Houndmills & London: MacMillan Education.

Lemstra, W. (2006). *The Internet bubble and the impact on the development path of the telecommunication sector*. Delft: Delft University of Technology, dissertation.

Lemstra, W. (Ed.) (2007). *ReActies. Het effect van paradigma verschuivingen. (ReActions. The effect of shifting paradigms)*. The Hague: Ministry of Economic Affairs.

Mangold, N.N. (2006). *Privacy? Leuk voor bejaarden (Privacy? An issue for elderly people)*. Retrieved April 5, 2007 from http://www.marketingfacts.nl/berichten/20070219—privacy—leuk—voor—bejaarden/.

MinEZ. (2006). *Nederland in verbinding. Beleidskader voor de elektronische communicatie. (The Netherlands connected. Policy framework for electronic communications)*. The Hague: Ministry of Economic Affairs.

Nussbaum, E. (2007). *Say everything*. Retrieved July 3, 2007 from http://nymag.com/news/features/27341/.

Ostrom, E., Gardner, R. et al. (1994). *Rules, Games and Common-Pool Resources*. Ann Arbor: University of Michigan Press.

Perez, C. (2002). *Technological revolutions and financial capital: the dynamics of bubbles and golden ages*. Cheltenham UK: Edward Elgar.

Tweede Kamer der Staten-Generaal. (2007). *Vragen van de leden Gerkens (SP) en Bouchibiti (PvdA) aan de Minister van Justitie over virtuele kinder porno via het online game Second Life. (Questions in the House of Representatives to the Ministry of Justice on the issue of virtual child porn)*. February 23rd. The Hague: Tweede Kamer (The Dutch House of Representatives), Vragen, nr. 20060708170.

Vree, W.G. (2003). *Internet en Rijkswaterstaat: een ICT-infrastructuur langs water en wegen. (Internet and the Directorate for Public Works and Water Management: and ICT-infrastructure alongside water and roads)*. Delft: Delft University of Technology, inaugural speech.

Wilson, J. (2006). 3G to Web2.0? Can Mobile Telephony become an architecture of participation? *Convergence*, 12, 229-242.

A SUFFICIENT DEGREE OF SECURITY IS A PRECONDITION FOR PRIVACY, BUT IN ITSELF IT IS NOT ENOUGH. AFTER ALL, PRIVACY REQUIRES FURTHER-REACHING AGREEMENTS SURROUNDING THE AUTHORIZED STORAGE AND HANDLING OF PERSONAL AND COMPANY-RELATED INFORMATION.

From Civil Servant

Thoughts about Identity, privacy and virtualisation

Hans M. Pronk

ABSTRACT
This paper is a first order elaboration of a discussion between René Wagenaar and myself about the development of future scenarios for governments. Its purpose was to formulate the (research) questions that could help provide more insight into the role of, among others, the government.

My relationship with René goes back to my time as a student at Erasmus University of Rotterdam, where René was a lecturer at the time. Between the late 1980's and 1995, the two of us worked at the FBK. After I left to work at VKA, we have always stayed in touch, both professionally and at a more personal level.

INTRODUCTION
It was during my time as a student at Erasmus University of Rotterdam (EUR) that I first made René's acquaintance. At the time, he had just started working there, and he taught a number of classes in information science at the economics faculty. After I graduated, I continued to work at the Management Department of EUR until 1995, which was also the department where René was working during that period. We worked together on a number of occasions, for instance in a study into interconnectivity in the messaging infrastructures that existed at the time. During that time, we developed a friendship that has lasted over the years. We shared a passion for art, music and social issues. After I left to work at Verdonck, Klooster and Associates, our cooperation continued. I participated, for example, in a number of 'think tanks' during his time at KPN, and we regularly exchanged ideas about the relationship between government and ICT. In January 2007, he invited me to join a brainstorm, this time in Brussels, now with regard to future scenarios about the role of ICT. On our way back, we discussed the day and the scenarios that had been presented

extensively, and agreed to investigate and elaborate the subjects we had discussed. Unfortunately, it was not meant to be.

For this publication, I have taken the notes I made in Brussels and attempted to put our thoughts and ideas to paper, with a focus on the questions and issues. As such, it is a collection of concepts, thoughts and ideas that we felt were relevant in the overlap of our respective fields of expertise. They are intended as stepping stones towards further study and deeper analysis, rather than as fully grown position papers.

Will Thomas Watson be proven right after all?

In 1943, Thomas Watson (IBM) made his famous statement "I think there is a world market for maybe five computers". Also this claim has long been regarded as a sign of short-sightedness, developments in the area of platforms and cloud-computing place his statements in an entirely new light. The current combination of networks and ICT systems are powerful enough to implement the models that have been worked out in the 1990's on the basis of the notion that 'the network is the computer'. Current SaaS developments are a first step in that direction. As far as end-users are concerned, Software as a Service (SaaS) are the way in which ICT functionalities will increasingly be provided to the users. An good example of a SaaS solution is the Basecamp product by a company called 37signales (www.basecamphq.com). Basecamp offers users a complete set of online project management tools. Because these tools are provided from a central location, end-users do not have to install and maintain software or servers. The tools are offered as a subscribed service.

As far as the providers of these Saas service are concerned, platforms and Internet-scale computing (or cloud-computing) are becoming increasingly relevant. The providers of services like Basecamp are specialized in the development and management of their own applications. From their point of view, the systems and networks on which these applications run are merely a facility that they need to provide their services. Cloud-computing of Internet-scale computing involves the large-scale provision of high-quality underlying systems and network. One of the company's that are very active in this area is Amazon, for instance by offering access to virtual servers (EC2 or elastic computer cloud), storage (S3 or simple storage systems) and database services. This means that companies like 37Signals no longer have to purchase or manage their own servers.

The phenomenon of cloud-computing that is now being pioneered by companies like Amazon put the Thomas Watson's statement in an entirely new context for me. If we realize who the players are in this so-called cloud-space and what the qualities are that they need to possess to operate effectively in the computer market, we see that their number is indeed small. It is in particular the 'massive' nature of these kinds of operations that makes them suitable for high levels concentration similar to for example energy generation. Unlike energy generation is it also possible to provide these services to a global market. Current players like Amazon, Google, Microsoft, IBM and Sun, to name the most prominent players, have the technical qualifications as well as the scale that is needed to carry out these kinds of operations at the level of excellence and costs (due to the massive economy of scale) that the market demands. It become clear that it is in particular in this area of operational excellence that the current smaller providers of ICT resources fail to perform at the required level.

What emerges is a three tier model of -1- cloud-computing, -2- platform players and -3- the owners of the intellectual property. The bottom layer is filled by the new generation of cloud-gods. Why are they called cloud-gods? At this layer, the actual computing takes place and, as we mentioned, the room that is available in this layer will remain limited. After all, how many Googles can there be? That's why. On the layer of platform the num-

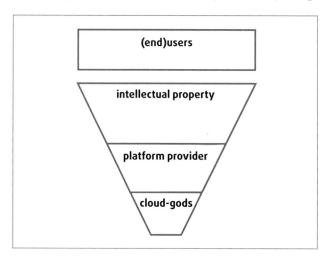

Figure 1. Three tier model

ber of potential players is also low, although here, unlike in cloud-space, it is easier to create added value via context-related knowledge and skills. The cloud and the platform layer together provide the environment in which IP owners can ultimately create the real economic added value, based on the two underlying layers.

And in the end Thomas Watson may have been right after all!

The question is, however, what it means if this added value will be created on the basis of these resources. In the case of physical goods it is always possible to use the physical presence as a starting point. However, with the increased use of virtual goods, these mechanisms no longer work. Concepts like 'MADE IN XXXX' become meaningless. In addition, legislation is (often) based on location, e.g. it is determined at a national level and sometimes at a higher level (EU, UN). At the moment, in the case of Amazon's EC2 and S3 services, it already is no longer possible to determine where exactly one's data is being stored or where the server images are run, other than that it is within the EU. As soon as a part of the actual data processing takes place at the client end-point, it becomes even more difficult to tell. Where is the profit or added value generated? And which legislation applies? The important thing, at any rate, is the Amazon S3 / EC2 exist and are being used, and that this usage will only become more important over time.

Furthermore, it is interesting to investigate whether there is a relationship between the presence of these cloud-gods and prosperity, or rather, whether the presence of these kinds of organizations it is economically advantageous to a country. In theory, The Netherlands should be in an excellent position to benefit from this presence. After all, the AMS-IX, the Amsterdam Internet Exchange, is the largest of its kind, guaranteeing good cost-effective access to all the relevant Internet infrastructures. In addition to network access, however, energy is also an important production factor in these types of operations.

The country's status as an energy distribution hub should present opportunities in this respect. And in view of the short distances there are plenty of locations available. On the other hand, the question is whether energy can be acquired at price levels that are low enough. Rumours that Google and Microsoft are investigating connectivity in locations that provide very cheap and green energy, like Iceland, are something of an indication of the relevance of this question.

It remains to be seen whether the presence of cloud-gods with a country's borders actually represents major economic benefits. One of the determining factors may be a guaranteed access to these resources. With regard to the storage of data, one can imagine that legislation alone may lead to a data storage model per country, at least concerning data that have a certain status or that are subject to legal restrictions.

Identities and virtualisation

One of the consequences of the emergence of virtual worlds is that the users of these worlds increasingly have multiple online personalities. At the moment, there is a one-to-one relationship between a physical person and his or her various avatars. However, this relationship will become progressively less straightforward. If we look at intelligence agents, this process has already begun. After all, the agent on the one hand displays autonomous behaviour, while on the other hand representing the user's alter ego. It is not clear how these kinds of artefacts should be dealt with. Even now, there is a legal problem with regard to autonomous vehicles. The core question is who is responsible, for example in the case of accidents. Is it the supplier of the software, the manufacturer of the vehicle, or its owner? Without answers to these questions, a large-scale introduction of these kinds of vehicles, despite the promises in terms of road safety and environmental benefits, will not be possible. Vehicles at least have the advantage of being physical entities. When the agents are completely software-based, it will be even more difficult to create an airtight legal framework that will do justice to the problems involved. An interesting thought experiment is the case in which the owner of a software agent that has a certain level of autonomy passes away. As long as the owner is alive, the data of the software agent are protected by privacy legislation, among other things. However, as soon as the owner dies, there is no longer a natural person to which privacy legislation applies. One of the questions that arises is whether all the actions that have been carried out by the software agent should be openly available to all. Depending on the kind of actions, this might make for an interesting into the lives of people.

In addition to these questions, the phenomenon of multiple avatars is a new and tricky problem for governments. Confronted with it, the standard reaction appears to be one of denial. Basically, the very existence of the problem is ignored, which does not make it disappear, because it is a growing phenomenon with which governments will at some point have to deal. The first steps in this direction are already visible. Especially with regards to fighting crime, at a European level legislation is being set up that prohibits the creation of a false identity with the goal of meeting minors in the physical world. What remains interesting in this context is, of course, the term false identity, because one of the characteristics of the virtual is the ability to remove the restrictions that are imposed by the physical reality. The very term false identity would imply that there is such a thing as a genuine virtual reality. It is possible to imagine an official virtual identity, or a formally established connection between a virtual and a physical identity, or rather several virtual identities, with an emphasis on several. A kind of more generic DigiD that can also be applied by non-government entities. It needs to be pointed out here that the trend with regard to identity management is not towards a central identity provisioning. The keyword in this respect is user-centric identity management, where the management of the (virtual) identity is in the hands of the user himself. Due to the developments with regard to the OpenID and Oauth standards, this is already technically feasible. A number of governments are conducting experiments involving a connection between the more user-centric approach that is facilitated by OpenID and the more federal approach of, for instance, DigiD. It seems worthwhile to investigate to what extent the various strengths and weaknesses of the environment can be combined, in order for governments (and the business community) to be able to arrive at a balanced decision regarding future developments.

In addition to the issue of identity, there are also problems surrounding the virtual worlds themselves. Due to the immense (media) success of environments like SecondLife, Habba Hotel and WoW, an awareness is emerging about the existence of these networks. This is another area where there are more questions than answers, in particular with regard to the role of government. Here, too, the questions are first and foremost of a legal nature. Is virtual (child) pornography covered by existing legislation? What was ultimately the intention of the legislator when the legislation was crated? And is it possible to apply existing legislation to the virtual world as is? Another phenomenon is the emergence of new (virtual) money flows. SecondLife already is responsible for a total turnover of hundreds of millions linden dollars every day. Through a connection with the 'real' dollar, this virtual money has actual value in the physical world. Ultimately, new financial institutions will emerge within these virtual worlds. The American government already has taken action against Linden Lab, the company that brought us SecondLife, when it became clear that money was being laundered via virtual casinos on a massive scale. In all virtual worlds it turns out that fully virtual goods also represent a genuine value, and this value can be translated into monetary value. In worlds like SecondLife, the link with 'real' money is established in the world itself, but also in other worlds where such a link is not explicitly established, markets emerge, usually hosted by platforms like eBay or Marktplaats, where virtual goods can be traded. The generation of value, which traditionally took place in the physical world, is also transferred to these new virtual worlds.

The question that arises in this respect is what the role of governments is with regard to the emergence of these kinds of new economic frameworks. Ultimately, the money that is being spent in these worlds is 'virtual'. Does that mean they have become banks? To what extent can existing legislation be applied or does it need to be modified?

It is remarkable that, despite the fact that all the objects that are traded are in fact all software, buyers view them as genuine objects, and they are traded as such. In other worlds, people feel they do not own software, but a helicopter/house/plot of land. When we look at the kinds of objects/goods that are being traded, they can be divided into a number of classes. The most important classes are skill sets and virtual objects. The value of skill sets is based on the fact that in many virtual worlds there is a connection between the game options and the time/experience a player has in such a virtual world. In the case of online car races, for instance, top range cars only become available to players who have managed to reach a certain score. Many players do not have the inclination or the time to acquire the necessary skills, and instead buy a virtual software agent that has already been trained by another user. The other class involves the trade in 3D models that can be used in such a virtual world. Examples are all manner of clothing, but also furniture, houses, cars, etc., that can be introduced into the SecondLife environment and used as object within that environment. To produce skill sets, a provider needs to have sufficiently skilled players that develop these skill sets. To do so in a cost-effective manner, the wages have to be sufficiently low. It would appear that that is why these kinds of skill sets are primarily being developed in China and India. The situation with regard to virtual object is different. These involve a creative process in which the hourly wage is not the determining factor. Based on this, it is assumed that, in light of the good reputation of Dutch design, there are excellent opportunities in this area. Questions that arise here are related to the way the Dutch creative sector manages to make the best possible use of the opportunities available in this area, and which role the government can and maybe ought to play here.

Privacy and the public space

Increasingly, electronic surveillance systems are used by governments for law enforcement purposes. The large-scale availability of, on the one hand, communication channels in the form of fibre optic infrastructures and, on the other hand, sufficiently cheap cameras, for example, has made it possible to deploy very large-scale video surveillance networks that possess the ability to monitor the public space around the clock. Augmenting this camera infrastructure with innovations like automatic facial recognition opens new possibilities for governments to track citizens all the time. Although, until a few years ago, there was widespread public resistance to the use of these kinds of measures, due to the current threat of terror this resistance has been reduced. Further developments in this area are taking place in the field of pattern recognition. Research is already being conducted into the automatic recognition of behaviour that may lead to suicide, with the aim of enhancing safety in London's subway system. By adding these possibilities with regard to pattern recognition to the existing mix of surveillance networks, a situation may emerge in which citizens are being tracked all the time and their behaviour is being assessed automatically for signs of what a government considers suspicious of undesirable behaviour.

By establishing additional links with extra information that can be read, for instance, from RFID tags, communication devices, physical movement patterns (congestion charge/public transport chip card), payment behaviour, etc., a system can be created that makes it possible to keep track of and interpret the behaviour of citizens in public space. In principle, such a system can be a powerful tool with which governments are able to guarantee public safety far better than it can at present.

The questions that arise as a result of these developments are first of all related to control issues. Basically, at the moment it is only those who develop technology who determines what kind of behaviour is 'interesting'. There is no or insufficient awareness with regard to what these kinds of systems can and cannot do. One of the major risks, for instance, is the fact that these kinds of systems are to a large extent based on automated interpretations of behaviour.

What is at any rate lacking with regard to public space is a framework that indicates what is permissible in this context. Such a framework can also help promote discussion with the public 'at large' about what are and are not acceptable ways of controlling public space. The government, as a steward of public space, eventually will have to create clear legislative guidelines, in particular in view of the impending possibilities of automated pattern recognition and assessment.

Needless to say, the same applies to the virtual public space. Due to the nature of the environment, virtual public space is very susceptible to large-scale automated surveillance. It is a public secret that the United States routinely observes e-mail and other Internet-related traffic. The Dutch justice department uses similar means. For the benefit of surveillance, the Dutch ISPs have to spend (a lot of) money to make their networks suitable for surveillance, and they are legally obliged to store all kinds of traffic information. The costs involved in implementing all this are transferred to society. The question is, of course, whether the relationship between the effectiveness of such measures and the costs involved in implementing them makes it possible to be competitive at a national level, in view of the investments that have to be made.

In addition to the issue of control, there is, of course, also the issue of privacy. As mentioned earlier, what is acceptable in this area has come under considerable pressure. Whereas twenty years ago it was inconceivable that people would be obliged by law to carry a form of identification, now it is a fact of life. In any case, existing legislation pays insufficient attention to the privacy-related issues that have emerges as a result of recent technological developments. Here, too, research should focus first of all on the implications of new technologies. The question then becomes how we can safeguard the level of privacy that is considered socially acceptable, given these and other developments in the area of ICT. Even now, it is possible that the existing communication tools have (latent) possibilities that may make it easier to eavesdrop on others. And in the light of the increasing miniaturisation, those possibilities are more likely to increase than decrease. At any rate, public awareness of these kinds of problems at the moment is limited.

Conclusions

ICT is only a tool. However, due to the nature and possibilities of this new tool, completely new realities have emerged in lots of areas. Importantly, many of our current systems and environments are based on the (economic) reality of the pre-ICT world. Due to the new possibilities with regard to large-scale processing and communication, many of the old constraints have been removed or significantly reduced. Whereas in the old world, privacy was protected by the simple fact that large-scale tapping and surveillance was prohibitively expensive, these intrinsic protection mechanisms no longer apply. In addition, new dependencies are being created that never existed in the past and that in particular have economic consequences. When we look at government, for the coming years this implies a continuous orientation on its role and responsibilities for the Dutch economy and the possibilities for government itself to benefit fully from the opportunities provided by the new tools and (virtual) realities. The fascination that René and I shared focused in particular on this area. The house of Thorbecke was built in and for a society characterised by Stone Age information technology. That world no longer exists, and the future is already here. Based on all three topics discussed in this contribution, we formulated a number of research questions early 2007 with regard to the changing relationship between government, citizen and ICT. None of those questions has become less relevant. And because the future is already here, we still need to answer them if we are to give direction to our future.

ARE WE DOING THE RIGHT THINGS, ARE WE DOING THE RIGHT THINGS IN THE RIGHT WAY, HOW CONSISTENT AND RESPONSIVE DO WE TREAT OUR CUSTOMERS, DO WE HAVE THE RIGHT PARTNERS, IS IT SMART TO OUTSOURCE MORE TASKS.

From Civil Servant

'If only we knew what we knew...'
ISO 15489, Sarbanes-Oxley, MoReq, 5015.2-STD – what next?

Kees van der Meer

ABSTRACT

The ISO 15489 standard on records management, the Sarbanes-Oxley law, the Model Requirements for ERMS and the US DoD 5015-2 STD were published in 2001 and 2002. This led prof. dr. René Wagenaar and me to discussions about whether or not these can been seen as building blocks for records management and archives. Although that is an uncommon view, it proved to be useful. It gives an amusing view of interoperability and stability. As a next step, we investigated related building blocks, predicting the list of technical building blocks to be extended in years to come. In addition, the properties of possible building blocks are too varied to be commonly used in business situations. The size, version typology, flexibility and longevity of building blocks for records management and archives are essential and they still have to be investigated and agreed upon.

MEMORY INSTITUTIONS AND THE SCIENCE OF INFORMATION

To know what is known is a topic in information science. The science and art of information is the expertise of memory organizations, like records management offices, archives (which selects the records to be kept in the future), and libraries. They store information for future use, preserve it and make it accessible. Over time, a great deal of experience has been gathered: records management offices and archives existed before the birth of Christ and libraries have been around for centuries. The goals and tasks of memory institutions have been very clear since time immemorial.

ICT AND ARCHIVES

ICT has had a profound affect on records management offices and archives. These organizations handle and store printed works and other physical objects that are regarded as documents. However, due to ICT, they have also needed to cope with electronic 'documents' of digital data (people who work with printed books full of mathematical tables may feel uneasy about the term digital data for electronic information, but that is the term being used). In the days of typing rooms, nearly all information was printed or written. Records were managed meticulously. However, in recent decades, the computer brought about changes.

— Nowadays, it is easy to generate word-processed documents. As a result of this, the number of documents that has to be managed, stored and made accessible has increased enormously.

— The increase in word-processing capacity has been accompanied by a tsunami of volatile information items, like informal drafts, e-mail notifications and memos. There is a danger that comes with the volatility of this type of sources: people may be inclined to discard information after handling it. They will hardly remember afterwards that it ever existed, until it is needed for some other reason, at which point archives prove their value.

— Access to the archives can be granted to users from all over the world: ubiquitous access to archives! Picture Australia, for example, provides access to a photo collection (Australian-only) of some 100 organizations. Picture Australia does not own any of these photos: it can be regarded as an archive without its own collection. The one-counter principle of the Dutch government is based on a similar idea: wherever official public information is stored, citizens ought to have access to it.

These are but a few examples that show that ICT has fundamentally changed the requirements and rationale of the way information is collected and stored.

The importance of records management and archives

As the saying goes: you don't know what you have until it's gone. What happens if we have to do without records management and archives? The collapse of the WTC towers in New York provides a stark example. The business records in records management offices and archives were gone; both the paper-based and the electronic records. The survivors had to try and reconstruct their activities over the past months and years from memory or from scratch (Cox et al, 2001), providing a very clear indication of the value of records management and archives.

For governments, from communities to states, the situation would not be better. Governments are powerless without records management and archives. For instance, the principle of 'equal treatment of all citizens' implies that all transactions, for instance the official responses to requests from citizens, need to be archived. Everybody understands the importance of this.

Building blocks for records management and archives

Both businesses and governments place high demands on records management and archives. Experience shows, that there are advantages to using building blocks, for obvious reasons:
— Use of tested-and-proved components,
— Ease of maintenance of components,
— Sharing costs to develop and maintain the components,
— Interoperability between organizations.
In other words, this is an area that is worth investigating.
In 2001 and 2002, four complex artefacts for records management and archives were published that can be seen as generic building blocks.

ISO standard for records management

ISO standard 15489, the ISO standard for records management, describes business requirements for records management[1]. The business requirements are the core of the standard. It was based on the Australian standard AS 4390. The standard contains the cause for records management and archiving in terms of types of benefits, procedures, staff education, accessibility, system requirements and others. It provides a basis for comparing and discussing records management and archives. This standard has been accepted in various ways by organizations all over the world, which makes the standard valuable.

Sarbanes-Oxley law

When the American company Enron collapsed and Arthur Andersen, one of the largest accountancy firms in the world, had to close down, this debacle, referred to as the Enron/Andersen debacle, was partly based on irregularities with records management. As a result, a law was made, approved, and signed in the US that has a profound impact on records management and archives: the Sarbanes-Oxley law ('SOX'). It requires every organization to periodically review policies and procedures on records management, to support the records management programme at the executive level, and to guarantee the technical demands needed to keep records, among other things.
The Enron/Andersen debacle, a high profile corporate scandal, has provid-

ed records managers and archivists with a foot in the door of the boardroom and the attentive ear of senior management.

Model Requirements for ERMS
MoReq is short for the Model Requirements for Electronic Document and Record Management. The MoReq Specification is a model specification of requirements for Electronic Records Management Systems (ERMS). MoReq was formulated under the supervision of the European Commission. It describes functional requirements with regard to issues like the storage and description of the records, accessibility, folder management and version management, safety and security, and disposal at the end of a record's life cycle. It can be used as an overview to functional requirements for suppliers and developers, and also to audit existing ERMS, and if outsourcing is considered, as a specification of the services to be procured. MoReq is widely known.

US standard on RMA's
The US DoD standard 5015.2-STD is more or less the counterpart of MoReq. It defines the basic requirements based on operational, legislative and legal needs that must be met by records management application products (RMA's) that are acquired by the US Department of Defense and other US government organizations. It includes requirements for RMA's for classified records. This standard, too, is widely known.

Research! (1)
The above-mentioned four generic building blocks for records management and archives were published in 2001-2002. The section of Information Systems (an education and research group in the department of Computer Science, at which I worked) had contacts with the group of prof. dr. René Wagenaar. I had previously worked in memory institutions for some 10 years, and prof. dr. René Wagenaar had a lot of experience with and insight into the role of ICT in business and governance.
The motive of one of the discussions, which later led to more discussions, was the applicability of principles of information systems design to building blocks for memory institutions. There was no formal research proposal; the discussions began by coincidence. We discussed the generalized design building blocks for records management and archive information

systems several times. I was just deeply interested, I do think that prof. dr. René Wagenaar was both interested and amused, and I discussed the item in some of my courses.

One can (and we did) compare the building blocks to the entities in an information systems design methodology, which was an uncommon step[2]. There is no strict relationship between the four building blocks, but it is not necessarily incorrect to compare them to information systems design artefacts. And it results in an interesting point of view.

A 'cascade' approach to controlling information systems design has the consecutive steps global design, functional design, technical design, coding, testing and implementation. If we compare these steps with the four building blocks, we get following result:

— ISO standard 15489 for records management and the Sarbanes-Oxley law can evidently be compared to a global design of the real system (RS) in which the information system (IS), according to any RS-IS representation, should fit. In a way, they represent a generalized result of requirements engineering for records management.

— The MoReq for ERMS and the US DoD standard 5015.2-STD on RMA's can evidently be compared to the functional design of the information system. In a way, they are a generalized result of functional demands for ERMS and RMA's (they are nearly the same).

One amusing point of view derives from standards construction. One of the requirements of a new ISO standard is that there are two independent implementations. The double and apparently unrelated work to construct both ISO standard 15489 for records management and the Sarbanes-Oxley law means that it is possible to indicate a common ground for the global design of records management. The double and apparently unrelated work to construct both MoReq and the US DoD standard 5015.2-STD means that it is possible to indicate a common ground for the functional design of ERMS and RMA's, i.e. for records management information systems. In each of the four cases, the supporters of the one building block will only have to agree on the overlapping domain of the adjacent building block.

One more amusing point of view derives from the stability of the building blocks. They are less stable than one might assume. The ISO standard on records management was established in 2001, it was preceded by the Australian standard of 1996 and it is expected to be succeeded by an updated and revised version in 2008. The SOX law of 2002 has not been changed; jurisprudence probably has the effect of keeping its effects up-to-date. MoReq for ERMS was established in 2001. It is being redrawn and MoReq2 has been promised to be available in 2008. And the most recent standard, the US DoD standard 5015.2-STD on RMA's of 2002, was the fastest to be replaced: there is a new version of 2007.

The supporters of each side need not only agree on the adjacent building block, they will have to stabilize their own building block by agreeing on its content first.

Related building blocks

Again, my computer science point of view merges with the point of view of prof. dr. René Wagenaar.

In information systems design, in a cascade approach, after the business requirements engineering phase and the functional design phase, comes the technical design phase. What are the building blocks for the technical design of records management and archives information systems that we have? Quite a few ICT standards are used today. There are some 150 ISO standards for storage media, WORM-disks and rewritable storage media, with different sizes and different chemical components. There is the ODMA model to connect applications, persistent identifiers for web-based information, the XML syntactic data model family including XSLT and XPath &c., the OAIS model (ISO standard 14721) for durable data sets, OAI-PMH to harvest metadata, various metadata element sets like the Dublin Core (ISO standard 15836), EAD and the Metadata for records model (ISO standard 23081), query languages, and PDF and other data formats[3]. Nevertheless, the answer is incomplete. There are elements in MoReq and in the 5015.2-STD that do not correspond to a technical building block, while on the other hand there are information science standards that could turn into building blocks but that are not yet stable and commonly used. That is an important conclusion, which indicates that the number of technical building blocks or standard components must be expected to increase in the coming years.

Moreover, the longevity of these standards needs to be investigated. The information in memory organizations should be fit to be kept for centuries. In sharp contrast, the half-life of common ICT tools and software may be some five years, which is anxiously short for memory organizations. The standardization process takes time. However, the idea that 'by the time things are standards, they are obsolete' does not automatically lead to thinking about durable standards. What will the optimal lifetime be of a standard? At present, ICT standards will last for five years. Memory organisations cannot do with that. Although ideas on backward compatibility of standards have been published, the issue of longevity of standards has too seldom been raised and not many people are aware of the problem (Egyedi and Loeffen, 2002, and Egyedi and Heijnen). Having said that, public awareness could change rapidly. Would it not be great if lots of electronic life insurances (with a life time of 30 years) would prove to be unreadable in the near future? At least, from this scientific point of view...

RESEARCH! (2)

The business case of building blocks for records management and archives is clear. Standard building blocks that are available are wanted for obvious reasons.

The technology readiness level of building blocks in general, however, is low. It has been suggested that a standard component can – should? – consist of ICT components, procedural components and human (e.g. cognitive) components. It has also been stated that a standard component should be easily recognizable and maintainable. For the records management and archival world the following questions want further research.

— What would be an acceptable size for a standard component? And how to measure the size?

— We could end up with 'standard' components available in all versions, sizes, materials, and colours, resulting in a first-class version management problem. How to control that?

— Should we aim at 'flexible' building blocks, being about as solid as sandwich spread? (That was a suggestion at a dinner).

— Finally, the question of longevity or durability must be considered. Memory institutions want information to last for many years and sometimes even for many centuries. If records management offices and archives would be updated with the speed of their present 'building blocks', our history would be a black hole...!

CONCLUSION

'If only we knew what we knew…'. In order to answer that, the digital age led to brand new requirements and a new way of thinking for memory organizations.

The systems development line of thinking is interesting to relate ISO 15489, Sarbanes-Oxley, MoReq and 5015.2-STD, and whatever will come next.

From the point of view of the functional design elements, the store of technical building blocks or standard components is severely incomplete. We must expect that their number for the purpose of records management and archives, necessary to know what we knew, will increase in the next years.

Next to that, one must expect that these ICT standards will be a base of standard components that might be characterized by maintainability and recognisability and with size, version typology, flexibility and longevity characteristics that are waiting to be investigated.

Prof. dr. René Wagenaar and I were of a different faculty. We did not meet often enough. I found a listening ear for these (and other) ideas; I got approval and alternatives and feedback. All mistakes in these ideas are my own. For the progress of thinking I thank prof. dr. René Wagenaar; with a deep understanding of business needs and ICT developments; interested; sometimes witty, always cheerful.

[1] Information on the goal and content of ISO standard 15489, as well as on the three other building blocks, is easily found on the World Wide Web.

[2] A bibliographic search in INSPEC – the bibliographic information service on Physics, Electronics and Informatics – and in LISTA – the bibliographic data base Library, Information Science & Technology Abstracts – shows the relationship we describe in this article seems to be uncommon even in November 2007.

[3] Like in footnote 1, information on goal and content of each of these ISO and non-ISO standards can easily be found on the World Wide Web.

REFERENCES

Cox, R. J. et al. (2001). The day the world changed: Implications for archival, library, and information sciences. First Monday 6 (12). http://rstmonday.org/issues/issue6—12/cox/index.html (accessed 27 November 2007).

Egyedi, T. M., & Loeffen, A. G. A. J. (2002). Succession in standardization: grafting XML onto SGML. Computer Standards & Interfaces 42(2), 279-290.

Egyedi, T. M., & Heijnen, P. Scales of standard dynamics. Change in formal, international IT standards. http://www.open-std.org/jtc1/sc22/open/n3894.pdf (accessed 27 November 2007).

Biographies

Nitesh Bharosa MSc is a PhD candidate at the Information and Communication Technology section ate Delft University of Technology. René chaired his graduation committee and later his promotion. Together they were developing a proposal for research on Information Architectures for Disaster Management.

Roger Bons is consultant for the Strategy & Business Change department of ING Group, Amsterdam, the Netherlands. Prior to that he has worked for Philips Electronics. He was a PhD candidate and colleague of René at Rotterdam School of Management of the Erasmus University.

Dr. Harry Bouwman is Associate Professor at the Information and Communication Technology section of Delft University of Technology. René was the chair of the section. Together we were involved in management of the section and worked on research in the domain of Mobile Communications, business models and 3G+mobile technology.

Eric Bun MSc is a graduate in Systems Engineering, Policy Analysis and Management at Delft University of Technology. He took part in a project supervised by René Wagenaar, on which this chapter is based.

Prof Christer Carlsson, Director of the Institute of Advanced Management Systems Research, and a professor of management science at Abo Akademi University in Abo, Finland. He is a Fellow of the International Fuzzy Systems Association, an Honorary Member of the Austrian Society for Cybernetics and an Honorary Chairman of the Finnish Operations Research Society. He is the author of 4 books, and an editor or co-editor of 5 special issues of international journals and 12 books; he has published more than 240 papers.

Drs. Koen van Dam is a PhD candidate at the Energy & Industry group at the Delft University of Technology, working on a framework for agent-based models of infrastructures using a generic ontology. René was co-author of his very first scientific publication.

Prof. em. dr. Patrick Dewilde is Professor emeritus in Electrical Engineering and the former Scientific Director of ICT Delft Research Centre of Delft University of Technology. He co-operated with Rene in the management of the Research Centre and had many stimulating discussions.

Dr. ir. Gerard Dijkema is Associate Professor of Energy & Industry. In research and education he specializes in innovation for sustainability in industry and infrastructure networks. René inspired him to think of ICT and sustainability.

Elizabeth Dominguez is Vice Chairperson at the Department of Mathematics and Computation at the University of Havana. She has been a scientific collaborator at the EURIDIS Institute, where she also came to know René.

Jeffrey Gortmaker MSc is a PhD candidate at the Faculty of Technology, Policy and Management of Delft University of Technology. René was his promoter and contributed to many discussions over the years.

Eric van Heck is professor of information management and markets at Rotterdam School of Management, Erasmus University. In 1997 René was appointed as professor in Amsterdam, Eric was his successor in Rotterdam. Since then we had several discussions about the role of online auctions, the use and impact of the next telecommunication infrastructure, and the critical success factors of virtual merchants and its applicability in practice. These discussions took place in lecture rooms, university coffee corners, E-dispuut meetings, conference meetings around the world (Barcelona, Bled, Hawaii, Xian), and during excellent diners or at a terrace nearby the Lake of Bled. Discussions were intense but always ended with humor (and a good glass of wine or beer).

Ralph Feenstra MSc is a PhD candidate at the Faculty of Technology, Policy and Management of Delft University of Technology. He holds a MSc in systems engineering, policy analysis and management. His PhD research is focused on service composition methods for multi-actor networks. René was his promoter and contributed to many discussions during the years as supervisor of this research project.

Dr. ir. Erwin Fielt is a researcher at the Telematica Institute in the areas of electronic business and government. René was Erwin's PhD supervisor during his study on electronic intermediaries, and Erwin works with René's group in the area of business models for electronic services.

Prof. dr. John Groenewegen is professor Economics of Infrastructures of Delft University of Technology. René and I shared interest in the institutional design of information systems. Also our common background of Erasmus University Rotterdam provided complementary ideas about economic and managerial issues of the firm.

Guadalupe Flores Hernández received her Master degree from Universidad Politécnica de Madrid, and is now working as a consultant in the mobile telecommunications domain. René co-supervised her Master graduation project on Mobile Web-services, which she executed at the Information and Communication Technology section of the Delft University of Technology.

Prof. dr. Lorike Hagdorn is a Professor at the Economics and Business Administration Faculty, where René held a chair for some years after 2002. Together, they worked at the Erasmus University of Rotterdam (EUR) on research in the area of information management and logistics.

Helle Zinner Henriksen is Associate Professor in the field of digital government at the Center for Applied ICT at Copenhagen Business School. She is involved in the research project ITAIDE. René participated in one of the ITAIDE workshops.

Kenneth Henry is Instructor and PhD candidate at the Department of Decision Sciences and Information Systems at Florida International University in Miami, Florida, USA.

Dr. ir. Paulien M. Herder is an Associate Professor at the Energy & Industry section at Delft University of Technology, and she was Director of Education for the Faculty of Technology, Policy and Management until September 2007. She worked with René in developing the new MSc program for Information Architecture.

Wout Hofman (1959) has been active for many years as an ICT architect in many application areas, including transport, customs, production and government. He is currently a senior consultant with TNO ICT. He is the author of a number of books, the latest of which contains a foreword by René.

Dr. Martijn Hoogeweegen is a principal consultant for the Strategy & Business Change department of ING Group, Amsterdam in the Netherlands. René Wagenaar, together with Peter Vervest, supervised Marijn s PhD project at the Rotterdam School of Management of the Erasmus University.

Dr. Marijn Janssen is an Associate Professor within the Information and Communication Technology section of the Technology, Policy and Management Faculty of Delft University of Technology. René chaired this section and he supported me to develop the necessary competencies to become an associate professor. They collaborated intensively in the field of e-government and ICT-service engineering.

Dr. ir. Wil Janssen is a research fellow at the Telematica Instituut, working on service innovation and internet Technologies. Together with René Wagenaar, he supervised Erwin Fielt s PhD thesis, and organized several conference workshops with René on topics like e-business and service engineering.

Dr. Els van de Kar is Assistant Professor at the Faculty of Technology, Policy and Management of Delft University of Technology and an independent consultant in service design. Els worked with René in the Service System Engineering research program on e-services and mobile services.

Bram Klievink MSc is a PhD candidate at the Information and Communication Technology section of the Technology, Policy and Management Faculty of Delft University of Technology. René shaped the opportunities for his research on the coordination of public-private cooperation in service-delivery, in which René identified a fruitful research direction.

Tim de Koning MSc is a graduate in Systems Engineering, Policy Analysis and Management at Delft University of Technology. He took part in a project supervised by René Wagenaar, on which this chapter is based.

Ir. Norien Kuiper is an IT architect at the Center for Process and Product Development of the Dutch Customs and Excise Administration. She completed the part-time study Technology, Policy and Management. She met René Wagenaar during the ICT lectures.

Dr. Rolf Künneke is associate professor and head of the section Economics of Infrastructures of Delft University of Technology. As members of the same Department 'Infrastructure

Systems and Services', René and I were involved in various management activities. In the field of research we had joint interests with respect to designing information infrastructures and the role of public values in ICT.

Dr. ir. Marc M. Lankhorst is leader of the Service Architectures expertise group of the Telematica Instituut. He is also project manager of the B-dossier project on integrated, demand-driven e-government services, to which René and his group contributed their extensive expertise on intergovernmental cooperation.

Ronald Lee is Professor at the Department of Decision Sciences and Information Systems at Florida International University in Miami, Florida, USA. Prior to that he was Hoogleraar and Professor and Director of the Erasmus University Research Institute for Decision Information System (Euridis) in Rotterdam, the Netherlands, where René was also a researcher.

Dr. ir. Zofia Lukszo is Associate Professor at the Energy & Industry group at the Delft University of Technology. She leads the Intelligent Infrastructures subprogram of Next Generation Infrastructures and worked closely with René in this context. The first ideas and the strategy of Intelligent Infrastructures subprogram was formulated during many very pleasant and inspiring discussions with René.

Dr. René Matthijsse is a principal consultant at Verdonck, Klooster & Associates (www.vka.nl) and associate professor Information Technology and Auditing at the Free University of Amsterdam. Professor René Wagenaar and the author worked together at KPN and initiated several research projects and business development initiatives at policy level in the public sector. Also, René Wagenaar was co-promoter with the academic dissertation of the author (email: rene.matthijsse@vka.nl).

Dr. K. van der Meer is associate professor of the department of software engineering, faculty EWI, Delft University of technology, and guest professor at the section of Library and Information Science at Antwerp University. In the time span after the publication of the four building blocks, at occasions like the aftermath of the DITSE Betade research programme, WEIP meetings, D-CIS laboratory projects, and at other occasions, the last one shortly before his untimely death, we discussed this line of thinking and the consequences.

Dr. Andreas Mitrakas is Head of Administration at the European Network and Information Security Agency (ENISA). In 1995, he worked on EDICON, an EU-funded project on EDI managed by René. In 2007, René co-authored a chapter in the book Secure eGovernment Web services (IGI Publishing, 2007), which Andreas co-edited.

Ton Monasso BSc is a student of Systems Engineering, Policy Analysis and Management at Delft University of Technology. He took part in a project supervised by René Wagenaar, on which this chapter is based.

Vu Nguyen is PhD candidate at the Department of Decision Sciences and Information Systems at Florida International University in Miami, Florida, USA.

Prof. dr. Bart Nieuwenhuis is part-time Professor at the School of Management and Governance of the University of Twente and owner of K4B Innovation. Bart cooperated with René when they worked for KPN. Bart and René jointly developed R&D Strategies for Internet and mobile service innovations.

Gerti Orthofer is a Research Assistant at the Institute of Informatics in Business and Government (Johannes Kepler University Linz) and she was involved in the conference organisation of EGOV 2005 and EGOV 2006. There she got known René as a very innovative and committed person in the field of E-Government.

Hans Michael Pronk is a principal consultant/partner at the Dutch consultancy Verdonck, Klooster & Associates, and he works on what he calls 'everything Internet'. His motto: 'The future is already here, it's just not widely distributed yet!' Hans worked with René at Erasmus University of Rotterdam, and he has been involved in projects with him ever since.

Mark de Reuver MSc received his Master degree from Delft University of Technology, and is now PhD candidate at the Information and Communication Technology section of Delft University of Technology. René co-supervised his PhD research on governance dynamics in value networks for next generation mobile services.

Dr. Uldrik Speerstra is a Project Director at the Faculty of Technology, Policy and Management at Delft University of Technology. He worked with René in developing the new MSc program for Information Architecture, and he chaired the 2006 Information Architecture evaluation committee.

Prof. dr. Yao-Hua Tan is Professor at the Information Management group of the Department of Economics and Business Administration of the Vrije University Amsterdam. He is also coordinator of the research project ITAIDE. René participated in one of the ITAIDE workshops.

Roland Traunmüller is Professor Emeritus of Linz University and former director of the Institute of Informatics in Business and Administration. He founded 2001 the annual EGOV conference series as a main focus of the European R&D community. In that way a fruitful cooperation with René Wagenaar has developed.

Drs. Jolien Ubacht is an Assistant Professor at the Information and Communication Technology section of the Technology, Policy and Management Faculty at Delft University of Technology. René chaired this section and was promoter of Jolien s PhD thesis on Regulatory Practice in Mobile Telecommunication Markets. In her role as coordinator of the management of educational affairs of the section, René was an enthusiastic sparring partner in the design of educational innovation.

Pim Veldhoven MSc is a graduate in Systems Engineering, Policy Analysis and Management at Delft University of Technology. He took part in a project supervised by René Wagenaar, on which this chapter is based.

Dr. Arjan van Venrooy is Managing consultant and partner at Verdonck, Klooster & Associates. René was a member of his promotion committee and both were members of the Center for Public Innovation, a cooperation of universities and the business community. Arjan and René did both research and talked a lot about the role of ICT with regard to new forms of inter-organisational public service provisioning.

Alex Verheij BSc is a student of Systems Engineering, Policy Analysis and Management at Delft University of Technology. He took part in a project supervised by René Wagenaar, on which this chapter is based.

Professor dr. Peter Vervest is Professor of business networks at the Department of Information and Decision Sciences at RSM Erasmus University. He is partner of D-Age, information technology consultants and investment advisors. He worked with Professor René Wagenaar since the late 1980s on innovative value chain management tools and methods. Together they developed the Port of Rotterdam management game, they organized summer schools on messaging technologies and applications, and supervised PhD students.

Pirkko Walden, Deputy Director of the Institute for Advanced Management Systems Research (IAMASR), Leader of the TUCS Mobile Commerce Laboratory, is a professor of marketing and information systems at Åbo Akademi University. She is an Area Editor of Journal of Decision Systems and is serving as a reviewer for several international journals and international conferences. She has published 2 monographs, 2 edited books and more than 100 articles in journals and conference proceedings. Her research interests are focused on electronic and mobile commerce.

Prof. dr. ir. Margot Weijnen is professor for process and energy systems engineering and head of the Energy & Industry section. In her positions as chair of the Infrastructure Systems & Services department of the TPM Faculty and as scientific director of the Next Generation Infrastructures Foundation, she especially valued his deep personal involvement with the ICT section and his perseverance in inspiring the section to establish an innovative research program which gained recognition in Europe. As a colleague she had many informal discussions with René on the strategy of TPM and NGInfra, and always enjoyed his buoyant personality and sense of humor.

Prof. dr. Maria Wimmer is professor and chair of the research group eGovernment, University of Koblenz, Institute for IS Research, Germany. She co-organizes the EGOV conferences and cooperated with Rene in the European Union funded eGovRTD2020 project in which we had many profound discussions.

List of Publications René Wagenaar

Heer, F.J. de, Wagenaar, R.W. and Tip, A. (1976). A dispersion relation for forward scattering. *Journal of Physics B, 9,* 269-274.

Heer, F.J. de, McDowell, M.R.C. and Wagenaar, R.W. (1977). Numerical study of the dispersion relation for e-H scattering. *Journal of Physics B, 10,* 1945-1654.

Blaauw, H.J., Wagenaar, R.W., Barends, D.H. and Heer, F.J. de (1980). Total cross sections for electron-helium scattering, *Journal of Physics B, 13,* 359-375.

Wagenaar, R.W. and Heer, F.J. de (1980). Total cross sections for electron scattering from noble gas atoms. *Journal of Physics B, 13,* 3855-3864.

Wingerden, B. van, Wagenaar, R.W. and Heer, F.J. de (1980). Total and differential cross sections for elctron-H_2 scattering. *Journal of Physics B, 13,* 3481.

Bruijn, D.P. de, Wagenaar, R.W. and Los, J. (1982). A parallel slit electron detection system. *Review on Scientific Instruments and Methods, 53,* 1020-1029.

Wagenaar, R.W. (1984). *Small angle elastic scattering of electrons by noble gas atoms.* Ph.D. Thesis, University of Amsterdam.

Riele, H.J. te and Wagenaar, R.W. (1985). Numerical solution of a first kind fredholm integral equation arising in electron-atom scattering. *International Series of Numerical Mathematics, Ed by G.Hammerlin and K.H. Hoffmann, 73,* Birkhauser Verlag Basel, 224-234.

Wagenaar, R.W. and Heer, F.J. de (1985). Total cross sections for electron scattering from Ar, Kr and Xe. *Journal of Physics B, 18,* 2021-2036.

Bouman, J. and Wagenaar, R.W. (1986). Kantoorautomatisering en verder: ontwerpaspecten bij datacommunicatie netwerken. *Informatie, 28(10),* 801-810.

Wagenaar, R.W., Boer, A. de, Tubergen, T. van, Los, J. and Heer, F.J. de (1986). Absolute differential cross sections for elastic scattering of electrons over small angles from noble gas atoms. *Journal of Physics B, 19,* 3121-3143.

Wagenaar, R.W. (1986). *Computer performance modelling using Petri nets* (Philips Technical report series, No. 43, 246).

Wagenaar, R.W. (1988). Netwerkdiensten: SURFnet als voorbeeld. ROM, 1, 4.

Wagenaar, R.W. and Dissel, H.G. van (1989). Kwaliteit van Informatiesystemen: onmogelijk te beoordelen? *Nieuwsbrief voor kwaliteitsverbetering,* 1(1), 3-5.

Dissel, H.G. van and Wagenaar, R.W. (1990). De Informatiesysteemfunktie in de jaren negentig. *Computable,* 29-30.

Sheombar, H.S. and Wagenaar, R.W. (1991). The strategic impact of EDI on logistical organization. *Proceedings of the 4th International EDI conference* (pp. 208-228). Bled, Slovenia.

Wagenaar R.W., Sol, H., Wierda, F. and Streng, R.J. (1991). *The Rotterdam Port Community.* Case study conducted for DGXIII of the Commission of the European Communities.

Wagenaar, R.W. (1991). User Requirements on electronic mail. EEMA Briefing, 3(6), 11-13.
Wagenaar, R.W. (1991). EDI: zegen of vloek? Nieuwsbrief Telematica, Jaargang 2(5), 1-3.
Wagenaar, R.W. (1991). Simulatiespel 'Port of Rotterdam' schept duidelijkheid over EDI. Polytechnisch tijdschrift, 46(5), iA10-15.
Sheombar, H.S. and Wagenaar, R.W. (1992). EDI induced redesign of coordination in logistics. International Journal of Physical Distribution and Logistical Management, Special Issue of EDI and Electronic Order Entry systems in Logistics Management, 22(8), 4-15.
Wagenaar, R.W. (1992). Business Network Redesign. Proceedings of the 5th International EDI Conference, Bled, Slovenia (pp. 390-404).
Wagenaar, R.W. (1992). Electronic Trading. Proceedings of the Workshop on Frontiers in Electronic Commerce (pp. 21-25). SEI Center for Advanced Studies in Management, The Wharton School, University of Pennsylvania.
Wagenaar, R.W., Lee, R.M. (1992). Panel on International Telecom Infra-structures: Development and Policies. Proceedings of the 12th ICIS Conference, Dallas (pp. 279-288).
Wagenaar, R.W. and Pronk, H.M. (1992). ADMD Interconnections within Europe: status and developments. Proceedings of the EEMA Annual Conference, Paris (pp. 212-218).
Bons, R.W.H. and Wagenaar, R.W. (1993). Interactieve EDI in Nederland (EDIFORUM/EURIDIS, EURIDIS reprint RP 93.09.01).
Bons, R.W.H., Wagenaar, R.W. (1993). Interactieve EDI kansrijk bij real-time dialoog. Telecommagazine 7, 8(7), 63-65.
Goetsch, E. and Wagenaar, R.W. (1993). Financiele EDI kan de banken buitenspel zetten. TelecommagazinE, 8(6), 31-37.
Heijden, H. van der and Wagenaar, R.W. (1993). Value Added Information Services. Proceedings of the 6th International conference on EDI, Bled, Yugoslavia, ed J.Gricar (pp. 207-222).
Heijden, H. van der, Wagenaar, R.W. and Nunen, J. van (1993). Organisational redesign through telecommunications: exploring authority shifts in agency realationships. (Management Report Series, 155, ERASM, 12p).
Wagenaar, R.W. and Pronk, H.M. (1993). ADMD European Interconnection matrix. Annual EEMA Conference, Montreux.
Wagenaar, R.W. (1993, 8 juni). Research directions on EDI, 6th International EDI Conference, Bled, Yugoslavia.
Wagenaar, R.W. (1993, 3 juli). EDI over X.400, EEMA Annual Conference, Montreux
Wagenaar, R.W. (1993, 13 oktober). EDI en transport, presentation bij Mees and Pierson.
Wagenaar, R.W. (1993, 1 november). Doing Business using Open-EDI, presentation tijdens EURIDIS Symposium.
Wagenaar, R.W. (1993, 14 december) Toegevoegde waarde van ISDN presentation tijdens EURIE '93.
Bons, R.H. and Wagenaar, R.W. (1994). Barrieres voor EDI sneller slechten: een introductie in Open-EDI. Telecommagazine 9(5), 51-53.
Bons, R.H., Lee, R.M., Wagenaar, R.W. and Wrigley, C. (1994). Computer Aided Design of Interorganizational Trade Scenarios: A CASE for Open-EDI. Proceedings of the Seventh International EDI-IOS Conference (180-193), Bled, Slovenia.
Heijden, J.G.M. van der, Nunen, J.A.E.E. van and Wagenaar R.W. (1994). Process Authority Redesign and Electronic Markets. Electronic Markets, 11, 9-10.
Hoogeweegen, M.R., Nunen, J.A.E.E. van and Wagenaar R.W. (1994). EDIALYSIS: A Decision Support System for Assessing costs and benefits of Electronic Data Interchange. Proceedings of the First European Conference on IT Investment Evaluation (129-134). United Kingdom: Henley College.

Lee, R.M., Bons, R.W.H., Wrigley, C.D. and Wagenaar, R.W. (1994). Automated Design of Electronic Trade Procedures using Documentary Petri Nets, *Proceedings 4th Conference on Dynamic Modelling and Information Systems (DYNMOD IV)*(137-150), The Netherlands: University of Technology, Delft.

Saxena, K.B.C. and Wagenaar, R.W. (1994). *Critical Success Factors of EDI Technology Transfer: A Conceptual Framework* (ERASM Management report series, No. 200).

Wagenaar, R.W. and Heijden, J.H. van der (1994). EDI Induced Business Redesign: a modelling approach towards improved intercompany coordination, *Research Forum of the 5th World Congress of EDI users*, Brighton.

Wrigley, C.W., Wagenaar, R.W. and Clarke, R. (1994). Electronic Data Interchange in International Trade: Frameworks for the Strategic Analysis of Ocean Port Communities. *Journal of Strategic Information Systems*, 3(3), 211-234.

Wrigley, C.D., Wagenaar, R.W., Gricar, J. and Swatman, P. (1994) Panel on Inter-organisational Business Simulation and Gaming: Rethinking IS Curricula. *Proceedings of the 15th International Conference on Information Systems* (476-477). Vancouver.

Wagenaar, R.W. (1994, 4 maart). *EDI and Business Process Redesign*. Presentation voor de studievereniging Vespucci, Delft.

Wagenaar, R.W. (1994, 29 april). *EDI and Business Process Redesign*. Presentation voor de board of directors van Aspa BV.

Wagenaar, R.W. (1994, 30 septemmber). *Business Process Redesign*. Presentation voor de management staff Terminal Operations van de NV Luchthaven Schiphol.

Wagenaar, R.W. (1994, 13 oktober). *Innovations in Telecommunications: Managing from the Warroom*. Presentation in het kader van de TopTech Master Class.

Bons, R.W.H., Lee, R.M., Wagenaar, R.W. and Wrigley, C.D. (1995). Modelling Inter-organizational Trade Procedures Using Documentary Petri Nets. Competence Centre Electronic Markets, University of St-Gallen, Switzerland. *Electronic Markets*, 4,13-14.

Bons, R.H. and Wagenaar, R.W. (1995). Een introductie tot Open-EDI. *Handboek Telematica*, Samson.

Bons, R.H., Lee, M.R., Wrigley, C.D. and Wagenaar, R.W. (1995). Modelling Inter-organisational Trade Procedures using Documentary Petri Nets. *Proceedings of the 28th HICCS Conference Hawaii* (pp. 189-198).

Bons, R.W.H., Lee, R.M., Wagenaar, R.W. (1995). Obstacles for the development of open electronic commerce. *Proceedings of the second Edispuut Workshop 1995 'Academic Research on Electronic Commerce'*, Edispuut.

Heijden, J.G.M. van der, Wagenaar R.W., Nunen, J.A.E.E. van and Bosch, F.A.J. van den (1995). Redesigning Process Control Mechanisms Using EDI: An Agency-theoretic Perspective. *Proceedings of the 28th HICCS Conference Hawaii* (pp. 388-397).

Heijden, J.G.M. van der and Wagenaar, R.W. (1995). Information technology and the structure of markets. *Proceedings of the second international workshop on electronic markets*, Ermatingen.

Heijden, J.G.M. van der and Wagenaar, R.W. (1995). *Information technology and the structure of markets* (Mangement Report Series 230, ERASM, 21 pp).

Hoogeweegen, M.R. and Wagenaar, R.W. (1995). Assessing Costs and Benefts of EDI. Proceedings of the 8th International Conference on EDI and Inter-Organisational Systems, Bled, Slovenia, ed. Clarke, Gricar and Novak (pp. 1-11).

Hoogeweegen, M.R., Teunissen, W.J.M., Vervest, P.H.M.and Wagenaar, R.W. (1995). The expected costs and benefits of EDI in the modular supply chain. *Proceedings of the Doctoral Consortium of the 16th ICIS Conference, Amsterdam.*

Hoogeweegen, M.R., Wagenaar, R.W., Nunen, J.A.E.E. van and Bens, W.E.J.M. (1995). Kosten en Baten van EDI investeringen, *Informatie, 37*(1), 41-50.

Hoogeweegen, M.R., Wagenaar, R.W., Bens, W.J.E.M., Nunen, J.A.E.E. van (1995). Het bepalen van kosten en baten van EDI-investeringen - naschrift. *Informatie.*

Lee, H., Wrigley, C.W. and Wagenaar, R.W. (1995). Electronic Marketplace with Multimedia Representation in the Florist Chain. *Proceedings of the 1995 Pan Pacific Conference on Information Systems, Singapore.*

Saxena, K.B.C. and Wagenaar, R.W. (1995). Critical Success Factors of EDI Technology Transfer: A Conceptual Framework. *Proceedings of the 4th European Conference on Information Systems, Athens (pp. 57-74).*

Saxena, K.B.C. and Wagenaar, R.W. (1995). Global transfer of EDI Technology. *Proceedings of the 8th International Conference on EDI and Inter-Organisational Systems, Bled, Slovenia, ed. Clarke, Gricar and Novak (pp. 136-156).*

Wagenaar R.W., Tulder R. van (1995). *Omgaan met Dilemma's: zeven Cases in Strategie en Informatie Technologie in Mainport Rotterdam.* Kluwer Bedrijfswetenschappen.

Hoeve, J.H., Heijden, J.G.M. van der and Wagenaar, R.W. (1996). De invloed van Informatietechnologie op het marktmechanisme. *Informatie, 38*(5), 63-67.

Hoogeweegen, M.R. and Wagenaar, R.W. (1996). A method to assess expected net benefits of EDI investments. *International Journal of Electronic Commerce, 1*(1), 73-95.

Hoogeweegen, M.R., Teunissen, W.J.M., Vervest, P.H.M. and Wagenaar, R.W. (1996). The expected costs and benefits of EDI in the modular supply chain. *Proceedings of the 29th HICCS Conference Hawaii (pp. 302-310).*

Hoogeweegen, M.R., Streng, R.J. and Wagenaar, R.W. (1996). A comprehensive approach for assessing the value of EDI. *The 4th European Conference on Information Systems, Lisbon.*

Wagenaar, R.W. and Saxena, K.B.C. (1996). Global transfer of EDI Technology: A Multi-Level Approach. *Chapter in the book Global Information technology and Systems Management: Key issues and Trends*, ed Palvia P, Palvia S. and Roche E.M. (pp. 395-424). Ivy League Publishing, Nashua USA.

Wagenaar, R.W. (1996, 21 november). *De virtuele koopman.* Presentation verzorgd in het kader van het 5-jarig bestaan van de City Ring Amsterdam.

Wiersma, T., Heijden, J.G.M. van der and Wagenaar, R.W. (1996). Electronische markten en hun voordelen, voorwaarden en belemmeringen. *Informatie, 38*(4), 16-19.

Bons, R.W.H., Lee, R.M. and Wagenaar, R.W. (1997). Designing trustworthy inter-organisational trade procedures. *Proceedings of the 10th International Conference on EDI and Inter-Organisational Systems (pp. 39-70).* Bled, Slovenia.

Creemers, M.R., Gerrits, H. and Wagenaar, R.W. (1997). Systeemarchitectuur banken is erf met kippenhokken en schuren. *Automatiseringsgids, 12*(21), 15.

Meijs, C. and Wagenaar, R.W. (1997). Verschuivingen in marktmechanismen onder invloed van Informatie-technologie. *Agro-Informatica, 10*(3), 5-8.

Hoogeweegen, M.R., Teunissen, W.J., Vervest, P.H.M. and Wagenaar, R.W. (1997). Towards EDI Enabled Cost Efficient Supply Chain Flexibility. *Proceedings of the Americas Conference on Information Systems (pp. 640-642).* Indianapolis, USA.

Wagenaar, R.W. (1997). *De virtuele koopman: ontwikkelingen in het elektronisch handelsverkeer vanuit strategisch en economisch perspectief.* Inaugural book to accept position as professor at the Free University Amsterdam.

Wagenaar, R.W. (1997). Innovative business models towards the adoption of wide-scale electronic commerce in business to consumer markets. *Proceedings of the 15th International Communications Forecasting Conference.* San Francisco, USA.

Wagenaar, R.W. (1997, 18 februari) *Virtualisering van waardeketens.* Opening adress op het seminar Nieuwe Media, Maarssen.

Wagenaar, R.W. (1997, 20 februari). *Belemmeringen voor elektronische handel.* Presentation in het kader van de Postdoctorale opleiding Informatiemamagement, Heemskerk.

Wagenaar, R.W. (1997, 14 maart). *De virtuele koopman: ctie of werkelijkheid.* Inaugurele rede, Amsterdam

Wagenaar, R.W. (1997, 9 april). *De burger dicteert, de overheid serveert.* Keynote speach op de Vakbeurs IT en Overheid, Jaarbeurs Utrecht.

Wagenaar, R.W. (1997, 25 juni). *Innovative business models for the adoption of Ecommerce within consumer markets.* Presentation verzorgd op de 5th International Telecommunications Forecasting Conference, San Francisco.

Wagenaar, R.W. (1997, 16 september). *Ontwikkelingen in Electronic Commerce.* Presentation op uitnodiging van de CAG branche groep Retail ten overstaan van een groep accounts van PTT Telecom in het MediaPlaza.

Wagenaar, R.W. (1997, 21 oktober). *De virtuele koopman, ctie of werkelijkheid.* Presentation ter gelegenheid van de opening van het PTT-Telecom districtskantoor regio Hengelo.

Wagenaar, R.W. (1997, 9 december). *Business to business Ecommerce.* Presentation gehouden op uitnodiging van Stichting Ediforum t.g.v. de lancering van het Electronic Commerce Platform Nederland in het Promenade Hotel, Den Haag.

Bons, R.W.H., Lee, R.M. and Wagenaar, R.W. (1998). Designing Trustworthy Interorganizational Trade Pocedures for Open Electronic Commerce, *International Journal of Electronic Commerce,* 2(3), 61-83.

Hoogeweegen, M.R., Streng, R.J. and Wagenaar, R.J. (1998), A comprehensive approach to assess the value of EDI, *Information and Management,* 34, 117-127.

Wagenaar, R.W. (1998) De virtuele koopman, *Interface,* 2, 1-3.

Wagenaar, R.W. (1998, 23 maart). *Van tikken naar Transacties.* Presentation gehouden op 23 maart 1998 op uitnodiging van district Rotterdam in Hotel New York.

Wagenaar, R.W. (1998, 16 april). *De virtuele koopman: ontwikkelingen rond Ecommerce.* Presentation gehouden op uitnodiging van de Stichting IBO in het Slot Zeist.

Wagenaar, R.W. (1998, 21 april). *Electronic Commerce: quo vadis?* Presentation gehouden op het Internet Congres in de RAI, Amsterdam.

Wagenaar, R.W. (1998, 23 april). *Electronic Commerce in perspectief.* Presentation gehouden op uitnodiging van de studievereniging Pantha Rei in het Randstad Congrescentrum Amsterdam.

Wagenaar, R.W. (1998, 6 mei). *Virtual Communities.* Presentation gehouden tijdens het PDN congres in het Evoluon, Eindhoven.

Wagenaar, R.W. (1998, 22 september). *De toekomst van de Elektronische snelweg.* Presentation gehouden ter gelegenheid van het 10-jarig lustrum van het Expertise Centrum in het Vredespaleis, Den Haag.

Wagenaar, R.W. (1998, 30 september) *Ecommerce in strategisch en organisatiekundig perspectief.* Presentation gehouden op uitnodiging van Meneba in het MediaPlaza, Utrecht.

Wagenaar, R.W., Wolthuis, R. and Nieuwenhuis, L.J.M. (1999). ICT Service provisioning for Electronic Commerce, *Proceedings of the Interactive Summit of the ITU Telecoms Conference Geneva.*

Hoogeweegen, M.R., Teunissen, W.J.M., Vervest, P.H.M., Wagenaar, R.W. (1999). Modular Network Design: management support for the virtual organisation, *Decision Sciences* 30(4), 1073-1103.

Wagenaar, R.W. (1999). Vertrouwen als smeerolie, *Computable*, 44-46.

Wagenaar, R.W. (1999, 11 oktober). *Myths and Realities of Ecommerce,* pannellid tijdens het Interactive Symposium van de ITU Telecom Conference, Geneva.

Wagenaar, R.W. (1999, 25 oktober). *Mcommerce: trends and market opportunities.* Presentation gehouden op het European Mobile Commerce Congres, Amsterdam.

Wagenaar, R.W. (1999, 9 december). *Web sites zijn blikvangers, maar wat hoort er achter te zitten?* Presentation gehouden tijdens het jaarlijkse symposium van de Association of Business Engineers, Zoetermeer.

Wagenaar, R.W. and Mooi, E. (2000). Ecommerce ontwikkelingen binnen het MKB.

Wagenaar, R.W. (2000, 26 april). *Electronische handel: klant aan de knoppen.* Presentation gehouden binnen de collegecyclus Een brede kijk op ICT, georganiseerd door Focus.

Wagenaar, R.W. (2000, 21 juni). *Dansen in de porseleinkast.* Presentation gehouden op het jaarlijkse Nationaal Overleg Telecommunicatie, Utrecht.

Wagenaar, R.W. (2000). *Nieuwe ontwikkelingen rond ICT.* Presentation gehouden tijdens de opening van het onderzoekscentrum Vuturenet van de Vrije Universiteit Amsterdam.

Lee, R.M., Bons, R.W.H. and Wagenaar, R.W. (2001). Refereed Conference Proceedings, *IFIP Conference on Ecommerce,* Zurich.

Wagenaar, R.W. (2001, 13 februari). *Breedband oprit naar de digitale snelweg.* Presentation gehouden tijdens de perslancering van BabyXL, Arena Amsterdam.

Wagenaar, R.W. (2001, 4 mei). *Ontwikkelingen rond Elektronische Marktplaatsen.* Presentation gehouden op het ECP.NL symposium, Den Haag.

Fielt, E., Faber, E., Janssen, W. and Wagenaar, R.W. (2003). On exchange design and electronic intermediary acceptance. In Lechner, U. (Ed.), *Proceedings of the Tenth Research Symposium on Emerging Electronic Markets* (pp. 143-158).

Ferguson, W.J., Gordijn, J., Janssen, M. and Wagenaar, R.W. (2003, 30 september). *E-Services Workshop Panel.* Pittsburg, USA, Discussion Panel First International E-Services Workshop, ICEC 03.

Janssen, M. and Wagenaar, R.W. (2003). From Legacy to Modularity. A Roadmap towards modular architectures using webservices technology in e-government. In *Electronic Government.* Berlijn: Springer.

Janssen, M., Wagenaar, R.W. and Beerens, J. (2003). Towards a exible ICT-architecture for Multi Channel Service Provisionering. In *Proceedings of the 36th Annual Hawaii International Conference on System Science.* (pp. 1-10). Los Alamitos CA: IEEE Computer Society.

Janssen, M., and Wagenaar, R.W. (2003). Towards a Reference Architecture for a Virtual Business Counter. In *Proceedings of the First International E-Services Workshop, ICEC 03* (pp. 91-97). Pittsburg: Carnegy Mallon University.

Janssen, M., and Wagenaar, R.W. (2003). Towards a reference Architecture for a virtual business counter. In Gordijn, J. and Janssen, M. (Eds.), *Proceedings of the First International E-Services Workshop, ICEC 03* (pp. 91-97). Pittsburg: ICEC.

Wagenaar, R.W. and Ali Eldin, A.M.T. (2003). Information Systems for a Connected Society. In *Towards a Component based Privacy Protector* (pp. 1-5). Klagenfurt, Oostenrijk: University of Maribor Press.

Wagenaar, R.W. and Ali Eldin, A.M.T. (2003). Towards a Component based Privacy Protector Architecture. In *Proceedings 15th Conference on Advanced Information Systems Engineering* (pp. 1-11). Klagenfurt, Oostenrijk: University of Maribor Press.

Wagenaar, R.W. and Ali Eldin, A.M.T. (2003). Towards a Component based Privacy Protector Architecture. In *Proceedings of the 15th Conference on Avanced Information Systems Engineering.* (pp. 1-11). Maribor: University of Maribor.

Wagenaar, R.W. and Ali Eldin, A.M.T. (2003). Towards Privacy Protecting Mobile Business Applications. In Palma dos Reis, A. and Isaías, P. (Eds.), *IADIS International Conference Proceedings* (pp. 1047-1050). Lissabon, Portugal: IADIS.

Wagenaar, R.W. (Eds.). (2004). *Netnomics - Kluwer online*.

Ali Eldin, A.M.T., and Wagenaar, R.W. (2004). A Fuzzy logic based approchad to support users self-control of their private contextual data retrieval. In Leino Timo (Ed.). *Proceedings of the 12th European Conference on Information Systems (ECIS)* (pp. 1-12), Turku, Finland.

Ali Eldin, A.M.T., Berg, J. van den and Wagenaar, R.W. (2004). A Fuzzy Reasoning Scheme for Context Sharing Decision Making. In Marijn Janssen, Henk Sol and René Wagenaar (Eds.), *Sixth International Conference on Electronic Commerce ICEC04* (pp. 371-375). ACM.

Ali Eldin, A.M.T. and Wagenaar, R.W. (2004). Towards Users Drive Privacy Control. In W. Thissen, P. Wieringa, M. Pantic and M. Ludema (Eds.), *Proceedings of the IEE SMC'2004 Conference* (pp. 4673-4676). Den Haag: IEEE.

Bruijn, J.A. de, Wagenaar, R.W., Voort, H.G. van der and Wendel de Joode, R. van (2004). *Shared services in de overheid*. Atos, Den Haag.

Dam, K.H. van, Ottjes, J.A., Lodewijks, G., Lukszo, Z. and Wagenaar, R.W. (2004). Intelligent Infrastructures: Distributed Intelligence in Transport System Control; an Illustrative Example. In W. Thissen, P. Wieringa, M. Pantic and M. Ludema (Eds.). *Proceedings of the 2004 IEEE International Conference on Systems, Man and Cybernetics: Impacts of Emergence Cybernetics and Human-Machine Systems* (pp. 4650-4654). Madison, Wisconsin, USA: Omnipress.

Fielt, E., Janssen, W., Faber, E. and Wagenaar, R.W. (2004). Confronting the design and acceptance of electronic Intermediaries: A case study in the maritime sector. In Marijn Janssen, Henk Sol and René Wagenaar (Eds.), *Sixth International Conference on Electronic Commerce ICEC04* (pp. 392-410). ACM.

Goedvolk, E.-J., Faber, E. and Wagenaar, R.W. (2004). Towards a framework for understanding the effectiveness of digital content exploitation strategies. In Janssen, M., Sol, H. and Wagenaar, R.W. (Eds.), *Sixth International Conference on Electronic Commerce ICEC04: Towards a New Services Landscape* (pp. 239-244). ACM.

Gortmaker, J., Janssen, M. and Wagenaar, R.W. (2004). The Advantages of Web Service Orchestration in Perspective. In Janssen, M., Sol, H. and Wagenaar, R.W. (Eds.), *Sixth International Conference on Electronic Commerce ICEC04* (pp. 506-515). ACM.

Janssen, M. and Wagenaar, R.W. (2004). An Analysis of a Shared Services Centre in E-government. In Ralph.H. Spraghue Jr. (Ed.), *Proceedings of the 37th Hawaii International Conference on System Sciences 2004* (pp. 1-10). Hawaii: IEEE.

Janssen, M. and Wagenaar, R.W. (2004). Developing Generic Shared Services for e-Government (pp. 31-39). *Electronic journal of e-government*, 2(1), 31-38.

Janssen, M., Sol, H.G. and Wagenaar, R.W. (Eds.). (2004). *Proceedings of the Sixth International Conference on Electronic Commerce ICEC04*. Delft: ACM.

Matthijsse, R. and Wagenaar, R.W. (2004). Shared services in de overheid *Overheids Management*, 10, 262-265

Saxena, K.B.C., Janssen, M. and Wagenaar, R.W. (2004). CRM in E-government: Learning from Netherlands. In Sirohi, R.S. and Gupta, M.P. (Eds.), *Towards E-Government: Management Challenges* (pp. 99-108). New Delhi: TaTa McGraw-Hill.

Daskapan, S., Eldin, A.A. and Wagenaar, R.W. (2005). Trust in mobile context aware systems. In Khalid S. Soliman (Ed.), *Proceedings of the 5th International Business Information Management Association Conference on Intenet and Information Technology in Modern Organizations: Challenges and Anwers* (pp. 813-819). Cairo: International Business Information Management Association.

Eldin, A.A., Wagenaar, R.W. and Bouwman, W.A.G.A. (2005). Towards Dynamic Control of Users Privacy. In Khalid S. Soliman (Ed.), *Proceedings of the 5th International Business Information Management Association Conference on Intenet and Information Technology in Modern Organizations: Challenges and Anwers* (pp. 401-406). Cairo: International Business Information Management Association.

Feenstra, R.W., Janssen, M. and Wagenaar, R.W. (2005). M-government safety services: Evalution of alternatives from stakeholders' perspectives. In onbekend (Ed.), *Proceedings of the First European Conference on Mobile Government* (pp. 1-9). Brighton: University of Sussex.

Fielt, E., Faber, E., Janssen, W. and Wagenaar, R.W. (2005). Designing for acceptance: Lessons from two electronic intermediaries in the Dutch insurance industry. In Prof. Dr. Tan, Y.H. (Ed.), *Proceedings of the 12th Research Symposium on Emerging Electronic Markets* (pp. 241-262). Amsterdam: Vrije Universiteit Amsterdam.

Gortmaker, J., Janssen, M. and Wagenaar, R.W. (2005). Accountability of Electronic Cross-Agency Service-Delivery Process. In Wimmer, M.A. and Traunmuller, R. (Eds.), *Proceedings of the 4th International Conference EGOV 2005* (pp. 49-56). Berlin: Springer.

Gortmaker, J., Janssen, M. and Wagenaar, R.W. (2005). Towards Requirements for a Reference Model for Process Orchestration in e-Government. In Gamper, J., Polasek, W. and Boehlen, M. (Ed.), *Proceedings of the TED Conference on e-Government* (pp. 169-180). Bolzano-Bozen Italie: Springer.

Janssen, M., Kuk, G. and Wagenaar, R.W. (2005). A Survey of e-Government Business Models in The Netherlands. In Li, Q. and Liang, T-P. (Eds.), *Proceedings of the Seventh International Conference on Electronic Business* (pp. 496-504). Association for Computing Machinery.

Matthijsse, R., Bruijn, J.A. de, Voort, H.G. van der, Wagenaar, R.W. and Wendel de Joode, R.van (2005, januari-februari). Shared services centers bij de rijksoverheid: Big bang of zachte dwang. *Tijdschrift voor Informatie en Management*, 6, 17-25

Matthijsse, R.P.H.M., Bruijn, J.A. de, Voort, H.G. van der, Wagenaar, R.W. and Wendel de Joode, R. van (2005). Shared Services bij de rijksoverheid: Big bang of zachte dwang. TIEM, 1, 16-25

Matthijsse, R.P.H.M. and Wagenaar, R.W. (2005). Shared services: synergie tussen organisatie en informatie. *Overheids Management*, 1, 8-10.

Vrancken, J.L.M. and Wagenaar, R.W. (2005). An Evolutionary Approach to Road Pricing. In onbekend (Ed.), *Proceedings of the 5th European Congress on ITS* (pp. 1-7). Hannover: ITS Europe.

Wagenaar, R.W. and Janssen, M. (2005). Development in intelligent support for e-commerce negotiation applications. *Electronic commerce research and applications*, 4(4), VII-VIII.

Wagenaar, R.W. (2005, 15 augustus). E-Government: The Road Ahead., *Seventh International Conference on Electronic Commerce*. Xian, China.

Wagenaar, R.W. (2005). Journal of the Peoples, University of Bangladesh.

Wendel de Joode, R. van, Bruijn, J.A. de and Wagenaar, R.W. (2005). Sustainability of virtual communities: How to deal with structural conjcts in Hybrid OSS communities. In L.A. Ripamonti (Ed.), *Proceedings of the Workshop F: Development and sustainability of online business communities.* (pp. 57-61). Milaan: D.I.CO. Università degli Studi di Milano.

Wendel de Joode, R. van, Bruijn, J.A. de and Wagenaar, R.W. (2005). Sustainability of virtual communities: how to deal with structureal conjcts in 'hybrid' OSS communities. In LA Ripamonti (Ed.), *Proceedings workshop F: Development and sustainability of online business communities. 2nd International Conference on Communities and Technologies* (pp. 57-61). Milaan: D.I.Co. Università degli Studi di Milano.

Ali Eldin, A.M.T. and Wagenaar, R.W. (2006). A privacy preference architecture for context aware applications. In *Proceedings the 4th ACS/IEEE International Conference on Computer Systems and Applications* (pp. 1010-1013).

Daskapan, S., Vree, W.G. and Wagenaar, R.W. (2006). Emergent information security in critical infrastructures. *International Journal of critical infrastructures (ijcis)* 2(2/3), 247-260.

Fielt, E.J., Jansen, W.P.A., Faber, E. and Wagenaar, R.W. (2006). Towards a Design Theory for Electronic Ineetermediaries. In Tanniru, M., Tjiang, T-P., Shaw, M.J., Zeng, D. and Chau, M. (Eds.), *Proceedings of the 5th Workshop on e-Business, Milwaukee, Wisconsin, USA* (pp. 1-12).

Gortmaker, J., Janssen, M. and Wagenaar, R.W. (2006). Adaptivity of Public Service networks. In Scholl,.J., Andersen, K.V. and Gronlund, A. (Ed.), *Electronical Government Communication Proceedings of the Fifth International EGOV Conference 2006* (pp. 225-232). Linz (At): Trauner Verlag.

Gortmaker, J., Janssen, M. and Wagenaar, R.W. (2006). Coordinating Cross-agency Business Processes. In Anttiroiko, A-V., and Malkia, M. (Eds.), *Encyclopedia of Digital Government* (pp. 237-243). Hershey: Idea.

Janssen, M., Gortmaker, J. and Wagenaar, R.W. (2006). Web Service Orchestration in Public Administration: Challenges, Roles and Growth Stages. *Information systems management*, 23(2), 44-55.

Janssen, M. and Wagenaar, R.W. (2006). Unraveling Shared Services using Simulation. In s.n. (Ed.), *Proceedings of the 7th annual International Conference on Digital government Research* (pp. 404-405). San Diego, CA.

Janssen, M. and Wagenaar, R.W. (2006). Business Engineering of Component Based Systems. In Lycett, M., Cesare, S. de and Macredie, R.D. (Eds.), *Development of Component-Based Information Systems* (Advances in Management Information Systems, 2) (pp. 166-181). New York: M.E. Sharp.

Janssen, M. and Wagenaar, R.W. (2006). Enterprise Architectures as Knowledge Sharing Instrument: Concepts and Challenges. In *Knowledge Transfer e-Government* (Schriftenreihe Informatik, 20) (pp. 82-91). Linz: Trauner Verlag.

Matthijsse, R.P.H.M., Venrooy, A. van and Wagenaar, R.W. (2006). Organiseren en implementeren van samenwerking. *Overheidsmanagement*, 3(19), 66-68.

Matthijsse, R.P.H.M., Venrooy, A. van and Wagenaar, R.W. (2006). Vorming van een netwerkoverheid. *Overheids Management, 9,* 216-219.

Wagenaar, R.W. (2006). Governance of Shared Service Centers in Public Administration: Dilemma's and Trade-offs. In s.n. (Ed.), *Proceedings of the ICEC 06, Eith International Conference on Electronic Commerce* (pp. 354-363). New Brunswick, Canada: University of New Brunswick.

Wagenaar, R.W., Matthijsse, R., Bruijn, J.A. de, Voort, H.G. van der and Wendel de Joode, R. van (2006). Implementation of Shared Service Centres in Public Administration: Dilemmas and Trade-offs. In V.J.J.M. Bekkers et al. (Ed.), *Information and communication Technology and Public Innovation* (Innovation and the Public Sector, 12) (pp. 141-158). Amsterdam: IOS Press.

Wagenaar, R.W. (2006, 25 april). Waar blijft het E-government lab? *De Staatscourant* (pp. 10-10).

Ali Eldin, A.M.T., and Wagenaar, R.W. (2007). Towards Autonomous User Privacy Control. *International Journal of Information Security and Privacy* 1(4), 24-46.

Bharosa, N., Janssen, M. and Wagenaar, R.W. (2007). Enterprise architecture evaluation: a case study on the purposes of enterprise architecture for e-business. In Khosrow-Pour Mehdi (Ed.). *Proceedings Managing Worldwide operations and Communications with information technology* (pp. 834-844). Vancouver: IGI Publishing.

Bouwman, W.A.G.A. and Wagenaar, R.W. (2007). Mobile Service bundles, Mobile Service Compositions and the Role of Fuzzy Logic. In P. Waldon, R. Fuller and J. Carlsson (Eds.), *Expanding the Limits of the Possible* (pp. 145-159). Abo: Painotalo Gillot.

Fielt, E.J., Janssen, W., Faber, E. and Wagenaar, R.W. (2007). Exchange Design Patterns for Electronic Intermediaries. In H. Oster, Schelp, J. and Winter, R., (Eds.), *Proceedings of ECIS 2007* (pp. 155-166).

Feenstra, R.W. Janssen, M. and Wagenaar R.W. (2007). Evaluating Web Service Composition Methods: The need for including Multi-Actor Elements. *The Electronic Journal of e-Government, 5, 2,* 153-164.

Gortmaker, J., Janssen, M. and Wagenaar, R.W. (2007). Requirements on Cross-Agency Processes in E-Government: The Need for a Reference Model. In Mittrakas, A., Hengeveld, P., Polemi, D. and Gamper, J. (Eds.), *Secure E-Government Web Services* (pp. 217-232). Hershey, Pensylvania, USA: Idea Group Publishing.

Janssen, M., Duin, P.A. van der, Wagenaar, R.W., Bicking, M. and Wimmer, M. (2007). Scenario building for E-government in 2020. In: *Proceedings of the 8th annual international Digital Government Research* (pp. 296-297). New York: ACM.

Janssen, M., Duin, P.A. van der, Wagenaar, R.W., Bicking, M., Wimmer, M., Dawes, S. and Petrauskas, R. (2007). Scenario building for E-Government in 2020: Consolidating the results from regional workshops. In Sprague Jr., R.H. (Ed.), *Poceedings of the Fortieth Annual Hawaii International Conference on System Sciences* (pp. 1-10). Los Alamitos California: IEEE.

Janssen, M., Huizer, E.A.J., Duin, P.A. van der and Wagenaar, R.W. (2007). The Results of a Scenario Building and Road Mapping Workshop for e-Government in 2020. In Remenyi, D. (Ed.), *Proceedings of the 7th European Conference on E-Government* (pp. 219-228). Reading, UK: ACI.

Janssen, M., Wimmer, M., Bicking, M. and Wagenaar, R.W. (2007). Scenarios of Governments in 2020. In Codagnone, C. and Wimmer, M.A. (Eds.), *Roadmapping e-Government Research: Visions and Measures towards innovative Governments in 2020* (pp. 55-84). Clusone, Italy: E-Gov.RTD2020 Project Consortium.

Janssen, M., Kuk, G. & Wagenaar, R.W. (2008). A Survey of Web-based Business Models for e-Government in the Netherlands. *Government Information Quarterly, 25*(2), 202-220.